Managing Strategy
in the Real World

Managing Strategy in the Real World

Conclusions and Frameworks from
Field Studies of Business Practice

R. Jeffery Ellis
Babson College

Foreword by
Robert J. Allio

Lexington Books
D.C. Heath and Company/Lexington, Massachusetts/Toronto

Library of Congress Cataloging-in-Publication Data

Ellis, R. Jeffery.
    Managing strategy in the real world.

    Bibliography: p.
    Includes index.
    1. Strategic planning. 2. Decision making. 3. Problem solving. I. Title.
HD30.28.E45   1988   658.4'012   87-4259
ISBN 0-669-15898-4 (alk. paper)

Published simultaneously in Canada
Printed in the United States of America
Casebound International Standard Book Number: 0-669-15898-4
Library of Congress Catalog Card Number: 86-46409

The paper used in this publication meets the minimum requirements of American National Standard for Information Sciences—Permanence of Paper for Printed Library Materials, ANSI Z39.48-1984. ∞™

88 89 90 91 92 8 7 6 5 4 3 2 1

For my dear father and mother

Contents

Figures and Tables   xi

Foreword   *Robert J. Allio*   xiii

Preface   xv

Part I.   Setting the Scene   1

1.   Concerning Discontinuity   3

    The Environment and Discontinuity   4
    This Study   6

2.   Managing Response   11

    The Strategy and Planning School   11
    The Decision-making School   13
    The Organizational Schools   18

3.   Defining the Study   25

    Discontinuity   25
    Corporate, Administrative, and Operating Responses   27
    Complex, Divisional, and Simple Settings   31
    Response   36

4.   Researching Response   43

    Research Design   43
    Sites and Responses   50

Part II.   Collected Data   61

5.   Prosper's Coal Venture   65

Coal and Prosper   66
Beginnings   69
Development   73

6.   Atlas's Coal Venture   79

Formation   79
Directions   84
Impetus   87

7.   Prosper's Catalytic Cracker   93

Instigation   93
Preliminaries and Proposal   97
Approvals   101
Contrasts   104

8.   Atlas's Scenario Planning   107

Origins   108
Cassandra and Percival   111
The Oil Crisis   113
Prosper's Scenario Planning   117

9.   Prosper's Use of Rotterdam Prices   121

Special Factors   122
Reorientation   124
European Organization   126
Dissemination   129

10.   Prosper's and Atlas's Management of the Embargo   135

Managing Supply   136
Organizing Supply   137
Crisis   140
Responses   143

11.   Further Responses in Complex Settings   151

Interoil   151
Columbus Bank   155
DeVito Power   159

12. **Generaltex's Industrial Products Division**   165

The Industrial Products Division   165
Demand Surge   167
Cost Inflation   168
Recession   171
Cash Shortage   173
Postscript   175

13. **TCA's National Lighting Division**   177

The National Lighting Division   178
Inflation Beaters   179
Far Eastern Vehicle Bulbs   183
Safety Legislation   188

14. **Further Responses in Divisional Settings**   193

Carolvale Division and Ronson Division   193
Weld Division   199
Container Division   202

15. **Responses in Simple Settings**   209

Jackson Mines   209
Schumacker   212
Suza Cars   215

Part III.   Analysis and Implications   221

16. **Reviewing Response**   223

Response and Discontinuity   223
Corporate, Administrative, and Operating Responses   231
Complex, Divisional, and Simple Settings   235

17. **Finding Solutions**   243

The Three Rs   245
Realignment   247
Reemphasis   251
Replication   255

18. **Solving Problems**   261

The Analytic and Derived Modes   263
General Results   264

Uses of the Analytic Mode 268
Uses of the Derived Mode 269
Balancing the Modes 273

19. **Developing Initiatives 277**

A Constant Process 279
The Phases of Response 284

20. **Using Situational Factors 295**

Contextual Focus 296
Start-up Focus 301
Maturation Focus 304

21. **Implications 313**

Implications for Management 314
Implications for the Organization 321
Implications for Strategy 324
Implications for Research 328

Author Index 333

Content Index 337

About the Author 341

Figures and Tables

Figures

1–1. Pfeffer and Salincik's Causal Model of Organizational Environments 5

2–1. Summary of Findings from Some Major Studies of Decision Making   17

5–1. Selected Chronology of Prosper's Entry into the Coal Industry   70

5–2. Prosper's Coal Group Organization, Early 1979   75

6–1. Selected Chronology of Atlas's Entry into the Coal Industry   81

6–2. Atlas's Coal Organization, 1979   91

8–1. Scenarios Presented within Atlas in 1972   112

10–1. Prosper's Supply Function Structure   138

10–2. Atlas's Supply Function Structure   139

12–1. IPD's Organization   167

13–1. National Lighting Division's Organization   178

20–1. A Map of People and Groups in Atlas's Coal Venture   305

20–2. A Map of People and Groups in Prosper's Use of Rotterdam Prices   306

Tables

3-1. Corporate, Administrative, and Operating Responses   29

3-2. Probable Features of Complex, Divisional, and Simple Settings   32

4-1. Responses in Complex Settings   51

4-2. Responses in Divisional Settings   54

4-3. Responses in Simple Settings   57

5-1. Examples of Prosper's Subsidiaries and Their Principal Activities   69

6-1. Examples of Atlas's Subsidiaries and Their Principal Activities   82

7-1. Oil Demand by Order of Distillate   96

7-2. A Forecast of Catalytic Converters   104

12-1. Comparative Income Statements   172

16-1. Researched Responses   226

16-2. Features of Complex, Divisional, and Simple Settings, as Amended   238

17-1. Finding Solutions: The Three Rs   246

17-2. Use of the Three Rs in the Researched Responses   248

18-1. A Comparison of the Analytic and Derived Modes   263

18-2. Some Instances of the Modes in Each Response   266

19-1. The Three Phases Compared   286

19-2. The Commencement of Each Phase in Each Response   288

20-1. Parties, Vested Interests, and Effects on Prosper's Rotterdam Pricing   308

Foreword

Robert J. Allio

Today's institutions need vastly deeper knowledge and understanding of how to handle effectively the increasingly novel and disruptive pressures that surround them. This book shows how responses that accomplish strategy and change it with the times can be better managed. This is important because survival and strengthening demand progressively finer and more timely responses to meet competitive and environmental challenges.

More specifically, *Managing Strategy in the Real World* is concerned with those common and critical situations where managers need to meet extraordinarily taxing irregularities in their environment or where they desire to take their organizations into different directions of development. By studying the managerial and decisional processes of organizations, an understanding of management is presented that addresses many of the often slighted conceptual insufficiencies and implementation problems of common approaches.

Jeffery Ellis provides a more complete perspective for managers and academics that treats the process of strategy formation in its fullness. This scholarly work is a practical complement and deepening of existing knowledge found by intricately and systematically examining strategic decisions and analyzing them for the patterns and forces that are fundamental to their successful functioning. It should not be a surprise that applying strategy as it is presently described in management writing fosters the frequently reported unimplementable plans, rigidity, blind spots, and frustrating rituals, because most reported approaches largely disregard the actual nature of the decisional and managerial processes that lie at the heart of organizational thought and action.

Indeed most of what can be read on the critical question of strategy and its implementation proceeds from the simplest possible assumptions concerning management action. This is because researchers have too often been courted only to the perceptual and quantifiable that can be captured in questionnaires

Robert J. Allio is visiting professor and area head of Strategy Formulation at Babson College in Wellesley, Massachusetts and founder of Robert J. Allio Associates, consultants to management of Duxbury, Massachusetts.

and analyzed electronically. This bias in research method has deflected attention from many vital and fundamental questions concerning how strategy actually takes place. Dr. Ellis has sought to remedy some of this imbalance by a study that first observed thoroughly the process of strategy formation in the field in detail in some of the world's leading companies, recorded those data for others to appraise, and then analyzed those data systematically.

As a result, Dr. Ellis reports much that has not been described by others and goes further to present his findings in ways comprehensible to managers and operationalizable by researchers with similar and perhaps harder methodological preferences. In this study, the messiness of reality is not sidestepped but made to influence usefully the findings that are presented. Jeffery Ellis's models, frameworks, and conclusions simplify the world as it is and do so in ways that are both practical for managers and testable by researchers.

Here is a study of unusual originality and value. Managers, consultants, and researchers can find many previously unstated insights as to how strategic situations can be managed. Findings are useful because the rigors of this study are methodologically as well as theoretically relevant to the real world. Progress in the practice and research of strategic management depends on deeper knowledge of how strategy actually forms and is administered in organizations. Jeffery Ellis takes us an important step forward in this vital quest.

Preface

This book was inspired in 1973 as I spun above London in the Post Office Tower Restaurant on the evening of my engagement to my future wife. This was also the day when OPEC decided to price oil unilaterally. Unromantically, part of our conversation was speculation on the challenges facing corporations of steeply increased oil prices. Nearly to the day, fourteen years later, forward-thinking executives explored how to manage the implications of a possible new era heralded by October 1987's precipitous, worldwide decline in equities. The world shifts continuously but regularities can be found as how to manage the strategic process of change within corporations more skillfully and effectively.

As this book shows, discontinuities are merely the occasional and sensational triggers for a perpetual flux that proceeds within surviving institutions. Multiple and complicated agendas constantly flow and interact profoundly within corporations as managers struggle to deliver competitive advantage. The future whole of each of our organizations results inscrutably from countless initiatives that must span all levels and units and must differ widely in their scope, time frames, risk, and appropriate vision. This book addresses essential elements of that complex process.

I began reading around this captivating question of how corporations could handle the qualitatively different world that faced them. I was struck at how little was published that dealt with these managerial challenges in a well-informed and genuinely useful way. Without recorded knowledge, how could practitioners pass on their skills, how could the thoughtful reflect on how the process could be improved and how could we know how and what to teach aspiring managers? Concerning the critical process of strategy formation, there were a number of unmistakably deep and reliable studies, but, overall, little knowledge had been reported. It was equally startling how limited my initial battery of statistical and hard data gathering tools were to the research task.

To assist my mission, numerous prople shared their wisdom with me magnanimously and with great patience. Many knew, I think, that more powerful learning would come later in more intimate ways. It was in observing clinical researchers who could create impact on those for whom I especially care when the subtleties and nuances of the creation of knowledge finally became apparent with most fullness. Over these years many professors have raised thought-provoking questions in my mind that have required the conjunction of both life's experiences and disciplined research to begin to answer satisfactorily. Thus, one allusion to Kafka in an MBA class eventually prompted in me an entirely different and deeper understanding of causality as well as recognition of its twin, interdependency. The journey has been remarkable and intellectually liberating. It will continue.

The years since 1973 have also taught me forcefully why studies that incorporate depth descriptions of actual practice are few. Such work is time consuming and requires vastly more grist to get to the grain. This approach is aberrant in business school academia where rewards, value systems, resource allocations, and even the structure of the industry itself arise from and define only exceptionally the research methods and output of work of this character. If managers like the intent of this study—to address the world of practice as it really is from the standpoint of managerial process—the resources required to do more and go further are nearly beyond most academics, but results would be easily realized by only very small but well-targeted corporate support.

As readers will find, this work goes deeper than a distillation of what managers report as effective. It reveals, through exhaustive observation and systematic analysis, fundamental processes governing the practice of strategy. For this study, how organizations within corporations managed major strategic situations was investigated thoroughly in the field. The results of this research were then condensed as in-depth case studies from which the findings were derived analytically. In this book, fourteen such strategic challenges are described at length from four of the world's largest and most vital companies, and nine other intriguing situations are examined fully but written-up in less depth. Throughout, the emphasis is on discovering and presenting what managers can do to handle better these continuing and critical challenges.

Conclusions, frameworks, and methods for strategy are derived, therefore, from extensive and rigorous study of real world practice. Many insights are offered to benefit managers as an antidote to the often mechanical prescriptions that have marred many efforts at strategy. The work provides much that will be of methodological as well as content interest to some academics and, as an advance in knowledge, will provide also a source of hypotheses for researchers.

More specifically for managers and consultants, this book presents practical knowledge concerning effective management of strategy. Fundamental to this process is the finding of solutions, the solving of problems, the developing of initiatives, and the using of situational factors. *Responsive management,* a style or approach to managing, is introduced that shows how higher performance or revisions in the development of an organization can be achieved practically, actively, flexibly, and sensitively through the stimulation and adoption of initiatives and the use of an overall structure promoting these characteristics and processes. Observations are made on the managing of corporate, administrative, and operating challenges, and of managing in complex, divisional, and simple organizational settings.

For management academics and researchers, original findings and perspectives are presented on the management of strategy and its associated decision processes. The naturally incremental, uncertain, evolutionary, and situationally specific aspects of managing strategy are examined thoroughly. External validity is stressed, as are findings that generally permit their statement as hypotheses testable empirically in subsequent work. Results show how: even radical outcomes issue from the application of only seven main elemental choice processes; cybernetic, cognitively limited, and satisficing decision making operates interdependently with planning and analysis; decisions are driven according to a three-phase structure by three conjoint managerial processes; and situational factors determine where and when a response originates and its characteristics. Contingencies are examined for types of responses and types of organizations.

Written to be readable by both managers and academics, some eighteen of the twenty-one chapters apply equally to both audiences. Managers may choose to skim chapters 3 and 4, but academics may find these chapters to be of special interest. Most of chapter 21 is particularly pertinent to the manager audience but should also prove of interest to the academic.

My chief debt is to the many corporate executives who gave unstintingly of their time and information to make this book possible. It is unfortunate that confidences make it impossible to acknowledge these many people by name. Norman Berg, Professor at the Harvard Business School, was a special inspiration, perhaps unknowingly, for this study. Derek Abell, Dean IMEDE, Switzerland, assisted with entry to one important research site. J. Constable, Director General of the British Institute of Management, and Chris Harling, Professor at IMEDE, Switzerland, provided encouragement and advice in the early stages of the project. Many other academics helped occasionally in many ways, but, with apologies, these are too many to acknowledge individually. The Social Science Research Council of Great Britain provided funds for some of the fieldwork reported in this book. The Rotary Foundation awarded a scholarship for a year of study at the Harvard University Graduate School of Business Administration which proved formative for this work. Conclusion of the project was made possible by the invaluable support of the Board of Research of Babson College.

Bunny Sutherland typed most of the manuscript and labored with constant good humor over successive drafts. I am grateful also to the word-processing personnel at Babson College for the typing of three chapters. Thanks are due to my wife, Sue, and my two sons, Grant and Christopher, for equably tolerating occasional poor humor, and to my mother, who unselfishly made it possible for me to work for concentrated periods of time. Sue, in particular, perceptively responded to the comments of the copy editor, constructed the indexes, and arranged for much of the typing. Thanks are also due to Lexington Books for professional and helpful assistance in the final stages of the manuscript. Weaknesses or errors that may be found in this book are those of the author.

Permission was granted by Harper and Row, New York, for reproduction of figure 1–1 from Jeffrey Pfeffer and Gerald R. Salincik, *The External Control of Organizations: A Resource Dependence Perspective*, 1978, and by the *Sloan Management Review*, for the use of material in chapter 21 of this book from my paper "Improving Management Response in Turbulent Times," Winter 1982 (pp. 3–12).

He who learns must suffer. And even in our sleep pain that cannot forget, falls drop by drop upon the heart, and in our despair, against our will comes wisdom to us by the awful grace of God.

—Aeschylus,
Agamemnon

Part I
Setting the Scene

But doth suffer a sea-change
Into something rich and strange.
—William Shakespeare,
The Tempest

The first part of this book sets the scene for this lengthy study. Chapter 1 states and justifies a basic premise underlying the study: that business organizations are experiencing environments that are not only changing more rapidly but, in particular, are increasingly subject to sudden irregularities or discontinuities. The focal question guiding the study is formulated as: How are discontinuities and their associated responses managed in business organizations?

As a prelude to the construction of a study to examine this question, chapter 2 reviews existing literature relating the management of organizations to changing environments. Three general schools of thought are discussed in chapter 2: strategy and planning, decision making, and organizational studies. Much is found in this review that seems provisionally of interest to the study, but no synthesis or definitive conclusions can be drawn from these diverse fields to provide an obvious basis for the development of the study.

Chapter 3 systematically develops a conceptual and propositional framework to guide the development of the study overall. Working from existing literature, the framework that is originated helps interpret the respective relevance and interrelationships of the separate schools of thought embraced in chapter 2. Nine general propositions are developed that collectively relate to (1) the likely general structure and nature of discontinuity and response in an organization, (2) the likely distinctive forms of response that are possible, (3) the types of organizational settings within which response can take place, and (4) the likely nature and character of decision-making processes under discontinuity. The remainder of the study works from and systematically examines these four sets of propositions.

Reflecting these propositions, chapter 4 describes the method and design of the study and introduces the sites and responses that were investigated in the fieldwork. Part I, therefore, fully documents the motivation for the study, background work, the definitions and viewpoints formative in its design, and how and where the subject of the study was investigated through extensive fieldwork.

1
Concerning Discontinuity

How are the extreme, sudden challenges that have been experienced in recent years managed? How do managers take their organizations into different directions of development? These are simple questions that address continuing and ubiquitous matters of concern to managers, academics, researchers, and all those whose fortunes are tied to the well-being of businesses. "Strategy!" or "Planning!" are likely answers, but this study has examined many situations in depth and has found that the concepts and techniques that comprise strategic planning provide only a partial and usually only a minor role. Systematic or rational decision making might be another answer, but was found to be a poor descriptor of what actually did or could have happened. The techniques and perspectives of the various fields within organizational studies were observed also to be used only infrequently, and produced only fragmentary answers to the overall challenges that the above questions posed managers. This work, through carefully derived and analyzed data faithful to what actually occurred in significant action taken by professional managers in leading and smaller corporations, challenges assumptions underpinning much that has been written about the practice of management.

Decision processes were found to be quintessentially incremental, uncertain, evolutionary, and situational. It followed from the analysis of decision processes and from observation that managers met major challenges through a practical, active, flexible, and sensitive pursuit of a series and collection of sometimes relatively independent initiatives. Solutions to problems were often partial, inelegant, obvious, imperfect, and nonoptimal. A willingness to take limited risks, together with a boldness in attempting the unknown and a readiness to experiment, were often important characteristics for management. A preparedness to change one's mind, an ability to learn from mistakes, and a receptivity to shifts in circumstances were significant attributes for decision makers. An awareness of the interests of others and an alertness to shifts in organization and environment were usually critical for successful response.

When a company was confronted by the need for response or change, a process was found that mainly involved a stimulation of suitable initiatives from the directly involved levels of the corporation, followed by adoption and support of the most constructive initiatives. A free atmosphere, a supportive culture, and a loose structure seemed useful in the stimulation of initiatives. Adoption of initiatives reflected a combination of internal and personal forces that encouraged the constructive and discouraged the unhelpful and destructive.

Responsive management is proposed for managing when wholesale revisions to existing streams of development are required or when major disruptions need to be met. A hands-off attitude, carefully tailored motivation systems, and a nonprotective organizational structure are proposed. A hands-off attitude encourages managers at many levels in an organization to develop initiatives. A carefully tailored motivation system encourages managers to present and support their initiatives. A nonprotective organizational structure forces managers to experience real problems arising from change and to create solutions accordingly.

A company's success depends upon the way it seizes opportunities and fits the character of its times. This chapter identifies discontinuities requiring additional flexibility and major corporate adaptation into new ways of thought and action as characteristic of the challenge facing corporations in the present and foreseeable future. In times of increasingly frequent and severe sudden changes occurring outside of a corporation's control, the skills of managing such challenges will be of increasing importance. Yet almost no studies have focused primarily on this topic, and much of what has been written is normatively based rather than subjected to the rigors of careful observation and systematic analysis.

The Environment and Discontinuity

The central premise on which this study is based is that organizations are experiencing environments that are not only changing more rapidly but, in particular, are increasingly subject to sudden irregularities. It has long been recognized that environments have become susceptible to "dynamic properties arising not simply from the interaction of identifiable component systems but [also] from the field itself."[1] Further, it is generally accepted (1) that environments are increasingly turbulent, (2) that organizations are increasingly less autonomous, and (3) that the actions of other organizations are increasingly more important.[2]

Various dimensions of organizational environments have been recognized in literature and usefully synthesized by Jeffrey Pfeffer and Gerald R. Salancik[3] as three structural characteristics: concentration, the extent to which power is widely dispersed; munificence, the availability or scarcity of resources; and interconnectedness, the number and pattern of linkages or connections. These three structural characteristics determine the extent of conflict or interdependence among social actors, which in turn determines the level of uncertainty in the environment. These structural characteristics and relationships among social actors are presented by Pfeffer and Salancik as a causal model, as reproduced in figure 1–1.

A number of trends of apparent long-term stability can be identified to characterize the evolution of the environment over time. For example, Herman Kahn and Anthony J. Weiner[4] propose a multifold (interconnected) trend toward (among other things): increasingly sensate (pragmatic) cultures; accumulation of scientific and technological knowledge; institutionalization of change, especially research, development, innovation, and diffusion; worldwide industrialization and modernization; increasing affluence and leisure; urbanization; increasing literacy and education; an increasing tempo of change; and an increasing universality of these trends. It is common to speak of the advanced nations entering a "post-industrial society," characterized by Daniel Bell[5] as one of professional, technical, and scientific occupations, information technology, abstract theory, future orientation, and where the axial principle is the codification of theoretical knowledge.[6] It is postulated that the overall trends and general characteristics of the contemporaneous environment, such as those noted above, shape and drive components of the causal model of the generalized dimensions of an organization's environment proposed by Pfeffer and Salancik (figure 1–1).[7] Inspection suggests that concentration, munificence, interconnectedness, interdependence, and conflict are likely, in general, to trend individually and collectively toward the production of increasing uncertainty. Application of this model of multifold trends and characteristics to this causal model of environments suggests further, however, that uncertainty is

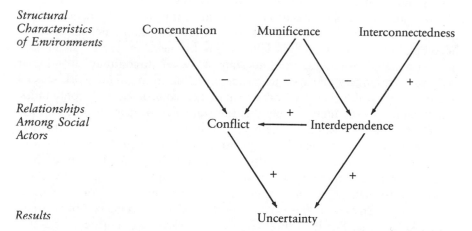

Figure 1–1. **Pfeffer and Salancik's Causal Model of Organizational Environments**

likely to become not only greater but to present, on average, challenges of progressively greater irregularity.

H. Igor Ansoff,[8] for example, presents four major trends in the twentieth century and shows, in particular, that "there has been a dramatic shrinkage of the time lag between invention and full market penetration [and] that the rate of invention has been accelerating." Further, Ansoff states that complexity is intensifying because of the increasing number of actors and the influence of actions brought to bear through intermediate partners.[9] From these and other observations, Ansoff hypothesizes: "During the twentieth century the key events in the environment . . . have become progressively (1) novel, (2) costlier to deal with, (3) faster, [and] (4) more difficult to anticipate."[10]

Another major viewpoint conveyed in Ansoff's *Strategic Management*[11] is that "uncertainty" or "environmental turbulence" occurs with different intensities. Five levels of environmental turbulence were posited, where the highest was termed "creative" and characterized by events that are discontinuous and novel, a rapidity of change shorter than the firm's response, a visibility of the future as only partially predictable weak signals, and by the presence of unpredictable surprises.[12] The central property of this extreme case is, therefore, the presence of partially predictable or unpredictable and novel events for which prior adaptation or preparation is largely impossible. This phenomenon and how managers achieve the flexibilities and adaptations that such discontinuities demand is the subject of this study.

This Study

The principal motivation for this study was, therefore, the recognition that discontinuity or sudden change is a phenomenon of relatively increasing importance but one for which present knowledge is limited and inconclusive. For a complex of reasons, work was delineated to business "for-profit" institutions and formulated around the focal question: How are discontinuities and their associated responses managed in business organizations? This work seeks a theory of practical, operational value to managers confronted by discontinuities. Examination of the literature permits the statement of general propositions, which are examined through extensive, depth fieldwork. Analysis of the field data in the light of the general propositions and the logical development of the research findings of others results in original findings. On the basis of these findings, some general implications of operational quality are made for those who need to manage major adaptation or achieve new levels of flexibility.

The position taken in this work is one faithful to and cognizant of research-based knowledge. Purely normatively inspired views on management action are avoided where those views might overlook the complexities of organizational processes. It is hoped that the observations of actual managerial practice made in part II and the findings presented in part III can form the basis for further development of knowledge by other researchers concerning organizational reaction to environmental change.

In summary, it has been possible in this book to:

Examine briefly the possible relevance of previous research and writing on strategy and planning, decision making, and organizational studies to the managing of response to discontinuity. It is found that each of these schools offers useful insights for this study but, both individually and collectively, prior studies provide neither a sufficient basis for the progress of the study nor an integrated nor consistent view of the managing of a corporation beyond existing flexibilities or through different directions of development. To appreciate properly the respective importance of the disparate but potentially relevant schools of thought, to devise a study that builds on and explicates present knowledge, to refine and elaborate existing knowledge, and to suggest fresh emphases or directions, it was judged necessary to develop logically and also from this literature and elsewhere a framework to guide the study.

Derive a conceptual and propositional foundation from which to conceive and design the study. The first set of propositions relates to the overall likely character and configuration of a response. The second set of propositions indentifies three basic types of response: corporate, administrative, and operating. A third set of propositions defines three distinct types of organizational settings within which a response can arise and form. Finally, a fourth set of four propositions addresses expectations concerning the nature of decision processes under discontinuity. This is presented in chapter 3.

Formulate a research design and method that allows examination of the propositions in ways that are rigorous and yield results of operational value to managers and to researchers. Conduct field observation in a sample stratified by type of organizational setting and by type of response, with several matched paired responses and other sample controls. This is presented in chapter 4.

Investigate a total of twenty-six instances of managing response, with fourteen of these responses researched in clinical depth. These field observations are written up as extensive textual summaries which provide a basis for the substantiation of findings. Summaries are presented in sufficient depth for managers to gain insights from their reading. They may also provide source data for analyses of how organizations handle change according to analytic perspectives different from that employed in this study. These data are presented in chapters 5 to 15.

Review observations recorded in the fieldwork for the extent to which the basic determining and distinguishing propositions for response of chapter 3 can be refuted, provisionally accepted, or modified. A proposed model of response in terms of various general steps is discussed, together with the proposed fragmented pattern of subresponses around an organization. Acceptance of responses as characterized by novelty, instability, and compression is also discussed. Distinctions between corporate, administrative, and operating responses are commented upon and developed further. The concept of complex, divisional, and simple organizational settings is found to be basically sound, but an amendment to improve the explanatory power of this organization contingency view on managing response is developed. These results are presented in chapter 16.

Find, on the basis of the fieldwork conducted for this study, that even radical changes in organizations employ solutions that are close to the experience of the decision makers and represent small steps from the status quo. Indeed, only seven elemental processes of choice were found to explain how all the responses investigated in this study came about by realigning, reemphasizing, or replicating elements already in existence "near by." These seven processes can be readily identified by managers in live situations, and it is believed that they can be operationalized also for the purpose of further research. This is presented in chapter 17.

Show how solving problems was achieved by the joint use of two distinct modes of managerial action: planning and analysis on one hand, and a cybernetic, satisficing (the "good enough" solution), trial-and-error mode of action on the other. Each of these modes was found to have unique uses in response, and managing response required a balancing of the two modes at each point in time and through time. Generally, the experimental or trial-and-error mode dominated because of the high uncertainty that was typical in response, with planning providing coherence and analysis the necessary factual and interpretative input. These two modes are explained and their particular uses as found in the fieldwork identified. Again, the results are believed to be readily usable by managers and management researchers for their respective purposes. This is presented in chapter 18.

Present responses as the developing of initiatives driven, according to a three-phase structure, by the application of three conjoint managerial processes. A pattern of antecedent circumstances was present in all responses before a definite commitment was made by management to design a response to a then reasonably well-defined problem. Second, development occurred in a typically involved and iterative manner until a "prototype" was originated to resolve the problems posed by discontinuity that a sufficient body of management approved. Third, the response maturated as this prototype was put into force, refined in its details, and incorporated into the organization as a whole. Responses were driven through these three phases by an evolutionary process dependent on the contribution of the time and other resources of managers, and propelled by the conscious or perhaps unconscious choice of managers to elect their usually scarce resources for the progress of the particular response that materialized. This is presented in chapter 19.

Find that situational context both originates and determines responses. An overall focus apparently determines which response arises when, and the overall character of a response. Just where a response originates in an organization is also found to depend on local situational features, to include the professional background and personality of the respective managers. Finally, the pattern of the various parties and their various motives and vested interests apparently produce many concluding details of a response. This is presented in chapter 20.

Conclude that managing response should be a practical, active, flexible, and sensitive process of stimulation of initiatives and adoption of selected courses of action. This is presented in chapter 21. Implications of this study for subsequent research are also presented in chapter 21.

The agenda for the study is therefore substantial, but the account is written to be readable without esoterica, obscurity, or pomposity. The intention is that the text be understandable to an educated layman with a basic appreciation of managerial processes.

Notes

1. F.E. Emery and E.L. Trist, "The Causal Texture of Organizational Environments," *Human Relations*, Vol. 18, Fall 1965, p. 32.

2. Shirley Terryberry, "The Evolution of Organizational Environments," *Administrative Science Quarterly*, Vol. 12, March 1968, pp. 590–613.

3. Jeffrey Pfeffer and Gerald R. Salancik, *The External Control of Organizations: A Resource Dependence Perspective* (New York: Harper and Row, 1978), p. 68.

4. Herman Kahn and Anthony J. Weiner, *Toward the Year 2000: A Framework for Speculation* (New York: Macmillan, 1967).

5. Daniel Bell, *The Coming of Post-Industrial Society: A Venture in Social Forecasting* (New York: Basic Books, 1973), p. 117.

6. References to the "post-industrial society" are legion. Of particular relevance to the field of strategy is H. Igor Ansoff, *Strategic Management* (New York: John Wiley and Sons, 1979), p. 34.

7. Pfeffer and Salancik, op. cit.

8. Ansoff, op. cit., p. 33.

9. Ibid., p. 34.
10. Ibid., p. 35.
11. Ibid., pp. 60–64.
12. H. Igor Ansoff, *Implanting Strategic Management* (Englewood Cliffs, N.J.: Prentice–Hall, 1984) pp. 10–15.

2
Managing Response

T he ability of institutions to manage in prevailing conditions is questioned by many writers. Warnings include the counterintuitive nature of many problems.[1] Present theoretical models of cause and effect are considered too simple, since subtle interdependencies outside of the models amplify small errors and create second, third, or higher order disturbances around expectations.[2] A perspective of the "whole system" is acknowledged to be required, an opposing philosophy to the reductionist approach to knowledge which has characterized most thought over past centuries by splitting problems into progressively smaller parts.[3,4]

Need for a revised outlook is said to bring about its own problems. Donald A. Schon observes that many actions are "anti-responses" where the discomfort of reality is wrongly corrected by its rejection.[5] According to Schon there is a need for institutions to learn and change by an open-ended, flexible, and adaptive approach to knowledge, because every problem will be new. He comments: "The here and now provides the test, the source and the limit of knowledge . . . existential theory building must grow out of the here-and-now of this situation, must be nourished by and tested against it."[6]

How relevant are present perspectives on managing an organization in relation to change in its environment to the problem of managing sudden and novel departures from pre-existing conditions? Three sets of knowledge seem relevant to the problems of managing decision processes in discontinuity, to be termed here as (1) the Strategy and Planning School, (2) the Decision-making School, and (3) the Organizational Schools.

The Strategy and Planning School

As change speeded up, and as external factors increased in their importance, systematic ways have been found to manage the link between corporation and environment. Strategy and the related field of business policy satisfied this need by "expressing a persistent concept of the business so as to exclude some possible new activities and suggest entry into others."[7] A skillful matching of the strengths and weaknesses of the corporation with the opportunities and threats confronting it is sought in the perspective. The business of the company—its markets, products, and other matters—is regarded as variable and to be reassessed continuously as circumstances alter. Planning formalizes review of the corporation and its external circumstances, and also aims at coordination of functional areas within a single business and coordination of several businesses within a diversified corporation.

Strategy and Planning in Discontinuity

For its success, a strategy relies on the accuracy and specificity of its view of the future. Shifts through sudden change weaken that reference point and challenge the key assumption on which the concept depends. Many writers proposed means of accommodating "disturbances" within the strategic planning framework. For events which are uncertain but to which a range of probabilities can be assigned, *contingency planning* was described by Russell L. Ackoff and others.[8] Plans are drawn up for each eventuality so that they may be implemented according to the development of circumstances. In situations where events are so uncertain as to be incapable of probability assessment, Ackoff noted that preparations cannot be made directly, but can be made indirectly through *responsiveness planning*.[9] Such planning is directed toward designing an organization and a system for managing it that can quickly detect deviations from the expected and respond to them effectively. Responsiveness is thereby built into an organization. Equivalent approaches have been described. For example, H. Igor Ansoff proposed a *flexibility objective* which includes external flexibility through a diversified pattern of product markets and suppliers, and internal flexibility through liquidity of resources.[10]

Some dissatisfaction with strategy and planning emerged in the 1970s noting increased rates of change and less predictability. Strategic planning, the most rigid manifestation of the strategic viewpoint, was viewed by some as too structured and somewhat inapplicable. More adaptive approaches to planning have been proposed where varying mixtures of contingencies, monitoring systems, links with environmental assumptions, frequent updates, and qualitative analysis have been incorporated.[11] Managing strategic surprise by watching for and responding to weak signals of imminent threats has been advocated.[12]

As a means of dealing with more uncertain environments, H. Igor Ansoff, Roger P. Declerk, and Robert L. Hayes proposed *strategic management* as opposed to *strategic planning*.[13] Strategic management is a term that has enjoyed wide adoption and is usually conceived as incorporating matters beyond products and markets (the focus of strategic planning), places greater emphasis on constant surveillance of the environment, and usually implies a more complete and more systematic link with implementation than many authors had embraced before.[14,15] Bernard Taylor and J.R. Sparkes proposed an equivalent approach in *policy analysis,* which is presented as a systematic procedure for revising and reassessing policy in the face of change.[16] Thus the stance of literature on strategy and planning in the face of greater uncertainty in the environment has been primarily one of devising further systematic procedures to incorporate into existing corporate planning systems.

Incrementalism

While the concept of strategy and planning (particularly when modified as noted above) will continue to be a useful and a rational approach to managing environmental change, a contrasting perspective has also been reported by some researchers. H. Edward Wrapp asserted that good managers don't make policy decisions.[17] He saw advantages in managers' avoiding policy straitjackets and leaving statements of purpose deliberately imprecise. Such vagueness was able to embody inconsistencies through time which conveniently permitted expediencies or changes of direction.

Charles E. Lindblom observed what he termed *incrementalism,* where decision makers reacted to changes in a piecemeal fashion; any unity arose naturally or fortuitously rather than in a planned conscious way.[18] Lindblom recognized an opportunistic process where the administrator made a series of choices based on limited comparisons and incomplete data.

A similarly indefinite approach to management has been recognized by many other writers. Henry Mintzberg corroborated the more incremental view on strategy making.[19] James Brian Quinn stated that "muddling" processes are, in fact, purposeful, politically astute, and effective management practices[20] and that "managers *consciously* and *proactively* move forward *incrementally.*"[21] (Quinn's emphases) Richard Tanner Pascale described *ambiguous management* (especially in Japan) and showed it as an essential viewpoint.[22] Michael B. McCaskey described managing in "more complex, interconnected, unsettled and ambiguous" conditions, for which he argues that traditional functions such as directive control are diminished and others such as creative conceptualization are enlarged.[23]

The Decision-making School

The concept of strategy and the procedures of strategic planning embody what has been termed *rational decision making.* Systematic generation of alternatives, calculation of pay-offs, and a consistent basis of evaluation of possible outcomes underlie strategy and planning prescriptions. As Simon noted, "There is a complete lack of evidence that, in human choice situations of any complexity, these computations can be, or are in fact, performed."[24] Herbert A. Simon's seminal work observed that lack of information and a frequent inability to analyze complex circumstances led decision makers to *satisfice* rather than to *optimize*.[25]

Studies of Decision Making

Summaries of the findings of a representative selection of four important studies of actual decision-making behavior are presented in figure 2–1: the works of James G. March and Herbert A. Simon,[26] Richard M. Cyert and James G. March,[27] David Braybrooke and Charles E. Lindblom,[28] and John D. Steinbruner.[29] Although the selection of works in the figure embraces private enterprise, public management, and a presidential foreign affairs decision, all the works are consistent in describing a real decision-making process that is distinct from that assumed in "rational decision making." Among other things, a sequential, nonexhaustive, local, nonoptimal, reactive, crisis-instigated, loosely structured type of problem solving was observed by all the writers.

The less systematic type of decision making described by writers probably issues from their commitment to study real management activities in detail. Such workers have not assumed, as Henry Mintzberg states, that the integrated systematic approach "*can* work and *is* appropriate."[30] The few researchers who have adopted a more descriptive view on method and who have worked in large corporations have added insights to the findings of the workers noted in figure 2–1 according to their respective focus of inquiry. Some examples not already cited include Alfred D. Chandler's study of strategy and structure,[31] Joseph L. Bower's study of the resource allocation process,[32] Robert W. Ackerman's study of the management of social challenge,[33] Richard Normann's study of the management of growth and renewal,[34] and Henry Mintzberg's study of unstructured decision making.[35] Each developed a set of findings of mostly indirect relevance to this study, but they all described complicated and changing circumstances where problems were slowly solved in an interactive and uncertain manner over a considerable period of time.

But within the decision-making school the work of possibly greatest relevance to the focus of this study on decision processes in discontinuity is that of several researchers who have identified and commented upon a higher mode of decision making. This higher mode links with more creative, more irregular, more sudden, or more extreme kinds of organizational change. The next section reviews the various identifications that have been made of a higher mode of decision making and the insights that they provide.

Decision Making in a Higher Mode

Joseph A. Schumpeter, in 1947, spoke of an *adaptive response* when an economy, an industry, or a firm change within existing practices. A *creative response* was described by Schumpeter as "something that is outside of the range of existing practice."[36] Chandler cited this division in his study of strategy and structure of American enterprise.[37] Adoption of multidivisional structure at DuPont, General Motors, Standard Oil Company (New Jersey), and Sears Roebuck and Company were recognized as examples of creative responses. On the other hand, the companies were understood to be committing an adaptive response in the building of departmental headquarters or further field units as extensions of current activities along the lines of existing custom.

William J. Gore observed in 1964, also based on field research:

> The point is that we have two modes of decisional activity: activation of sanctioned patterns of structured behavior and consequent maintenance and reinforcement of the status quo; and activation of indigenous patterns of accommodative behaviors which result in the loosening of commitments supporting existing structures and the introduction of potential changes.[38]

Gore also distinguished three types of decision: *routine*—"an habituated behavior pattern" such as triggered by a fire bell in a "drilled" and "prepared" institution; *adaptive*—a realignment of a routine pattern of behavior; and *innovative,* where an incompatible internal or external pressure has to be incorporated or withstood in the organization.[39]

Normann considered formulation of existing arrangements into the future with only minor adaption as *product variations,* and situations where existing circumstances needed to be substantially altered as *product reorientations.* Normann also argued that this basic distinction is widely generalizable: "Adaptive specialization and adaptive generalization are obviously analogous to Kuhn's 'normal problem solving' and extraordinary problem solving, to Buckley's 'homeostasis' and 'morphogenesis' and to our own concepts of product variation and reorientation."[40] In a similar vein, Philip Selznick identified this higher form of corporate change as *critical decisions,*[41] March and Simon likewise referred to *programmed* and *unprogrammed* decisions,[42] and Eric Rhenman distinguished *disturbance* and *irreversible change.*[43]

Insights provided by the above researchers on the processes underlying what they have individually termed creative responses, unprogrammed decisions, innovative decisions, reorientations, critical decisions, and irreversible changes incorporate considerable consistency. Common themes included how such decisions do not usually come naturally and are often motivated by crisis, how goals influence the process, how stress and the role of the generation of alternatives are prominent, and how the part played by people, as decision makers, and the specific characteristics of the situation within which the decision takes place are often crucial.

Crisis. March and Simon noted that: "Individuals and organizations give preferred treatment to alternatives that represent continuation of present programs over those that represent change."[44] They attributed the state of affairs to the

March and Simon, *Human Problem-Solving*
(1)   Optimizing is replaced by satisficing to underline the extent that only satisfactory levels of the criterion variables are attained.
(2)   Alternatives of action and consequences of action are discovered sequentially through search processes.
(3)   A repertoire of action programs is developed by organizations and individuals, and these serve as the alternatives of choice in recurrent situations.
(4)   Each specific action program deals with a restricted range of situations and a restricted range of consequences.
(5)   Each action program is capable of being executed in semi-independence of the others—they are only loosely coupled together.

Cyert and March, *Behavioral Theory of the Firm*
(1)   Quasi-resolution of conflicts
      • Local rationality
      • Acceptable level decision rules (rather than optimizing)
      • Sequential attention to goals
(2)   Uncertainty avoidance
      • Feedback–react decision rules
      • Negotiation with institutions in the environment
(3)   Problemistic search
      • Problem motivated
      • Simple concepts of causality
      • Subject to bias
      • Local perspective
(4)   Organizational learning
      • Goals adapt with experience
      • Some aspects attended to above others
      • Tendency for repetition until inadequacy demonstrated

Braybrooke and Lindblom, *Disjointed Incrementalism*
(1)   *Margin Dependent Choice* focused on:
      • Incremental alteration of existing social states
      • Policies whose known or expected consequences differ incrementally from the status quo.
      • Examination of policies proceeds through comparative analysis of no more than the marginal or incremental differences in the consequent social states rather than through an attempt at more comprehensive analysis of the social states.
(2)   Restricted variety: the policy analyst attends to a smaller variety than all possible policies that might be imagined.
(3)   Restricted number of consequences are considered for any given policy—limited to those for which the policy analyst has tools.
(4)   Adjustment of objectives to policies
(5)   Problems are transformed as data clarifies issues.
(6)   Analysis and evaluation together follow a serial pattern.
(7)   Since policy analysis is incremental, exploratory, serial, and marked by adjustment of ends to means, it is to be expected that stable, long-term aspirations will not appear as dominant critical values in the eyes of the analyst.
(8)   Social fragmentation of analysis and evaluation which takes place at a very large number of points.

Steinbruner, *Cybernetic Paradigm Amended by Cognitive Theory*
(1)   Vaguely specified conception which posits nominally articulated, preservative values, and which does not yield a coherent preference ordering for alternatives states of the world under trade-off conditions
(2)   Uncertainty controlled by focused attention and programmed response
(3)   No alternative outcome calculations
(4)   No updated probability assessments
(5)   Not a causal learning process but instrumental
(6)   Collective decisions fragmented into small segments and treated segmentally
(7)   Process dominated by established procedure
(8)   Tendency to set up decision problems in terms of a single value
(9)   Tendency to associate a single outcome with the available alternatives
(10) Tendency to restrict information to a relatively limited number of variables

Figure 2–1. Summary of Findings from Some Major Studies of Decision Making

individual or organization not searching for the more original solution until the "present course is in some sense unsatisfactory."[45] Chandler similarly observed of his depth studies: "In all three companies, it took a sizable crisis to bring about action. Yet all three presidents had received proposals for reorganization before that crisis made their usefulness apparent."[46]

Goals. To overcome a process that would otherwise "be slow and halting at best,"[47] March and Simon emphasized that goal clarity and determined deadlines would focus and hasten. Other writers, however, observed that "goal ambiguity" is intrinsic to problems of this general type. Gore specifically defined innovative decisions as "where there is not only lack of agreement upon the pattern relevant to achieving a goal but also disagreement about goals as the ends of activity."[48] Normann preferred visions "as intuitive ideas of reasonable future states"[49] over explicit goals so that the type of step-by-step learning associated with reorientation could take place. A more bounded aspiration would have been, to Normann, more stultifying than motivating.

Stress and Alternatives. March and Simon hypothesized that unprogrammed decisions are ones where initiation of alternatives is a vital part. The importance of this activity was contrasted with programmed situations where selection of one course of action from a set of alternatives is characteristic.[50] Gore placed this mechanism in an organizational context and noted that the situation is "further complicated because the choice is not between two major alternatives but between hundreds of small ones that have limited and localized effects." Selection from among them was regarded as the source of stress that was recorded as prevalent in innovative decisions: "Whose claims should be honored and whose ignored?"[51]

Gore recognized that innovative decisions expose clashes of purposes and divergent activities that would not otherwise emerge in an organization in the normal run of business. They typically involve "uncomfortable changes in status, role, and the patterns of activity" and are recognized as a "stressful experience."[52] Addressing synthesis between learning and the development of knowledge and growth of corporations, Normann saw tensions, misfits, and imbalance as both progenitor and outcome of reorientation and growth in general. Structure, control systems, environment, and reward systems were seen to potentially impoverish or enrich such development. A dialectic process between alternatives is specified in which tensions and misfits play a constructive part in identifying problems and propagating solutions or opportunities.[53] March and Simon noted that frequently a new organization is created for the purpose; this step is said to avoid innovation's being "hampered by tradition and precedent."[54]

People. Fundamental to Normann's conception of the growth of business was the core group of individuals in the corporation in question.[55] Their interactions and combinations of roles was seen as intrinsic to the generation of business ideas and associated needs of growth in an organization. A parallel, although different, emphasis on particular personnel was also described by Chandler.[56] The creative response of forming separate divisions in a company was found to take place where individual innovators had an intimate contact with the problem, and where they were given or took the time to study it. Particularly interesting is Chandler's finding that the personality and training of the innovators was a factor in stimulating response. Most of the prime movers in the reorganizations were engineering graduates "who showed the greatest interest in systematizing and explicitly defining organizational relationships."[57] However, he recorded that undoubtedly more important was a rational, analytic view of the problems of industrial administration that existed widely in the enterprises he studied.[58]

Context. The factors of a personal or historical nature that influence a decision were termed *situational context* by Bower. Factors that influence decisions (specifically resource allocations) associated with the formal organization, the system of information and control used to measure performance of the business, and the systems used to measure and reward performance of managers were termed *structural context*.[59] In his study of the process of resource allocation in a multidivisional firm, Bower found that these situational structural forces not only played a part in deciding outcomes but were also modified by managers to facilitate desired outcomes among subordinates.

The Organizational Schools

Organization theory generally recognizes organizations as systems of internal relations existing within a larger environment from which the organization draws inputs and discharges outputs. Literature taking this "general systems" view provides many valuable insights to the conceptual and propositional framework of this study to be developed in chapter 3 and to which the work of W. Ross Ashby is particularly relevant.[60] James D. Thompson's[61] propositional study of organizations as bounded but open systems within an environment is a central example of this perspective. The roots of the classic works of Chester I. Barnard's *The Functions of the Executive*[62] and Simon's *Administrative Behavior*[63] can be traced to the ideas of general systems theory.

Relationship of Organization and Environment. Studies concerning the relationship of organizations with their environments showed, in particular, that an organization's internal structure is contingent upon determining features of the organization's environment. Raymond Miles and Charles Snow provide a good review of this research literature.[64] For example, it has been shown, among other things, that organizations with nonhierarchic structures are better suited to faster changing environments, and that high-performing organizations show higher differentiation of functions associated with a higher state of integration between the functions.[65] It is reported that matrix and modular organizational forms are suited to rapidly changing environments[66] because of complex interdependencies and needs for high information-processing activity.[67] A general conclusion of this work is that organization structure is contingent on characteristics of the environment and, further, that when elements such as environment, technology, social systems, dominant coalitions, and formal organizational arrangements fit together consistently and congruently, organizational effectiveness tends to result.[68] Studies of organizational structure tend to focus on adjusting to a generalized level of environmental change, while discontinuity represents significant departure from such a generalized level. Findings in this subarea may therefore be considered suggestively relevant rather than directly relevant.

Adaptation. Studies embraced in the above discussion of the relationships of organization and environmental change fall within the "information complexity perspective."[69] In this perspective, investigators are concerned with "the impact of uncertainty or the ability of organizational participants to make decisions, and in consequent organizational restructuring to cope with uncertainty."[70] The second major approach in organizational theory "treats environments as consisting of resources for which organizations compete."[71] This resource dependence perspective is exemplified by the work of Jeffrey Pfeffer and Gerald R. Salancik[72] but embraces also the field of industrial organization such as the work of Richard E. Caves; for example.[73] Paul R. Lawrence and Davis Dyer consider adaptation as a synthesizing concept between these two perspectives as "the process by which an organization and its environment reach and maintain an equilibrium ensuring the survival of the system as a whole."[74] Adaptability requires both efficiency and innovation, and is hypothesized by Lawrence and Dyer to link with strategy type (prospector, defender, reactor, and analyzer[75]) and organizational form. Again, the perspective is long-run equilibrium and not adaptability in the face of irregularities around general stabilities.

Organization Development. A substantial body of literature takes the view of diagnosing, designing, and executing change in organizations. A panoply of methods have been developed for improving organizational effectiveness, including management training devices, methods of conflict resolution, systems for organization design, measurement tools for attitudes, climate, and processes, and approaches for intervention in the workings of organizations.[76] Several examples of these techniques played a part in the responses to discontinuity investigated in this study. Their application, however, facilitated responses fragmentarily and little was provided by them as to how to manage response in an overall sense.

Management of Crises. Crises have, of course, been ever-present in corporate life, and research in that area might be expected to provide findings of value to managing in sudden change. All investigations in crisis management take one of two perspectives.[77] The first is a perspective that recognizes crises as the result of past mismanagement and concentrates on what should have been done to avoid the crisis.[78] A small body of literature takes a second perspective, which recognizes crises as possible features of even well-managed corporate life. That research has concentrated on methods of reducing the organizational stresses and related "inefficiencies" that crises bring about.[79] Studies have not attempted development of a theory that explains the development and appropriate management of crises from an organizational or decision process standpoint.

To address the research topic of managing response, it is necessary to build a conceptual and propositional foundation that will help to appreciate the respective importance and possible interrelationships of these potentially relevant but disparate schools of thought. With that conceptual foundation, and the definition and clarification presented by it, a study can be devised that builds on and explicates present knowledge and serves also to refine and elaborate that knowledge and to suggest fresh emphases or directions. The next chapter develops this conceptual and propositional foundation.

Notes

1. Jay W. Forrester, *Urban Dynamics* (Cambridge: MIT Press, 1969), pp. 10–11.
2. F.E. Emery and E.L. Trist, *Toward a Social Ecology, Contextural Appreciation of the Future in the Present* (New York: Plenum Press, 1973).
3. Russell L. Ackoff, *Redesigning the Future* (New York: John Wiley and Sons, 1974).

4. Basil John Alexander Hargraves and Jan Dauman, *Business Survival and Social Change* (New York: John Wiley and Sons, 1975).

5. Donald A. Schon, *Beyond the Stable State* (London: Maurice Temple Smith Ltd., 1971).

6. Ibid.

7. Kenneth R. Andrews, *The Concept of Corporate Strategy* (Homewood, Ill.: Dow Jones–Irwin, 1971), p. 28.

8. Russell L. Ackoff, *A Concept of Corporate Planning* (New York: John Wiley and Sons, 1970).

9. Ibid.

10. H. Igor Ansoff, *Corporate Strategy: An Analytical Approach to Business Policy for Growth and Expansion* (New York: McGraw–Hill, 1965), pp. 56–58.

11. Ronald N. Paul, Neil B. Donavan, and James W. Taylor, "The Reality Gap in Strategic Planning," *Harvard Business Review,* May–June 1978, pp. 124–130; Michael L. Johnson, "Strategic Planning—Is That What You're Doing?" *Industry Week,* November 27, 1978, pp. 94–97; John C. Faulkner, "Strategic Plans: Made to be Broken?" *Management Review,* April 1979, pp. 21–25; "The New Planning," *Business Week,* December 1978, pp. 62–68; and "The Corporate Strategy Problem," *Management Today,* October 1979, p. 87.

12. H. Igor Ansoff, "Managing Strategic Surprise by Response to Weak Signals," *California Management Review,* Winter 1976.

13. H. Igor Ansoff, Roger P. Declerck, and Robert L. Hayes, *From Strategic Planning to Strategic Management* (London: John Wiley and Sons, 1976), p. 44.

14. Dan E. Schendel and Charles W. Hofer, eds., *Strategic Management* (Boston: Little, Brown, 1979).

15. Arnoldo C. Hax and Nicolas S. Majluf, *Strategic Management: An Integrative Perspective* (Englewood Cliffs, N.J.: Prentice–Hall, 1984).

16. Bernard Taylor and John R. Sparkes, *Corporate Strategy and Planning* (London: Heinemann, 1977).

17. H. Edward Wrapp, "Good Managers Don't Make Policy Decisions," *Harvard Business Review,* September/October 1967, pp. 91–99.

18. Charles E. Lindblom, "The Science of 'Muddling Through,' " *Public Administration Review,* Spring 1959, pp. 79–88.

19. Henry Mintzberg, *The Nature of Managerial Work* (New York: Harper and Row, 1973), pp. 132–164.

20. James Brian Quinn, "Strategic Goals: Process and Politics," *Sloan Management Review,* Fall 1977, pp. 21–37.

21. James Brian Quinn, *Strategies for Change—Logical Incrementalism* (Homewood, Ill.: Irwin, 1980).

22. Richard Tanner Pascale and Anthony G. Athos, *The Art of Japanese Management* (New York: Simon and Schuster, 1980).

23. Michael B. McCaskey, *The Executive Challenge: Managing Change and Ambiguity* (Boston: Pitman, 1982), p. 177.

24. Herbert A. Simon, *Administrative Behavior* (New York: Free Press, 1976), p. 104.

25. Ibid.

26. James G. March and Herbert A. Simon, *Organizations* (New York: John Wiley and Sons, 1958).

27. Richard M. Cyert and James G. March, *A Behavioral Theory of the Firm* (Englewood Cliffs, N.J.: Prentice–Hall, 1963).

28. David Braybrooke and Charles E. Lindblom, *A Strategy of Decision: Policy Evaluation as a Social Process* (New York: Free Press, 1963).

29. John D. Steinbruner, *The Cybernetic Theory of Decision* (Princeton: Princeton University Press, 1974).

30. Henry Mintzberg, "Policy as a Field of Management Theory," *Academy of Management Review,* January 1977, pp. 88–103.

31. Alfred D. Chandler, Jr., *Strategy and Structure, Chapters in the History of the Industrial Enterprise* (Cambridge: MIT Press, 1962).

32. Joseph L. Bower, *Managing the Resource Allocation Process* (Homewood, Ill.: Irwin, 1972).

33. Robert W. Ackerman, *The Social Challenge to Business* (Cambridge: Harvard University Press, 1975).

34. Richard Normann, *Management for Growth* (New York: John Wiley and Sons, 1977).

35. Henry Mintzberg, Duru Raisinghani, and André Théorêt, "The Structure of Unstructured Decision Processes," *Administrative Sciences Quarterly,* June 1976, pp. 246–275.

36. Joseph A. Schumpeter, "The Creative Response in Economic History," *The Journal of Economic History,* November 1947, pp. 149–159.

37. Alfred D. Chandler, Jr., op. cit., pp. 349–388.

38. William J. Gore, *Administrative Decision Making—A Heuristic Model* (New York: John Wiley and Sons, 1964), p. 30.

39. Ibid., p. 131.

40. Richard Normann, op. cit., p. 75.

41. Philip Selznick, *Leadership in Administration* (New York: Harper and Row, 1957).

42. James G. March and Herbert A. Simon, op. cit., pp. 209–210.

43. Eric Rhenman, *Organization Theory for Long-range Planning* (London: John Wiley and Sons, 1973).

44. James G. March and Herbert A. Simon, op. cit., p. 173.

45. Ibid.

46. Alfred D. Chandler, Jr., op. cit., p. 375.

47. James G. March and Herbert A. Simon, op. cit., p. 187.

48. William J. Gore, op. cit., p. 132.

49. Richard Normann, op. cit., p. 97.

50. James G. March and Herbert A. Simon, op. cit.

51. William J. Gore, op. cit., p. 142.

52. Ibid., p. 185.

53. Richard Normann, op. cit., pp. 52–138.

54. James G. March and Herbert A. Simon, op. cit., p. 187.

55. Richard Normann, op. cit., pp. 122–138.

56. Alfred D. Chandler, Jr., op. cit., pp. 389–400.

57. Ibid., p. 392.

58. Ibid., p. 394.

59. Joseph L. Bower, op. cit., p. 71.

60. W. Ross Ashby, *Design for a Brain* (London: Chapman and Hall, 1952); *An Introduction to Cybernetics* (London: Chapman and Hall, 1956).

61. James D. Thompson, *Organizations in Action* (New York: McGraw–Hill, 1967).

62. Chester I. Barnard, *The Functions of the Executive* (Cambridge: Harvard University Press, 1938).

63. Herbert A. Simon, op. cit.

64. Raymond Miles and Charles Snow, *Organizational Strategy, Structures and Processes* (New York: McGraw–Hill, 1978), Appendix.

65. These are the central findings of, respectively, Tom Burns and G.M. Stalker (*The Management of Innovation,* London: Tavistock, 1961) and Paul R. Lawrence and Jay W. Lorsch (*Organization and Environment: Managing Differentiation and Integration,* Cambridge: Harvard University, Graduate School of Business Administration, Division of Research, 1967).

66. Stanley M. Davis and Paul R. Lawrence, *Matrix* (Reading, Mass.: Addison–Wesley, 1977); Douglas C. Basil and Curtis W. Cook, *The Management of Change* (New York: McGraw–Hill, 1974), p. 29.

67. Jay R. Galbraith, *Designing Complex Organizations* (Reading, Mass.: Addison–Wesley, 1973).

68. Some works that variously demonstrate this conclusion in addition to those cited immediately above include: Joan Woodward, *Industrial Organization: Theory and Practice* (London: Oxford University Press, 1965); Jay W. Lorsch and John Morse, *Organizations and Their Members* (New York: Harper and Row, 1974); Charles Perrow, *Organizational Analysis: A Sociological View* (Monterey, Calif.: Brooks/Cole, 1970); and E.L. Trist, G.W. Higgens, H. Murray, and A.B. Pollock, *Organizational Choice* (London: Tavistock, 1963). Jeffrey D. Ford and John W. Slocum, Jr., review the work of the "Aston Group" and related work relevant to this conclusion in "Size, Technology, Environment, and the Structure of Organizations," *Academy of Management Review,* October 1977.

69. Paul R. Lawrence and Davis Dyer, *Renewing American Industry: Organizing for Efficiency and Innovation* (New York: Free Press, 1983).

70. Howard E. Aldrich, *Organizations and Environments* (Englewood Cliffs, N.J.: Prentice–Hall, 1979), p. 110.

71. Ibid.

72. Jeffrey Pfeffer and Gerald R. Salancik, *The External Control of Organizations: A Resource Dependence Perspective* (New York: Harper and Row, 1978).

73. Richard E. Caves, *American Industry: Structure, Conduct and Performance* (Englewood Cliffs, N.J.: Prentice–Hall, 1972).

74. Paul R. Lawrence and Davis Dyer, op. cit., p. 295.

75. Raymond Miles and Charles Snow, op. cit.

76. A bibliography of organization development perspectives and techniques is provided in John P. Kotter, *Organizational Dynamics: Diagnosis and Intervention* (Reading, Mass.: Addison–Wesley, 1978), particularly pp. 1–3.

77. Stephen J. Andriole, ed., *Corporate Crisis Management* (Princeton: Petrocelli, 1985).

78. Richard Austin Smith, *Corporation in Crisis* (New York: Doubleday, 1963).

79. Carolyn Smart, ed., *Journal of Business Administration,* Special Issue: "Studies on Crisis Management," Spring 1978.

3
Defining the Study

C hapter 1 showed that the environment of organizations has an incipient capacity for change, and proposed that environments were generally becoming more likely to display severe, sudden changes or discontinuities. Chapter 2 examined literature relevant to managing organizations in relation to their environments. This chapter presents, first, a conceptual and propositional framework to help interpret the extensive and detailed data collected for this study and to provide a basis for the development and statement of findings. Second, three distinct types of response to discontinuity are identified for which many aspects of managing discontinuity are proposed to be distinctively different. Third, three types of organizational settings are described which are presupposed to condition the form and progress of the management of a response. Last, some general propositions are developed, using the review of chapter 2, relating to decision processes under discontinuity. Taken together, these four sets of propositions guided the design and progress of the study.

Discontinuity

An organization is viewed as a system of cooperative activities of more than one person for the accomplishment of a common goal.[1] This unit exists in an environment defined as "the external conditions and influences that affect an organization's life and development."[2] There is a closer *working environment* of customers, supplies, labor, and the like, and a more removed *broader environment* of competitors and trends that affect the system of organization and working environment.[3] A surviving organization is one where the match of rganization and total environment embodies sufficient flexibility to withstand environmental challenges, and also one that adapts appropriately through time to environmental change.[4] *Strategy* is this configuration of an organization with its environment, and the goal formation, resource allocation, and other means that produce that configuration.

When environmental change exceeds the flexibility of an organization, or when environmental change exceeds the rate or conflicts with the direction of adaptation, this is termed *discontinuity*.[5,6] Where the organization is a continuing entity, one or more *responses* by members of the organization are necessary to achieve a sufficient attainment of goals or strategy.[7] Response is brought about by a number of subresponses that collectively adjust the system of organization and environment until it again functions so that it can satisfactorily meet the goals of the then organization members.

Response to discontinuity is, therefore, likely to involve the taking of unprecedented actions in poorly understood circumstances. The environment is likely to be characterized by major uncertainty, and the organization's actions by significant deficiencies in structure, systems, intelligence, and processes. Intense organizational activity is likely, therefore, to take place. The efficiency and effectiveness of the decision processes, or the activities and constituent actions that produce responses, must, therefore, be critical to the future of the organization.

Environmental change cannot be expected to map one-to-one into the internal structure of an organization—different parts would be expected to be differently affected. This differentiation holds several implications for the expected pattern of activities within an organization responding to discontinuity, particularly in more complex settings:

> *Asymmetry and situational specificity.* Discontinuities yield asymmetric organizational activities dependent upon the specific conjunctions of the respective parts of an organization with their respective environments at each point in time.[8]
>
> *Situational specificity* prompts local, idiosyncratic initiatives.[9]
>
> *Synthesis.* These fragmented and local activities constituting specialized parts of a response (subresponse) are expected either to work within or collectively yield a synthesized whole.[10]

Thus, any one response would generally be one of several taking shape within any large, multifaceted organization and would generally be itself the result of a number of discrete activities around the organization.

It is advanced from several sources that organizations faced by the need for response to a discontinuity experience novelty, instability, and compression. These basic aspects of response are noted below, together with the central managerial implication that results from each of them.

> *Novelty.* The tendency for sudden change to arise from progressively further afield (geographically, technologically, societally, and otherwise) results in progressively greater novelty in decision-making circumstances. It may be presumed, therefore, that discontinuity imposes the need for revised organization structure, systems, or processes, either temporarily or permanently.[11]

Instability. The disturbed system of organization and environment would be expected to experience successive disturbances (of possibly decreasing amplitude) before a new stability is attained. Indefinite, ambiguous, and inspirational decision making is, therefore, likely to be commonplace.[12]

Compression. Time pressures, coupled with the extremity of the situation, may be expected to incline actions towards the expedient, conservative, and natural when those tendencies are possible.[13]

The above discussion can be summarized as a set of three propositions relating to the overall determinant of a response:

Proposition 1. The process of discontinuity and response can be represented as a model of (1) an environment of an organization possessing an incipient capacity for discontinuity, this capacity potentially resulting in (2) a discontinuity that (3) exceeds the flexibility or adaptation of the organization so that its members' goals can no longer be satisfied adequately, making (4) a response necessary that (5) involves a collection of subresponses to (6) realize a viable organization whose members' goals are, once again, satisfactorily met.

Proposition 2. The pattern of overall response, particularly for more complex cases, is likely to display some fragmentation into asymmetric and situationally specific parts (subresponses) and embody correspondingly some syntheses of these respective parts or dissemination of subresponses to one or several parts of the organization.

Proposition 3. Discontinuity and the associated response are characterized by novelty, instability, and compression.

Using this background of determining features for response and the examination of potentially relevant literature presented in chapter 2, it is possible to develop general propositions relating to the decision processes within response. First, however, it is useful to examine two major considerations expected to affect the overall nature or form of a response—whether a response is corporate, administrative, or operational, and whether it takes place in a complex, divisional, or simple organizational setting.

Corporate, Administrative, and Operating Responses

From the third paragraph of this chapter, discontinuity renders either or both the operations and adaptive mechanisms of an organization insufficient to meet goals satisfactory to the organization's members. It follows, therefore, that response can occur only according to three distinct cases:

1. *A corporate response* involving adjustment of the number of strategically independent businesses in a diversified corporation

2. *An administrative response* involving the introduction of revised structure or new systems or processes to a business (structure is defined in this work as "first, the lines of authority and communication between the different [managers] and, second, the information and data that flow through these lines of communication and authority," after Alfred D. Chandler)[14]

3. *An operating response* amending the operations of an organization

Six features thought to be of importance to response were examined to determine the nature and extent to which they may vary according to these three types of response:

1. Structural change
2. Goal definition
3. Constituent subresponses
4. Source and nature of required expertise
5. Personnel and their interrelationships
6. General atmosphere characterizing a response of each type

Table 3–1 notes the expected differentiation by type of response for each of these six features, and the following paragraphs expand upon them. In part, the hypothesized relations reflect the expectation that definition of tasks and related matters increases toward the shorter term time horizon where cause and effect relationships are better understood, and that progressively more determinant management action follows correspondingly.[15]

Corporate Response. Corporate responses add operations distinct to those contained in the existing structure and which therefore probably will be separately organized as an independent unit. Because the intention to diversify is explicit and, later, the diversification is specifically known, goals are highly specific in terms of overall purpose. How the diversification is to be achieved, however, is highly uncertain because of the level of ignorance present in entering a new business. A set of precisely defined subresponses following from the overall goal is rarely possible, because the management will not have had direct experience of the new business. (Even a well-researched acquisition probably will present some surprises, despite the fact that a detailed set of intentions for the acquired company may have been developed before the acquisition.) It is probable that a special management team will be selected to manage a diversification. Personnel from outside the organization may well be recruited deliberately to avoid imposing a set of behaviors from the old organization that would be inappropriate for the new. The general atmosphere, therefore, most likely will be

Table 3–1
Corporate, Administrative, and Operating Responses

	Corporate Response	Administrative Response	Operating Response
Structure	An added structure independent of the original structure	A revised structure	Expedience around existing structure
Goals	Clear ultimate goal will be expressed	Unclear goals will exist until ambiguities are resolved, then general principles will be established	Goals apparent; perhaps day-to-day survival
Subresponses	Subresponses will follow from goals but cannot be predetermined in detail	Subresponses will be translated from goals in an uncertain and evolving manner	Subresponses often will be mostly less than obvious, and extreme actions sometimes will be required
Expertise	Management expertise will have to be obtained by specific means (a project team, for example)	Management expertise will be found by revising behavior of present incumbents	Management expertise may be challenged but will almost always be adequate
Personnel	Special or outside personnel probably will be required	Mainly the same managers with different relationships; outsiders possibly added	A set from the same personnel, perhaps supplemented with others
Atmosphere	Clear mission, but needing learning and experiment	Introspection and reeducation	Clear tasks, ingenious solutions, and expedient, high-pressure working conditions

one of clear mission (a precise, ultimate goal) coupled with learning and experiment (detailed prior planning will not be possible).

Administrative Response. Administrative responses typically embody a revised structure—either or both different patterns of authority and communication and different patterns of information and data. Clear goals are often difficult to determine at an early stage because it takes time for the ambiguities in such situations to be resolved. When a final goal of reorientation is expressible it will often take a rather general expression of principle rather than a set of detailed plans or prescriptions. Examples might be that the organization must decentralize, must be more sensitive to cash flow, or must make an independent contribution to earnings from all its constituent businesses. Translation of general statements of reorientation into practical subresponses occur usually bit-by-bit in an uncertain and, often, evolving manner. Because reorientation of existing operations must involve existing personnel, the need is to bring about revised behavior in present incumbents, although the process might well be enhanced by bringing in outsiders who bring the new perspective with them. The general culture, therefore, most likely will be one of introspection (to determine what reorientation is needed), testing (to translate the reorientation into specific actions), and reeducation (to bring about revised behavior in existing personnel).

Operating Response. Operating responses typically involve expedient changes of and around the regular structure of the organization. Goals may be simply those of day-to-day survival and organization of the company's position in the circumstances. Goals are, therefore, typically both clear and near term. Subresponses necessary to achieve goals are somewhat obvious but possibly require ingenuity under time pressure. Mostly, the same personnel will be involved who usually manage the operations, but supplementary staff and supplementary management may be introduced. Established relationships among personnel may be disrupted during an operating response, but if circumstances are temporary the organization may be expected to return to its original pattern of relationships. The general atmosphere, therefore, most likely is one of clear tasks (maintaining operations day-to-day), ingenious solutions (extreme circumstances prompting extreme actions), and expedient, high-pressure working relations (mostly the same decision makers but experiencing short-term irregularities in relationships).

Another set of propositions may now be added to the others stated earlier:

Proposition 4. Three distinct types of response exist (corporate, administrative, and operating) and the details and circumstances of the response situations differ according to each type. In particular:

> *Proposition 4.1.* Corporate response involves an added structure, clear overall goals, and loosely defined subresponses. Special arrangements are necessary to obtain needed expertise, and the overall atmosphere is one of learning and experiment.

> *Proposition 4.2.* Administrative response involves revisions to structure, unclear goals, and emergent, uncertain subresponses. Needed expertise requires revised thinking from present organization members; introspection and reeducation characterize the general atmosphere.

> *Proposition 4.3.* Operating response involves expedience around an existing structure, apparent goals, and sometimes obvious but generally extreme subresponses. Response is managed by prior organization members and, while tasks may be clear, ingenious solutions employed under high pressure are often characteristic.

Complex, Divisional, and Simple Settings

Response is proposed to proceed differently depending on the organizational setting within which it takes place. Numerous classifications of organizations have been made[16] but literature classifying business corporations is relatively small. Excluding multinational cases,[17] three types of corporations have been identified: the multidivisional corporation, consisting of several strategically independent businesses; the complex firm, with a fully established internal structure; and the simple firm, with a fragmentary structure constituting a one-man show.[18] A business organization is an operationally complete system of organization and associated environment and, therefore, several business organizations can exist (perhaps interdependently) within a complex or within a multidivisional firm. Leaving aside the instance of an infantile firm with little or no formal structure, three distinct business organizational settings within which a response can arise and take place can be deduced from the above classification of corporations: first, a *complex setting* where a response embraces several business organizations interdependently within a corporation; second, a *divisional setting* where response takes place independently within one business organization within a corporation; and third, a *simple setting* where response is confined to one independent business organization.

Another case is also possible where a response might take place largely within only a part of an operationally complete business organization. An example would be where a functional department (such as marketing, manufacturing, or finance) executes a response independent of the rest of the organization. This situation could occur in either complex, divisional, or simple organizational settings, and it is provisionally concluded that the features of such a *functional response* overwhelmingly reflect, nevertheless, the overall type of organizational settings within which such a situation occurs. It would be expected, in general, that the long-run structural and cultural factors would dominate the everyday workings within all parts of an integrated operating company. Thus the overall nature of response would be expected to prevail even in such a functional response, with the exception, of course, of some absence of corporatewide interactions.

Complex, divisional, and simple types of organizational settings were examined for several distinguishing features. Basic organizational parameters (operational form, size, horizontal and vertical organization, and the presence of specialist staff functions), technical features (product markets and complexity of operations), and culture (values, leadership style, and rewards and performance measurements) were selected. General expectations were determined for each type of organizational setting as suggested by research and writing concerning each of these features. Expectations were also derived concerning the nature of discontinuity and response that is thought to be generally likely according to each of these three organizational settings. A summary of these expectations is provided in table 3–2 and the following paragraphs.

Table 3–2
Probable Features of Complex, Divisional, and Simple Settings

	Complex Setting	Divisional Setting	Simple Setting
Organization	*Diverse*	*Focused*	*Simple or incomplete*
Operational form	An independent complex of several operational units (departments, subsidiaries, etc.) all mutually dependent on each other in some way	One of a portfolio (managed through a central corporate office) of largely independent operational units (divisions)	A single, independent operational unit
Size	Large	Medium	Small
Horizontal organization	Each department subsidiary, etc., might have its own organizational form	A single established organizational form such as functional or matrix	Functional or inexplicit
Vertical organization	Many levels of management	A medium number of levels of management	A small number of levels of management
Specialist staff functions	Many staff functions	A few staff functions within the division but probably many in the central corporate office	Few staff functions, if any
Technicality	*Complicated*	*Controlled*	*Confined*
Products and markets	Many diverse products (although related)	A few quite similar products and a few quite similar markets	Single (or few) products, single (or few) markets
Operations	High complexity	Medium complexity	Medium or low complexity
Culture	*Rigid*	*Professional*	*Personal*
Values	Institutional and well entrenched	Professional with few sacred cows	Revolves around leading personalities
Leadership style	Amorphous and institutionally sensitive	Strong professional leadership	Strong personal leadership
Rewards and performance measurements	Diffuse and relatively gently enforced	Tightly defined and strictly enforced	Largely unformalized or administered on personal grounds
Discontinuity/ Response	*Complicated*	*Systematic*	*Improvised*
Discontinuity	For corporate and administrative responses the significance may be misconceived	Usually immediate, with alternative managerial views on the nature of the problem relatively rare	Extreme, immediate, and readily interpreted for its significance
Impact	Impacts can be localized within the corporation	Impact usually pervades most of the division	Impact usually disrupts the company as a whole

Table 3–2 (continued)

	Complex Setting	Divisional Setting	Simple Setting
Comprehension	Difficult to comprehend because of diverse organization and complicated technical circumstances (external and internal)	Relatively straightforward to comprehend because of focused organization and controlled technical circumstances	Simple to identify but perhaps difficult to understand because of limited expertise and resources
Response	Substantial and wide-ranging in the organization. Decisions taken in an incremental, testing fashion in high complexity and high uncertainty.	Problems investigated and relatively comprehensive decisions put into effect, with difficulties that arise dealt with as necessary within moderate uncertainty	Large investment of time and other resources (relative to company), tightly managed under high risk because of vulnerability and limited expertise
Programs	Difficult to implement within a complicated structure of many levels and many departments, subsidiaries, etc. and operations of high complexity	Relatively straightforward to implement within a complete, well-regulated structure and operations of medium complexity	Implementation tests ingenuity because of organizational limitations, although operations are of medium or low complexity

Complex Setting. A complex setting may be described as organizationally "diverse," technically "complicated," and culturally "rigid." Organizationally, a complex structure is an independent complex of several operational units (departments, subsidiaries, selling companies, and so on) which are mutually dependent on each other in some way. Such organizations are usually of large size, embody a mix of individual units, each with its own organizational form, and have many levels of management and many specialist staff functions. Technically, such a setting usually incorporates the manufacture of many diverse products which are sold to many diverse markets, although all the products and markets will be within one industry, and high operational complexity. Culturally, the organization's values are likely to be institutional and well entrenched, leadership styles are likely to be amorphous and institutionally sensitive, and rewards and performance measurements are likely to be diffuse and relatively gently enforced.

As a result of the size and diversity of complex settings, the nature of response can be expected to be complicated. While situations that require operating responses are immediate, it is expected that situations requiring corporate or administrative responses are sufficiently wide-ranging and interconnected to need extensive judgment. Misconceptions are expected to be characteristic and, because of the variety and geographic dispersion of complex settings, can often be localized in one or more parts of a total structure. A response in a complex setting may be expected to be a process that is substantial and wide-ranging, where decisions are taken in an incremental and testing fashion in high complexity and high uncertainty. Implementing subresponses would generally be expected to present difficulties, because many levels and many departments and subsidiaries are likely to be involved in highly complicated circumstances, both internally and externally.

Divisional Setting. A divisional setting may be described as organizationally "focused," technically "controlled," and culturally "professional." Organizationally, a divisional setting is one of a portfolio of largely independent operational units managed through a central corporate office or headquarters. Such organizations are usually of moderate size, embody a single organizational form (such as functional or matrix), and have a "medium" number of levels of management and a few specialist, staff functions, but with extensive support or control functions centered at the corporate office. Technically, such a structure usually incorporates manufacture of a few quite similar products which are sold to a few similar "served markets," and moderate operational complexity. Culturally, the organization's values are likely to be professional with few sacred cows, leadership styles are likely to be strong and professional in technical terms, and rewards and performance measurements are likely to be tightly defined and strictly enforced.

As a result of the focused organization and narrowly defined business of divisional settings, it is expected that the managing of a response to a discontinuity would tend to be relatively systematic. The intensity with which discontinuities strike such structures may be expected to be high and immediate, because the "slimmer" organization allows the discontinuity to challenge the heart of the business. This means that there is less chance in divisional settings of discontinuities being misconceived or differently perceived by their managers, and the tight coordination of operations typical of divisional settings means that responses could often pervade the whole organization. A response in a divisional setting is expected to be a process where problems can be investigated and relatively comprehensive decisions can be put into effect. Identification of the need and likely form of response are expected to be relatively straightforward, although often requiring intensive, high-pressure work.

Simple Setting. A simple setting may be described as organizationally "simple" or "incomplete," technically "confined," and culturally "personal." Organizationally, a simple setting is a single, independent operational unit. Such organizations are usually of small size, embody a single organizational form which is probably functional, and have a small number of levels of management and few specialist staff functions (if any). Technically, such a setting usually incorporates manufacture of a single (or few) products which are sold to a single (or few) markets, and low or medium operational complexity. Culturally, the organization's values are likely to revolve around those of the leading person or persons, leadership style is likely to be personal also, and rewards and performance measurements, if they are formalized, are likely to be loosely defined and administered on personal grounds.

The often incomplete management structure and often single products and markets typical of a simple setting suggest that the impact of a discontinuity on such a setting is likely to be extreme but readily understood. Presumably it is likely, because of the limited product markets served by a simple setting, that discontinuities can often disrupt the entire unit and more usually threaten its survival than in the complex and divisional cases. The limited range of expertise and resource slack supposedly common in simple settings also suggest that management skills and organizational resources are likely to be particularly stretched. It follows that identification of the need and likely form of response are likely to be straightforward but difficult to accomplish. These circumstances combine to suggest that response in simple settings may be expected to show managerial ingenuity for which the term *improvised* might be a suitable descriptor.

A third set of propositions can now be advanced concerning response according to possible contingencies introduced by the structure and nature of the organizational setting within which it takes place.

Proposition 5. The form and nature of response is contingent upon the type of organization setting within which it takes place, of which three types can be differentiated: complex, divisional, and simple (excluding the multinational and infantile cases).

Proposition 5.1. In complex settings (as defined and described above), the response can be termed loosely as *complicated*.

Proposition 5.2. In divisional settings (as defined and described above), the response can be termed loosely as *relatively systematic*.

Proposition 5.3. In simple settings (as defined and described above), the response can be termed loosely as *improvised*.

The meaning of these terms—*complicated, relatively systematic*, and *improvised*—was indicated in the above paragraphs and in table 3–2. With the background of the first set of propositions concerning the probable determining features of response, the second set differentiating corporate, administrative, and operating response and this third set relating to organizational contingencies, it is now possible to develop a fourth set of propositions relating to the nature and form of the decision processes that constitute a response.

Response

In chapter 1 the focal question which this study seeks to address was stated as: How are discontinuities and their associated responses managed in business organizations? An answer requires study of where decisions originated, how decisions were made, the underlying activities and general shape of those decisions, and what influenced the form and nature of those decisions. In summary, it is necessary to make a study of the decision processes that took place in organizations under discontinuity. *Decisions* are regarded here as actual output that modifies the interface of the organization with its environment—not decisions as they are formulated or as they are intended to be implemented, but outcomes as they actually occur. In the context of this study, *response* is equivalent, therefore, to the aggregate of decisions or realized output that reinstate the relationship of the organization to its environment so that the goals of its members are met satisfactorily. Similarly, *subresponses* are equivalent to the significant intermediary collections of actions that modify the organization: environment interface.

Earlier in this chapter it was reasoned that response for an organization would typically involve a fragmentation into asymmetric and situationally specific subresponses with an associated synthesis or dissemination of those subresponses, and further that response would be characterized by novelty, instability, and compression. It has been argued and shown generally that the operation of synoptic, optimal, systematic, or objective decision making is less likely than under more stable conditions.[19] It is posited here that incremental, satisficing, unstructured, and situational views of managing organizations through environmental change are likely to provide a more accurate overall description of managing response.[20]

Four related priorities for investigation were suggested for this investigation of decision processes under discontinuity:

1. the source and general form of solutions employed to achieve response[21]
2. the character and functioning of decision making in the finding and incorporation of those solutions
3. the nature and general structure of the decision process
4. the influence and role of situational factors in the overall response

The review in chapter 2 of prior work potentially relevant to this study and the development of ideas in this chapter permit some preliminary conclusions to be drawn concerning each of these four areas.

First, the system characterization of compression, fragmentation, and disaggregation are likely to pressure solution finding to the close-by and to small steps from the status quo. Novelty and compression encourage the more apparent and also more secure options of the familiar, close-by, and nearer term, where possible. Instability encourages small steps forward to prevent further unpredictable interactions and instabilities.

Second, novelty, instability, and compression even more than usually can be expected to take decisions beyond the cognitive limits of decision makers. Conditions for bounded rationality are likely to be, therefore, richly present, and decision making may be expected to be substantially characterized by satisficing and related decision making concepts. Simultaneously, the highly uncertain conditions surrounding response are likely to prompt intensive analytic efforts and also the use of planning or other frameworks to provide coherence for a necessarily complex situation.

Third, the general structure or process of the response may be expected to incline toward the unstructured or loosely structured, with a tendency for numerous irregularities. Novelty is likely to induce several initiatives before successful combinations are found. Instability is likely to cause several loops and modifications in the design of a particular response. Compression may be expected to intensify activity and exacerbate the above complexities. Only overall patterns concerning decision process can be expected to be generalizable.

Fourth, asymmetry is judged likely to force specific situational factors to be determinant for an individual response, in terms of both its development and the final outcome. Compression may additionally force decision makers to find solutions in or close to the specifics of a particular situation and also to fit those solutions closely with the specifics of situations.

A set of related propositions can now be advanced concerning managing response:

Proposition 6. Decision processes find solutions close to the experience of the decision maker(s) and represent small steps from the status quo.

Proposition 7. Satisficing and other nonoptimal approaches to decision processes better describe solving problems in response, but depend upon some analysis and also upon rational frameworks for coherence.

Proposition 8. Decision processes are complex and irregular and can be described only as general conceptual patterns.

Proposition 9. Situational factors are determinants of decision processes and outcome.

This study explores this set of propositions relating to decision processes under discontinuity by evaluating them against fieldwork and recorded data. As part III of this book is to show, these propositions are mostly upheld, but deeper examination of the literature for each of them and more detailed analysis of the data collected for this study permits these general propositions to be deepened significantly. The analysis in part III provides findings of sufficient resolution to be usable by managers and also of sufficient definition to be mostly restatable as testable hypotheses with which subsequent researchers can work.

The four sets of propositions advanced in this chapter were used to formulate a research design for their useful examination. Chapter 4 details how the study was approached, how it was structured, how precautions were taken to ensure data of high reliability, which companies and responses were investigated, and other relevant matters.

Notes

1. A classic definition of an organization, first proposed by Chester I. Barnard in *The Functions of the Executive* (Cambridge: Harvard University Press, 1938), pp. 8–22, 73.

2. Kenneth R. Andrews, *The Concept of Corporate Strategy* (Homewood, Ill.: Dow Jones–Irwin, 1980), p. 60. This basic definition of an environment reflects the orientation of those applying systems concepts to business organizations, such as William Evan ("The Organization Set: Toward a Theory of Interorganizational Relations," in *Approaches to Organizational Design*, ed. James D. Thompson, Pittsburgh: University of Pittsburgh Press, 1966) and works concerning general systems theory, such as G. Sommerhoff, "The Abstract Characteristics of Living Systems," in *Systems Thinking*, ed. F.E. Emery (Harmondsworth, Eng.: Penguin Books, 1969), p. 155.

3. The general concept of a closer, more directly interactive environment and a broader, still influencing but more contextual environment has been widely noted in fields as diverse as marketing (for example, Philip Kotler, *Marketing Management, Analysis, Planning and Control*, Englewood Cliffs, N.J.: Prentice–Hall, 1976, pp. 21–44—core systems, publics, and macroenvironment); strategic management (for example, Thomas Wheelen and J. David Hunger, *Strategic Management*, Reading, Mass.: Addison–Wesley, 1984, pp. 68–82—task environment and societal environment, and John H. Grant and William R. King, *The Logic of Strategic Planning*, Boston: Little, Brown, 1982, pp. 28–29—internal, operating, and general environment); and organization development (for example, John P. Kotter, *Organizational Dynamics: Diagnosis and Intervention*, Reading, Mass.: Addison–Wesley, 1978—task environment and wider environment).

4. James D. Thompson (*Organization in Action*, New York: McGraw–Hill, 1967) provides a useful conceptualization of means available to coalign an organization with its environment.

5. In order to be state-determined, it is necessary to regard the organization and its environment as one integral system (W. Ross Ashby, *Design for a Brain*, London: Chapman and Hall, 1952, pp. 36–41). "Discontinuity" described a relative situation where the organization's means of managing change at that time are inadequate to the satisfactory maintenance of the total system. Ashby (*An Introduction to Cybernetics*, London: Chapman and Hall, 1956, pp. 221 and 224) defines the situation of discontinuity more rigorously as when anticipation is impossible or when the organization's action cannot be completed before the outcome of the disturbance starts to be determined.

6. H. Igor Ansoff (*Implanting Strategic Management*, Englewood Cliffs, N.J.: Prentice–Hall, 1984, pp. 14–15) described four distinctive stages of evolution of a corporation according to progressively faster changing environments, namely: *management by control* (when change was slow); *management by extrapolation* (when the future could be predicted as extrapolation); *management by anticipation* (when discontinuities appear but can be managed by anticipation and response); and *management by flexible/ rapid response* (when changes develop too rapidly to permit timely anticipation). This study recognizes discontinuity as the exceeding of an organization's flexibility and adaptability relative to the one state-determined system of organization and environment (see above). Discontinuity, according to this formulation, is therefore equivalent to Ansoff's fourth category but admits discontinuity to be possible during any of Ansoff's four stages of evolution according to the relativity of the change to the means of the organization to manage it. Ansoff was concerned chiefly with describing overall conditions progressive through time. Chapter 1 of this book is therefore consistent with his conclusions.

7. In Ashby's (1952) vocabulary, this is the restoration of essential variables to acceptable values.

8. Asymmetry follows because organizations are loosely coupled (Herbert A. Simon, *Administrative Behavior: A Study of Decision-Making Processes in Administrative Organization*, New York: Free Press, 1945, p. 274; and Howard E. Aldrich, *Organizations and Environments*, Englewood Cliffs, N.J.: Prentice–Hall, 1979, pp. 76–86). Ashby (1952, op. cit., p. 157) notes that a system "neither divided into permanently separated parts nor so wholly joined that every event always influenced every other . . . showed a richer and a more intricate picture, one in which interactions and interdependencies fluctuated."

9. By extension from asymmetry, one-to-one mapping of the variations in the environment into the organization cannot occur. At the institutional level it is widely and variously found that total situations are resolved by their being split into smaller parts, which are then treated somewhat independently. For example, John D. Steinbruner (*The Cybernetic Theory of Decision*, Princeton: Princeton University Press, 1974, p. 87) found that decisions are split into small segments and treated segmentally. Richard M. Cyert and James G. March (*A Behavioral Theory of the Firm*, Englewood Cliffs, N.J.: Prentice–Hall, 1963, p. 119) report feedback react decision rules where objectively interdependent decisions are largely treated independently. David Braybrooke and Charles E. Lindblom (*A Strategy of Decision: Policy Evaluation as a Social Process*, New York: Free Press, 1963, pp. 104 and 127) describe a fragmentation of analysis and policy-making in the realm of public administration.

10. It is widely recognized that decisions constitute a number of subdecisions (see Eberhard Witte, "Field Research on Complex Decision-Making Processes—The Phase Theorem," *International Studies of Management and Organization*, Summer 1972, pp. 156–182; Henry Mintzberg, *Nature of Managerial Work*, New York: Harper and Row, 1973, p. 257; and Henry Mintzberg, Duru Raisinghani, and André Théorêt, "The Structure of 'Unstructured' Decision Processes," *Administrative Science Quarterly*, June 1976, pp. 246–275), and that higher level action programs embrace lower level programs (James G. March and Herbert A. Simon, *Organizations*, New York: John Wiley and Sons, 1958, p. 149).

11. This is drawn by deduction from the environmental contingent theories of organization, of which an early summary is provided in Paul R. Lawrence and Jay W.

Lorsch, *Organization and Environment: Managing Differentiation and Integration* (Cambridge: Harvard University, Graduate School of Business Administration, Division of Research, 1967); theories of progressive structuring relative to environmental demands concerning certain organizational variables (for example, Jay R. Galbraith, *Designing Complex Organizations*, Reading, Mass.: Addison–Wesley, 1973); and as prescribed for crisis decision units by Carolyn Smart and Ian Vertinsky in "Designs for Crisis Decision Units," *Administrative Science Quarterly*, December 1977, pp. 640–657. The importance of novelty is addressed extensively by Alvin Toffler in *The Adaptive Corporation* (New York: McGraw–Hill, 1985), pp. 67–89.

12. As a consequence of patterns of delays and the multiple levels that exist in the combined, loosely coupled (Howard E. Aldrich, op. cit.) system of organization and environment, second-order negative feedback loops (Jay W. Forrester, *Industrial Dynamics*, Cambridge: MIT Press, 1961) or the algedonic feedback of Stafford Beer (*Platform for Change*, Chichester, Eng.: John Wiley and Sons, 1975) of possibly damped oscillation would be predicted cybernetically after a discontinuity. Similarly this is a property of Ashby's ultrastable system (1952, op. cit., pp. 80–99).

13. This conclusion is consistent with findings from behavioral decision making, human problem solving, and organizational decision making. For a review of relevant findings, see Gerardo R. Ungson and Daniel N. Braunstein, eds., *Decision Making: An Interdisciplinary Inquiry* (Boston: Kent, 1982).

14. Alfred D. Chandler, *Strategy and Structure: Chapters in the History of the American Industrial Enterprise* (Cambridge: MIT Press, 1962) p. 16.

15. An example of the importance of using the "right" approach to decision is provided by Frank E. Harrison (*The Managerial Decision-Making Process*, Boston: Houghton Mifflin, 1975, pp. 284–285): "The uncertainty regarding the cause-and-effect relationships associated with the probable outcome still worked for a judgmental rather than a computational strategy . . . given the 'wrong' approach it was almost axiomatic that the final choice would be incorrect." The terms *judgmental* and *computational* refer to Thompson's four-way classification of decision (James D. Thompson, *Organizations in Action*, New York: McGraw–Hill, 1967, pp. 134–135).

16. A review of different classifications of organizations is provided by Richard H. Hall in *Organizations: Structure and Process* (Englewood Cliffs, N.J.: Prentice–Hall, 1982) pp. 28–48.

17. The multinational case has been addressed by Lawrence E. Fouraker and John M. Stopford, "Organization Structure and Multinational Strategy," *Administrative Science Quarterly*, June 1968, pp. 57–70: Jay R. Galbraith and Daniel A. Nathanson, *Strategy Implementation: The Role of Structure and Process* (St. Paul: West, 1978), pp. 121–124; Derek F. Channon, *Multinational Strategic Planning* (New York, AMACOM, 1978), pp. 22–50; and Donald H. Thain, op. cit.

18. Bruce R. Scott, in "Stages of Corporate Development" (Cambridge: Intercollegiate Case Clearinghouse, Harvard Business School, 1971), after Alfred D. Chandler (op. cit.) and Donald H. Thain ("Stages of Corporate Development," in *Concepts for Corporate Strategy*, ed. John W. Bonge and Bruce P. Coleman, New York: Macmillan, 1972, p. 427) proposes this three-stage model of business organizational development of corporate structure. Henry Mintzberg's much more broadly based study (*The Structuring of Organizations: A Synthesis of the Research*, Englewood Cliffs, N.J.: Prentice–Hall, 1979, pp. 305–313 and 380–430) is generally corroborative of the models of Thain and Scott.

19. It has been argued by several writers that incremental processes are more appropriate for unstable environments. See, for example, Henry Mintzberg, "Strategy-Making in Three Modes," *California Management Review*, Vol. 16, No. 2 (1973), pp. 44–53; Carl R. Anderson and Frank T. Paine, "Managerial Perceptions and Strategic Behavior," *Academy of Management Journal*, Vol. 18, No. 4 (1975), pp. 811–823; Kenneth J. Hatten and Dan E. Schendel, "Strategy's Role in Policy Research," *Journal of Economics and Business*, Vol. 28, No. 3 (1976), pp. 95–102; and Paul C. Nutt, "Models for Decision-Making in Organizations and Some Contextual Variables which Stipulate Optimal Use," *Academy of Management Review*, Vol. 1, No. 2 (1976), pp. 147–158. That view is supported empirically by James W. Frederickson, "The Comprehensiveness of Strategic Decision Processes: Extension, Observations, Future Directions," *Academy of Management Journal*, Vol. 27, No. 3 (1984), pp. 445–466, and James W. Frederickson and Terence R. Mitchell, "Strategic Decision Processes: Comprehensiveness and Performance in an Industry with an Unstable Environment," *Academy of Management Journal*, Vol. 27, No. 2 (1984), pp. 399–423.

It is also understood that environmental uncertainty links with more organic rather than mechanistic organization structures. See Tom Burns and G.M. Stalker, *The Management of Innovation*, (London: Tavistock, 1961). Also, for example, progressive interdependency links with more complex organization designs. See Jay R. Galbraith, op. cit.

20. In 1968, for example, Shirley Terryberry ("The Evolution of Organizational Environments," *Administrative Science Quarterly*, Vol. 12, No. 4 (1968), p. 598) wrote: "Since uncertainty is the dominant characteristic . . . it is not surprising that emphasis in recent literature is away from algorithmic and toward heuristic problem-solving models, that optimizing models are giving way to satisficing models, and that rational decision making is replaced by disjointed incrementalism."

21. It follows from Ashby's "Law of Requisite Variety" (W. Ross Ashby, 1956, op. cit.) that change in the environment of an organization must be accompanied by change in the organization to return the organization to a similar or equivalent state. Ansoff (1984, op. cit., pp. 27, 382, and 457) uses the law of requisite variety in his discussion of discontinuity.

4
Researching Response

T he first part of this chapter outlines the research approach—how the study was conceived in its practical details and how the research was conducted. The remainder of the chapter describes the sites and responses that comprise the data base for this study.

Research Design

Preliminary fieldwork was conducted to determine the most satisfactory way to formulate and structure the research. An exploratory sample of seven challenging discontinuities was investigated. In addition, about twenty interviews were held with senior academics, consultants, and managers, all of whom had some direct or indirect experience of handling the kinds of challenges which are addressed by this study. This early work was pursued until a sufficient understanding of the research problem was achieved to formulate how it should be conceived and executed as a study.[1]

It soon became apparent in the preliminary fieldwork that several important considerations were critical to the successful completion of the intended study:

A clear focus on a primary unit of analysis was indicated so that efforts could be optimized and results could be consistent.

A thorough understanding of the company's preexisting strategy, of the background and interrelations of the leading actors for a given response, and of the industry and wider environment within which the response took place was found to be necessary.

The depth of data necessary to the study indicated that it was essential to work with situations where detailed data could still be acquired but where ephemera could be recognized.

The intricacy, uniqueness, and complexity of individual situations showed the need for thorough data collection and the dominant use of detailed but flexible research instruments.

The great variation that could exist from one situation to another demonstrated the need for a sample design incorporating a pattern of controls so that situations could be compared and contrasted effectively.

It was also clear that the same design needed to embody both opportunities for depth investigation and a sufficient breadth of experience to identify clearly overall patterns in the data.

It also became apparent that the inherent risks of subjectivity in the research field necessitated a full documentation of data and an explicit basis for the development of findings.

Details of the design and administration of the study are noted below.

Research Concept

Response as Unit of Analysis. Adjustment by a large, complex organization to an overall discontinuity was shown to be accomplished by a collection of several responses occurring in different parts of the organization and embracing quite different time frames. No one response represented, therefore, a direct mapping of the environmental mismatch into the organization or a full answer to the situation. Residual mismatch and additional tensions that could be introduced by a response might or might not be fully or partially addressed by other simultaneous or subsequent responses. The overall position could, therefore, be very complex, but it was found to be relatively straightforward to identify discrete, bounded responses in time and space which both provided a feasible research domain and fitted with managerial realities.

By focusing efforts on responses and constituent subresponses as delimited parts of the total field, energies could be concentrated and priorities clearly determined. Parts of the research field essential to the response but not directly part of it could be treated suitably as essential context. Such an approach to research in complex organization is common. For example, Richard M. Cyert and James G. March comment: "Simplify the conception by focusing on the participants in a particular 'region'—either temporal or functional [and] for a particular decision we can identify the major coalition members."[2] In similar terms F.E. Emery and E.L. Trist[3] describe the *focal system* and Ludwig von Bertalanffy[4] describes the *leading part* in complex systems.

This concept of a response and its constituent subresponses as the primary unit of analysis fitted managerial realities. It was the individual responses and constituent subresponses and their sequential relationship from one to the other that was the focus of thought and action for the managers involved. Responses and their subresponses occurring through time and at various places within the total organization were prominent in the minds of management and represented the primary vehicles by which organizational adjustment to environmental change was accomplished.

Context. The intrinsically complex nature of responses presented many other research challenges. Research was necessary into the structure and workings of the organizations investigated, the detailed developments in the environments of those organizations, and into the wider history of the situations investigated. Only with this background or context could reliable and adequate judgments and reasonings be made.

These considerations indicated the benefits of organizing the research effort into a number of phases. Phase I constituted a series of exploratory discussions to determine the nature of the sampled company's business and environment and the general pattern of environmental change that the company experienced. Phase II involved a thorough search of secondary sources on the company and concerning the selected responses. Phase III embraced the series of depth interviews and related check backs and so on necessary to describe accurately the selected responses. Sometimes some overlap and exchange among these phases was a practical necessity.

Middle Time Period. Preliminary fieldwork showed that the best course was to examine situations that were neither contemporaneous nor historic. The alternative of researching current events was less rewarding in that it was difficult to reliably decipher substance from noise in the multifarious and often confusing actions and opinions that interplay. Indeed, experience showed that it would even be difficult to select apparently embryonic responses with any confidence that they would proceed to some satisfactory end point. At the other end of the spectrum, a historical method employing, say, twenty-five years of elapsed time would filter out all temporary traces and create a quite different character of findings. It would have to employ, for example, a method almost wholly confined to enduring written evidence and thereby inevitably exclude many matters of decision process.

The precise meaning of the term *middle time period* varied from instance to instance. Probably ideal was research some two or three years after a response was largely concluded. However, since the more complicated responses developed intensively for several years before that time and could be traced to several years preceding that intense development, fieldwork was undertaken some four or five elapsed years after much of the "starting action" took place for these complicated cases.

Disadvantages necessarily accompanied the choice of a middle time period for the study. Evident among these was the loss of data points. First, there was the possibility of exclusion of subresponses that were not recognized as major and of those that started but did not come to a conclusion, although such inconclusive subresponses might be a recurrent and important part of making responses. Care was taken, therefore, to identify incomplete or subordinate subresponses and to document their relevance accordingly. Second, there was the loss of respondents from the group of involved decision makers due to resignations, departures, and reassignments to far-off parts of the world. In practice this was not found to be a problem. No essential respondents were lost, and because several respondents were used for investigating each response and data were cross-checked among them, complete and reliable information was acquired for each response.

Data Collection

Personal interviewing was found in the preliminary fieldwork to be the most informative method of data collection for this study. The main reason has already been noted by Henry Mintzberg et al.: "The best trace of the completed process remains in the minds of those people who carried it out."[5] Other evidence such as company correspondence is partial in extent and mainly devoid of its motivational context and the pattern of decision and reasoning that led to its production. As Chester I. Barnard has commented: "It is a perplexing fact that most executive decisions produce no direct evidence of themselves and that knowledge of them can only be derived from cumulation of indirect evidence."[6] Barnard further observes: "The fine art of executive decision consists in not deciding questions that are not now pertinent, in not deciding prematurely, in not making decisions that cannot be made effective, and in not making decisions that others should make."[7] James G. March and Herbert A. Simon similarly acknowledge the importance of inaction or "doing nothing."[8] These aspects of decision processes would be lost to a method confined to direct physical evidence or even to the exclusive application of fixed research instruments.

Because of the depth and complexity of the research field, interviews needed to be largely unstructured. Senior managers recounting major issues also needed an uninhibiting medium within which to communicate the fullness of their thinking. It was more useful for the respondents to tell the researcher what was important in a way that was natural to the respondent. Adopting the respondent's vernacular and seeking as much empathy with the respondent's circumstances as possible were found very useful in collecting detailed data and achieving a deep understanding of the research topic. Major interviews usually took four or five hours.

A study embodying personal interviewing as its primary method also has its drawbacks. Outstanding among problems is the risk of lapses of memory or the more insidious bias of exaggeration or coloring of incidents by informants. Another risk is distortion by the researcher's improperly gathering and interpreting facts given by respondents. The following steps were taken to minimize these potential problems associated with unstructured interviewing:

> Several sources of information were used to develop the data. Ten or more informants were often consulted to gather data for the deeper and more

important cases, and company records and other written sources were used whenever it was helpful and possible. Using multiple sources served to cross-check information and to open up inconsistencies that were later resolved by further fieldwork. Care was taken also to embrace all the major perspectives or viewpoints that existed in the company for a particular response.

Repeated interviews were conducted with nearly all central respondents, sometimes three or more times. This served to double-check earlier information and to reconcile any incompatibilities or uncertainties that may have arisen from information gathered from other respondents.

Tailor-made protocols were constructed before every interview, including the check-back interviews. These protocols were important in establishing research priorities reflecting the prior knowledge gained of the situation under investigation, the stage of knowledge of the response as a whole, and the apparent inconsistencies or weaknesses of information provided in earlier fieldwork. Protocols were used as a checklist and as an aide-memoire during the unstructured interview to ensure that the main points were embraced as they were understood before the session commenced.

Interviews were tape-recorded whenever it was possible to do so, which it was for most of the formal interviews in the more important sites. The contents of the tapes were later reviewed not only for the factual information but also for erratic manners of speech, emphases, and hesitations that might suggest other dimensions in the response. Where manual notes were taken, these were also annotated after the interview in an equivalent manner to the tape-recorded data.

All the fieldwork was conducted by the researcher himself so that potential problems of misperception in the translating of collected data from one researcher to another were avoided.

The researcher is confident of the accuracy and quality of the data collected for this study. The fieldwork conducted in the more important and deeper cases, in particular, is believed to represent field research of special quality.

Probably crucial to the level of cooperation enjoyed during fieldwork in most sites was the official sanction that had been secured from the top of the organization in question. Access was obtained to executives and information within sites with the official written consent of the chairman or divisional president. A mentor was also obtained for the larger, more diverse sites who assisted with practical matters and with the interpretation of fine detail of the institution.[9] To gain such access and make such arrangements took several months of careful preparation and use of personal contacts in the more important cases.

Also key to achieving a full understanding of the situations was the need to gain the full confidence of the respondents, be trusted with confidential viewpoints, and gain as many viewpoints on a situation as possible. A somewhat surprising conclusion is that a wide variety of formats and venues was sometimes helpful in this regard. Interviews were conducted not only in offices and conference areas but also informally at times in restaurants, in respondent's homes, in lounges during residential, off-site training courses, in the evening, and sometimes at weekends. Interspersing the interviewing schedule with these less formal and more social formats seemed to gain trust and encourage candor.

Sample Design

To manage the diversity inherent in the topic of this study, a mixed sample of twenty-six responses in fourteen corporations was selected. A matching of research sites and individual responses across the sample provided controls that afforded a satisfactory basis on which to compare and contrast the responses. As well as a number of examples of complex, divisional, and simple organizational settings and of corporate, administrative, and operating responses, the sample contained matched pairs or groups of either sites or equivalent responses or both, by industry, by theme (social, crisis, and so on), and by other potential sources of variation.

Because of the complexity of the research situations and the need to understand fine details, it was necessary for fieldwork within a site to embrace several months and for working relationships to be measured in years in some cases. Rather than commit total research efforts to fieldwork of this intensity, the decision was made to conduct the work with a mix of two levels of depth. A total of fourteen responses were investigated in depth in four corporations and twelve responses were investigated in lesser depth in a further ten corporations. The lesser depth fieldwork enabled a broadening of the study and served as a check on the external validity of the fieldwork of more intensive depth.

The four corporations and fourteen responses researched in depth in this study were selected to include (1) successful, respected corporations, (2) representative experiences of responses, and (3) examples that apparently constituted good practice. In this regard, the four corporations selected for depth study met the following requirements: (1) membership among the largest hundred corporations in the world, (2) very well-regarded management—all four can claim vanguard, enduring contributions to the theory and practice of management, (3) strong and strengthening performance—all four not only came out of the 1970s in better shape than they entered the decade but also generally outperformed their respective industries, and (4) sustained financial success—all four companies have shown generally stable and improving profit performance (with some cyclicity) over several decades. What was observed in this study might be presumed to feature steady, long-term good practice and not a set of ephemeral ideas that received only short-term success such as might be true for the newer microelectronic or computer companies. Selected responses were those of which the involved organizations were quite proud. The management of the corporations believed they had "done a good job," and in nearly all cases figurehead managers received substantial advancement beyond the conclusions of the strategic decisions researched here.

The lesser depth work forms an assortment of different types of business and national locations grouped according to whether the responses took place in complex, divisional, or simple structures. The twelve responses constitute a varied assortment to include demand falls and surges, social and government actions, labor relations problems, a salmonella outbreak, and exchange rate losses. They include also reorganization, introduction of new systems, finding of new markets, retrenchment, and others which together represent a mixture of administrative and operating responses. The corporations were situated in a total of six countries.

While several controls were sought among the combination of depth and lesser depth corporations and responses investigated in this work, an assortment of experiences was deliberately sought also. This policy of variety (1) gave some grounds for an assessment of the applicability of findings by type of organization setting and by type of response, (2) presented several research ideas that would not otherwise have become apparent and thereby improved the depth and refinement of findings, (3) acted as a discipline to generate findings of sufficient generality to be a contribution outside of the narrow circumstances of the four research sites investigated in depth, and (4) supplied additional opportunities for the testing of research ideas than would otherwise have been possible.

Two approaches were used to compile this sample of ten sites for lesser depth investigation. Five sites were obtained by requesting cooperation from senior executives participating in the advanced management program and the program for management development at the Harvard University Graduate School of Business Administration. As a sample of five organizations drawn in a different way to that of the depth fieldwork, this approach provided some check on possible biases that the personal selection of the depth and other lesser depth sites may have introduced. Researcher contacts and initiatives obtained cooperation from the other five sites investigated in lesser depth.

For this lesser depth work, site visits were made and depth interviews were conducted with more than one leading participant in the response in most cases. Although the number of interviews was limited in this lesser depth work, those that were conducted were all extensive and usually exceeded four or five hours. While the lesser depth work is not as thoroughly researched as the depth cases, the researcher is fully confident of the accuracy of the factual content of the case descriptions that will be presented in later chapters.

The data collected for this study of response to discontinuity are presented in part II of this book as textual descriptions of the observations made in the fieldwork. While these written accounts inevitably constitute the writer's judgments concerning raw data acquired in the researched sites, the extensive reports have been produced to make the basis of findings for this study as explicit as possible. Readers can evaluate the evidence for the analysis and conclusions drawn from the data. The careful writing and presentation of a full account helps derive an analysis faithful to the whole situation, and also serves as a discipline on the risks of subjectivity inherent in a research study where fixed instrumentation and measurement are an impossibility.

Sites and Responses

The sites and responses constituting the data for this study will be introduced briefly in the following pages as fieldwork in complex settings, fieldwork in divisional settings, and fieldwork in simple settings.

Fieldwork in Complex Settings

Seven responses in two corporations were researched in depth, and three strategic decisions in three corporations were researched in lesser depth as examples of responses in complex settings. Table 4–1 summarizes details.

Sites. For the depth fieldwork in complex settings, appealing subject matter was seen in what is probably the most sudden and extreme event of recent decades—the oil price increase and embargo of 1973 and 1974, along with the associated, long-term ramifications of a revised supply position for crude oil. Full research access for this project was secured with two of the world's largest oil companies.

To suggest associations of well-being and size, the two researched oil companies have been disguised as *Prosper* and *Atlas*. The companies were selected for their similarity to each other in order to maximize research controls. They are comparable with respect to stage of development, structure, and interests, and both have their headquarters in the same city. Within a small population of mature and specific institutions, a perfectly controlled pairing is obviously unattainable. While their respective similarities are noticeable, the most significant difference between these corporations is that Prosper is relatively abundant in owned crude-oil supply compared to its marketing operations, whereas the inverse relationship between owned crude and marketing needs exists for Atlas.

Corporations researched in lesser depth as complex organizational settings included another oil company (Interoil), a large bank (Columbus Bank), and a power station supplier (DeVito Power). These corporations are located in the United States of America and Western Europe, The United States of America, and Italy, respectively.

Table 4–1
Responses in Complex Settings

	Business	Location	Situation	Response	Type
Depth Fieldwork					
Prosper Oil	Oil–fully integrated international	Europe	Threat to oil supply Price differential between light and heavy products	Entry to the coal industry Investment in a catalytic cracker	Corporate Administrative
			Excess capacity and need to add value	Adoption of Rotterdam prices	Administrative
			Dislocation of supply	Rescheduling of supply	Operating
Atlas Oil	Oil–fully integrated international	Europe	Threat to oil supply Lack of investment confidence	Entry to the coal industry Introduction of scenario planning	Corporate Administrative
			Dislocation of supply	Rescheduling of supply	Operating
Lesser Depth Fieldwork					
Interoil	Oil–fully integrated international	USA and Western Europe	Floating foreign currency and associated corporate losses	Derivation of management system	Administrative
Columbus Banking Corporation	Banking	USA	Social outcry at planned branch closing	Formation of public affairs department	Administrative
DeVito Power	Power station supply	Italy	Loss of sole market	Sale to the Middle East and related product and organizational change	Administrative

Responses. The unilateral pricing of oil by the Organization of Petroleum Exporting Countries (OPEC), the quadrupling of the price of oil in a few months, and the associated embargo of the Organization of Arab Petroleum Exporting Countries (OAPEC) in late 1973 were the precipitating events of a suddenly new environment to which the oil industry had to respond. A full analysis could constitute a substantial volume in its own right. A total of seven responses (four in Prosper and three in Atlas) were, therefore, selected for study as being of special importance and together contained at least one corporate, one administrative, and one operational type of response for each company.

It was relatively straightforward to decide upon matched corporate responses as both companies entered the coal industry at approximately the same time and in direct response to a similar interpretation of the oil supply trends. A subtle and complex process of establishing these businesses was evident in both sites. Prosper's and Atlas's entry to the coal industry were selected as the two matched corporate responses for depth study.

Matching pairs of administrative responses was more difficult, because the two companies were at different stages concerning the then crucial question of the relative availability and price attractiveness of company-owned crude oil. Before 1973 Prosper had a relatively advantageous position with respect to the supply of owned crude. The events of 1973 and 1974 suddenly made that supply less available and less attractive and the priority response for Prosper was, therefore, the addressing of this issue. The two most important means of adjustment to the revised environment for this company were selected for depth investigation and may be briefly described as:

1. investment in a catalytic cracker to increase output of lighter products such as gasoline at the expense of heavier products such as heating oils
2. adoption of Rotterdam Prices (free market prices) in international marketing subsidiaries for internal control and motivation purposes

Investments in secondary refining capacity (a general term for catalytic crackers and other means of manufacturing higher value, lighter end products from heavier, baser raw material) had been made by Atlas some five or more years before 1973. Atlas's investment decision for increasing the proportion of light products in their output was reviewed for comparison with Prosper's experience but could not, because of the substantial elapsed time, be researched in depth. Similarly, Atlas's equivalent response to Prosper's adoption of Rotterdam Prices (the abandoning of cost-plus transfer prices in favor of market-based prices) occurred in the 1960s and was therefore reviewed but also could not be investigated in depth. For Atlas, the priority response was to find a way of handling the increasing uncertainty that tighter supply of crude introduced, having already incorporated responses suiting the corporation to conditions of limited crude availability. In this connection, introduction of a scenario planning system was probably the most important response for the Atlas oil company. Its selection as an administrative response for depth investigation was further strengthened by a prima facie process similarity with the introduction of free market prices for internal control and motivation at Prosper.

Prosper's and Atlas's response to the 1973 embargo through their supply operations offered for study an apparently cardinal instance of operating response. The Organization of Arab Petroleum Exporting Countries' embargo put highly complicated shipping and distribution supply operations of both companies into disarray. Ways in which the supply departments wrestled with these circumstances were examined for both companies as examples of operating responses.

Responses in complex settings researched in lesser depth included: the derivation of a management system at Interoil in response to floating exchange rates and associated corporate losses; the organization of a public affairs department at Columbus Bank in response to a social outcry regarding a planned branch closing; and the development of export sales to the Middle East and associated product and organizational change at DeVito Power in response to the loss of the company's sole market. All are examples of administrative responses.

Fieldwork in Divisional Settings

Seven responses in two divisions were researched in depth and five responses in four divisions were researched in lesser depth as examples of responses in divisional settings. Table 4–2 summarizes details of these divisions and responses.

Divisions. The two divisions researched in depth for the study are disguised as the Industrial Products Division of the Generaltex Corporation and as the National Lighting Division of the TCA Corporation.

The Industrial Products Division, referred to as IPD, manufactures and markets petroloids. These are petrochemicals which use certain petroleum products as well as some nonpetroleum minerals as raw materials. Generaltex, one of the world's largest textile companies, and IPD are both based in the United States of America. IPD synthesize some two thousand petroloid end products by numerous specialist finishing methods which adapt the material to many forms. Petroloid products have a large number of indispensable applications which provide unique possibilities for customers in numerous industries.

The National Lighting Division, a bulb manufacturer, pairs with the Industrial Products Division of Generaltex. National Lighting is similar to IPD in being within a parent company in the textile industry and has similar size and product diversity. The most noticeable difference between the two divisions is that National Lighting is in a low-growth, mature industry, standing in contrast to the moderate growth situation at IPD.

Table 4–2
Responses in Divisional Settings

	Business	Location	Situation	Response	Type
Depth Fieldwork					
Industrial Products Division	Manufacture and sale of petroloids (specialist chemicals)	USA	Economic boom stimulating supply shortages	Selective sales and manufacture	Administrative
			Energy cost increases	Price rises	Administrative
			Economic recession and withdrawal of demand	Cost cutting and sales stimulation	Operating
			Cash shortages at corporate level from economic circumstances	New management systems	Administrative
National Lighting Division	Manufacture and sale of bulbs	Great Britain	Weakening of customer demand	Imaginative advertising campaign	Administrative
			World industry competition	More cost effective manufacturing	Administrative
			Increasing demands for safety at work	Redesigned machinery and formation of safety committees	Administrative
Lesser Depth Fieldwork					
Carolvale Division	Package vacations	Great Britain	Demand fall	Demand stimulation and contraction of operations	Operating
Ronson Division	Package vacations	Great Britain	Demand fall	Demand stimulation and contraction of operations	Operating
Weld Division	Heavy welding sets	Great Britain	Demand fall customary markets	Demand stimulation and contraction of operations	Operating
Container Division	Cardboard containers	Great Britain	Government imposed three-day week	Rearrangement of work pace and conditions	Operating
			Surge in demand	Revision of supply and demand conditions	Operating

Divisions researched in lesser depth included two involved in assembling and selling foreign vacation excursions (Carolvale Division and Ronson Division), one division which manufactures and sells welding sets mainly for use in oil field development (Weld Division), and one division which manufactures and sells cardboard containers (Container Division). All these divisions are located in Great Britain and operate in highly international contexts.

Responses. In 1973 the fortunes of IPD began to alter. Their oil-based raw material costs more than tripled during calendar 1974. United States interest costs also increased substantially, together with IPD's plant replacement costs, which doubled from early 1974 to the end of 1976. Productivity improvements could no longer compensate for cost inflation, and the need to increase prices became evident.

The pattern of events in late 1973 and in 1974 was also disruptive in other ways. Customer expectation of price increases in late 1973 and early 1974 caused a surge in demand as customers bought ahead to avoid future price increases and to ensure supplies in an atmosphere where advance buying was, in itself, creating shortages of specific items. A large backlog of orders accumulated in the first half of 1974 allowed the plant to work at full capacity for the first three quarters of 1974. Before the backlog was completely satisfied, however, demand swung violently in the opposite direction. The world recession of 1974 to 1975 was beginning to take hold, and customers who had bought ahead earlier now had excessive inventories. For a period of time in 1974, IPD received practically no orders. The abrupt fall in demand placed the company in an unprecedented situation.

Economic prospects appeared grave for IPD by that third quarter of 1974, but for Generaltex as a whole the position appeared even graver. While IPD was still working at full spate in the middle of 1974, the other divisions in Generaltex were already into recession. The demand for textiles had taken a nosedive and there seemed no short- or medium-term prospect of management's improving performance in most of the sectors in which Generaltex was involved. The efficient management of cash flow is important in normal times, but in the economic conditions of 1974 its maximization was vital to the well-being of the group as a whole. As a high growth division, and with the appearance of a long-term future of above average profitability, IPD had historically been a cash recipient of corporate funds. The new cash-short circumstances which Generaltex confronted resulted in a reversal in this relationship with IPD. The division was now required to be a cash contributor to corporate funds.

Four distinct but related responses emerged for investigation at IPD from this pattern of events:

1. demand surge
2. cost inflation

3. recession
4. cash shortage

The second and fourth represent administrative responses, and the first and third are operating responses.

As IPD, National Lighting experienced relative stability up to 1973, although there have been recent incidents which have disturbed the assumption of regularity underlying the business up to the middle seventies. First, there was the rapid and substantial increase in energy costs after 1973 which threatened to reduce markedly the demand for bulbs. Second, there was a flood of foreign imports of vehicle bulbs entering the division's domestic market. Third, challenges had arisen from recent legislative changes. Legislation on factory safety produced some particularly challenging difficulties.

Three responses were therefore selected for investigation in National Lighting:

1. Inflation Beaters—an imaginative advertising and marketing campaign that was launched to arrest the risk of a diminished demand for bulbs

2. Far Eastern vehicle bulbs—how the division reacted to recover its share of the vehicle bulb market which had been dramatically overwhelmed by low-cost imports from the Far East

3. safety legislation—how the division met standards imposed by the enforcement of new safety legislation

All are examples of administrative responses, which reflects National Lighting's apparent immunity from operating responses because of its technologically stable environment and the fact that corporate responses are inappropriate to a division whose charter is delimited to given products and markets by its parent company (as is also true of the Industrial Products Division).

Responses in divisional settings researched in lesser depth included demand stimulation and contraction of operations at Carolvale Division, at Ronson Division, and at Weld Division in response to demand falls, and rearrangement of working schedules at Container Division in response to government imposition of a three-day work week, and also in response to a surge in demand. All are examples of operating responses.

Fieldwork in Simple Settings

Four responses in three corporations were researched in lesser depth as examples of responses in simple settings. Table 4–3 summarizes details of these corporations and responses. The simpler organizations and simpler circumstances meant that less information needed to be gathered than for the complex and divisional structures. Fieldwork of any greater depth was therefore unnecessary

Table 4-3
Responses in Simple Settings

	Business	Location	Situation	Response	Type
Jackson Mines	Iron ore mining	North America	Uncooperative working atmosphere	Labor relations improvement	Operating
			Demand fall	Contraction of operations	Administrative
Schumacker	Pet foods	Germany	Salmonella outbreak	Public relations and product development	Operating
Suza Cars	Car manufacturers	Great Britain	Safety legislation and supply difficulties	Design and sale of a new product range	Administrative

to obtain data of comparable quality to that of the depth investigations, because information was both more accessible and more understandable.

Corporations. Corporations (disguised) researched as simple settings included an iron ore mining company (Jackson Mines), a pet food manufacturer (Schumacker), and a specialist automobile manufacturer (Suza Cars). These corporations are located in North America, Germany, and Great Britain, respectively.

Responses. Responses in simple settings include: the contraction of operations at Jackson Mines in response to a demand fall; the improvement of labor relations at Jackson Mines in response to an uncooperative working atmosphere; a public relations campaign and product development effort at Schumacker to survive a salmonella outbreak; and the design and sale of a new product range at Suza Cars in response to a series of adverse trends, including safety legislation and supply problems.

The fundamental test of the research method is its ability to generate reliable data of useful quality and depth. The writing of precise descriptions of what was found in the researched companies was recognized as a part of the research method, helping to clarify and double-check details. A textual presentation of observations was found essential to represent the data. Summary statistics, flow charts, and other means of data summary would have all compromised important character. A standardized format (such as uniform headings) would have risked misrepresenting the balance between different facts. Consequently, each description is presented uniquely to reflect, as effectively as possible, the complex sequences and shades of meaning important to each situation. All the depth studies have been approved by the researched companies as faithful accounts of what actually transpired. The following chapters 5 to 15 present these researched accounts.

Notes

1. Raymond A. Bauer, "Exploring the Exploratory Sample," *Harvard Business Review*, March–April 1973, p. 131.

2. Richard M. Cyert and James G. March, *A Behavioral Theory of the Firm* (Englewood Cliffs, N.J.: Prentice–Hall, 1963), p. 27.

3. F.E. Emery and E.L. Trist, *Towards a Social Ecology: Contextual Appreciation of the Future in the Present* (New York: Plenum Press, 1973).

4. Ludwig von Bertalanffy, *General System Theory, Foundations Development, Applications* (New York: George Braziller, Inc., 1968), Equation 3–26.

5. Henry Mintzberg, Duru Raisinghani, and André Théorêt, "The Structure of 'Unstructured' Decision Processes," *Administrative Science Quarterly,* June 1976, p. 248.

6. Chester I. Barnard, *The Functions of the Executive* (Cambridge: Harvard University Press, 1938), p. 193.

7. Ibid., p. 194.

8. James G. March and Herbert A. Simon, *Organizations* (New York: John Wiley and Sons, 1958), pp. 175–177.

9. The value of arrangements of this sort is demonstrated, in particular, in William Foote Whyte's classic sociological study, *Street Corner Society* (Chicago: University of Chicago Press, 1943), p. 357.

Part II
Collected Data

It is a capital mistake to theorize before one has data.
—Sir Arthur Conan Doyle,
Scandal in Bohemia

In the first part of this book the study's motivation, prior research findings, definitional, conceptual, and propositional background, and research design were presented. The second part of this book presents summaries of the data collected for this study against which the propositions noted in chapter 3 can begin to be evaluated. In chapter 3, differentiated sets of propositions were presented:

1. Those relating to an overall model and the general nature of responses (propositions 1 to 3).
2. Those relating to the three different types of responses—corporate, administrative, and operating (proposition 4).
3. Those relating to the three distinctive organizational settings—complex, divisional, and simple (proposition 5).
4. Those relating to the decision processes in response—small steps, close to the experience of the decision makers, satisficing choices, general conceptual patterns, and situational specificity (propositions 6 to 9).

To assist interpretation of the data in relation to the propositions, the textual accounts of the respective responses embraced in this study have been organized as follows:

Data relating to the depth fieldwork in Prosper and Atlas, the two large, integrated oil companies responding to the challenges of the mid-seventies, are presented first in chapters 5 to 10. Collection of this data in one body of consecutive chapters provides a thorough documentation of two corporatewide perspectives on responding to essentially similar environments and discontinuities. A convenient opportunity is thus afforded at the end of chapter 10 to review provisionally the model of response, the likely overall companywide pattern of responses, and the general nature of response (propositions 1 to 3 of chapter 3).

The accounts of response in Prosper and Atlas are ordered, further, to introduce first two corporate responses (chapters 5 and 6), then three administrative responses (chapters 7 to 9), and finally two operating responses (chapter 10). It is possible, therefore, at the end of chapter 10 to preliminarily review also the soundness of proposition 4 concerning the main characteristics and distinctions of corporate, administrative, and operating responses with the benefit of the sample control of just two paired sites.

Prosper and Atlas comprise two of the five complex organizational settings investigated in this study. The next chapter concludes the research in complex settings by examining the further three responses in three more organizational settings (lesser depth cases). A brief and provisional summary of observations relating to complex settings is, therefore, provided at the end of chapter 11. The next three chapters (12 to 14) address response in divisional settings, and chapter 15 addresses response in simple organizational settings. A summary of the observations relating to divisional settings is, therefore, presented at the end of chapter 14, and a similar summary relating to simple settings is given at the conclusion of chapter 15. By way of summary, observations relevant to proposition 5 of chapter 3 relating to the characteristics of the host organization for response are reviewed in three parts after the accounts of response for each type of setting have been concluded (chapters 11, 14, and 15).

Commentary concerning the propositions relating to the decision processes in discontinuity (propositions 6 to 9, given in chapter 3) is made at the conclusion of most chapters. Observations are made according to aspects that have been particularly evident in the response(s) described in the chapter, or as such commentary seems helpful in the cumulative exposition of observations concerning decision processes. It is possible to make gradually more refined statements relating to decision processes as successive chapters build evidence for them.

The following accounts attempt to retain the sense of complexity of actions as they take place in the investigated organizations, but also are written to be readable. It is hoped that, as output from thorough field research, the chapters comprising part II of this book can stand as significant accounts of management as it is practiced, useful to others seeking an improved understanding of management processes according to perspectives other than the specialized one adopted for analysis of the data for this particular study.

The writing and publication of the following summaries of observations were judged an essential part of the research effort. The data on which the findings were generated were, thus, made explicit. Subsequent parts of this study are, therefore, more than anecdotal in the support of findings. All the findings reported in this study can be evaluated against these fully documented descriptions of actual decision processes as they occurred in the sites.

5
Prosper's Coal Venture

T he Organization for Economic Cooperation and Development study on coal (1978) commences with the sentence: "A massive substitution of oil by coal will be required of industrial societies and developing countries alike if they are to sustain in this century even modest economic growth in a setting of moderately increasing energy prices."[1]

The Workshop of Alternative Energy Strategies, however, raises doubts on the ability of the world to attain a massive substitution: "The pertinent question is whether coal will be produced soon enough, given the long lead times, the large financial investments involved, the need to attract more manpower for deep mines by improving working conditions, and the increased productivity resulting from technological development."[2] Moves into coal by the large oil companies including Prosper and Atlas, must be examined in the context of developments that were taking place and heralded in the world coal industry. Oil companies were expected to play a formative part in these changes.

After a brief introduction to the coal industry and to the Prosper Oil Company, the management of Prosper's entry will be discussed. As an example of a corporate response, it will show the process by which a separately organized venture was developed in the company. It will be shown that:

Motivation for entry to the coal industry arose from fear of the long-run viability of the company without the use of coal as a potential source of crude oil.

A team removed from the normal organizational framework was a vital part of the move.

Only outline terms of reference and budget approvals were used to control the strategic initiative in its early stages.

Many favorable outcomes arose from tentative or uncertain steps taken by the management.

Management of autonomy from and dependence on the mother company was critical to the success of the venture.

Although the process was often a departure from the detailed planning and forethought advocated in most management writing, Prosper executives mainly consider that the company managed its entry to the coal business well, and they are satisfied with the structure and performance of this new part of Prosper's worldwide operations.

Coal and Prosper

Coal and Oil

The extent to which coal will gain ground in the future is widely debated, but that it will increase in importance is seldom disputed. Mel Horwitch talks of constrained abundance.[3] Although addressing the United States specifically, his observations are probably more generalizable. Constraints arise from investment, environmental, and political barriers. Abundance relates to conservatively estimated exploitable reserves sufficient to meet demand for 235 years[4,5]— some 6 percent of total reserves.[6] A vision of coal in the future, however, must also take into account effects of new industry participants, new technologies, and the fact that large reserves exist in the industrialized nations and also among nations at this time sympathetic to the industrialized West.[7,8]

Renewed importance of coal has been described as likely to be an Indian summer.[9] Its role is sometimes thought to be that of a bridge between the realization that there are limitations in oil resources and the introduction of large-scale new energy forms in the next century. International coal trading is likely to be a major aspect of economic growth, especially when looking from the European perspective of the companies investigated in this study. The high cost of coal produced in Western Europe by nationalized concerns is unlikely to find a place in world markets. Conversely, coal brought to Europe from less expensive sources may be highly competitive. The more variable quality of coal deposits over oil and their probably greater range of applications (although currently less selective) suggests further promise.

To realize potentials for an international coal business plays into the hands of the oil majors. They have the sizable financial resources essential to open mines, lay railways, construct port terminals, and build maritime transport, while independent coal companies do not and nationalized participants are, practically speaking, prevented from making overseas investments. Coal regenesis is also likely to combine new technologies for which oil majors have a head start in expertise as well as resources in some cases—fluidized bed combustion in power generation, gasification, liquefaction, slurry pipelines, oil production by gasification synthesis, and, more distantly, coal-fired magnetohydrodynamics and fuel cell generation.[10] Perhaps the most apparent strength of the Seven Sisters (the largest oil companies) is their several decades of experience in integrated, large-scale, worldwide shipping,[11] processing, and marketing of petroleum products—coal being a solid hydrocarbon and oil or petroleum its liquid equivalent hydrocarbon.

Hindsight permits the above observations. The future of coal was less certain in the early 1970s and before 1973 such insights would have seemed unduly speculative. In 1974, only 9 percent of coal produced entered international trade (233 million out of 2,513 million metric tons.)[12] Interest in coal was so low that even reliable information on reserves was limited until the World Energy Conference published estimates in 1977.[13]

The advanced notions of coal's future described above were appreciated only in the vaguest terms, if at all, by most decision makers, both oil company experts and energy experts generally. Prosper's subsequent experience shows how a successful business was developed within a partially understood environment from somewhat undefined beginnings to a resilient form. For this reason, and others, the case material on Prosper's entry to the coal industry is a useful initial step in generating an empirically based understanding of corporate response. What follows is a description of how the entry came about—its major phases, subdecisions, events, and influences.

The Prosper Oil Company

As is the case in the other major oil companies, Prosper is engaged in all phases of the oil and natural gas industry, including exploration, production, shipping, refining, marketing, chemicals, plastics, and research. All of these activities are closely integrated and, together with some nonoil interests of less importance, are undertaken around the world. The company is therefore very large, ranking within the top twenty companies in the world as measured by almost any criterion. It is, of course, organizationally complex, with holdings in more than a hundred major subsidiaries in about forty countries and with total, including indirect, holdings in more than five hundred companies in about eighty countries.

The predominant cultural norm prevailing in Prosper Oil can be described as entrepreneurial. The company's personnel enjoy bold, large, high-risk investments, and executives like to claim firsts in the industry. As a result, the company is aggressive in its outlook. Its operations have been enlarged frequently by rather spectacular and complex acquisitions as well as by large-scale and somewhat novel investments in exploration, production, refining, and marketing.

The corporation is governed through a board of directors and an executive committee in the corporate headquarters. The board consists of a number of senior presidents and presidents. The primary responsibility of the higher level appointments is corporate strategy and policy. Presidents each have formal responsibility for a part or parts of the business. These individual assignments are either solely functional (for example, accounts), solely geographical (for example, Southeast Asia), or more commonly a combination of both and possibly designated also by a group diversification interest (for example, coal). The board confines its function to policy matters and meets infrequently. The day-to-day business is done at the level of the executive committee, which meets monthly and comprises the presidents on the board but excludes the senior presidents.

There is a third governing tier below the executive committee which is a series of bridging committees, one for each of several logical subsets of the company's strategic management. This third level is manned by a mixture of presidents and general managers (who have a managerial status immediately below that of the presidents). Examples of bridging committees are the policy review committee, the organization committee, and the trading policy committee.

The group as a whole is managed through one company, Prosper Operations Incorporated. This body has its own staff in support of such activities as accounts, finance, corporate planning, engineering, public affairs, and research and development. Prosper Operations also has direct ownership (whole and partial) of a multitude of subsidiary companies. Additionally, many of these companies have their own subsidiaries, so that several layers of companies often exist. The several hundred corporate entities are clustered and ordered hierarchically in a fashion that has been described as a cascade.

Prosper's numerous subsidiaries are of two kinds: functional and geographical. The former are typically worldwide; examples are Prosper Distribution Incorporated, Prosper Coal Incorporated, Prosper Tanker Incorporated, Prosper Exploration Incorporated, Prosper Chemicals Incorporated, and Prosper Trading Incorporated. Geographically differentiated subsidiaries are typically responsible for operations within national boundaries and usually perform several activities. Examples of geographical subsidiaries with their principal activities are given in table 5–1.

The organizational structure of each subsidiary and the details of its reporting relationships vary from case to case depending upon specific needs. Larger national companies generally have their own boards including representatives from the main company. National companies are grouped into areas such as Scandinavia or the Benelux, France, and Switzerland, and then grouped into regions such as Western Europe or Africa. These area and regional groupings have small but highly qualified staffs who act in directive, analytic, and coordinate roles.

The Prosper Oil Company therefore embodies the features of a complex organization as described in chapter 4. It may justly be described as organizationally diverse, technically complicated, and culturally rigid. Prosper's entry to the coal industry, and Prosper's other responses presented in later chapters, may therefore be recognized as examples of responses in a complex organization.

Table 5–1
Examples of Prosper's Subsidiaries and Their Principal Activities

	Principal Activities
Societe Francaise des Petroles Prosper	Oil refining and marketing, France
Prosper Petrolleri	Oil processing and supply, Turkey
Prosper Benzin	Marketing, Austria
Prosper (Oil Exploration, North Sea) United Kingdom	Oil and gas exploration, United Kingdom
Prosper Petroleum Development of Japan	Oil exploration, marketing, refining, natural gas liquefaction, Japan

Prosper's Entry to the Coal Industry

Nineteen seventy-eight was the first year of profit for Prosper's coal business. The initiative to pursue coal as a new source of earnings became formal in the spring of 1974, when the board approved the setting up of a small task force for the purpose. Results for 1978 were encouraging, and the management of the company as a whole was satisfied with the steps that had been taken.

The development of Prosper Coal can be described in such a way as to appear a carefully planned operation. The fact is that there was a great deal that had to be learned, and outcomes did not always materialize exactly as they had been planned. Some happenings were actually accidental, and others were more the result of propinquity than of any greater rationale. The general feeling in the company is that Prosper's actions have turned out better than those of competitive oil companies' moves into coal. A chronology of selected events in Prosper's development of a coal business is noted in figure 5–1 (countries are disguised).

Beginnings

The possibility of entry into the coal business was first seriously considered as limitations on the long-term supply of oil became evident in the company during the 1960s. Debate reached a critical level with the publication of the 1971–1981 ten-year plan in 1970. The stimulus was mainly one of seeking substitute sources of crude oil, that is, by liquefication of coal. In particular, Prosper's chief geologist became well known in the company for his view that coal would become a major source of crude by the turn of the century.

Within about two years after completion of the ten-year plan, management became conscious of the potential near-term and medium-term viability of coal operations. New oil price levels pertaining from late 1973 could be expected to increase energy prices across the board. The potential of a higher price for coal boosted the profitability of coal operations to a level meriting capital

1971	A ten-year forecast prepared by the corporate planning department precipitates serious discussion on oil substitutes.
Spring 1974	The board formalizes the intention of entry by designation of a small group of senior managers charged with investigating opportunities in coal.
Summer 1974	A budget proposal is submitted to the board and a request for ultimate staffing levels at headquarters of thirty-five persons of management rank within five years is submitted to the organization subcommittee. Both requests are approved.
Spring 1975	Several approaches are made by the task-force members to companies and to governments, to obtain involvement in coal activities.
Summer 1976	Rand Coal Mines Pty. (South Africa) is acquired. This is the Prosper Coal Group's first step into managing coal operations. It yields approximately four million tons per annum.
Spring 1977	Joint venture with a coal-mining venture in Alberta, Canada, commences with Prosper's share amounting to 1.5 million tons per annum.
Spring 1978	Prosper Indonesia begins production planned to reach three million tons per annum.
Summer 1978	A 50 percent share of Johannesburg Coal Pty is acquired, representing about six hundred thousand tons per annum to Prosper.
Spring 1979	Production is started at the wholly owned Winifred Mines development in Queensland, Australia, at the rate of two million tons per annum, bringing Prosper's coal interest to 11.1 million tons each year.

Figure 5–1. Selected Chronology of Prosper's Entry into the Coal Industry

investment. Circumstances were now propitious for the start of a coal business. Members of the newly formed policy and strategy committee, the board, and other members of the senior management became strongly interested in Prosper's entering the coal business towards the end of 1973.

Team Formation

In the winter of 1974, the president in charge of planning at Prosper presented a paper to the board recommending the establishment of a small team to investigate starting a coal business in exploration, production, and marketing. The proposal and the general business idea were accepted in principle, and two specific decisions were made. The first was that the president who presented the paper should be charged with overall responsibility for the venture. The second confirmed that a small team should be formed under this president to further examine the coal business and, if the indications were good, to begin the company's participation in that industry.

There were no explicit terms of reference, although there was some implicit notion among the board members concerning the probable size of the investment and its cash flow. These notions were not committed to paper and were accepted in the general sense of the board members' provisionally satisfying themselves that the project showed promise. Details of the size and cash flow would be expected to materialize as the project got off the ground, and would be presented as capital investment proposals to the Executive Committee at the appropriate times.

The president charged with responsibility for the coal investigation chose a colleague with whom he had worked within Prosper as the leader of a small team. The appointee was known and trusted by the president from their years together in another functional area, and he was also known to have personal attributes thought to be relevant to a project of this sort. Above all, the team leader had a reputation for being tough and commercially oriented. He was known to have an independent mind and strong opinions. He could not easily be swayed from a job in hand. This was felt to be important for a fledgling business within a mighty company with an exclusive oil mentality.

The team leader was primarily responsible for the selection of his small group of managers. He was conscious of the need not only to find people with whom he could relate satisfactorily but also to incorporate complementary skills and expertise which were essential to the task but which he did not necessarily possess himself. Two candidates seemed natural appointments.

One candidate was well known in the company because his studies as a consultant had acquainted him with many members of the senior echelons of the organization. This experience had equipped him with a rich appreciation of procedures within Prosper. Probably of even more account, this manager had a familiarity with the informal way in which things were accomplished in the company. For these reasons, he was selected as a member of the coal team.

The other candidate was Prosper's sole coal geologist. He had joined Prosper only two years previously, although he was near retirement. The chief geologist at Prosper had met him at the 1970 World Geologists' Conference, having known him for some time before that. With the general thought that some time in the near future Prosper would enter the coal business, and knowing that, in any case, his knowledge and perspective would make him a useful member of the geologists' group, the chief geologist had recruited this coal specialist into Prosper. This coal geologist therefore became the third member of the team.

Each team member had an essential part to play, the leader seeing himself as the tough businessman and negotiator, the former company consultant as the internal diplomat, and the coal geologist as the contributor of knowledge on the coal business. It is worth noting at this juncture that two members of the team had no technical knowledge of coal. They were, however, known and trusted members of the company and familiar with its internal workings.

Early Days

There was a perceived need to quickly demarcate the issues concerning the proposed move. As the circumstances have been described by one member, the team sat down on the first day to completely clear desks, blank paper, and deliberately vague terms of reference. The team members soon concluded that the liquefaction of coal was not economically feasible for many years and should not affect decisions at this early stage. Within a few days it had been provisionally concluded, however, that the coal business was commercially viable in the immediate future. The team then set about establishing parameters for Prosper's involvement in coal.

In this connection, future worldwide energy demand was estimated (noted in the review distributed by the corporate planners at Prosper) and a view determined on the proportion which Prosper Coal could reasonably expect to hold. This gave the team a five-year target figure of ten million tons per annum, representing about 5 percent of the revenue of Prosper Oil attributed to Europe. It was expected that the coal business would be a significant separate part of the total operations of Prosper within five years from 1974.

The next issue to receive careful attention by the team was the method of coal acquisition (where and how to obtain the coal). It was decided that the United States should be excluded from their search for reserves. The American Prosper company had already acquired large reserves in that country, and it would have been politically insensitive to encroach upon their domain. It was also acknowledged that the U.S.S.R., China, and the U.S.A. owned about two-thirds of the world's known coal reserves. Consequently, only the remaining third was available to Prosper companies outside of the United States.

Within that available third of world reserves, there were considerable limitations on potential areas of operation in that all European reserves were controlled by state coal companies. The most auspicious areas for operations were soon determined to be Australia, Canada, Indonesia, South Africa, and some countries in South America. By the middle of 1974 individual plans were made by the coal team for each of these regions of the world. Although definite, in the sense that intentions were quantified, the plans represented a statement of purpose to be modified as circumstances merited.

The noncoal members of the team were becoming acquainted with the coal industry during these early days. They were gaining an appreciation for distinctions between coking coal (harder, higher quality coal mainly used in steel making) and steam coal (lower quality coal mainly used in electricity generation) and for the significance of technical terms such as *in situ* (the total reserves in the location in question) and *mineable* (that part of the reserves which can be sold in the prevailing market demand circumstances). There was much homework done; the important terms and concepts were mastered within a few months. The team was also aided in this process by extensive discussions with the nationalized coal monopolies of Europe. Those companies were not generally encouraged to exploit reserves outside of their national boundaries and, as a result, they were prepared to act as consultants and advisers.

It was also during this period that the team began to construct proposals for further staffing and a budget presenting financial intentions. The budget was a substantial exercise. It was not designed as a document to be submitted for approval of a specific amount of money against a specific future cash flow. It was more a statement of the likely aggregate picture, presented with the intention of gaining outline approval of the board for the ultimate designation of monies needed for entry into the coal business. For each particular move, the coal group would be required to submit a specific proposal.

The request for staffing was couched in terms of provisional approval for a team of thirty-five managerial or specialist members in about five years. This was more than the immediate needs but gave the team a desirable flexibility to respond to staffing needs as they might arise for reasons other than were presently envisaged. The board approved the budget outline and the manpower request.

Development

In fact, Prosper's first involvement in coal activities arose from an initiative that predated by a short while the establishment of the team at corporate level. The South African subsidiary had commenced coal exploration in that country in 1972. Prosper–South Africa had approached one of the larger coal-mining groups and an agreement had been reached on joint exploration. This effort was to be largely financed by the Prosper subsidiary, but with a view to ultimate collaboration with the coal-mining group in actual mining. The funds for this venture had to be approved by Prosper's main board, but they had been forthcoming and at a time when an intention to enter the coal business had not been formalized. The exploration was fruitless—no mineable coal reserves were found.

Although this was technically the end of the intended collaboration, some months later, in 1973, the South African mining company decided to develop some reserves and approached Prosper to join them as a partner. The offer was accepted, and this joint venture became the company's first involvement in coal-mining operations. Although preceding any formulated strategy development of a coal business by Prosper, it did, however, fit within an entry strategy formulated by the latter half of 1974.

Strategy

Prosper Coal decided to seek out specific types of opportunities. These were as follows:

participation in existing mining ventures with other companies or consortia

acquisition of existing coal-mining operations

rights to explore virgin territory and to develop any discoveries

purchase of existing reserves for development

coal training entered by any appropriate method

Under this broad strategy, a series of approaches were made to foreign governments and foreign companies wherever potential seemed to exist. The plan, constructed in the early days of the project, formed the framework for these initiatives, but the mood was one, essentially, of the coal team's exploring whatever avenues seemed propitious.

Many initiatives did not materialize, including one where negotiations proceeded for a considerable time with a European communist nation. The intention there was for Prosper to trade internationally a proportion of the nation's coal output, but the idea did not come to fruition. However, other initiatives came about more forcefully than anticipated. Intentions to contract for a specific amount of coal would often need to be compromised upwards or downwards if a particular government was only prepared to negotiate for some other quantity. Individual efforts also frequently proceeded faster or more slowly than planned, and such vicissitudes had to be accepted by Prosper's management.

Other variances to plan also occurred. At one time there was an intention to limit the future coal operations to just coking coal. Then the feeling emerged in the company that this may have long-term risks because improvements in the furnace reduction methods in the steel industry might reduce growth and profit potential in that sector. Views were constantly changing on this, and a balance between coking and steam coal was eventually considered the best policy.

Organization

The original team of three was soon expanded. First, economic assistants and younger coal geologists were added, and then the organization gradually developed a full range of expertise and a formal structure. The flexible and informal beginnings reflected the primary aim of establishing a coal business. When a range of coal activities was assembled, the need veered towards the managing of these activities as a business.

A headquarters organization gradually became established, and a commercial manager was appointed in 1977 whose initial function was seen to be the consolidation of the business. His priorities were:

1. establishing a formal structure
2. reinforcement and development of the coal group's relationships with Prosper affiliates
3. review and ordering of manpower requirements
4. a longer term examination of ultimate destination
5. the strengthening of planning, targeting, and budgeting practices on an annual basis

Overall, a progressive ordering and strengthening of the coal company's structures, procedures, strategy, and other matters were put into effect. A diagrammatic representation of the structure of Prosper Coal in 1979 is given in figure 5–2. This figure shows a commercial side of the business (split into management functions) existing in parallel with a technical side (split into operational specialisms), and a general manager (plus staff) maintaining liaison with Prosper Oil.

Autonomy and Dependence

A guiding principle in organization was to establish autonomy from Prosper's oil business. Considerable difficulties were anticipated by the coal team in relation to the rest of the oil company. As one might expect, the different departments in the oil company wanted responsibility for the equivalent functions in the coal business. For example, the exploration department wanted responsibility

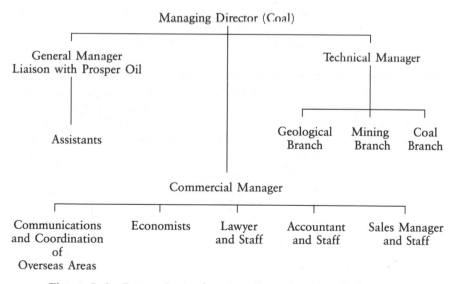

Figure 5–2. Prosper's Coal Group Organization, Early 1979

for the exploration tasks in the coal group. The claim carried some force, since the exploration group of Prosper Oil had earned a superlative regard within the company.

The coal group resisted encroachment from other parts of the oil company. Their policy was to accentuate the differences between the operations associated with each mineral. The reality of these differences is usefully illustrated in the field of exploration. The relationship between the costs of production and exploration are quite different for each case. For oil, it is usually necessary to drill seven to eight thousand feet; for coal, it is usually sufficient to drill six to seven hundred feet. In production, the exact positioning of an oil well is not critical. For coal, the siting of the mine entrance can make a substantial difference to the costs of extraction and can actually influence the volume of mineable reserves.

Although the policy of total independence from the oil operations of Prosper was sacrosanct, it did not prevent the coal group from consulting specialist departments where advisable. For example, when it was thought likely that it would be necessary to construct two hundred miles of railway in South America, the engineering group of Prosper Operations Inc. was contacted. The department had been involved in the largest and most demanding civil engineering projects in the world, as well as in the construction of many stretches of railway.

There was also a general rule that all personnel recruited for the coal operations were to be drawn from the coal industry. There were exceptions where specific "coal instincts" were not obligatory and the isolated situations where a synthesis of expertise could be beneficial. For example, personnel from the shipping function of the company have been recruited for the coal group. Prosper holds a leading position in the shipping of wet cargoes and natural gas. It was natural that the coal shippers should have access to that expertise in the expectation that each could learn from the other.

Observation of the inherent differences between the oil and coal businesses had yet deeper consequences for Prosper's fledgling coal enterprise. It became evident that the management of Prosper Oil had a natural instinct when it came to oil. It was possible to present them with any problem in the oil business, and they had a capacity to relate to it. This was true even if they did not know the facts of a particular situation. For coal, of course, the matter was quite different; in many cases, the instinct for oil would lead decision makers astray. The efforts of the coal group have since ensured that almost all of the senior management of Prosper have been down coal mines and talked with members of the industry at all levels. The aim is to make the distinction between the two different businesses an instinctive realization to all of management.

Achievement

In 1979, about five years after its inception, Prosper Coal was involved on three continents in about twenty mines. It was structured and operating as a full-fledged company of some considerable size by the standards of the coal industry. Despite the immensity of Prosper's oil interests, the coal business accounted for almost 5 percent of the total company—the board's initial goal was achieved. Over about the same time period, Atlas management also entered the coal industry and set and achieved the same goal as Prosper. The sequencing and patterning of events in Atlas were, however, even more complex than in Prosper.

Many consistencies with the propositions concerning the management of response given in chapter 3 were suggested by the facts of this case description. Perhaps most evident was the relative lack of finely detailed planning. While formal planning and strategy formulation were important in the response, more dominant was a process that may be summarized as "learning by doing," using minimally constraining strategy and pursuing a wide range of opportunities with nonspecific intentions in the expectation that some would materialize. The Atlas Company's entry into the coal industry, described in the next chapter, even more strongly displays the presence of these informal processes, but also strongly indicates the importance of other phenomena characteristic of managing response proposed in chapter 3.

Notes

1. *Steam Coal—Prospects to 2000*, International Energy Agency, Organization for Economic Cooperation and Development, 2 Rue Andre-Pascal, Paris, 1978.

2. *Energy—Global Prospects 1985–2000*, Report of the Workshop of Alternative Energy Strategies, Massachusetts Institute of Technology (New York: McGraw–Hill, 1977).

3. Mel Horwitch, "Coal: Constrained Abundance," in *Energy Future*, ed. Robert Stobaugh and Daniel Yergin (New York: Random House, 1979).

4. *Energy—Global Prospects 1985–2000*, op. cit.

5. *The Coal Option*, Shell Briefing Service, Shell International Petroleum Company Ltd. (PA/012), London, England, January 1978.

6. *Steam Coal—Prospects to 2000*, op. cit.

7. *Coal Technology for Britain's Future* (London: Macmillan, 1976), pp. 14–15.

8. *Steam Coal—Prospects to 2000*, op. cit.

9. "Minerals and Their Markets," *Financial Times*, January 16, 1979.

10. Donald E. Carr, *Energy and the Earth Machine* (New York: W.W. Norton, 1976), p. 70.

11. *Steam Coal—Prospects to 2000*, op. cit.

12. *Energy—Global Prospects 1985–2000*, op. cit.

13. Ibid.

6
Atlas's Coal Venture

At the end of the seventies the management of Atlas could reflect with satisfaction on the progress of their entry into the coal business. The earliest steps had been taken in the autumn of 1971 and, after eight years, the Atlas International Coal Company was managing a traded volume of over five million tons per annum. It was also exploring in five countries around the world and had other ventures concerned with proven reserves expected to come shortly on stream. It was probable that Atlas, outside of its United States holdings, would be trading up to ten million tons of coal per year by 1983, and that it had existing holdings and operations with the potential to reach fifteen million tons per year in the late 1980s.

The company's coal operations were on the way to realizing a fully integrated concept. Shareholdings had been acquired in a custom-built coal terminal. The company had become engaged in coal shipping and marketing. In addition, it had mounted a significant research and development effort in association with other companies. As an illustrative example, it had purchased a minority interest in a designer and manufacturer of specialized coal-handling equipment and obtained a substantial share in a large program researching the liquefaction and gasification of coal. Yet this considerable development took place amid uncertain initiatives, alterations in direction, and other deviations from the textbook prescriptions of careful research, detailed planning, and systematic actions. Following is a description of the corporate response of Atlas's entry to the coal business, which is to be compared with the equivalent response of the Prosper Company described in the preceding chapter.

Formation

Development of Atlas Coal was less straightforward than that of its Prosper equivalent. The company first intended a slow entrance observing its preferred method of operations in the oil business, that is, by obtaining exclusive license for exploration, development, and production, and then marketing the product.

All these operations were to be performed exclusively by Atlas, utilizing their skills in exploration to find reserves that were as yet unproven. This method was less expensive than buying into existing operations and avoided the associated problems of working with partners. Circumstances eventually made it desirable to use the faster but less preferred method of joint ventures as well as the exploration route. In addition, an early attempt was made to enter trading as well. That initiative was dropped when the oil price increase brought about a general resurgence of interest in coal that made it impossible for a newcomer to proceed. Coal trading, however, was incorporated into the Atlas coal business at a later date.

The strategic move to enter the coal business saw two quite distinct phases. From about 1972, after board level initiative, a small informal team of (mainly younger) managers succeeded in getting the project off the ground. In early 1975 a formal and functionally based structure was adopted and senior managers were introduced to the coal company. A chronology of the major events in Atlas's coal entry is given in figure 6–1. The listing illustrates these two phases; the first embraced the different directions, and the second consolidated the form that emerged.

To properly understand the way Atlas entered the coal industry it is necessary first to give some background to the Atlas Oil Company.

The Atlas Oil Company

Atlas Oil is international in the most complete sense of the term. Like the other majors, it has a fully integrated oil business and substantial additional investments in other energy forms and petrochemicals, as well as a few unrelated businesses of small current importance within Atlas.

Although the company has an extensive headquarters with centralized functions, the operations of the group as a whole are substantially decentralized into a large number of often autonomous subsidiary companies. Centralized functions at headquarters are largely managed as separate companies in a manner similar to Atlas's worldwide operating activities. Subsidiaries can be classified into two types: those termed support companies and those termed functional companies. The former supply services and advice to the functional companies, which are responsible for varied group operations in a designated geographical area.

There are about twenty support companies in Atlas. An example is Atlas Petrochemicals Inc., which supplies international coordination, planning, and technical information to the petrochemical subsidiaries. Other examples include oil manufacturing, oil refining, oil marketing, marine, natural gas, and coal. It is interesting to note that manufacturing, refining, and marketing are operated as separate companies, and that the structure emphasizes autonomy over close integration. Most of these support companies divide their responsibilities by

1971	The board approves formation of the "New Enterprises Group."
1972	A team of six is established. Exploration is commenced in Country A.[a]
Summer 1973	New Enterprises Group is prepared to enter coal trading.
Autumn 1973	Coal-trading plans fail. Company management recognizes urgent need to form a coal enterprise. Negotiations are concluded for exploration licenses in the six countries.
1974	Country B acquisition of coal deposits and their evaluation are commenced. Joint venture approach is accepted by senior management and results in: agreement on joint mining, transport and marketing of coal with a company in Country C; joint ventures in Countries B and C for development of proven reserves; research agreement with a company in Country D on coal liquefaction and gasification processes.
Spring 1975	Coal group is reorganized into a structural form with ambitious new managing director.
1975	Existing joint ventures are expanded and exploration is continued. A minority shareholding is acquired in a company in Country E, designers and manufacturers of coal-handling equipment. Several research and development programs get underway.
Autumn 1976	Exploration in Country A is finally terminated.
1976	A shareholding is acquired in an existing mining operation in Country C. A shareholding is also acquired in a coal terminal and mine in Country F.
1977	Further shareholdings in coal operations are acquired. Coal-trading volume exceeds one million tons for the first time. Development of Colombian reserves is deferred.
1978	Atlas's share of coal traded exceeds five million tons as the various projects described above move from pilot to full scale, or as they become fully incorporated into Atlas's accounts. Exploration and research and development activities are programmed into the future.

[a]The six countries are disguised as A, B, C, D, E, and F.

Figure 6–1. Selected Chronology of Atlas's Entry into the Coal Industry

region, so that the more detailed work relating to Europe, Asia, and other geographical areas is performed in regional headquarters in those parts of the world.

An individual functional company's or subsidiary's responsibilities are generally confined to one country but might include certain international activities necessary to national operations. The activities of a particular company may cut across almost all of the parts of the oil industry and the other businesses in which Atlas is engaged; or they may be limited to just one small part of Atlas's business. Examples of functional subsidiaries are listed in table 6–1.

Table 6–1
Examples of Atlas's Subsidiaries and Their Principal Activities

	Principal Activities
Atlas Great Britain	Oil production, oil marketing, oil manufacturing, natural gas production, manufacturing and marketing, research, and tankers operated from Great Britain
Atlas Nippon Exploration	Oil and natural gas exploration in and from Japan
Atlas de Raffinage	Oil manufacturing, France
Atlas Malawi	Oil marketing, Malawi
Atlas Guatemala	Chemical operations based in Guatemala

It is an important principle to Atlas that functional companies should have considerable autonomy. In many cases they have their own boards and are independently managed, for all practical purposes. The Atlas group is primarily governed by a board of directors. That board works as a committee, with each director having multiple responsibilities which might include one that is geographical, such as Asia or Africa, one that is a business area, such as oil exploration or chemicals, and one that carries overall responsibility for a central headquarters activity such as corporate planning. A member of the main board would also generally be a member of one or more of the subsidiaries' boards of geographical companies such as Atlas Australia.

The structural form and the accompanying management philosophy have given this company the flexibility to grow very large. Its size is conveyed by its status as one of the Seven Sisters, but membership in the sorority alone is insufficient to convey the true significance of its size. Bigness is an inculcated value and a guiding sense in the company. Related to this is also a genuine internationalism embodied in its culture. Many languages and many nationalities are typically encountered in company corridors. Oil and energy are the major business of Atlas, but commitment to its role as a responsible international institution is an important factor in Atlas's corporate behavior.

Like the Prosper Oil Company, the Atlas Oil Company represents a complex setting—the company is organizationally diverse, technically complicated, and culturally rigid. Entry to the coal industry described in this chapter is therefore an example of response in a complex setting, as are the other responses researched in Atlas and presented in later chapters.

Tourism or Coal?

Atlas's entry into the coal business first gained deliberate form in a more widely conceived initiative to develop new enterprise. A group had been set up to examine the matter in general terms and to advise on possibilities. A board president, who was also responsible for corporate planning, headed up this team.

Coal and tourism were two suggestions shortlisted for consideration by the board. The president took up the subject of entry into coal and pushed for its approval. As a result, further development work was agreed for both coal and tourism, and it was decided that a general manager should be appointed for that purpose, reporting to the president of planning and new enterprises.

The general manager appointed by the board president was an executive who had been very successful in Atlas. He had recently returned to the head-quarters after managing one of the largest national subsidiary companies for a number of years. His reputation was as a great "ideas man," and he was considered to be something of a philosopher on the condition of the world. One of his colleagues described him affectionately as "a bit of an iconoclast." He was also near to his retirement, and it is probable that he was prepared to adopt a more forthright stance on issues than would a younger man.

After the general manager had discussed the two possible ventures of coal and tourism with Atlas's larger subsidiary companies, the opinion was formed that tourism would not be a fruitful business. In contrast, the prospect of a move into coal was received with enthusiasm by some major subsidiaries. There were several reasons for the positive way in which the proposal was received. Foremost, apart from its possibilities as a profit opportunity, was a sense of kinship or affinity. This was particularly true in countries such as South Africa and Australia that have large, privately owned coal-mining sectors in their economies.

For Atlas's board the appeal of coal was probably a realization of the enormous disparity between the amounts of known coal reserves and known reserves of other nonrenewable sources of energy. The company was conscious that, on the basis of a number of years of sustainable consumption, coal reserves could be measured in centuries, but that oil, uranium, and gas reserves could be measured only in decades. The feeling was that company-owned coal would be a useful hedge against an unknown energy future. Reserves might be used as a traded commodity or processed by Atlas into gas or oil, but preconceptions on the way they would be used were not formed at this early stage.

The Team

The board had approved the establishing of a small team to develop a coal business in late 1971. The team was to be headed by the newly appointed general manager. In the early part of 1972, the general manager began to select five staff members from Atlas personnel. These included a generalist whose role was visualized as coordinative, a transportation manager, a business analyst with an American business school background, a planning and information manager who had worked with the general manager, and a marketing specialist. By Atlas's standards it is reasonable to describe the group as unrepresentative, in that they were more individual, more adventurous, and less conformist than the Atlas norm. As a team they worked well, with the more innovative suggestions of some team members moderated by those with a greater sensitivity towards the conservative perspective of most of Atlas management.

From the earliest point in the development of the coal business, the importance of people was recognized. At the start, its only asset was the people involved in the venture. The need to attract first-rate managers into the coal organization was accentuated by the requirement to attain high credibility within the rest of the Atlas organization.

The need for credibility was most important at the level of senior management and especially on the board, whose members were necessarily to act as paymasters for the project. Here, after all, was a part of the company which might request investments totalling nearly a billion dollars. Yet coal was an area about which the board had scant knowledge and little reason for confidence in their judgments beyond that of confidence in the people themselves. There was a dilemma in this problem in that Atlas's paternalistic attitudes ensured secure, rewarding, and known career paths. Personnel of the highest caliber could not be expected to commit to the uncertain future of the coal group. Such a career risk was simply not worth taking for most individuals. These considerations promoted the need to create an appealing atmosphere in the coal organization to assist in overcoming as much of this resistance as possible.

The need for a target or goal became apparent. This would help to focus and motivate the team's efforts and to reinforce commitment with the company's management as a whole. For coal to receive internal support it would have to attain a critical level of importance within Atlas. In practice, this meant the promise of contributing a significant proportion to total Atlas profits and at least as much as other new Atlas ventures. It was decided by the team that a goal of achieving a 10 percent share of profits in ten years and 5 percent in five years met this criterion. This level would also provide motivation. Management accepted that the goal could be compromised, in the short run, in recognition of shifting opportunities and developments in an uncertain situation.

Directions

In the early days the development of the coal business took place along three paths. The most important one was an effort at an exploration route. Another was the attempt to introduce a coal-trading business. Finally, a joint venture approach became the most advantageous in the middle seventies, after the catalyst of imposition of the 1973 oil price increases and after mainly unrewarding experiences with the exploration and trading attempts at entering the coal industry.

Exploration

The predominant thinking of the board for the shape of Atlas's future in the coal business was for the acquisition of coal reserves, with a view to later development. In contrast to the prospect of developing a business in coal in the immediate term by acquisition or joint venture, the chosen perspective was equivalent to the way the company had developed its oil business. Traditionally, leases had been taken on areas of land where oil was expected or known to exist. These were then explored by means of drilling, and the reserves and the crude oil were ultimately produced, traded, and marketed. It was a decisive way of operating and one which the company knew and understood. It also took advantage of the company's very definite skills in exploration and project management.

Entry by exploration also had many practical and long-term financial advantages. The company's geologists believed that there were many deposits in the world which were not delineated and which could be highly profitable in the near future. There were many parts of the world where there were known to be deposits but where coal-mining companies had no interest. Historically, adequate supplies of low-price coal had always been available near to industrial areas. Many industrial nations were now emerging, with economies based on oil, but without indigenous coal or oil reserves. More efficient transportation also offered the chance that coal from, for example, Southern Africa could be delivered to Europe at prices competitive with those of Germany and Britain.

If inexpensive leases or mining rights could be obtained on remote prospects in which the traditional coal industry had no interest, it followed that deposits found to have potential could be exploited in due time. This was an inexpensive way of obtaining entry to the coal business, and it carried the practical advantage that there were many decision points. The feelings of senior management were distinctly in favor of this slow but stronger approach. More risky joint ventures and acquisitions were not favored.

Accordingly, in late 1972 and early 1973 the group surveyed the nations of the world to determine where it was possible to acquire coal reserves but to withhold exploitation. It was found that only two countries permitted this approach. One was the United States and the other was South Africa. Ownership of reserves was the fundamental concept of importance to Atlas management, and only those two nations allowed the preferred approach in its fullest form.

Other nations were also interesting to management in that many of their governments were helpful and would accept acquisition of reserves but they mandated eventual mining. For such intermediate countries (Australia is an example), even this minor limitation on freedom was seen by Atlas management as a powerful disincentive to acquire reserves. The United States had to be excluded because Atlas's American company had already acquired coal deposits there. It would also have infringed upon the operating premises that exist between the American and European sections of the company.

In fact, Atlas was already contracted into a coal exploration project before the "coal team" was functioning. For historical reasons, Atlas had always had a close relationship with the government of a major country in Asia. It was known that there were substantial deposits of rather poor quality brown coal in that country, but it was also known that there was a proportion of better quality coal among the deposits. The government of that country gave Atlas exclusive exploration and development rights for a large tract of promising land. Atlas's geologists mounted an exploration rig during 1971 and 1972 and a considerable drilling program was instigated. The aim was to delineate the reserves in the hope of locating mineable, good-quality coal.

The senior management at Atlas held a strong commitment to this large exploration project and to the exploration route in general. Several other exploration projects had been agreed upon. Apart from the work in the first country, exploration licenses had been granted in two other countries and coal deposits had been acquired in a fourth country for immediate mining, where evaluation was in progress. Although working within the exploration route preferred by the company, the members of the new enterprises team had some reservations about the approach. Many preferred a joint venture or acquisition route and were in favor of immediately establishing coal-trading interests.

As understanding of the coal industry increased, senior management's commitment only to seek areas for exploration gradually softened. It became apparent that because of the wide abundance of coal and its underutilization relative to its extensive resource base, the intended method of operation by the company was not as attractive as had been previously supposed. The nature of circumstances was that even reserves with a high near-term potential may not be profitably operated for perhaps a century.

This was, of course, quite different from the position relating to oil, where even maximally expensive oil reserves, such as in the North Sea, were immediately exploitable at price levels holding before OPEC's unilateral pricing agreement came into effect. The company also came to the realization that the extent and quality of most coalfields was quite well understood, and that most deposits were already owned and had been for centuries. The position, again, was quite different from that of oil reserves, where the marginal barrel or ton was available for "discovery" and exploitation.

Trading

The exploration efforts did not require any significant involvement of the coal development team. The discovery and development of Atlas's own coal reserves was clearly a long-term prospect. The team of six persons needed a nearer term business to plan and to become involved in. Discussions coalesced towards setting up a coal-trading business. Such a business would fit well with the company's existing strengths as developed in the oil business.

Among the oil majors it is probable that Atlas has one of the strongest mercantile traditions. The servicing of contracts, the commissioning or hiring of tankers, and the worldwide management of its complex crude oil supply were well run and established activities. Entry into the coal-trading business in an initially limited way would give them a chance to experience the coal industry and to learn how it functioned. The character of the people and the companies are different, as are the ports, markets, physical properties of the commodity, and so on. Participation in coal trading would be a way to ease into hands-on experience.

The coal group spent the summer of 1973 gearing up for the move into coal trading. They needed to find coal sellers, shippers, and customers. Many "cold calls" were required, and the integrity of potential business associates needed to be carefully assessed. By the autumn of 1973, the company was almost ready to launch its coal-trading operation. It was to be mainly based on United States coal, because that was where the world marginal tonnage existed at the time.

It was at this critical juncture that the Middle East war started, and within months the price of petroleum had quadrupled. The world's suppliers of energy became universally aware of the higher prices that would prevail for energy. In particular, the coal industry became aware of the new profitability which coal activities had acquired. As a consequence, the world's marginal coal tonnage was no longer available for sale to newcomers to the industry. The tighter trading position even excluded a highly respected and wealthy company such as Atlas. The company's coal-trading plans were consequently put in abeyance.

Impetus

Despite foreclosing the coal-trading ambitions, the oil price increase gave a new impetus to the development of Atlas's coal business. It provided a validation of the initial reasoning behind entry, and lent a sense of urgency to the need to move. By this time, there was also an increasing awareness among senior management that the exploration approach was a long-term proposition and that it would not provide a vehicle for immediate entry. The new urgency, in turn, gave impetus to the joint venture and "buying in" approaches. But acquisition of companies whose managements had no inclination to be associated with Atlas was still not acceptable to senior members.

Joint Ventures

The shift in approach, from exploration for coal reserves and subsequent development to buying into joint ventures, came about gradually. It gained momentum from the end of 1973 after the oil price increase, but the earlier research findings of the coal group had already softened views. Additionally, disappointing results from the earliest exploration attempts had served to re-orientate opinions.

It was becoming apparent that coal exploration activity, although inexpensive in comparison to oil, was expensive in relation to the coal industry, where margins were lower. A series of fragmentary realizations and experiences such as this one, together with debates initiated by increasingly knowledgeable members of the coal group, influenced the gradual shift away from the strategy of ownership and exploration. Probably most important in bringing about the revised approach was the collapse of the time schedule that the company had judged to be comfortable for the development of a coal business. Previously a period of more than ten years was presumed for the development of the coal business, but the events of 1973 had caused the allowable time period for entry to be lessened.

A policy pertaining to joint ventures was developed around late 1973. It was decided that each venture would be relatively small. This allowed the infant coal company to limit its risks and confine itself to projects of manageable size. The activities were also selected for their value in providing management experience and launching the team steeply up the learning curve. The consequent absence of large mistakes would assist, too, in building internal credibility for the managers in the coal group.

In keeping with company tradition, the will of Atlas management was not to be inflicted forcibly upon the companies agreeing to joint venture operations with Atlas. This company always works from inside the system, harnessing the cooperation of the management teams of its partners. The intention was to find companies that would welcome the skills and resources of Atlas as complementary to their own existing business. Atlas is, after all, richly financially endowed and has the benefit of worldwide marketing operations, highly respected organizational expertise, and the technical and managerial skills which go along with these.

The intention was to encourage Atlas's local subsidiary companies to seek out sound joint venture opportunities in the coal industry. This did not preclude headquarters from originating its own ventures, but stressed corporate management's prime role as a catalyst to facilitate the entry of their overseas subsidiaries into coal. Although ideas originated predominantly from the headquarters-based team in 1971 and 1972, the group now increasingly involved the subsidiaries. The general idea of entry into coal was suggested to the subsidiaries in early 1973 in terms of the exploration route, and initiatives were invited. Readiness to enter by means of joint ventures was made known to them around the start of 1974, when proposals for local involvement were requested.

Many subsidiary companies greeted the joint venture idea with enthusiasm, and prospects were generated rapidly. This orientation was encouraged, and it became the policy of the headquarters-based senior coal management to staff and organize the international coal venture in such a way as to ensure that ideas would be mainly generated from the level of the foreign operating companies. This was mainly because detailed understanding of local conditions was so useful to the success of the individual operations.

The earliest joint arrangements arose during the efforts to obtain coal for trading purposes around 1973. An acquaintance had been made with a medium-sized coal-mining company. The company wished to expand its operations but lacked the funds to support growth. With the new mood within Atlas, the new enterprises team was able to negotiate a contract in 1974 which essentially involved prepayment for future coal supplies. The arrangement resulted in tradeable quantities of coal coming forward in 1975. The agreement was for participation in mining, transport, and marketing, and represented Atlas's first managerial involvement with actual coal operations.

By the end of 1974, other joint ventures had been agreed upon, including joint development of proven reserves in two of the countries with which exploration projects had been started and a technical research agreement with a company on the development of a coal liquefaction and gasification process. Other agreements and minority shareholding arrangements were concluded in later years. Particularly notable were contractual joint involvements with a company that designed and manufactured coal-handling equipment, shareholdings in a Southern Europe coal terminal and in an international coal-trading company, and various coal-mining agreements.

Consolidation

The coal group experienced the next major change in its operations shortly after making those first commitments to ongoing coal activities. In February 1975 the team leader's retirement fell due. The member of the board who had been assigned overall responsibility for the coal venture, and others in the company, felt that organization priorities should now begin to reflect that the company was rapidly emerging as an ongoing business. Most important in this reorganization was the appointment of a new leader for the group. Here the senior management selected a general manager who was in a career situation wherein he had everything to lose if the coal business was not successful.

The new manager was very young at thirty-two years for an appointment of this responsibility in Atlas. He was recognized as really "on the way up," and success in this appointment was crucial to his ambitions. His duties were seen to be the molding of the enterprise into a well-organized and smoothly functioning business, and his background in the company showed he had that perspective and ability. The needs, up to this time, had been less demanding in those rigors and were conceived as more of a mandate to generate ideas, move fast, and perhaps adopt some unconventional solutions. The general manager recognized one of his earliest priorities to be a reorganization that would meet the needs of efficient management and provide a framework for New Enterprise's growth into a viable business.

The original team was disbanded, although some of its members and others who had joined the embryo coal business under the old organization remained. The needs in the reorganization were seen to be for a functional structure and for the establishment of a solid, conventionally managed business. This philosophy would also meet the need for credibility for the coal business within Atlas. This had become an important issue as the operation developed and as the sums of money to be secured from the board grew larger and more frequent.

Reflecting this philosophy, several more established senior managers from Atlas's oil business were brought in to fill new functional slots. Previously the organization had been informal, and areas of interest for each member of the team had been loosely demarcated. The new organization was more robust and more professional and allowed the group to relate more satisfactorily with top management in foreign subsidiaries. The organization structure continued to develop and is shown as it was about three years after the reorganization in figure 6–2. As well as the normal functional breakdown between finance, marketing, and so on, the technical departments of exploration and engineering and technology are strongly represented.

From this period, a strategy for Atlas's coal business was consolidated and made evident in the pattern of commitments and projects. In common with its oil interests, the company was adopting a vertically integrated approach to the business. The company's perspective was wholly international, even though the international coal industry had traditionally been insignificant. There was also a major commitment to invest in research and development. The company's laboratories had earlier led strides in the field of petrochemicals and other applications of petroleum. The research and development laboratories had always had an indirect interest in coal as a member of the genera of mineral hydrocarbons. Atlas's decision to move into coal had served to stimulate and advance those efforts.

Achievement

By 1978 the Atlas coal business was beginning to be substantial. Atlas's mined and traded volume of coal exceeded five million tons in that year, and other ventures would be coming on stream shortly. Several promising exploration projects were also well under way, including initial participation in coal terminals, shipping, and marketing. The company was optimistic about its technical advances in several areas, for example, in coal slurries, mechanical handling, and other fields with considerable potential. With its experience accumulating in all facets of the industry, and with the rapidly increasing strength of its

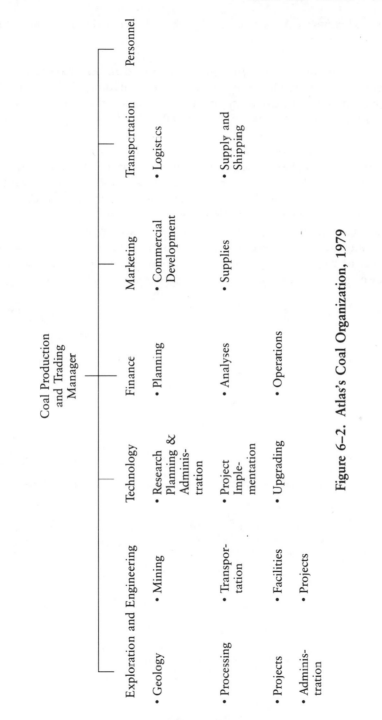

Coal Production
and Trading
Manager

Exploration and Engineering	Technology	Finance	Marketing	Transportation	Personnel
• Geology	• Research Planning & Administration	• Planning	• Commercial Development	• Logistics	
• Transportation	• Project Implementation	• Analyses	• Supplies	• Supply and Shipping	
• Processing					
• Facilities	• Upgrading	• Operations			
• Projects					
• Administration					

Figure 6–2. Atlas's Coal Organization, 1979

commercial contacts, Atlas considered itself well prepared to meet the projected increase in demand for coal.

Both Atlas and Prosper attained their goals for coal and created successful and promising businesses. How they achieved their outcomes differs in most details, but similarities exist. Among the more obvious distinctions is one of timing. In judging the two, it should be recalled that Prosper really only entered the picture when the 1973 oil price increase provided the impetus and more tangible sense of purpose than in Atlas. Preceding that impressionable event, Atlas's response had been susceptible to several conflicting pressures that were absent in Prosper. However, the same sense of evolution from bare beginnings to a maturity not conceived in any detail in the early phases of each initiative is observable. Other similarities also exist in the use of teams, the importance of individuals, issues of autonomy and dependence upon the mother organization, and others that will be expanded upon in later chapters when these two cases of corporate responses have been contrasted with the following examples of administrative and operating responses.

7

Prosper's Catalytic Cracker

pproval of a catalytic cracker converting heavier, baser oils to more valuable, lighter end products such as gasolines was a decision without precedent for Prosper. It was one of the most hotly contested decisions in the company's history. At issue was an environmental analysis which many managers did not believe, a very substantial investment at a time when capacity utilization for many existing fixed assets was hovering around 60 percent, and, most significant of all, a revised outlook on oil operations from one of maximizing volume to one of adding value.

This chapter addresses the first example of an administrative response—one concerned with adapting the operations of a business. In this respect the emphasis, unlike that of the corporate responses described in the two preceding chapters, is on the impacts of the proposed investment on the main business of the oil company. Internal decision processes, for example, dwell extensively on the fit of the project with existing operations and on the implications of the project for the organizational structure and its members. By comparison these were relatively minor matters in the entries to the coal industry. The response evolved from unclear expectations about future demand positions to a statement of general principle that the construction of a cracker should be considered, through a cumbersome process of analysis and debate, to a final proposal for a catalytic cracker of specific size and location. The decision processes took place within highly formalized procedures for capital investments that exist at Prosper as in other large corporations. As this account demonstrates, however, much that was formative for the response occurred informally.

Instigation

The majority of people in Prosper felt great enthusiasm towards the catalytic cracker project in 1979. Instigators of this substantial refining investment decision were confident and excited about the plant's projected financial return from 1980, when it was to go on stream. As a supplementary stage in the refining of oil, a cracker lightens oil products by cracking large molecules into smaller ones. Although the inputs and outputs of a specific installation are limited, in general terms heavy oils with baser end uses are broken into thinner products of higher value, suitable for more selective applications. In the aggregate, use of such facilities increases the proportion of expensive products, including aviation fuels and gasolines, and decreases the proportion of oils suitable only for under-boiler heating.

The Project

Justification for the catalytic cracker project is dependent upon a shift in demand patterns away from uses of heavier oil towards those that are lighter. The process is described as a "lightening of the barrel shape" in oil industry vernacular. The project's detractors were uncertain of this inherent planning assumption, but they became vehemently opposed when the size of the proposed cracker became known. At a capacity of fifty thousand barrels of oil per day it exceeded even the planners' forecast demand until the middle 1980s. Even accepting the established sales predictions, the cracker would be operated at less than capacity for five years or more.

The cracker in question was designed to be one of the world's largest, at an estimated cost of over half a billion dollars. Although the investment was small by the standards of exploration and development of the North Slope and the North Sea oil fields, it was a very substantial outlay by refining standards. As an investment in expectation of a trend to a lighter barrel, it constituted a reorientation and a novel view on investment in the refining sector. Previously, development of the refining business had followed a steady formula of building capacity by adding extra integrated units (of quite standard configurations) and by gradual technical evolution.

In converting heavier inputs to light distillates, the viability of the catalytic cracker is largely determined by the price differential between products like 3.5 percent sulphur fuel oil (a heavy base product) to premium motor oil (a light, high value product). The differential, in turn, depends upon a different supply and demand balance for each product. In early 1974, $40 per barrel was estimated to be the minimum differential justifying the investment. During 1978 the differential averaged more than $60 to $80 and it reached $130 during the cutoff of Iranian crude in 1979. It was not expected that sufficient cracking capacity would be available in Europe to bring about a balancing of supply and demand such that the differential would approximate profitability comparable to that of other products until the middle 1980s. Until that time the supply of light distillates was thought by many to have the potential of a highly profitable business.

From its inception, the rationale for the cracker was a combination of economic arguments and of its fit with Prosper's European facilities. Following outline consent from the executive committee and the main board for the development of a proposal, its details on location, cost, return, and other aspects were formulated as a formal capital investment proposal submitted to the executive committee. After further development, it went forward to the main board for formal discussion and action.

Corporate Planners

Enthusiasm for the catalytic cracker project ran highest in the corporate planning department of Prosper. The forecasters and planners had been largely responsible for the demand analyses which had prompted the company's decision. Members of the department were also responsible for the overall development of the project through to final approval by the main board in March 1977.

The function of the corporate planning department is, primarily, to analyze the oil industry environment and to examine how the company is reacting within the total supply and demand position. It reviews its conclusions in terms of potential investments. The supply department also analyzes the environment, but only in relation to nearer term, noninvestment issues such as the buying and selling of crude and products.

The corporate planning department is organized as four sections. There is a forecasting group of just over twenty persons which examines shipping and refining as well as the total energy picture. Another group of slightly more than twenty persons constitutes divisional group planning, which deals with geographical analysis, capital budgeting, and the control and coordination of the planning exercise of group subsidiaries. There is also a small group of half a dozen persons who act as advisers on all major projects (including the catalytic cracker investment), all diversification investments, and oil field developments. The work of the corporate planners makes considerable use of computer models, and there is a systems group responsible for their development and maintenance.

The corporate planning process in Prosper is essentially continuous and substantially informal. Nevertheless, it is organized around a well-established formal procedure. The forecasters compile annually, and sometimes more frequently, a survey of world energy demand and supply. The *World Review,* as it is called, is presented to the board and elsewhere within the company. It may be the primary vehicle for debate on planning issues, and it forms the context within which budget planning takes place. The *World Review* also forms the basis of analyses of the company's position in relation to world demand and supply and competition.

The work of the department heavily emphasizes a quantitative approach. It is peopled substantially by economists with an econometric bias, and liberal use is made of a comprehensive suite of corporate models. The long-term model for Europe is of particular importance because the logistical determinants of

Prosper's supply operations are simulated in considerable detail. The pattern of demand for all products is incorporated in that model, as are the refining facilities, shipping and handling costs, and other features necessary to comprehensive analysis. A nonquantitative approach, using political or social analysis for example, is subordinate in Prosper.

Origination

The realization of an ultimately lighter barrel had been assumed by some of Prosper's senior management for some years before the oil crisis of 1973. The higher prices of that year focused attention on the prospect and on introducing additional cracking capacity. In consequence of oil industry developments, the corporate planning review of 1974 specifically featured 1980 forecasts of barrel shape. Prosper's 1974 forecasts for the Organization for Economic Cooperation and Development in Europe, together with 1973 actuals, are reproduced in table 7–1. The uncertainty as to whether the sharply increased prices of late 1973 would continue into the future suggested to the planners that they should present two scenarios. One would incorporate the existing high price and the other would assume that the price would decline.

Naturally, the higher price scenario, assuming that the unilaterally declared price of the Organization of Petroleum Exporting Countries (OPEC) would not soften, showed a much greater proportion of lighter distillates than the low-price scenario, which assumed that prices would fall back to the levels operating in early 1973. Under the higher price scenario, approximately 3 percent of production was forecast to shift from fuel oil to light distillates in six years. This represented a small decline in fuel oil demand, and an annual growth of almost 5 percent in the demand for light distillates.

Reasoning behind the forecast change in barrel shape was quite simple. The increased price of oil favored other energy sources in applications where

Table 7–1
Oil Demand by Order of Distillate

| | 1973 Actuals | | 1974 Forecast | | | |
| | | | High Price Scenario | | Low Price Scenario | |
OECD Europe	Million Tons	Percent	Million Tons	Percent	Million Tons	Percent
Light Distillates	134	18.2	173	21.5	195	20.0
Middle Distillates	212	28.7	230	28.6	277	28.4
Fuel Oil	230	31.2	221	27.4	299	30.6
Other	162	21.9	181	22.5	206	21.0
Net Oil	738	100.0	805	100.0	977	100.0

the oil could be substituted. Potential for substitution was greatest in the case of fuel oil; coal could be used as an underboiler fuel, and nuclear and hydroelectric power could also be substituted in many applications. In addition, the increased costs of energy was thought most likely to suppress the growth of energy consumption at the heavier end of the barrel. Both industrial and domestic consumers were thought likely to reduce consumption by introducing economies in energy consumption, increased insulation, and other easily implemented methods. Coupled with expectations of economic recession, a buoyant market in light distillates was also forecast. It was known from experience that the demand for lighter distillates typically increases in recessions. The reason for this is the increased use of automobiles, probably the result of more leisure hours among the work force.

Consideration of possible future price differentials further increased the profit potential in the situation. In a production environment structured to the pre–1974 barrel shape, the reduction in fuel oil demand would result in a relative surplus of fuel oil and a relative scarcity of light distillates. Market pressures were expected to suppress fuel oil prices and stimulate light distillate prices. In short, a price differential would be expected to develop where market profit would swing in favor of light distillates. The economics of any move to increase the proportion of light distillates would depend largely upon the opportunity cost of uncracked fuel oil.

Prosper's corporate planning department considered these environmental characteristics and trends in relation to the company's existing facilities. Their conclusions were that Prosper was less equipped to deal with a lightening of the barrel than were most of its competitors. The disparity arose largely from Prosper's proportionally larger chemicals business. Naphtha was used as the major feedstock by Prosper, which reduced its availability, as compared to competitors, for the production of gasoline.

In conclusion, Prosper's competitors had greater flexibility and could meet a further shift to a lighter barrel. To satisfy the forecast pattern of demand, it was evident that some adjustment of Prosper's European refining operations was required. Despite the uncertainty in the forecasts, the newly established policy committee, the main board and the corporate planners believed that a more detailed analysis of the company's policies on cracking would be advisable. The corporate planning department was charged with the responsibility for a detailed examination of the foregoing situation. Following is a description of how that was accomplished.

Preliminaries and Proposal

The long-term planning computer model was invaluable in considering the company's response to lightening of the barrel. Initially the model was used to determine the feasibility of meeting the forecast demand changes without capital investment, by shifting towards the production of a lighter barrel. This could be achieved in a number of ways, including substitution of lighter crudes, re-arrangement of existing refining facilities, and small, selective investments in modifying existing processes which could yield an increase in the proportion of light distillates.

All of these options, and others, were tested on the model, and indications were clear that the level of demand could not be met without substantial investment in cracking capacity. (General talk in the oil industry proceeded along the same lines. For example, the *Petroleum Industry Review* advocated the building of crackers as a solution to the anticipated demand shift away from heavy products). The construction of cracking capacity would be a capital investment for Prosper and would thus have to be presented in a formal proposal to the executive committee. Meanwhile, subsequent events in the oil industry could be monitored to seek corroboration of the assumptions underlying the economic and financial viability of the move.

Key Questions

With a provisional view that an investment in a cracker was likely to be recommended, the planners' efforts next focused on the two key questions governing its viability. The first related to what the price differential was to be over the life of the plan. The second related to likely competitive actions on installing cracking, and how this might affect the profitability of the project.

The question of the extent of the differential between fuel oil and light distillates was heavily dependent upon views on the level at which crude oil buying prices would finally settle. As time passed, it became generally accepted that the OPEC–administered price levels were likely to be sustained, with only limited softening. Accepting this general level, the differential would then be influenced by the development of those trends which justified the company's more detailed analysis. Environmental trends were reinforcing the arguments through 1974 and 1975. Prosper's low growth forecasts were found to be close to actual results, unlike the more optimistic projections of most of the industry.

At the same time, governments were legislating price increases on fuel oils, which suppressed demand, produced oversupply, and lowered oil company selling prices. Equivalently, gasoline price rises were suppressed by governments because of their effect on inflation. Volume demand was therefore bouyant, and oil company selling prices relatively firm. For the oil companies, these actions increased the differential between fuel oils and light distillates. A computerized analysis on provisional assumptions had shown that at a $40 differential, at projected 1976 prices, it was feasible to consider investment in cracking facilities. The average market situation, through 1974 and early 1975, was of this order or slightly higher.

For the second question, concerning the probable actions of competitors, discussions within Prosper fostered the view that most companies would choose to invest later in crackers. Prosper's previous observation of their competitors' investment behavior had led them to conclude that most companies would invest in a project if it showed at least a 10 percent discounted cash flow return before tax. This represents a $40–45 differential between fuel oil and light distillates. This differential had existed since late 1976, and it was deemed reasonable to expect competitors to build crackers as soon as their projections showed that demand could not be satisfied from existing refineries. Some delay could be reasonably expected before most competitors constructed crackers, because of their already greater potential for refining light distillates and substantial opportunities for small modifications.

However, another factor became a limiting one: the capacity of the construction industry. Building delays could hold back the introduction of light-distillate production equipment for some years. It was concluded that a supply/demand equilibrium giving only an average return on capital would not occur until at least 1983. Up to that time, it was judged likely that the price differential between light distillates and fuel oils would result in an above average return on capital for extra cracker capacity.

The Proposal

With broadly favorable and encouraging answers to these questions, the corporate planners proceeded to develop a capital investment proposal. A number of factors had to be considered before projecting the specific cash flow over the life of the project. In particular, decisions had to be made on the type of process to be used for cracking, the logistics of the provision of the cracking facilities, and the capacity of one or more crackers. With these details, conclusions could be drawn on its effects on the group as a whole, as well as on the final financial details such as costs, revenues, taxes, and returns that would allow the final construction of the cash flow analysis. Type of cracker, logistics, and capacities were all interdependent and could be determined by details of Prosper's European supply operations.

Each type of cracking requires different inputs and produces different outputs. Costs vary between one type and another and between different capacities. The computer model was used to test the possibility of building several types, from hydrocrackers, the most selective and most expensive, to thermal crackers, which reside at the other end of the selectivity and expense spectrum. A weighing of all the relevant factors by the computer model demonstrated an advantage for catalytic cracking. A technical difficulty remained to be solved with this choice, because the method produces material which is high in olefins and low in octanes. Good quality motor oil must be low in olefins and high in octanes. As a result, it was judged necessary to blend complementary materials to yield a premium motor oil. To secure the supply of the appropriate product for this blend required the cooperation of the supply department and the subsidiary companies in Europe.

Logistics were also important. A fundamental decision was whether the cracking capacity should be a central or local facility. There was a choice between a large central cracker servicing almost the whole of the European market and several smaller, locally managed cracking facilities. These small crackers would be attached to the national affiliate companies with existing refineries. The handling, shipping, and storage costs were important in this decision, as were the economies of scale that would be associated with a larger central facility. In this respect the logistic decision was closely linked with the issue of capacity.

Provisional Conclusions

Details of the corporate planners' analysis will not be related here, but the final conclusion of the corporate planners was that a single catalytic cracker should be constructed. Its capacity was to be fifty thousand barrels per day, and it was to be situated in Sicily. The choice of Sicily was based largely upon the principle of central location. This single cracker would be able to link up with refining facilities on that island and would also be well placed to distribute products throughout southern Europe. A capacity of fifty thousand barrels of oil per day represented a large, above-average capacity unit, but others had been built of this size and larger. The proposed capacity was, in fact, some 50 percent larger than the optimum size indicated by the computer model. The recommendation assumed that the viability of the project would increase through the 1980s.

With these parameters defined, the corporate planners began to develop the capital investment proposal for presentation to the executive committee. The executive committee, as the second-level board, has, in practice, a shorter time perspective than the main board. Capital investment proposals follow a general format and need to be specific on financial details and deadlines. Guidelines on rates of return, evaluated by discounted cash flow techniques, have to be met for executive committee approval of a project. The assessment and timing of cash flow is mandatory to satisfy these requirements.

It was against these expectations that the corporate planners prepared their proposal. Definite commitments on specific financial outcomes were usually required, yet the uncertainty surrounding the project made it unrealistic to construct these in the usual way. Small changes in the demand pattern between fuel oils and light distillates would greatly affect cash flow and profit. A procedure was adopted where the long-term computer model was used to derive figures for the financial outcome under a full range of possible environmental developments. A chart was prepared which showed the pattern of returns on the different levels of capacity utilization. Another was constructed for different price levels under several scenarios, such as the limitation of supply by oil producers, these possibilities being extrapolated for various periods of time. Particularly memorable is one diagram that was tantalizingly named the cat's cradle. This showed the possible consequences of the installation of cracking capacity serving Europe to the mid–1980s for the entire industry.

Approvals

The enthusiasm of the corporate planners for the prospect of a cracker project was not matched in other parts of the company. One of the company's most vigorous and, at times, most heated debates emerged on the viability of the proposed investment.

Dissent

One problem was a view that higher prices and diminished growth were not to be permanent features of the oil industry. Some executives also felt uncertain that increased prices necessarily meant any significant change in the shape of the barrel. To accept the view necessitated rejection of a long-term trend of preference for oil rather than other underboiler energy sources. Oil has overwhelming advantages over substitute fuels. Compared to coal, it is lighter per calorific content and its liquid form makes for massive economies and ease in terms of transportation and storage. Oil is also cleaner to handle and to burn, which was increasingly important as environmental pollution standards became more stringent.

Further criticism for the project came from the sectional interests of the supply department. Under the comparatively recent decentralization proposals (around 1972), these people were to be managerially and financially responsible for the catalytic cracker. Opposition from the supply group became acute for several reasons. At an intuitive level, the project ran counter to the entire previous experience of refining. Traditionally the oil-cracking business had been one of slim profit margins, and the management approach had been one of cost minimization and modest, gradual improvements in production efficiency. A bold investment to yield higher returns would have been senseless in Prosper's historical circumstances. The department's past experience with a slow and evolutionary environment had also encouraged a practical and immediate-term perspective on operations. The spectre of a novel environment was not easily appreciated and was viewed as irrelevant to the immediate need to meet operating goals. The years 1974–75 were characterized by a large excess of refining capacity and, consequently, poor financial results. Additional refinery investment was not a rational development from this point of view and, in any case, opinion was that they could meet any likely demand over the coming decade with existing facilities.

Uncertainty facilitated competing arguments. In particular, the rationale for Prosper's entry into coal could be argued to be in conflict with the rationale for the cracker. The viability of the cracker was heavily dependent upon a suppressed price for fuel oil. Reasoning for the coal venture was based upon a high price for fuel oil, so that the large investments in mining and trading could be justified. The viability of the project in terms of its own internal logic was also criticized. By cracking heavier distillates into lighter ones, it could be argued that the price of the lighter end of the barrel would be suppressed by extra supply, and the price of fuel oils would be supported by a reduced supply.

In the meantime the project's supporters were alert to the need for urgency. Every year that the project was delayed substantially increased its cost, due to general inflation. Delay would also mean foregoing the best locations and best sites in favor of competitors. Most important of all, the forecast differential between fuel oil and light distillates would be expected to decline as oil companies brought extra cracking capacity on stream. The highest return on the proposed project would be in its early days, before the more hestitant oil companies had constructed extra capacity.

Executive Committee

The capital investment proposal for the fifty-thousand-barrel-per-day catalytic cracker in Sicily went forward to the September 1975 meeting of the executive committee. During that year the world economy was in recession following protracted low growth after the oil price increase. The forecaster's prediction of suppressed demand for fuel oils and stimulated demand for light distillate was fulfilled in microcosm during that year. The differential between 1 percent sulphur fuel oil and premium motor oil (98/99 octane) averaged nearly $70 on the free oil markets during the spring and summer quarters. The pattern of demand relationships described by the planners was demonstrated and could be plausibly interpreted as a portent for the future.

At the same time there were apparently contradictory trends. A surplus of crude oil in Europe and competitive pressures in a depressed market had reduced margins. The lower level of demand had rendered the retail end of the business too densely populated with outlets and depots. In combination, the light distillates sector of the market was showing a particularly poor financial performance. Also, largely because of overcapacity, the refining and tanker interests of Prosper had never been in worse financial circumstances.

The executive committee was, very largely, the company's most important organ for regulating capital investments. It was painfully evident to Prosper that it had too much in the way of capital investment in the face of the lower volume demand. Yet, more funds were committed to projects commissioned before the oil price rise, and when these were completed the excess capacity position would be aggravated further. Psychologically, additional capital investment was not welcome, particularly in the refinery sector, which was sometimes showing only a 60 percent capacity utilization. In a decision later described as bold by management, the executive committee accepted the cracker investment proposal and thereby initiated the planning of its technical details. Development of the project was to remain the responsibility of the corporate planners.

Final Planning

Planning of the final details of the project was a substantial exercise. In this task the corporate planning department largely acted as integrators and coordinators. Two particular aspects of the problem were demarcated. One was the work concerned with engineering problems that required help from the managers of the Sicily refinery, research and development laboratories, engineering department, purchasing department, and others. The second was concerned with the organizing and securing of commitments for demand and supply of goods from Prosper's subsidiary companies.

Analysis of the location decision proved particularly interesting. In addition to the internal logic relating to Prosper, the project had to be reviewed for its likely political effects. The analysis of balance-of-payments outcomes on potential host governments was complex, but labor and material availabilities and approval and construction lead times were also critical to the decision.

The final analysis of the demand and supply position for cracking capacity looked encouraging. Table 7–2 shows that, based on demand estimates and on the basis of known competitive actions, some five extra twenty-five-thousand-barrel-per-day crackers would be required in Europe by 1980, and fifteen by 1982. With a lead time of some three years from final investment decision, and with limits on construction capacity into the middle 1980s, this should mean good returns from Prosper's cracker, as competitors would be unable to enter in great numbers for some years.

The confidence of the corporate planning department was still not shared by other parts of the company. When the technical planning and the associated proposal was completed (some eighteen months after executive committee approval), the completed document went forward to the main board in March 1977. A project of importance like the catalytic cracker would have been so thoroughly discussed and monitored through its development that board approval would normally be assured. Seldom would such a proposal risk outright

Table 7–2
A Forecast of Catalytic converters
(25,000-barrel-per-day crackers)

	1976	1980	1982	1985	1990
In operation (1976)	80	80	78	75	70
Firm plans	0	20	20	20	18
Further requirement	0	5	15	40	90
Probable range for total	0	105–115	110–130	120–170	140–240

refusal at this late stage, but the catalytic cracker investment was so contentious that rejection was a possibility.

Every capital investment request put to the main board requires the signature of a main board president, as a sponsor of the project. In 1977 the atmosphere in the oil industry and within Prosper itself was such as to make it difficult to secure a signature. In the end the recommendation went forward with two signatures, the reason being that no board member would sign it unilaterally. An agreement was made between two members to the effect that one would be prepared to sign if the other also consented. In this way the two signees shared responsibility for putting the recommendation through the board. They were, in effect, communicating that they were of like mind that the project was sound and worthwhile, while accepting that the risks were high.

In retrospect, executives in Prosper note that the development of the catalytic cracker project proceeded at a rapid pace. From its initiation to main board approval took only three years, and the project was on stream in about six years from the inception of the idea. It was also felt by many executives that both the executive committee and the main board had been forthright in view of the uncertainty in the situation, the size of the proposed project, and the strength of adverse opinion that prevailed in parts of the company.

Contrasts

The research experience provided by Prosper's catalytic cracker response allows contrasts to be appraised in two respects: first, in relation to the corporate responses described in chapters 5 and 6; second, in relation to the comparable response made by Atlas some years before. Both these sources of contrast are discussed below.

Corporate Responses

Prosper's catalytic cracker and the coal situations allow some preliminary observations to be made concerning distinctions between corporate and administrative responses. For the administrative response described above, the challenge was one of amending existing operations to increase their suitability for the future. For the corporate responses described in chapters 5 and 6, the challenge was one of starting an independent business to compensate for the apparent fortunes in the original oil business. In all cases a team was distinguishable, but that for the cracker was in place within the existing corporate structure. An evolution to final form from uncertain beginnings applies to all these experiences, but a clearer understanding of the cracker existed than for the coal ventures. For the cracker it was a case of selecting from a wide range of identifiable options. For the coal cases, wholly different businesses might have suggested themselves. Those possibilities ranged from exploration through trading, might have involved hard or coking coals for steel making as well as mining of softer coals used in power generation and had quite different geographic scope. Unlike the coal responses, where attempts were made to accentuate independence, the cracker was inevitably concerned with fine matters of interdependence with Prosper's existing operations. When it was built and running, the flows of information, data, and physical products around Europe were considerably revised, and the expertise of the refinery managers had to be updated in order to run this high-technology plant.

Atlas

By the time a substantial price differential had arisen between light and heavy distillates, Atlas already had cracking capacity developed from a capital investment decision made in 1971. A partial explanation for the different time frames in which the two companies acted is provided by contrasting supply positions. For several decades Atlas owned relatively few inexpensive reserves of crude oil. Their marketing activities had developed strongly, but access to sources of petroleum had not kept pace. It was perhaps natural for Atlas to concentrate on maximizing returns from crudes by upgrading them. In this activity the company had long emphasized refining processes which add higher value to products. A respected group of technologists had arisen within the company by the late 1960s, and management was well used to the technical and commercial principles of such upgrading.

This pattern of external and internal circumstances was naturally auspicious for addition of secondary refining capacity. Enthusiasm on the part of technical specialists for the most modern cracking facilities was to be expected, considering their backgrounds and ambitions. Senior managers were receptive to such initiatives, because of the foundation of experience with high value products and because of their confidence in the technologists. As a result, the proposal to build a cracker was defined as a capital investment decision in the late 1960s, and this culminated in a hydrocracker (hydrogen is forced into oil molecules under high pressure) and related facilities. Generally speaking, a hydrocracker embodies higher technology than a catalytic cracker and achieves a greater conversion from heavy to light.

Atlas was, therefore, well prepared when a substantial premium could be commanded for light products in the marketplace. There may be a temptation to begin to conclude that Atlas was more forward-thinking and that it acted with more foresight. This may be the case. However, as other responses are examined, a rather different conclusion will be drawn relating to the specific situation in which Atlas's and Prosper's decision makers found themselves.

The next two chapters present two further depth accounts of administrative responses in complex organizational settings. Although both chapters address incorporation of management systems rather than a capital investment, many of the basic distinctions between corporate and administrative responses mentioned above are upheld. Also, commonalities with the decision processes characterizing this and the preceding responses are to be observed in the following two depth cases of administrative responses in complex settings that can be provisionally concluded to be consistent with the expectations of propositions 6 to 9 given in chapter 3.

8

Atlas's Scenario Planning

cenario planning is a method of analysis used to explore possible future
developments and change. In particular it seeks to identify interactions
in trends and events. Adoption of the technique in Atlas is a matter of
some pride to the planners who initiated it, and is generally thought to have
had a major impact on the ability of Atlas to manage successfully in the high
oil price and low growth environment of the 1970s. It presents an example
of an administrative response in that it modified the operations of the existing
oil business in line with the marked shifts in the environment.

In this instance, the adaptation was brought about by the introduction of
a management system serving to alter management's perceptions of their environment and hence their investment behavior. This contrasts with the example of the catalytic cracker investment described in the previous chapter, where
the reorientation was achieved by introduction of a facility for which a reorientation of managerial perceptions concerning the nature of the environment was
a necessary precondition. Despite the quite different substance of these two
responses, the case description suggests further "endorsement" of the large
distinctions between corporate and administrative responses noted in table 3–1,
and further observations consistent with the general patterns characteristic of
decision processes under discontinuity as indicated in the relevant propositions
of chapter 3.

The principal benefit of the scenario planning system is probably its efficiency in constructively focusing executives' attention on uncertainties in the
future environment. Scenario planning influences the selection of strategic project and the form they assume. It tends to shift decisions towards projects with
a greater viability in uncertainty. It generally favors those investments embodying greater flexibility. In the words of the Atlas planning department, investments
made under the scenario system are resilient to the range of possible outcomes
in the future.

It is certain, too, that the scenario method has facilitated investment in
an environment where lack of confidence could have markedly decreased
the will to invest. This planning system has been developed within Atlas, from

rather primitive beginnings, to a method of considerable conceptual depth and practical refinement. In particular, it has won serious recognition within the company on the strength of its demonstrated ability to quite precisely describe the events of 1973 as one of the scenarios constructed the year before.

Origins

The origins of the adoption and development of scenario planning at Atlas can be traced to 1968 when the board of directors for Europe commissioned a "long-distance look-ahead study" into the future of the company and the oil industry and also a study of the future to the year 2000. Senior managers were beginning to sense an uncertainty in the future. The commissioning of these studies represented the need for a careful and systematic analysis so that legitimate opinions could be determined on the nature of the unknowns. It was intended as a clarification of issues and a structuring and proportioning of the future uncertainties. Ironic though it may appear, the need for this study can be found in the questions which arose as a result of the successful growth of the oil industry in the post–World War II years.

Horsetailing

Throughout the decade of the 1960s the demand for oil had grown consistently at 7 percent per annum worldwide. This rate approximated a doubling in demand every ten years. Towards the end of the 1960s, forecasters were increasingly hesitant to continue to project this rate of growth. The feeling was that it had to slow eventually, since oil reserves must be finite. This hesitancy was represented in the graphs that were produced; most projections showed growth tapering off at some indefinite point in the medium-term future. Consistently, however, the high growth rates were maintained into the 1970s, and the graphs were progressively extended in the same form but with the tapering off shifting along the time axis.

When one year's projection was superimposed on those of previous years, the appearance became one of a horse's tail. Consequently, disbelief in the long-term maintenance of high growth rates in oil demand became known in the company as horsetailing. As the 1960s progressed, planners became increasingly uncomfortable at the continued projection of high growth into a future where oil supply was known to be finite and where the rate of consumption was overtaking the rate of discovery of new oil sources.

In 1968 it was decided that a study of the future to the year 2000 should be carried out by the Atlas corporate planning department. That department was already responsible for examination of the future environment as the stimulus to planning; the fit was logical. Atlas corporate planners are organized as a department that has been manned and structured in much the same way since the late 1960s, just before the time of the Look Ahead and Year 2000 studies.

It is a small unit of about thirty professional staff, comprising executives who command a high intellectual reputation within Atlas. The department is divided into two sections; one is concerned with the analysis of the industry and world energy trends, the other with the broader environment of business, including economic, social, and political developments working up to a twenty-year horizon. This central group of corporate planners serves the main board and the regional and functional coordinators within corporate headquarters. It also acts in an advisory capacity to the subsidiary companies which constitute the Atlas Group around the world.

Look Ahead

While the Look Ahead and Year 2000 studies had been commissioned separately under different managers, their common ground soon became evident and, consequently, they effectively fused together. Faced with the need to examine the future, it was perhaps natural for the people involved to adopt the scenario methodology. The team was well aware of the contemporary work of Herman Kahn and Anthony J. Weiner,[1] who probably have the strongest claim to transferring the method to the business sector from its origins in the military.

In the construction of scenarios the practitioner is forced to think logically into the future through a series of connected events. The range of outcomes from the occurrence of a particular event, together with the possibility of nonoccurrence, lead the scenario analyst to project a series of different futures.[2] One benefit of the method is that it is likely to identify a number of possibilities which would otherwise not be recognized. In practice, it is usual for a small number of generalized and more probable situations to be identified and described as individual scenarios. The method has proved more rewarding in Atlas than even many of its advocates presupposed.

The study group presented a paper to the board in 1970. The major finding was the high possibility of a future where the oil industry might face a limited production base and price inflation well above the generalized rates of other industries. The content of the paper surpassed even the more extreme expectations that had provided the motivation for the study. The future that was described in the report was practically the converse of the assumptions underpinning the workings of the industry at that time.

In the report discussed by the board, progressively decreasing prices and an unrestricted and increasing production supply were largely abandoned in favor of a future of high and increasing prices and low growth. The analysis had been derived largely by the scenario method, and four different futures were described. These had been formulated around combination of the seemingly two most crucial determinants of the energy future, namely the "host government take" and the rate of world economic growth. Host government take refers to revenue acquired by producer governments, mainly by levying taxes on production volume. The scenarios that were presented were defined as follows:

high host government take and high growth
low host government take and high growth
high host government take and low growth
medium host government take and medium growth

Three of the four scenarios were provocative in recognizing and highlighting oil as a diminishing resource. The importance of this viewpoint was greatest from the perspective of the producer governments who, with awareness of their rapidly reducing reserves, were almost certain to use the dual action of regulating production and price to increase their take. This assumption was incorporated in the three scenarios not describing the future in the same terms as the past.

Planning Use

The scenarios in the paper presented to the board were also pressed into service by the planners for their 1970–1971 annual review. The review was an Atlas publication (confidential to the company) that formed part of the integrated planning process used by Atlas, and was broadly the same as when consolidated in the 1950s and 1960s. Produced annually, the review was a central part of Atlas's planning process. It gave companywide voice to the planners' expectations for the future of the economies and of the industries in which the company had interests, as well as for Atlas's position within them.

Presentation of the review's main contents was made to the committee of presidents prior to its distribution. In practice, much of the material had been discussed already beyond the corporate planning department at the level of regional coordinators, functional and division heads, and the separate planning functions of the more important subsidiary companies.

After the review was approved by the main board, it was officially distributed in its final form and became the basis of planning throughout the company. With the review as background, each of the planning areas in Atlas, that is, each national subsidiary, each business division such as coal and natural gas, and each functional area formulated its individual plans. The more important of these planning areas had their own planning group, but their plans were typically constructed in the context of the global picture described in the Atlas review.

These individual plans were then aggregated at a regional level for Europe, Asia, and Africa. The regional coordinators fed information back to their constituent national entities as modifications were required in the light of the complete situation. A second level of aggregation took place as the regional plans, division plans, and functional area plans were put together to obtain a groupwide picture. The complex was then finely tuned as necessary. Capital investments were typically developed within the umbrella of the planning process, but were usually the subject of separate consideration. Capital investment projects of over $10 million had to be approved by the main board, but smaller projects could be decided by subsidiary companies according to established policy.

The review had always taken the form of a single forecasted future with commentary. The new scenario format constituted a radical departure of philosophy. The planner was now confronted with four futures and asked to test strategy against all these possibilities. More subtly, the intention was to induce decision makers to consider their plans in the light of a range of global outcomes in the oil industry. The scenario approach seemed a more satisfactory and realistic way of portraying a future which was becoming progressively more uncertain. In practice, most users of the scenarios tended to select just one of the four which seemed to them to be the most probable.

Cassandra and Percival

Despite managements' ready embrace of the revised planning philosophy of a range of futures, it was noted in 1970 and again in 1971 that the scenarios were having no tangible effect. The three of the four not reflecting the traditional oil world of low prices and high growth were ignored in all the plans submitted by the subsidiaries and other planning units in Atlas. In all cases the most optimistic scenario was the sole basis on which the plans were produced. Corporate planners and senior management were, however, becoming increasingly convinced of a discontinuity in the oil industry in favor of an environment of high prices and limited supply. Planning efforts were correspondingly further invested towards a scenario approach.

Predictions

Some individual analyses were performed by the corporate planners on areas of the business considered to be most at risk in a high-price and low-growth environment. Notably, papers were presented to senior management showing the imminent over-supply of shipping and refining capacity. The separate exercises were incorporated in an extensive report, written in 1972 and published for the upper levels of management in January 1973, which presented six scenarios and a deeper analysis of the future environment than the 1970 paper. Of course, the evolution of the report and the presentation of the separate analyses had promoted debate among senior management for almost two years preceding the publication of the full report in January 1973.

All six scenarios were based upon the premise of the imminence of an oil shortage relative to the existing rates of consumption and oil finds. The six were split into two groups of three scenarios, as shown in figure 8–1. The first group of three scenarios related to a world where there was a general awareness of an impending oil shortage. Scenario 1.1 described an oil crisis. Scenarios 1.2 and 1.3 described two general types of solution to an impending oil shortage. A private enterprise solution was posited for scenario 1.2, and a dirigiste or heavily government-steered solution for 1.3.

The second group of three scenarios was based upon no conscious awareness of an oil shortage. The first (scenario 2.1) related to low growth in the world economy, thereby indirectly solving the possibility of an oil shortage. The second (scenario 2.2) represented an easing of world growth and a "muddling through" in terms of oil supply and other forms of energy. The third (scenario 2.3) represented a world of uninterrupted growth rate accompanied by a high rate of discovery of new sources of oil. The last one was not believable to the planners, but one senior member of the planning group later observed that the credibility of the group across the company was saved by the inclusion of this one scenario, which was effectively a continuation of the historic situation.

The crisis scenario makes fascinating reading, given knowledge of the events of 1973. The planning team had conducted their analysis of the circumstances in the oil industry from the viewpoint of the major actors involved. It is a prescription in the construction of scenarios to think through circumstances by considering the possible actions of the influential parties. The major entities in oil supply and associated decisions were identified as the host governments of the oil exporting countries. Exploring their possible actions, the planners constructed a scenario of eerie prescience.

The analysis, completed in 1972, describes a crisis incorporating a quintupling of oil prices to over $10 per barrel, accompanied by a restriction of supply. This major event was forecast to occur within a space of a few months and to occur at least before the end of 1975. It is astounding to reflect that such premonitions existed of probably the most critical event in recent history. Perhaps even more interesting is the fact that, for planning and capital investment purposes, a planning exercise whose efficiency could rightfully be described in glowing terms was wholly ignored by the company which had sponsored it.

1: General awareness of an impending oil shortage
    1.1: An oil crisis
    1.2: Private enterprise solution
    1.3: Government-steered or dirigiste solution
2: No direct awareness of an oil shortage
    2.1: Low-growth world economy and correlated solution
    2.2: Easing of world growth and "muddling through" with energy
    2.3: Uninterrupted world economic growth with high rate of discovery of oil

---

Figure 8–1. Scenarios Presented within Atlas in 1972

Business As Usual

Of the six scenarios, only the one pointing to high growth and the high discovery of new oil was used by management up to the autumn of 1973. Although there was much sympathy among senior managers for the notion of a supply-constrained, high-price, and low-growth future, the company's reaction can be summarized as: Business as usual.[3] There was much evidence to support such a view. The productive capacity of the Middle East was not at a maximum, and there was also the prospect of Alaskan and North Sea production coming on stream. The price was, in fact, falling during the early part of 1973, largely as a result of intense competition among the successful and growing oil companies.

Recognizing the importance of the price of oil in the future, the corporate planners at Atlas staged a Delphi analysis on the issue in the company in 1972. Delphi analysis is a technique where several respondents record their views on the future independently but where results are fed back repeatedly to respondents until a consensus or general pattern is arrived at among participating experts. This poll of Atlas senior management opinion in 1972 on the price of oil over the next ten years resulted in not even one person citing a price above $2 per barrel. It was a view that was probably almost universally held; in fact, one of the foremost experts in the industry concluded in 1972 that the price of oil would decrease to $1 per barrel.[4] Consequently, orders for additional refining capacity and very large crude carriers continued to proceed at the same rate as before.

There is an opinion in Atlas's corporate planning department that it is a natural instinct for managers to select scenarios that provide a close fit with their particular microcosm of experience. The high-spirited historical character of the petroleum industry was largely enjoyed by the management of Atlas. There were massive challenges in terms of intense competition and high risk associated with capital investment, but managers were comfortable in dealing with these familiar aspects of the business. It was, perhaps, natural that unfamiliar challenges should be put to one side, especially when there was no certainty that events necessitating an altered view on the workings of the industry would materialize in any case.

Planners at Atlas have likened their predicament to Cassandra, the unregarded prophet, and to General Percival's defeat by the Japanese in 1941. Described as the "greatest debacle in the history of British arms," Percival's failure was due largely to his adamant refusal to switch seaward, south-facing defenses to resist a practically inevitable land-based attack from the Malay peninsula in the north. The general's justification for his decision was reported to be his belief that such a radical about-face of defenses would be bad for the morale of troops and civilians.[5]

The Oil Crisis

As the events of early 1973 unfolded, the realization of the possibility of a discontinuity along the lines of the 1.1 scenario became more evident within the corporate planning department. In fact, by the summer of that year the planning group became convinced of the impending reality of their crisis scenario. Their thinking for the short-term situation arose clearly from the fact that demand for oil had become very strong. In that year all of the noncommunist, industrialized world was experiencing high growth. It was rare that Europe, North American, and Japan were all in such a period of high growth simultaneously. Prices of most raw materials were increasing in response to demand pressures and, although the oil price had been decreasing over this period, an increase in the price of oil seemed likely.

Actions

The planning department, in July of 1973, took two important steps. The first was expression of the opinion, in the form of a special memorandum circulated among senior management, that all the scenarios should be dropped except the one pointing to the imminent discontinuity (scenario 1.1 in figure 8–1). The second was a request to the main board that a special meeting be convened to discuss the supply situation. A meeting was arranged for late August but was rescheduled to late September, and then postponed for a second time to late October. It is ironic that the pressure of managing the events preceding the unilateral oil price increase of the Organization of Petroleum Exporting Countries (OPEC) was the principal reason for the postponement of these meetings.

The storming of the right bank of the Suez Canal by Egyptian troops took the world by surprise, and at the beginning of October the Yom Kippur Arab–Israeli war was underway. By October 17, 1973, the member nations of OPEC had unilaterally imposed the price of the benchmark crude, and the Organization of Arab Petroleum Exporting Countries had declared the oil embargo.

The scenarios were presented (as they had been before) to the main board at the prearranged meeting at the end of October. The climate was, of course, propitious for acceptance of the discontinuity scenario and the accompanying low-growth future. There were dissenters to this view who thought that things would return to normal but the center of gravity in the senior management of Atlas was swayed toward acceptance of a continuation of the revised situation. A world was discussed where political power had shifted to the producing nations, giving rise to both limited supply and increased price. It also pointed to a world of recession and inflation for some years, as adjustments to the higher oil price took place gradually.

Consequences

Many management problems accompanied and compounded the low-growth and high-price situation after 1974. Timing and structure of decisions became more critical. Prior to 1973, errors of timing and scale had been quickly corrected by subsequent growth, leading executives to be accustomed to confident decision making. The realization that recent investment decisions had been completely misplaced was disconcerting and demoralizing. The need to lay up oil tankers and newly commissioned refining capacity involving many millions of dollars was unsettling to managers' perceptions of the soundness of their commercial judgment.

Consequently, business sentiment after 1973 was characterized by risk aversion. The problem was exaggerated by the cost inflation that occurred after the crisis. A famous example of the level of cost inflation for new oil sources is that of the Atlas tar sands project in Canada. The costs were estimated in 1977 at between $3 and $4 billion for a flow of about 12,500 barrels per day. This investment was greater than the total capitalization of any Canadian oil company in the middle 1970s. The risks were perceived as enormous and were entirely dependent upon the price of oil not decreasing in real terms. As a means of appraising decisions in terms of the risks of differing futures, scenario planning can play an important part in assessing the attractiveness of such high-risk investments in the high uncertainty surrounding the oil industry.

Benefits

In the prevailing business atmosphere of 1974 and afterwards, the corporate planning function at Atlas and the scenario approach enjoyed new respect. In the first place, the stature of the planning group had grown enormously in the light of their premature understanding of the events of 1973 and of the arrival of the subsequent environment of low growth and high prices. Second, in this period of higher uncertainty, the ideas, perspectives, and conclusions that the department were able to develop after careful study became of greater interest and use to executives.

The appeal of scenario planning to executives was its candor in making uncertainty explicit in a convenient and readily usable form. It was not offered in the nature of a forecast but more as a modest statement of the possible outcomes in the future. The previous planning which it displaced much more closely resembled a projection of numbers. The basis of planning and the associated task of capital investment planning and review had relied fundamentally on the use of discounted cash flow and related techniques. The cash flow was entirely subordinate to the revenue forecasts which were embodied into it as working assumptions. These in turn relied upon price and volume estimates.

A relatively junior executive would select a figure for price and, typically, another executive would use an estimate of volume. These two estimates would then be combined and the capital investment proposal planned and accepted on this basis. In other words, a single line forecast was obtained which invariably would not be exactly fulfilled. In a more certain environment, variations around this single outcome might well be acceptable. In the less certain business circumstances of the middle 1970s, such mechanical methods became unacceptable. They could not realistically appraise decisions in relation to the wider range of possible variations in the business environment.

Development

Motivated by the positive attitudes of Atlas senior management towards scenario planning and its obvious suitability to business conditions, the corporate planning department gradually developed its approach. Experience allowed several conclusions to be drawn concerning its improvement. Notable among the modifications was the practical need to reduce circulated scenarios to a manageable number. Experience showed that two scenarios is an ideal maximum, but three is manageable. The rather mechanical approach of matching upper and lower sets of outcomes in a few key variables, for example, host government take and world growth in demand such as was used from 1970 to 1972, was rejected.

The emphasis is now upon conceptualized scenarios that represent consistent sets of circumstances that each constitute probable outcomes. Typically, two scenarios are constructed that are designed as archetypes, each being close to the outer edge of the range of probable outcomes. In this sense, two ideal types are coined, but it is accepted that any specific situation is likely to be a mix of them both.

The instruction to the executive users of the scenarios has also been modified as the approach has become more established. It is now necessary that plans submitted by the company's planning areas are resilient to the published scenarios. The submitted plans are formulated, and later examined, in the light of achieving an acceptable return under each scenario and possibly also reflect a weighting in terms of the more probable outcomes in a given case. For example, plans where viability is biased towards high growth would probably be acceptable from subsidiaries in high-growth economies such as Mexico and Brazil, but the opposite bias in viability would be expected from companies in the lower growth European nations.

Endorsement and Fallibility

The scenarios presented in the annual review also form the basis of the appraisal of capital investment projects submitted for approval to the board. Capital investment proposals are now tested against the scenarios, and typically a matrix of outcomes according to the higher and lower range of outcomes is presented. Also, less probable, extreme outcomes, such as a breakdown of OPEC and the major lowering of oil prices, are treated as accident scenarios and are typically explicit in large capital investment proposals. A good capital proposal is now conceived as one that is resilient to the range of possible future outcomes. In other words, it must be viable under each working scenario and must be able to withstand the materialization of accident scenarios.

Before the dawn of the 1980s, the scenario approach to the appraisal of investment decision and to the annual planning exercise had become established within Atlas. There were dissenters in some parts of the company, but they were few and decreasing in numbers. Senior managers strongly endorse the scenario approach and insist upon at least a general assessment of strategic actions that takes into account the variety of possible futures. It would now be very unlikely that any capital investment proposal would be accepted that was based on a single line projection or one that was not resilient to the range of likely futures over its lifetime.

With the use of scenario planning, Atlas feels better prepared for high uncertainty. The method is expected to reduce the number of surprises, and the additional flexibility that is now embodied in capital projects should provide more resilience. Although the method is expected to be more efficient than any known alternative, it is not seen as invincible. In 1979 the fallibility of the system was demonstrated by the failure to anticipate the fall of the Shah of Iran, the associated interruption of supplies, and the expected reduction in future production levels. The possibility of disruption in Iranian supplies was mentioned in the preceding planners' review, but it was not developed into an accident scenario and Atlas was not as prepared for the Iranian eventualities as executives consider they should have been.

Prosper's Scenario Planning

Use of scenario planning within the range of possibilities of oil price and supply changes would seem then to be an efficient and perhaps natural tool. Prosper, however, did not develop use of the technique to nearly the same extent as Atlas. The catalytic cracker investment at Prosper, described in the last chapter, arose from a planner's review in early 1974 that employed two scenarios. Viability of the project was tested against several futures during development of the proposal, in a manner exactly comparable to scenario planning. Despite this example, the procedure of scenario planning was neither incorporated routinely in Prosper's planning and capital investment appraisal systems nor conceptualized to the same extent as in Atlas.

It is only possible to speculate on the reasons for the lesser commitment to scenario planning in Prosper. Among the more obvious is the personal predisposition of the personnel in the corporate planning function, who were more inclined to the quantitative, numerical approach to analysis, within which the more qualitative and subjective reasoning typical of much scenario work would not fit comfortably. A more objective explanation can be found, however, by considering the specific environment within which the company existed. In fact, the customary and continuing high crude availability for Prosper made their position less vulnerable to disturbance. Uncertainty in the case of Prosper was less important because of the cushion that this availability provided, and the need for highly developed scenario planning was both less evident and of lower priority.

An important response to the new circumstances of the petroleum industry of the same general systems type was, however, made by Prosper and will be discussed in the next chapter as another example of an administrative response. In Prosper's use of Rotterdam prices (free market prices for crude oil) as an internal control and motivation system, a similar mechanism of adoption and development is encountered as has been described above for Atlas's scenario planning system.

Despite the variety of responses that have been recounted in chapters 5 to 8, several patterns were common to them all. An entity already extant, even in some limited, parochial way, gained importance and grew to a full form as relevant to the respective corporation's needs (consistent with propositions 6 of chapter 3). Dominance of informal decision processes sympathetic to the general ideas of satisficing were reported to be dominant in the cases of the entries to the coal industry, formative for the catalytic cracker investment, and observed also in the scenario planning response, as the technique was experimented with in various parts of the company and at the various stages of its adoption (consistent with proposition 7 of chapter 3).

Also, a general evolutionary structure from ill-defined origins to a fully fledged maturity was noted for the preceding responses and observed in this response as well (consistent with proposition 8 of chapter 3). In both companies' entrance to the coal industry, in Prosper's catalytic cracker investment, and in Atlas's scenario planning, the responses were pushed and pulled towards completion by a momentum seemingly guided by the promise of their utility. Essential to the successful evolution of all these responses was the usually optional choice of managers to contribute individual efforts to the development of a particular response. This process of managerial contribution and choice occurred at various places in the organization and at several significant junctures in the evolution of each response. Prosper's adoption of Rotterdam prices for internal purposes, presented in the next chapter, clearly illustrates these phenomena also, and additionally provides a good opportunity to review the relevance of situational factors (proposition 9 of chapter 3) in managing response.

Notes

1. Herman Kahn and Anthony J. Weiner, *Toward the Year 2000: A Framework for Speculation* (New York: Macmillan, 1967).
2. Ibid.
3. Sir Winston Churchill, Speech at Guildhall, November 9, 1914.

4. Morris A. Adelman, "Is the Oil Shortage Real? Oil Companies as OPEC Tax Collectors," *Foreign Policy*, Winter 1972–73, pp. 69–107.

5. Noel Barber, *Sinister Twilight: The Fall and Rise Again of Singapore* (London: Collins, 1968).

9
Prosper's Use of Rotterdam Prices

> In the days before oil became so mixed with politics, a happy oil company
> was an integrated company, with its functions neatly bundled according
> to their geographical location. But now the demands of more exciting
> times have the industry reworking the organizational charts. . . . Several
> oil companies have reorganized to develop deintegrated, functional
> structures.[1]

P rosper was no exception to the general trend toward a separation of the
different functions comprising the large oil companies. How it achieved
this adaptation was, however, unique. An essential part of the task was
accomplished through the use of what are termed Rotterdam prices, and this
case description traces their adoption for internal control and motivation by
Prosper. The response is a third example of an administrative response to compare and contrast with the adoption of scenario planning in Atlas with which
it is paired, the catalytic cracker investment in Prosper, and the corporate
responses of the entries to the coal industry of Prosper and Atlas.

Rotterdam prices is a colloquial term for the prices that oils fetch in the
free market that developed in Rotterdam. Notorious for their eccentricity, the
existence of Rotterdam prices at all was at odds with the way the oil industry
operated over this period. The Oil company strategies of complete vertical integration meant that no significant quantities of the mineral were traded outside of the companies and, therefore, no open or free market existed until the
strategies weakened.

Introduction of the Rotterdam prices was a contentious issue in Prosper
during the 1970s. At the end of the decade, use of free market prices had sup-
planted the use of transfer prices for purposes of internal control and motivation. From its origins in the Netherlands subsidiary in 1970 and 1971, the
Rotterdam pricing system had, with modification, come into use in most European affiliates. In doing so, the marketing operations became effectively independent in their operations rather than fully integrated and dependent purely
on the products made available for them to sell by the combined effects of the
exploration, production, transportation, and refining operations as before. This
was a bold development for a company that had previously relied for its prosperity on an integrated approach where the marketing companies were essentially limited to selling what the refining activity produced.

Prosper's Netherlands subsidiary was the first to use Rotterdam prices internally. Special factors applied in the Netherlands, and these are believed to have been instrumental in the development of the system in that country. Without those national factors and the subsidiary's particular senior managers, it is possible that use of free market prices would not have been adopted through most of Prosper's international marketing subsidiaries.

Special Factors

Rotterdam Market

Rotterdam was the undisputed center for oil refining and trading in Northwest Europe since the start of the 1960s. The Netherlands oil industry serviced an international demand many times larger than the country's domestic consumption, marking Netherlands activities as distinctive. The internationally important free market in oil, situated in Rotterdam, was probably foremost in creating individuality in the Dutch internal oil industry.

The Rotterdam market was essentially the trade in oil products conducted outside the integrated oil companies in northwestern Europe. Originating in the 1950s, it gained significance in the 1960s when the United States–based oil companies began to develop Libyan crude. Sales to the American market were constrained by quotas until 1973. Most of the Libyan crude found its way to Rotterdam, and that city fast became the center of oil refining and storage for Northwest Europe.

The Libyan government had deliberately allowed smaller, independent American oil companies production concessions. These companies did not have European marketing operations and, consequently, traded a portion of their crude in Rotterdam. The market became established on these surpluses, and remained a marginal market heavily sensitive to short-term balance between demand and supply.

Activities were confined to a free market in spot deals (delivery within three weeks) as negotiated between individual buyers and sellers. The "hinterland" of the market was limited to six countries: the Netherlands, Belgium, Germany, Luxembourg, Austria, and Switzerland. This hinterland was referred to as the Rotterdam Six. Although volumes traded through Rotterdam grew steadily, it was estimated that only 5 percent or less of the total supplies of these six nations passed through the trade market in the late 1970s. However, the market was important in its influence on prices and on the oil industry in general.

Since 1968, sales and purchases in Rotterdam have been reported and published. The most widely used source were the quotations of the American company Platt's, which posted prices daily as a high, low, and mean for the major oil products. This daily information was colloquially termed *Platt's prices* or *Rotterdam prices*. The quotations represented marginal behavior for the oil industry as a whole. If all business was passed through, including long-term contracts, prices would certainly be different. The prices therefore had only a partial relationship with the costs of refined products and long-term economics.

Oil supply had been in surplus since the start of the free market through the seventies, with the exception of the short disruptions around late 1973 and late 1978. Consequently the Platt's prices had, with these exceptions, consistently been lower than long-term contract prices from the oil majors. Since 1974 the substantial excess in shipping and refining capacities had resulted in spot prices well below the average costs of production, transport, and refining of the products supplied to the market.

Prosper Nederlands

It was within a national industry dominated by the Rotterdam market that Prosper's Netherlands subsidiary worked. Known as Prosper Nederlands N.V., it was a small European company with production and marketing responsibility for natural gas, marketing of oil products within national boundaries, and management of the large refinery and storage facilities of Prosper at Europoort (but without financial responsibility for the latter). Oil marketing was the most important activity, employing about four hundred people, and it is the focus of this case description.

From 1970, the marketing function was organized on the basis of market streams. There were three: one for the retail automotive market and mainly constituting motor oil; one for wholesale, that is, supply to dealers in a wide range of sectors with such products as heating oils and agricultural products; the third stream was for industrial markets selling a range of products, but mainly lubricating and fuel oil. In 1970, some 30 percent of the subsidiary company's product turnover was accounted for by direct sales, with the remaining 70 percent being sold indirectly through dealers and distribution agents. The product mix reflected Prosper's position as a high-volume and low-value producer with abundant supply and little need to create extra value.

Although Prosper Nederlands always held between 10 and 15 percent of the Dutch market, with the main competition coming from other oil majors, proximity of the Rotterdam market created special competition. It is important to note that, unlike other European markets, except perhaps West Germany where the influence of the Rotterdam market was also high, some 15 percent of the market was held by independent oil companies. These were known in the oil industry as white pumpers, because their brand names were not established and were frequently transient. These small enterprises exerted considerable net influence on the behavior of the retail market.

The white pumpers operated by buying oil, usually as spot deals from the Rotterdam petroleum market, and selling through their own slim marketing and distribution organizations. Depending on particular market circumstances, these independent companies were usually able to buy petroleum at a lower cost than could be supplied by the majors to their own retailing organizations. Their marketing and distribution costs were also generally less than the majors because of their low overheads and flexible operations. The white pumpers tended, therefore, to sell at a price slightly below the oil majors. As a result, they often acted as price leaders, establishing pricing levels which the oil majors often had to follow, while maintaining a small premium. These small companies were particularly active in the motor oil and home heating oil markets.

Reorientation

New President

It was within this milieu that the newly appointed president of Prosper Nederlands contemplated his task in late 1970. The background of this appointment is pertinent to the issue at hand. Unconventionally, by the usual standards of the oil world, he had worked outside of the industry for many years. In particular he had acted as a broker on the Chicago Board of Trade commodity and futures markets and understood well how such free markets operated. Conscious that oil is, itself, a commodity, it was natural that he should bring some part of this perspective and training to his new responsibilities.

It was an immediate personal observation that the company for which he was now responsible could literally disband all its employees and make the same financial return. All that would be necessary was for him to retain his secretary, buy from the free market, and sell to the larger existing customers. It is reasonable to conclude that the president's views on the oil industry represented a dramatic reorientation that would have been highly improbable for an experienced oil man to have identified.

At this time the oil majors barely recognized the embryonic free market in oil. It was unimportant, hardly known, and was looked upon with some derision by most executives of the majors. After all, the oil industry had worked exceptionally well in its integrated form and showed little sign of requiring such novel devices. Most oil company executives would have admitted ignorance of the workings of free markets and would not have wished to learn of them.

The curiosity of the newly appointed President of Prosper Nederlands, regarding the oil industry and the Rotterdam market, functioned at several levels. First, he was fascinated at the circumstances which had brought about a commodity product such as oil to be merchanted through a vertically integrated operation, and how such a method of operation could be efficient.

Second, he was frustrated with the deficiencies that existed in the way the Rotterdam market operated, and he spent some time attempting to improve its workings and to introduce a market in oil futures. There was no daily free calling period where bids determined prices, as on the London Metal Exchange and other markets. Private deals were struck between buyer and seller based on perceptions of the drift of the market, and they were published at the end of the day. The secrecy of the Rotterdam oil market, and its increasing influence on the determination of prices in national markets, was a source of concern to several governments. As one chairman of a large oil company noted in personal conversation, the market sometimes took on the character of the tail that wags the dog.

At a third level, the new president was compelled to consider the bearing the market might have on his company, both in the sense of the advantages which the physical and psychological closeness of the Rotterdam market offered and the threats that its proximity presented. He was also compelled to react to the very real influence he felt that its increasing dominance must exert on the future structure of the Dutch market.

Fresh Viewpoint

The early days of his presidency were marked by bringing a fresh viewpoint to the outlook of the marketing executives. The challenge was put forward that, since it was possible for the same return to be made by dealing on the Rotterdam market, there was no need for the company's executives to continue to be employed. His purpose was to motivate the managers into findings ways to add value to the products. It was not an idle threat; any individual product markets might well have been "liquidated" if the challenge could not be met.

Shortly afterwards, late in 1971, the viewpoint was formalized by the introduction of a management system based on Rotterdam prices. Daily sales and marketing activities of the company were recorded in terms of their returns, relative to the Rotterdam prices for that day. This system then became the routine control and motivational system, in much the same sense as actual invoiced product costs or transfer purchasing prices might be employed in another company. The performance of the executives was appraised on this new basis, and the entire marketing activity of the subsidiary company began to behave in accordance with maximizing its returns on Rotterdam prices.

Also in the early part of his presidency, in 1971, a weekend meeting was convened at a quiet, rural hotel to develop a strategy for the company. The sense of determination at the meeting was probably heightened by the boldness of the outlook and challenge that was put to the upper levels of management present. During the scheduled proceedings and informal discussions, ideas were generated and debated. Ultimately a strategy crystallized.

It was articulated that, as well as the existence and increasing importance of the Rotterdam market, inflation would also have a great influence on the future structure of oil demand in the Netherlands. The thinking extended to the conclusion that inflation would result in the closing of many independent dealers and distribution agents, because these small and inexpertly managed companies would not have the financial resources to meet increasing costs. In their place it was expected that a more concentrated independent industry consisting of fewer, larger, better managed companies would arise.

It was further surmised that these larger, independent operations would be likely to have certain advantages over the oil majors, including Prosper's subsidiary in the Netherlands. First, their small size and low overheads potentially would make them more profitable. Second, more important, and related to the first point, they would be able to bypass the oil majors for their supply and deal directly with the less expensive Rotterdam market. They could have done this in 1970, but increased familiarity with the market, improved telephone communications, routine purchasing procedures, and an expansion of the size of the market would make this practice more common in the future.

If the Netherlands market did develop in this way, it would put considerable price pressure on the oil majors. Traditionally, retail prices had been established predominantly by the major integrated oil companies. The selling price to the dealer was determined from this retail price by allowing an appropriate margin for the wholesaling or retailing functions that were performed. In the future, it was probable that the pricing mechanism, particularly at wholesale level, would become progressively more influenced by Rotterdam market prices.

At the same time, it was likely that retail prices would be under less pressure than wholesale prices, and that dealer and distribution agent margins would be bolstered. A strategy of acquiring dealers was decided upon. In that way the activities of Prosper Nederlands would add value by profiting from a greater emphasis on the more attractive price levels likely to apply in the retail markets. Towards the end of the seventies, approximately 70 percent of Prosper Nederlands's sales arose from the retail market and 30 percent from wholesale—a reversal of the 1971 split.

Events confirmed that the strategy was based on valid premises—a steady level and growth in profits was returned by Prosper Nederlands. Use of Rotterdam prices—or more exactly the kind of thinking that it produced—had a bearing on deriving and accomplishing the strategy. It was this ability of the reorientation to motivate managerial behavior appropriate to the emerging circumstances of the oil industry that was particularly relevant beyond the Netherlands. Eventually, influence of the new president's thinking could be found throughout much of Prosper. Use of Rotterdam prices for internal control and motivation pervaded almost all of Europe within a few years.

European Organization

An essential stimulus to adoption of a Platt's system of pricing for marketing activities was provided when Prosper's international operations underwent a major organizational reemphasis at the start of 1974. For some years before that time, the planning and organization review committee had examined methods by which activities could be decentralized to the national subsidiaries. Historically the subsidiaries operated as part of the total integrated business and had only limited independence. Prosper followed a policy which optimized profits against production, refinery, and distribution costs. Now the emphasis went towards creating profits through locally managed marketing activities. Refineries and other parts of Prosper's operations were also gradually devolved to the foreign companies, where benefits of responsive local management outweighed advantages of centralized operation. In summary, from 1974 the subsidiaries received greatly increased autonomy and became newly independent.

Appropriate through this reorganization was, it seemed to expose inequities among different parts of Prosper. Developments of the middle 1970s further aggravated these problems. Use of the Rotterdam prices for internal control and motivation took on an unexpected validation in the light of (1) the reorganization recommendations, (2) the problems following in its wake, and (3) the thrust of the oil industry into the new era with loss of control of price and supply by the oil majors.

Transfer Prices

Prosper had always employed a policy of determining transfer prices (internal prices charged when materials pass from one part of the company to another) on the principle of covering costs for each of the departments. Transfer prices to the foreign affiliates arrived at in this way took on an increased importance after the reorganization. They now formed the cost foundation on which the financial performance of these newly independent marketing companies were to be assessed. Despite this fact, the method of transfer price determination was not modified in the reorganization, and continued on a cost-plus basis.

Worldwide events in the oil industry aggravated shortcomings of the system more than would otherwise have been the case. The sharp upturn in excess tanker and refining capacity, in the early years of the automony, had the effect of greatly increasing costs and therefore also product transfer prices to the marketing companies. Prosper's activities downstream from marketing attempted to recoup their cost on much lower volumes by considerably increasing unit transfer price and invoicing the subsidiaries accordingly. At the same time, the European oil industry was experiencing a relative surplus, and free market prices showed a considerable saving relative to the dramatically raised internal prices applying within Prosper.

Depressed consumer demand stimulated a readiness for the oil producers to supply with a small discount on the higher energy prices which then prevailed. As usual, the surplus was available on the spot market in Rotterdam, and the traded prices were attractive compared to those possible on longer term contracts. Naturally, white pumpers were active in these supply conditions. Combined with consumer price resistance, the small independents were able to exercise considerable competitive price pressure on the oil majors at both the retail and the wholesale level.

Losses and Demotivation

Combination of downward pressure on sales prices and upward pressure on the costs of internal purchases from the refining department made the marketing operations of the foreign subsidiaries inviable. The effects were strongest in the Netherlands, because of the proximity of the Rotterdam market. There, as in many other countries, the retail prices for most products were less than it was possible to buy them internally from Prosper. Profit was impossible on the internally invoiced cost of products, whatever action was taken. Yet ready profit opportunities existed if the Dutch company bought products on the open market. Judged within the narrow and short-term interests of the newly decentralized Prosper Nederlands, it was more advantageous to cease purchasing products—and theoretically to stop trading altogether.

Introduction of the Rotterdam pricing system to Prosper Nederlands, and the revised outlook on the oil industry that it stimulated among the managers using it, had well prepared the company for its new autonomy under the reorganization. The mechanism of the oil market and the method of operations of the independent companies was understood. Executives' frustration at operations that could only lead to accounting losses was almost allayed by use of Rotterdam prices for internal control and motivation purposes.

As soon as Prosper Nederlands had purchasing autonomy, the company choose to buy most of its needs from the free market rather than internally from the refining group. All other subsidiaries routinely settled for an annual contract from Prosper's refining group for 80 or 90 percent of their expected needs. Prosper Nederlands only contracted for 40 percent of its needs in this way, and announced that it would seek supply from the less expensive Rotterdam market for the remainder. The Dutch company's decision engendered considerable controversy in Prosper.

It was inexplicable in the minds of many senior managers that, despite the decentralization philosophy, it was in the group's interest for subsidiaries not to purchase the overwhelming majority of their needs from Prosper. Not to do so meant that nonvariable overheads such as shipping and refining capacity were being even further underutilized. In consideration of these arguments, and in response to factions, an accommodation was reached where 70 percent of anticipated annual requirements were required to be purchased from Prosper and the remainder could be purchased independently.

In the meantime, all management concerned with foreign subsidiaries was, however, becoming increasingly concerned about the effects of high internal prices for refined products. In the face of subsidiary marketing company complaints and frustrations, Prosper management reflected on a way by which marketing executives need not be restrained by demotivating factors that were beyond their control. Additionally they were beginning to feel a need for a better basis on which to compare performance from one company to another. Such comparisons were a critical factor in the efficient allocation of resources and in other important matters. A weight of opinion gradually began to emerge that the use of Rotterdam prices throughout Prosper might be the answer.

Dissemination

Recognition

An example of the viability of the use of Rotterdam prices was available in the Dutch subsidiary, and it demonstrated a capability to go some way in meeting managerial needs. Despite the reasoned arguments in favor of the introduction of the system, a crucial factor in its adoption by other subsidiaries was to be management's increasing acquaintance with it. The use of the system in the Netherlands subsidiary had served to educate management on its practical and theoretical validity. Word of the Netherlands company's introduction of the system, and its effects, gradually permeated the managerial ranks of the international marketing group.

Education concerning the system and its benefits and detractions occurred in the many ways that news of developments spreads through large organizations. The president and enthusiastic executives of the Dutch subsidiary spoke informally on the method when the opportunity arose, such as at various company meetings. There were also more formal opportunities for presenting the system's attributes, such as when a member of the executive committee visited the Dutch subsidiary. During the day, the president made a presentation on the progress and strategy of his company, with all analyses and evaluations expressed in relation to Rotterdam prices.

When interest in the system had reached a critical point, the president of the Dutch company was invited to make a presentation on his Rotterdam price system to leading executives from the regional and area managements, as well as to leading executives from the other national subsidiaries. Probably most influential in promoting adoption were advocates who had worked in or close to the Dutch company. Such managers had become familiar with the practical issues involved in implementing and maintaining the Rotterdam price system and had become convinced of the efficiency of the approach.

A particular example is one manager who had worked in the marketing function of the Dutch company in 1972 and 1973, had moved to an area coordination post for countries within the European region, and later moved to the management group responsible for overseeing all of Prosper's companies in

Europe. His persuasive efforts, and those of others, served to communicate the advantages of the system and strongly influenced its adoption by individual foreign subsidiaries and its acceptance by headquarters management. Prosper's organization, which often gives multiple appointments to a single manager and sometimes incorporates overlapping responsibilities, also assisted in the pace of dissemination of the system's use and its attributes.

Reactions to the use of the system were mixed among the international marketing executives. In the early days at the Netherlands company, the feeling might be described as one of skepticism, curiosity, and interest. It was seen, at a minimum, as a harmless development from the Prosper Group perspective and that it might, perhaps, be a worthwhile experiment. As its effects in the Dutch company began to be assessed, greater confidence developed, until what had been reticence was gradually replaced by a mood of acceptance.

In general, the use of the system provided an effective motivational and control procedure within the companies, and also provided a more independent yardstick for comparison between subsidiaries for area coordinators, regional managers, planners, and senior management. Some also felt that the performance bias it introduced in the subsidiaries was in line with the broader and longer term interests of the group. With the method, it was judged likely that subsidiaries would begin to emphasize products and marketing approaches most appropriate to the structure and trend of the oil industry and its markets. On balance, this was considered a more favorable arrangement than one based on internal costings which may reflect past investment decisions that had become partly outdated by industry developments.

Refinements in Adoption

Although systems like the one developed in the Netherlands have since been incorporated by most European subsidiaries, the process of adoption was not smooth. Even in 1979 there were many dissenting managers across the group, and some companies had not adopted the system while others had brought about important modifications in its details. Prosper shipping and supply functions were mainly still opposed. The perspective created by use of Rotterdam prices in the national marketing companies ran counter to an integrated view of the industry under which managers in the shipping and refining sectors of the company traditionally prospered and, in their terms, threatened to increase surplus capacity in their activities and show substantial losses on their financial statements.

There was also some initial resistance to adoption of the Rotterdam pricing system in many countries distant from the Rotterdam market, in part because the influence of the Rotterdam market was much less than in the Netherlands. In Switzerland, for example, irregularities in the transport costs of Rhine barge deliveries, and also the opportunity of alternative supply from Italian refineries, particularly through the pipeline between the two countries, were two demotivations. Depending upon precise circumstances, oil products from Italy were often less expensive in Switzerland than those from Rotterdam.

The use of Rotterdam prices in Prosper Switzerland would have much less relevance than their use in Prosper Nederlands. There was a natural reluctance on the part of those marketing excutives to adopt Rotterdam prices that would have generally shown a lesser margin than that available to Swiss independent oil companies. On the strength of these reservations from Switzerland, and other countries to which they applied, the notion of an "opportunity cost internal pricing system" emerged. Realization of this conceptual point was a key step in the wider and more efficient adoption of free market pricing within national marketing subsidiaries.

Theoretically speaking, the Rotterdam prices were the opportunity cost in the Netherlands, that is, the cost of the least expensive alternative. Using the lowest priced free market for oil products in a given country was exactly equivalent to the use of Rotterdam prices in the Netherlands. Encouraged by this viewpoint, in the middle seventies the Swiss subsidiary adopted an opportunity cost based system, used in an exactly equivalent way to that of the Rotterdam price based system in the Netherlands. Other subsidiaries in similar positions, such as those in Scandinavia, then adopted an opportunity cost based system.

Some subsidiaries continued to resist adoption of the Rotterdam pricing system or one that was keyed to opportunity cost. An example is the French subsidiary, where the government has always regulated to obtain a profit margin on oil industry costs. Consequently a transfer price greater than market buying prices never occurred in that country. This meant that there was no incentive to adopt a system like the one originated in the Netherlands. Great reluctance also occurred in Germany, where Prosper's company had an indigenous, "balancing" (small scale) refinery incorporated in its financial statements. This fact suppressed the use of Rotterdam prices as an internal system in Germany because the company recognized that its greater self-interest was a maximum aggregate financial performance. That objective was better served, in their opinion, by maintaining a marketing arrangement more sensitive to selling the products of its refinery and to maintaining it near capacity.

Despite these practical reservations, there still remained dissenters in the company who were acutely concerned about a system which they perceived as artificial. The accounts of the subsidiaries were still based on invoiced transfer prices, and Rotterdam prices or opportunity costs had no relationship with the accounting bases of the companies. Skeptical arguments were particularly fueled in the latter half of 1978 and early 1979. Western Europe was experiencing oil shortage, and spot deals on the Rotterdam market were going to highs above those of longer term contrasts. Also, Prosper's excess refining and tanker capacity had been reduced to manageable proportions. As a result, the internal transfer price for refined products showed promise of being, on average, below Rotterdam prices.

Despite these 1978 and 1979 reservations on the use of the Rotterdam price system, most Prosper executives consider that the use of the system strengthened operations through the 1970s. Regardless of the opponents of the introduction of the Rotterdam pricing and opportunity cost systems, the consensus within the international marketing organization supported the development. Most managers believed the method was beneficial as a motivational and control device, but most also conceded that it was difficult to assess in detail what its effects had been.

Caveat

Did Atlas enact a response equivalent to the use of Rotterdam prices in Prosper? In fact, there has never been a comparable management response. Like Prosper, though, Atlas decoupled refining and supply from marketing. The extent, however, of integration was never so extreme at Atlas. As a crude-short company it had always bought oil competitively and permitted subsidiaries to do so as well. Hence, internal pricing had always contained some sense of traded market values between one company and another (not the same as Rotterdam prices). Transition to independent pricing was therefore smoother for Atlas. An executive heading up supplies assumed responsibility for implementing a fully independent pricing, supply, and trading system within Atlas, and he was able to do so without any major disruption during the 1960s.

In the Rotterdam prices case, as has also been evident in the other responses presented this far, a process of gradual development of response from undistinguished beginnings to wide adoption has been observed. Acceptance of each response occurred step by step when needs were identified in respective parts of the organization, and the risks of implementation of a subresponse outweighed the problems management was seeking to rectify at that point. This process was driven at each increment by managerial needs resulting from the interplay of specific situational forces.

Specific factors were instrumental in starting responses, in giving them overall form, and in creating important details. For example, the personality and experience of the new president of the Dutch subsidiary and the special position of the Netherlands market were essential to development of the Rotterdam pricing system in Prosper. The relevance of such situational factors is to be observed in further accounts of responses presented in following chapters in accord with the propositions stated in chapter 3.

Having examined entry to the coal industry, the catalytic cracker investment, and introduction of the scenario planning and Rotterdam pricing systems, this study is now to look at the 'kernel' disruption of the oil industry for the 1970s. The 1973 oil price increase and the associated embargo most singularly signalled the dawn of the new era that put the volition behind all the observed responses in Prosper and Atlas. Attention is now turned to how the supply functions of Prosper and Atlas managed through the embargo during 1973 and 1974 and its associated dislocation of production, transportation, storage, and marketing.

Note

1. *Business Week*, August 18, 1975, p. 24.

10
Prosper's and Atlas's Management of the Embargo

C rude oil sourcing, storing, shipping, refining, and final shipping of products to markets were all the responsibility of the supply departments of Prosper and Atlas. Efficient integration of supply activities became a more complex managerial problem than ever during the late 1973 and early 1974 embargo of the Organization of Arab Petroleum Exporting Countries, when crude oil was not made available to the U.S.A. and the Netherlands (the center of the European oil industry) by the important Arab oil-producing nations. Consider, for example, that Atlas and Prosper each used over fifty different crude oils from about twenty countries across the world, owned or chartered about two hundred crude or product carrying vessels, utilized about fifty refineries and several pipelines, and marketed many oil products to over a hundred nations on all continents.

The responses by the managements of Prosper and Atlas to the 1973 embargo provide seemingly cardinal examples of operating responses to discontinuity. In both cases, the supply operations were severely dislocated and had to be realigned in highly uncertain, constantly changing conditions. Preceding chapters have described two corporate responses and three administrative responses and have found those responses to be broadly consistent with the expectations for corporate and administrative responses presented in table 3–1 and the associated text. The general atmosphere characteristic of corporate responses was reasoned in chapter 3 to be one of a clear mission, but also one of learning and experiment, and of administrative responses it was reasoned that the general atmosphere would be one of introspection and reeducation. For operating responses such as those to be presented in this chapter, it was generally expected that tasks would be clear but solutions ingenious, and that working conditions would be high pressure, embodying expedient actions.

The first part of this chapter provides essential background to the supply functions of the two researched companies as well as to the sequence of events associated with the oil crisis of 1973 and 1974. Descriptions of the responses to the embargo by the managements of Prosper and Atlas is then to be presented.

Managing Supply

The diverse activities of the supply functions of the large international oil companies have to be performed within constraints imposed by historic investments in capital equipment, including production sources, pipelines, harbors, ships, refineries, and storage. To minimize costs, these investments typically exploit economies of scale by building facilities as large as possible and as specific as possible to the characteristics of the crude to be shipped or of the crude to be refined for given end products. Even routinely, however, there are numerous variations around general expectations resulting from technical as well as natural considerations. There is a need, therefore, for frequent changes to schedules, inputs, and products and, despite the heavy emphasis on realizing economies of scale, the oil industry has organized itself to incorporate this essential flexibility. In fact, the short-term operations of the supply activities of the large, integrated companies can be regarded as the constant exercise of choice among many changing options.

It is useful to classify this wide range of managerial activities of the supply functions of companies such as Prosper and Atlas into three sets, according to the time frame which is required for initiated activities to have effect. The longest term includes exploration and investments in production, shipping, and refining capacities (where the decision point is higher and cross-functional and incorporates corporate planning in Atlas and Prosper, with the supply function providing input). Within a medium time frame the variables include principally contract decisions on crude oils, refined products, shipping, storage, and refining. In the short term, the operational phase, the supply function has to accomplish its responsibilities within the constraints imposed by earlier longer and medium-term commitments, and within the vagaries of throughput from wells, weather, accidents, and other irregularities. This account focuses on the short- or immediate-term time frame concerned with day-to-day operations.

The financial results of an integrated oil company are significantly affected by the efficient immediate-term operations of its supply department. The return from a national market is a function of the product mix which can be supplied to that market. Refining costs are partly determined by the particular crude input and product output. Minimization of storage and transportation costs affects return. Efficiency of the supply departments over the short run is largely a function of their ability to match demand and supply well at critical points in shipping, refining, and marketing. For example, choices can be made concerning which ships are used on which mix of routes (tankers can be quite specific not only to port terminal requirements, size, and quality of cargo but also to specific crudes, some of the more viscous of which need to be heated constantly during a voyage to retain their fluidity), and some choices can be made on the way a refinery is operated (some crudes can be substituted for each other, and the mix of refined products from a given crude input is flexible within limits).

Supply of crude to Europe from the Middle East generally requires a four-week voyage around South Africa (since 1967), and there is a need to plan loadings up a further month ahead. During this eight-week lead time, circumstances can alter radically. Further, a change in the rate at which oil is coming forward from the oil fields, weather delays in shipping, or the rate at which the finished product is accumulating at the refinery can all have significant implications for logistic operations. Consequently, to match supply and demand exactly, several short-term actions are often necessary. Rerouting of tankers occurs frequently. Spot deals and exchanges including additional purchases or sales of crude or products often take place in Western Europe, and short-term hire of extra storage, small product carriers, and other elements of the supply activity can resolve short-term problems.

Organizing Supply

As the Prosper and Atlas supply functions managed the same tasks in the same general environment, it would be reasonable to expect that the method of operations and the organizational structure of the supply functions of the two companies would be similar. Broadly, this expectation is fulfilled, but there are important differences in operations and in structure. Most significant is that the planning aspects of the supply function at Prosper were fully computerized as a linear programming model, while Atlas operated a manual system. This difference introduced distinctions in systems and in organizational structure.

Prosper

In Prosper the approach to managing the supply function was predominantly computer based. In the 1960s the stability in the oil industry and Prosper's margin of owned crude permitted consolidation of supply problems into a computer-based optimization model. The model's efficiency had brought about the complete displacement of manual systems by the early seventies.

Input to the computer system was comprehensive: it required data on stocks and forecasts of demand and supply of crude oil and products for all types and grades. In this respect, data were required from many parts of the company, including marketing subsidiaries, refinery managements, the shipping department, and others. When the information was assembled, it generally took a day to enter it into the computer. Typically, the program was run overnight, with the output ready for dissemination and use the next day.

The model's linear programming solution was comprehensive, detailing specific sources, ships, and destinations for each crude and product. Run monthly, the program gave aggregate results for each of the next three months and a week-by-week breakdown for the first month. The model's optimal solution then acted as an operating plan for the supply function's exact arrangements. Details were implemented by the operational staff. Any irregularities that arose, for example, from adverse weather or other discrepancies between the assumptions of the "blueprint" and actuals were adjusted by the operators without reference to the model.

The flexibility and need for initiative by operators was therefore limited by the detailed computer solution. Where operators' initiative was required to deal with irregularities, the necessary decisions had, generally, only minor implications. Consequently the activities of Prosper's supply function were substantially concerned with administering and maintaining the modeling exercise, and this was reflected in ways of working and organizational form. Potential untoward effects were: less integration between planners and operators, reduced appreciation for the wholeness of the problem among the staff, and the substitution of the complex optimization calculations in the model for more flexible human judgment.

The organizational structure of Prosper's supply function in 1973 is diagrammatically represented in figure 10–1. The operations division was the

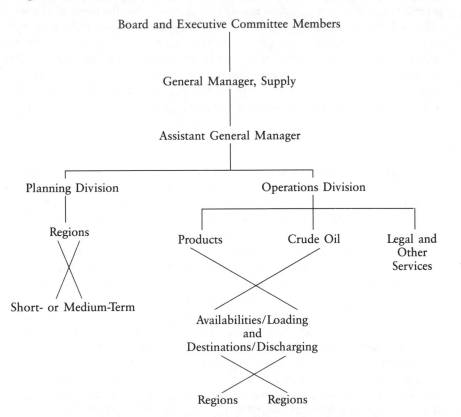

Figure 10–1. Prosper's Supply Function Structure

largest of the two divisions, containing about sixty staff members. This division split at the first level into products, crudes, and services (such as legal and import–export documentation). At the next level, the crude and products areas each split into availability to loading sections and destination to discharging sections. These subdivisions were then split at the lowest level into regions of the world.

The planning division within Prosper's supply function contained some forty persons and split first into regions and then into short- and medium-term time horizons. The short-term planning sections related to the time span of the optimization model and extended up to three months. The medium-term planners at Prosper worked within a time span of three months to approximately eighteen months. Beyond this period, responsibility fell within the corporate planning area under the assumption of the need for capital investment.

Atlas

In 1973 the supply function was organized in Atlas on the basis of three time horizons. The structure is diagrammatically illustrated in figure 10–2. A long-term planning division examined the supply and demand pattern for a period beyond two years. They were essentially concerned with problems requiring capital investment, and worked in close consultation with the corporate planning department in Atlas in studying future supply and demand patterns. More novel aspects of the supply situation tended to be initiated and led by the corporate planners as a result of their wider perspective and possibly greater influence with the board.

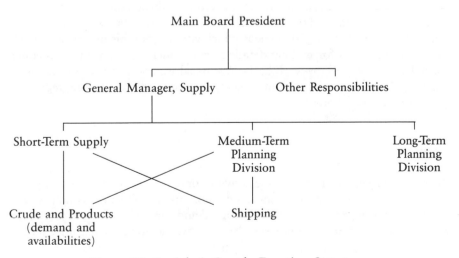

Figure 10–2. Atlas's Supply Function Structure

The medium-term planning division in the Atlas supply function had responsibility for a time period between six months and two years. Their area of influence covered circumstances that could not be solved by investment, but which still represented major commitments by the company. Examples of medium-term planning responsibilities are fixed-price contracts for supply or demand and tankage-leasing arrangements of one or two years. Often, concerns were for broad changes of emphasis or direction, but these did not involve capital investment. The perspective of the division was "whole world outside of the Americas" and "whole Atlas outside of the Americas," as was that of the long-term division.

The short-term division was fundamentally a logistic operation concerned with the mechanics of loading, delivering, shipping commissions, and related activities. It was split into two sections. The first, crude and products, dealt with the logistic operations of crude oil and products vis-à-vis availability, loading and destination. The second, shipping, was responsible for shipping arrangements, that is, the formulation and issuance of instructions to the marine department regarding when and where ships were required and what shipping capacity was necessary. Some subsidiaries operated independent supply operations, so that for the short-term the perspective at headquarters was just short of global. The staff in this short-term division of the Atlas supply function numbered about eighty-five, including secretarial and clerical grades, during the period of the supply embargo.

When the crisis struck in 1973, activities of Atlas's supply department were marshalled together under a well-established system. There was a monthly information gathering exercise where the subsidiary companies of the group submitted their requirements for crude and for products. At the same time, the availabilities were estimated by production personnel. Demand and availability were assessed for each month up to six months ahead; the position for the following six months and the next year were also assessed, but without monthly itemization. The planning document which issued from this monthly exercise provided guidelines for making detailed arrangements for a supply schedule formulated on a week-by-week basis. Appraisal was performed monthly at a meeting of supply department managers, with the current planning report as the basis of discussions.

Crisis

When the embargo of 1973 and the activities of the oil companies are analyzed, it becomes apparent that circumstances did not arise as suddenly as many would believe. Long-range tightening of oil demand and supply had been taking place for some time. Other factors were also at play, including increasing literacy and heightened political awareness of the oil-exporting nations. These were necessary, although insufficient, conditions to give rise to such a unified exertion of influence. Analysts of the oil crisis of 1973 have observed that the precursors of the crisis in fact extend specifically back to Libya and 1970.[1]

Run-Up

The newly instated radical government in Libya, under Colonel Quadaffi, confronted the oil companies during 1970 and managed to increase prices after ordering cutbacks in production. Libya's position was strong and was reinforced by the new regime's contracts with the USSR. The country offered high-quality crude at close proximity to the European markets. (Supply proximity had gained great importance following the 1967 closure of the Suez Canal.) The Exxon pamphlet on the Organization of Petroleum Exporting Countries (OPEC) summarizes background to the events of 1970 and 1971:

> Energy and petroleum demand by then were growing faster than anticipated. That, together with the disappearance of spare producing capacity outside the Organization of Petroleum Exporting Countries; a rupture and shutdown for many months of Tapline, the pipeline running from the prolific oil fields of Saudi Arabia to a Mediterranean port; a generally tight transportation situation, aggravated by the closure of the Suez Canal—combined to shift the balance of negotiating power in favor of the producing countries.[2]

The Tehran and Tripoli agreements of 1971 constituted the first significant assertion of the power of the oil-producing countries. The price increase to $2 per barrel from about $1 per barrel and the agreements on escalation and compensation for the devaluation of the dollar were a signal departure from the historic norms of the industry. The power of the oil producers was also shown throughout 1972 by the sudden progress in the long-discussed issue of participation, where host governments were able to acquire what amounts to an equity stake in their oil production. Aramco accepted a 20 percent participation in principle with the Kingdom of Saudi Arabia in March, and Iraq nationalized the Iraq Petroleum Company in the summer. Production cutbacks also began to occur over this period.

After Libyan cutbacks in 1970 and 1971, Kuwait was the second nation to restrain production, which it did in April 1972. In 1973 these various actions began to be felt in the marketplace. As the Petroleum Press Service reported in May 1973:

> Oil prices have been showing a strongly rising tendency in recent months. The causes are complex but they resolve themselves into two main groups: (a) host government pressures to raise the tax toll levied on crude oil exports; and (b) normal commercial factors, including the pressure of demand which has brought about temporary and specific shortages of crude and products.[3]

Other developments occurred in early 1973. First, the oil purchasers started to compete to buy ahead of expected price increases. Second, the major oil companies were uncertain over the possibility of losing control of a proportion of their oil through imminent participation agreements. Under the new participation agreements, the producer nations had greater freedom over their choice of customers, and smaller, independent oil companies were willingly bidding higher prices for supplies.[4] April 1973 also saw the President of the United States revoke the import quota that had previously suppressed demand for oil from the Middle East. Demand was thus stimulated, but there were even further cutbacks in oil production by host governments. Market pressures pushed prices higher, and a new high price of $5 per barrel and more was paid for Nigerian, Latin American, and Algerian crude by September 1973.[5]

In this escalating atmosphere, the supply functions of Atlas and Prosper were both experiencing nonroutine difficulties in the spring and summer of 1973. As the latter half of the year approached, it was recognized that shortages could become substantial and widespread unless avertive action was taken by the governments of consumer countries. By September, Atlas and Prosper were already working under supply acquisition difficulties and were beginning to prepare for an even tighter winter period while considering the possibilities of allocation of limited products among customers.

Embargo

Political developments in the Middle East finally precipitated the full oil crisis of 1973. Negotiations on prices had been proceeding between the oil companies and OPEC through September. A two-week standstill period was called for by the oil companies in October that was construed by the oil-exporting countries as a bargaining stand. On October 6, 1973, the Yom Kippur war started when Egyptian troops stormed the Suez Canal.

The Kuwait meeting of OPEC in October proved to be the turning point in the oil supply situation. On October 17, 1973, the Arab oil-exporting countries decided to use oil supplies as a weapon against Israel and its supporters in the war. A 5 percent reduction from their September exports was agreed upon for future months. This was to be followed by further reductions of 5 percent each month until Israel withdrew from the land it had occupied since 1967. Oil made available for export was allocated among consumer countries according to their policy stand in relation to the Arab–Israel War.

October 19th and 20th saw a clarification in the Saudi Arabian policy. With that country supplying some 40 percent of the total Arab oil production, it was in the strongest political and economic position and its decisions were influential throughout the Arab world. In fact, the cutback was decreed at 10 percent. Some industrial countries such as Britain and France were designated as "friendly" and were excluded from cutbacks, but a full embargo was confirmed for the United States of America and also for the Netherlands.

The United States and Netherlands embargoes included oil products processed elsewhere and then exported to those countries, as well as supplies to the United States Navy. For this reason, the proclamation included a number of third countries in the embargo, namely, the Bahamas, the Dutch Antilles, Canada, Puerto Rico, Guam, Singapore, and Bahrain, and also some specific refineries in Europe that supplied the United States or its navy.[6]

Precise details of the policy continued to alter as experience was gained in the workings of the embargo, but these began to be clarified at the Kuwait meeting on the 4th of November. An initial cutback of 25 percent was confirmed, and then successive cutbacks of 5 percent per month, although some modifications were made later. The decree included the assertion that oil supplies would be reinstated as national governments of the producing nations declared support for the Arab cause. Two days later, the European Economic Community (EEC) put out a strongly worded statement in favor of the Arab position. Consequently, all the countries of the EEC (except the Netherlands) became exempt from volume cutbacks.

Technical Challenge

It was within these complicated, often uncertain, and evolving circumstances that the supply functions of Atlas and Prosper set about the task of optimizing their positions. Each company's supply personnel needed to take a mass of complex and changing information and turn it into workable supply programs and tanker schedules. Generally speaking, the major oil companies were able to use Iranian oil to supply the Netherlands and Venezuelan oil to supply the United States. These modifications were, of course, quite easily accomplished by rerouting tankers. The effects of the reduced aggregate level of supply presented the real challenge to operations and logistics.

Low stock levels made circumstances very difficult, and shortages quickly arose from small variations in demand patterns which ordinarily would not have been important. Disruptions were frequent and extreme, as the uneven relationship between stock levels and the rate of demand cumulated through each level in the distribution channels all the way to the customer. Managing stock levels was also more difficult due to the very large and discrete, single deliveries that new tankers necessitated. Problems associated with low stock levels are considerable for oil refineries because sudden, uncontrolled closure of a refinery could be dangerous and would probably lead to damage. Even if there was no harm to the installation, it would take three or more weeks to restart the refinery, and the necessary cleaning and preparation that would be entailed would be expensive.

Variations in rates of supply had also created significant fluctuations in tanker freight rates and in the costs of other types of short-term capacity. Spot shortages and competition among electric utilities, independent oil companies, and other companies to buy ahead of anticipated price rises (later found to be a mere fraction of the massive price rises that came about eventually) wrought havoc in early 1973. Hectic attempts to acquire oil prior to the embargo had increased the cost of tanker freight by more than 700 percent from its low in the spring of 1972; acquisition of capacity was even difficult during the embargo. Afterwards, however, tanker prices went down more steeply than they had risen.[7]

Difficulties arising from the crisis were further compounded by the need to allocate available oil supplies among nations. The criterion of an equal sharing of the shortage among countries was applied by all the large oil companies. As Raymond Vernon has commented:

> In general, the international oil companies responded to the emerging situation with a conditioned reflex of entrepreneurs minimizing their risks at the margin. The patterns of oil distribution in the crisis, dictated by the principles of greatest prudence and least pain, were curiously nonnational.[8]

These principles of allocation constituted an overall constraint which further challenged the supply personnel in Atlas and Prosper.

Responses

Effects of the oil crisis and the modifications required to respond to them bear many similarities between Atlas and Prosper. Several differences do exist, however, particularly in terms of emphasis. Three sources of distinction were particularly pronounced: use of different non–Arab sources; presence of a computerized supply system in Prosper, where manual operations applied at Atlas; and restricted refining and storage facilities for Prosper, as much of its plant had been installed in the embargoed Netherlands.

The importance of the last point was considerable. Capacity in the remainder of Europe was correspondingly highly limited in relation to the volume of crude that maintenance of operations required. Facilities outside of the Netherlands in Northern Europe were planned for a relatively small throughput, and storage quantities, individually, were greatly inadequate in relation to the volume of oil carried in very large crude carriers. Localized storage problems therefore abounded and aggravated other problems for Prosper, precipitating additional shortages and emergencies of varying gravity.

Top Management

Broad involvement in the supply function responses to the embargo was common to both companies, and the need for it stemmed from characteristics of the situation as it evolved. First, the matter was of quite obvious high, short-term significance to both companies, and it had long-term ramifications in maintenance of working relations with the governments of host and consuming countries. The natural contact point between governments and the companies is the senior members of the board and, as a result, many important aspects of the situation materialized at that level in the company or were funneled through it.

The sensitive issues of the allocation of the scarce and critical resource among consumer governments was inevitably a top management decision in both Atlas and Prosper. Although the same decision of equal sharing of shortages among national markets was made in each company, each approach was different. In Atlas, the board instigated a group-wide cut of 8 percent of oil supplies to all customers compared to the September supply levels. The Prosper board consciously decided against implementing a universal, quantitative guideline of that sort, in the belief that its operation would introduce more problems than the adoption of a general principle of equal suffering among customers.

Top management in both companies also played an active role in details of the embargo, where their own ultimate authority in the companies and their detailed understanding of host governments were indispensable. An example of this situation occurred when an Arab oil-producing nation contacted a Prosper board member to offer a quantity of crude oil, conditional on the use of a particular carrier of that producer government. Acceptance of the offer not only required that suitable arrangements be made to integrate the consignment into the short-term supply operations but also signaled a new way of working, where the producer government encroached on the maritime transportation function, historically the exclusive domain of the oil companies and not the oil-exporting nations.

One particularly critical incident in Prosper's response to the embargo was when it became evident that a refinery operation in a consuming country ran the risk of uncontrolled closure through oil shortage. Only one week was available to secure crude supply, and it required a novel solution to an emergency that would have been unthinkable in normal times. To act in these rare circumstances, new contracts that could only be negotiated by top management using their ultimate authority were essential to gain supply at such short notice.

Boards also were obliged to be involved in sanctioning decisions that would otherwise have been routine. At one time Atlas wished to use a very large crude carrier flying the flag of an embargoed nation. It was the most suitably placed vessel from the aspect of normal scheduling considerations, but it was possible that the producing government involved would react against its use. The decision whether to use the ship in the normal way held the potential for a serious breakdown in the good relations between Atlas and the producer government, although the terms of the embargo did not extend to the use of ships. High-level judgment at board level on what might have been seen as a provocative act was necessary, as well as the high-level contacts that could be initiated from that level to test out opinions. In the end, the vessel was used without untoward consequences.

Decision Points

Thus, during the embargo, top management exercised more authority and used more initiative in day-to-day supply operations than would have been the case in normal times. The twin attitudes of increased initiative and of exercised authority extended throughout the organizational hierarchies in both companies. On the one hand, some otherwise minor considerations had to be referred higher because of novel ramifications. On the other hand, more decisions needed to be made more often, and these frequently incorporated uncommon qualities. Superiors were not always consulted who ordinarily would have been. Under the pressures of events, checking out all details at the appropriate point in the hierarchy became impractical in some cases.

The authority for subordinates to take the initiative to resolve details was a practical necessity and was readily delegated by superiors. At a senior level, but still below the board, there are several examples in Atlas. The need to state and work to a time limit and to formulate other practical aspects of the board's general dictate of a supply reduction of 8 percent of expected volume per customer, was the responsibility of the manager of short-term supply to implement. Examples of other actions that had to be made by the Atlas supply function included exceptional purchasing and trading of crude and the rerouting of tankers to avoid loading in the East Mediterranean. The latter decision was validated later when the Banias and Tartus pipeline terminals on the Mediterranean coast were destroyed in Israeli raids.[9]

Similar examples exist for Prosper. Details of operations which would otherwise have been referred to a higher level in the organization, where cost and efficiency would typically have been more carefully determined, were often settled at operator level. Deviations from computer blueprint and subsequent manual plans were usually managed at operator level during the embargo, through the exceptional use of split loads and of split deliveries, as well as through the substitution of crudes and products.

Realignment

The need for more decisions inevitably meant an increased workload for those working in immediate operations and short-term planning. The atmosphere was one of composure in both Prosper and Atlas, and largely constituted the realignment of priorities and resources, including manpower, to meet the needs of the situation. The way in which the adjustment in work levels was met in each company reflected the differences in the organizational structures and working systems, as well as in the different locations of crude sources, refining and storage capacities, and markets for each company.

In both Prosper and Atlas, the manpower needs were met by a realignment of the departments away from long-term considerations, which could not be planned effectively in any case, towards the short-term and immediate problems. The shift was less marked in Atlas, where a diversion of the energies of the medium- and long-term planners was adequate. This constituted a minor adjustment, since the interface between the respective sections had always been considerable and almost all the planners had been operators at some time. The disruption to routine methods of working were more marked in Prosper, largely because of the impossibility of using the computer optimization model and the company's switch from manual methods, some five years before.

Prosper's predicament was so critical at the height of the crisis that circumstances governing immediate decisions could change hourly. The optimization model generally needed at least one day for data preparation and input alone; it was of no value in such dynamic conditions. Over the years in which the model had been used, planners and operators had tended to lose an intuitive feel for the complex global situation which was more efficiently accommodated in the program.

The personnel most useful to operating without the computer were the original manual operators and planners whose importance had, over the years, receded within the supply function. They still had the feel of the total situation and had the most worthwhile contribution to make in the crisis. The most crucial extra work substantially fell upon this small number of employees, and they worked very long hours. Leadership went to them over this period, and the younger, computer-oriented, more specialized employees, who lacked a sense of the total picture, almost worked in tandem, although their working hours were also longer than normal. This observation should be appraised against the more complex supply problems encountered by Prosper in terms of their localized storage shortages, which demanded frequent adjustment of schedules.

Communications

Information needs were also more acute in the crisis, at its height. The customary monthly data-collection exercise on global stocks, demand, and availabilities became daily in both companies. Telex was used for this purpose, supported by telephone communications for changes as they arose during the day. Internal reports were also required more frequently, often containing information that was not usual, such as the names of tankers and their flags, and these were often handwritten and photocopied, ordinarily not tolerated in either Prosper or Atlas. Such reports often went up to board level, where they constituted an important source of information for consumer government enquiries—

they would generally have been of cursory interest. Less urgent reports relating to the longer term were often postponed or dropped.

The same needs for information and integration of the supply operations that prompted more reports also resulted in more internal meetings than usual. Special board meetings relating to the supply situation were convened by both Prosper and Atlas. The management of the Atlas supply function reports that a conscious effort was made to avoid too many time-consuming meetings but that occasional "matins" or "evensong" were convened. These were called to review the situation and to assemble coordinated sets of actions. More meetings than usual were reported by Prosper management, particularly at the level of the divisional managers and their immediate subordinates. Although not always formalized as a meeting, the increased frequency of review and assessment of the situation and a verification, or reassembly of priorities, was a common exercise and contrasted with what, in other times, had been a smooth monthly routine.

The need for rapid access to information, as well as for more frequent acquisition of such information, led to more intensive communications. The meetings and reports are, of course, symptoms of those needs, but day-to-day personal communications were also intensified. The constant flow of information among the executives involved was greater in terms of personal encounters and the use of telephones. Urgent needs prompted direct requests to the point where the information originated, rather than observation of conventional principles of hierarchy and protocol. In this sense, communication channels at all levels became more informal during the embargo at both Prosper and Atlas.

Operating response, as found in the two cases of response described in this chapter, fits with the general expectations presented in table 3–1. In both cases the situations were resolved by expedient actions around the original structure where administrative responses were found to be concerned with the actual revision of that structure and corporate response with forming an additional organization. Goals were indeed apparent in terms of day-to-day survival, but it was also observed that a supplemental goal to guide the specifics of response was also formulated (equal suffering for all customers). Extreme actions were required, as exemplified by the close involvement of top management in what would ordinarily have been regarded as purely operational issues. Needed programs were, however, mostly quite obvious. Involved personnel were those held in the regular structure, and expertise was generally found to be adequate, with the major exception of the computer operators at Prosper who could not relate to the frequent manual actions that needed to be taken in the hectic circumstances of the operating response. Operations after the response continued in the same way that they always had, even though the experience and understanding of it made some mark on the personnel involved.

This concludes the seven examples of response researched in the complex organizational settings of Prosper and Atlas. A further three responses in three corporations were researched in lesser depth as further examples of response in complex settings. These lesser depth examples are presented in the next chapter, where the influences of complex organizational settings on response are to be examined more closely.

Notes

1. Anthony Sampson, *The Seven Sisters: The Great Oil Companies and the World They Shaped* (New York: Viking Press, 1975); Adrian Hamilton and Christopher Tugendhat, *Oil, the Biggest Business* (New York: G.P. Putnam's Sons, 1975); Raymond Vernon, ed., *The Oil Crisis* (New York: W.W. Norton, 1976); Peter Hill and Roger Vielvoye, *Brandts Energy Crisis* (London: Robert Yeatman, 1974).

2. OPEC—*Questions and Answers* (New York: Exxon Corporation, undated).

3. *Petroleum Press Service* (Editorial), London, May 1973.

4. *The Petroleum Economist* (Editorial), February 1974.

5. Edith Penrose, "The Development of Crisis," in *The Oil Crisis*, op. cit., p. 49.

6. G. Lenczowski, "The Oil-Producing Countries," in *The Oil Crisis*, op. cit., p. 65.

7. Peter Hill and Roger Vielvoye, op. cit., p. 68–70.

8. Raymond Vernon, "An Interpretation," in *The Oil Crisis*, op. cit., p. 7.

9. Peter Hill and Roger Vielvoye, op. cit., p. 64.

11
Further Responses in Complex Settings

E ach of the following examples illustrates response in complex organizational settings, as do the preceding responses in Prosper and Atlas, but
these are researched in relatively lesser depth, as described in chapter 4. The response of an oil company, "Interoil," to foreign exchange losses
on corporate transactions is recounted first. The response of a large bank, "Columbus Bank," to a social disturbance and social issues in general is recounted
second. The response of a large power station supplier, "DeVito Power," to loss
of its sole market is recounted last.

Interoil

Interoil is another large, integrated petroleum company. It is not surprising that
the researched response carries a similar flavor to those described of Atlas and
Prosper. As an administrative response, it involves development and adoption
of a management system in a similar sense to the scenario planning and Rotterdam pricing initiatives given before. It does also carry its own unique features
of site and the specific intent of dealing with foreign exchange problems.

First Exposure

As with most international companies, Interoil not only bought and sold goods
from one country to another (involving currency exchange) but also borrowed
and invested interchangeably. During the period from 1968 to 1972, loans in
deutsche marks and Swiss francs were especially inviting, in that they offered
low interest and relatively high availability. At that time the United States dollar
was on the gold standard, as it had been since the Bretton Woods agreements
just after the Second World War. The rest of the world's major currencies, including the deutsche mark, were linked to this base in a constant relationship
that had been broken only for single currencies on a few isolated occasions

during the preceding twenty years. However, in the early 1970s the predictable arrangements began to be seriously threatened.

Pressures forced several critical readjustments among currencies that ultimately resulted in what was essentially a floating rates system which was to persist through most of the 1970s. The first major disruption was the floating of the deutsche mark in May 1971. That amounted to a considerable increase in its value as expressed in other currencies. In August 1971, the United States dollar was effectively devalued against the gold standard, thereby considerably altering its parity against strong currencies that had applied only three or four months before. In particular, loans and outstanding investment commitments denominated in deutsche marks and Swiss francs became much more expensive to service with the United States dollar, which was the currency denominated as the revenue base for Interoil and other oil majors.

Twenty years of exchange rate stability had naturally brought about routine currency conversions within Interoil's substantial movements of crude, products, and chemicals from one national operation to another. These comfortable ways were shaken in fiscal 1971 with the first exposure to foreign exchange risks. Results included a corporate profit-and-loss statement showing a write-off on such transactions reaching several tens of millions of dollars. At points throughout the organization, weaker currencies had been held at the expense of stronger ones. Particularly important to the company was the upward revaluation of the deutsche mark and Swiss franc loans held against assets in depreciating currencies, resulting in adverse liquidity and a weakened balance sheet.

Problems

If a culprit were sought for these losses in Interoil, it would have to be the Interoil treasury department. While the unprecedented nature of the circumstances did not merit any witch hunt, it was apparent that finding a solution to the serious situation would have to lie there. They were responsible for monetary transactions from one part of a company to another and for kindred tasks such as the management of cash holdings. Revaluations had been rare, and forecasting exchange rates and purchasing currencies as futures were inconsequential to preceding operations. Personnel in the department rallied to the challenges that they recognized as their own, but issues were more complex than anyone thought during the early stages.

Accounting conventions soon proved unhelpful. While not to be criticized in their own terms, the equal revaluation of assets and liabilities held in each currency produced inequities between patterns of revenues, costs, and investments that were at the heart of the 1971 losses. Uncertainty in the world at large had to be incorporated into the decisions. A managerial solution had to be found that brought about optimal actions under currency fluctuations.

Thus, attention turned early to forecasting exchange rates. With that information, it would be possible for managers to pace their transactions from one currency to another. They would avoid denominations about to devalue, but maximize holdings in those about to revalue. However, attempts at forecasting short term deviations were fruitless. The approach was abandoned as unworkable.

Among these problems and attempts at their solution, there arose a realization that a wider and deeper initiative was required. Interoil controllers across Europe and North America were gradually brought into the efforts to find a solution. A general posture was adopted of getting these "outsiders" involved up to the state of knowledge of the treasury department, without preconceiving the potential extent of their final cooperation or involvement. The stance was one of communicating problems and ideas in both directions so that the best possible decisions could be made at each point in time. The system gradually improved during this period.

As experience accumulated, there was a realization that a determined, more systematic effort at finding a solution was necessary. Understanding reached a level where a more structured approach was feasible, when only a much simpler and more tentative experimental sense of the problem was possible at the start. The decision was made to form a study group within the treasury department, comprising one full-time and four part-time people. It was an international group comprised of people from corporate headquarters in the United States and from the European headquarters.

Ten separate topics were selected by this group and split up among the members. Each then produced analyses or recommendations that were passed around and discussed. Particularly important to the progress of the study group were meetings held every two months or so, when problems were hammered out behind closed doors. The breakthrough came when it was recognized that the exchange rate problem, although rightly to be solved by them, was in fact a policy-level matter.

Dog and Pony Show

Early basic research conducted by the study group was concerned with a careful evaluation of exactly how floating exchange rates were affecting the company. Observing the wide influences at multiple levels and the centrality of most transactions to crucial day-to-day affairs prompted the realization that the problem had to be viewed from the perspective of the corporation as a whole. That meant that top-level management would have to support any solution.

The problems for the study group then became threefold: researching all the details that would be necessary to the construction of a workable recommendation to put to senior management; convincing each level of superiors that such a recommendation was necessary; and educating and preparing management at all of the affected operating parts of the company about the implications that the recommendations held for them. The answer to the latter two was what is lightly referred to in the company as a Dog and Pony Show.

Colloquialisms aside, a slide presentation was assembled, carefully tailored to a primarily nonfinancial audience. Influences of translation of assets and liabilities on financial statements was shown, as was the effect of fluctuations of exchange rates on transactions from one country to another. The former had to be accepted as an unalterable business risk in the short run, but the latter was recognized as a factor that should be taken into account in day-to-day affairs. Responsibility for such transactions was therefore to be devolved to the operations managers involved throughout the company. No one, for example, had a clearer idea of price elasticities in local markets that could compensate for disadvantageous transaction trends. If profits could not be sustained by managers in the face of currency situations, it was reasoned, losses should nevertheless affect their financial records so that appropriate investment or other decisions could be made in the future.

The package of slides and recommendations was assembled in final form and presented in late 1974. The mood was auspicious for its acceptance. Losses from 1971 remained an acute problem in the minds of senior management. Since that time, foreign exchange losses had been shunted around Interoil's profit centers because no one wanted to inherit them, and the need for clarification of the issue was seen to be important by almost everyone.

A centrally based system was proposed to support the operating managers with their additional responsibility. The treasury department committed itself to compiling and distributing a weekly anticipation of exchange rate movements. Although a forecast in a sense, research and study group work produced the conclusion that a system incorporating probability distributions was feasible and useful in that it incorporated a measure of the uncertainty while presenting management with a workable guide. The report was also to incorporate movements in the futures market that would allow managers to buy currencies at fixed rates several months ahead, and to show the premiums that such an insurance incurs.

It is relevant to note that most managers in Interoil had an engineering background. They were well able to deal with the statistical complexities of the proposed report—perhaps more than with the commercial and economic arguments that underpin currency fluctuations. Executives were not expected to use treasury department projections automatically. Judgment was expected to be applied to this information before action was taken, as in any other situation where managers had total responsibility for their decisions.

Signature

The response culminated in a memorandum detailing the system and instructions as a directive to managers. After approval by the chairman of the board, the document was forwarded over the signature of the chief financial officer. From that moment in early 1975, the system was in place and functioning. With only minor "teething troubles," as users learned its details and ramifications, the system remained in place into the 1980s with only small modifications. As the treasury department executives scanned the annual reviews of other major oil companies, they judged from the size of their competitor's foreign exchange losses that Interoil was probably well ahead on the management of currency instabilities.

Columbus Bank

Columbus Bank is one of the foremost members of the United States and international banking industry. The case description focuses at a more local level around a need to incorporate an integrated approach to social problems in the United States. In particular, problems surrounding the planned closure of a local branch office played a role in the development of a response through organizational change. This administrative response accomplishes the changes desired by the top executive mainly through the introduction of a new organizational system.

Appointment

Local banking operations in the United States are highly regulated. Both state and federal bodies can control numbers and sizes of branches as far as they relate to the proper provision of banking services to the community. Partly, these conditions reflect a need for government to meet social demands for banking, as sometimes articulated through consumer lobbying institutions or other organized groups. In the coalition model, social groups, government agencies, legislative steps, and the banks themselves move as one body that, on occasion, creates a cumbersome set of mutual interests.

With a consciousness of these circumstances and that they probably constituted an increasing trend, the president of Columbus Bank appointed a manager of promising ability in the area of social problems. With a distinguished career in the top echelons of government and with truly outstanding academic credentials, the appointee was readily recognized throughout the company as a man with a brilliant mind and as an important addition to management. With three levels of vice presidents in the organization, he was appointed to the top level as senior vice president, one step below the president. Responsibilities were, in practical terms, unspecific at the beginning, but many thought that he might be heir apparent to the chief executive officer and that early days were deliberately open ended so that he might "learn the business."

Clarification of the new senior vice president's responsibilities followed about one year later with the background of memorable social challenges confronted at the bank. Attempts at closure of a small and declining branch in Wilmington, a town near Columbus, precipitated a reorganization in the company. Although many senior managers felt that the change in management structure was an independently planned event by the president to reflect general developments, it is probable that the Wilmington disturbance at least served to confirm it. Among other things, the "Wilmington Issue" illustrated the breadth, interconnectedness, uncertainties, and irrationalities (as perceived by many managers) of social matters.

Disturbance

In the minds of most managers and citizens, the Columbus Bank had an impeccable record in social responsibility. It had special funding arrangements, liberal lending policies, and allowed deficits to be shown on accounts of businesses started and run by racial minorities. Federal government affirmative action goals for recruiting women, blacks, and Hispanics had always been surpassed, and several bank managers and loan officers were drawn from these population groups. For these reasons it was all the more inexplicable that the press and New York–based lobbyists should select Columbus Bank for attack.

At the time of the case, Wilmington was a neighborhood fast receiving a reputation for lawlessness. Looting and arson had become commonplace, and it was known in the bank that the branch had been the subject of a litany of acts of vandalism and robbery. The rapidly changing demographic structure of the area had reduced demands for bank services until the branch became unprofitable (even before allocation of overhead) in late 1977.

Decline of business was quite sudden and widely reported. Riots in Wilmington in the summer of 1977 produced an exodus of citizens and businesses. Cash transactions practically ceased after the riots, and the contents of over half the safe deposit boxes were reclaimed by their owners within a few months. After the summer, the two other large banks in the area announced closure plans for their branches from January 1, 1978. Columbus followed with its statement seven days later, declaring that the branch would be closed also from January 1st.

January, the start of the United States tax year, is the customary time to announce retail closings and openings. It was perhaps natural that all the bank's branches in the area would be nominated for the "axe," since all had experienced the same economic changes. However, from a social point of view there was the loss of three prestigious retail locations in a locality desperate to hold on to all vestiges of respectability. From the standpoint of the regulatory bodies, there was the risk of removal of all full-service banking facilities from the neighborhood. For the banks, there was the risk of being the last outlet and having the full force of social action groups, government agencies, and politicians demanding that an unprofitable branch remain open despite being subject to losses and to crime. For Columbus Bank, in particular, there was the risk of a social disturbance that might tarnish its reputation—especially important to United States banks since they are tightly regulated by state and federal political agencies capable of making life difficult for an irresponsible bank.

The initial steps satisfying federal requirements were made by Columbus Bank to close the branch. At the same time, the Wilmington branch was offered to the Supreme Bank, which was run by blacks predominantly for the purpose of meeting the needs of the black community. The Supreme Bank was in receivership already, but the state was supporting its deficit to meet social goals. Supreme expressed interest in acquiring the Wilmington branch. However, further uncertainties (primarily financial and thereby embracing state funding authorities) had to be overcome before an agreement could be made for Supreme to acquire the Wilmington branch of the Columbus Bank.

It is interesting to observe that the traditional methods of managing branch closures did not hint at the disruption that was to follow. A letter to customers informing them of the news led to only about a score of technical inquiries. There were no complaints received through the traditional channels. However, the energetic *Columbus Courier*—a widely read newspaper proud of its endeavors in investigative reporting—ran a story on the closure of the Columbus Bank's branch in September 1977.

The Columbus Courier journalist constructed a damning argument against the Columbus Bank, although properly consulting the bank's public relations department and basing his article on selected details supplied by them. It was claimed that Columbus Bank was deserting the declining neighborhood, thus contributing to its demise. It was noted in the article also that the action was being taken without even the redeeming justification that profits were not being made on the operation. Such actions were asserted to be against the precept of social responsibility. The willingness to hand over the branch to Supreme was given as further evidence of complicity. Columbus Bank's decisions and their handling had inadvertently sparked off a media campaign in the wake of which followed confrontation with lobbying groups. One important risk arising from the hostile press coverage was possible alienation by government regulatory bodies on whose goodwill many of Columbus Bank's successes were crucially dependent.

Community groups, many of which were previously unknown to management, began to contact the Columbus Bank. This culminated in October with a meeting between the management and representatives of the various associations. The request was made for Columbus Bank not to leave its branch and for the Supreme Bank not to enter the town. Later, Wilmington Social Action, a local chapter of the statewide Social Action Group claiming ten thousand members, became active. This group contacted congressmen, regulatory authorities, and national campaigners in order to rouse public interest but, most important of all, they contacted the Federal Deposit Insurance Corporation—the regulatory body whose approval was essential to Columbus Bank's plans. It was at this point that the head offices were besieged by shouting and gesticulating demonstrators and well-equipped television crews.

Structural Change

The circle was now complete, with full media coverage, several professional social lobbying groups supplying researched papers, a general public alerted to another example of "big bad business," and regulatory bodies possibly needing to moderate their decisions to reflect the opinions of the active populace. It seemed that any action or statement made by the bank was capable of interpretation in derogatory terms. An adverse reputation in regulatory bodies, media, and the public at large had to be avoided. To respond to the challenges, it was necessary for the bank to act in an integrated way, sensitive to the complexities and volatility of the situation.

It was around this time that the president enacted the change in organizational structure. The new senior vice president was given formal authority over public affairs and therefore became directly responsible for dealing with the Wilmington issue. At the same time, he was made officially responsible for all the bank's relations with the public and regulatory bodies. The reorganization was quite major. All the functions of public relations, advertising and communication, and executive recruitment and selection were given to him. With these resources, it was felt that he could develop and implement the integrated public affairs strategy for the many sides of the social, political, and regulatory milieu in which the bank was increasingly having to deal. Conceptually, the president and the senior vice president saw the need to consciously manage the company's social circumstances as systematically as had been traditionally necessary for economic and business problems.

The Wilmington situation served further to reinforce the authority of the new position and structure, reemphasizing its purpose. Exigencies as well as the nature of the problem made it advisable to designate the newly incorporated appointee with full presidential authority to deal with the branch closure and its ramifications. This gave him power to "subpoena" any personnel and documents as necessary and to convene any meetings at any time according to needs. Further, any instructions issued by the senior vice president of public affairs in connection with Wilmington were to be regarded with the same authority as those originating from the president himself.

Review

Little more could have been done to consolidate response than the actions described in the section above. Gradually a way was found, by influencing opinions and reconciling competing interests, for the branch to be closed at the end of 1978. Thus the initiated response succeeded. But the branch closure was more significant at Columbus Bank for its role in bringing about a new and systematic way of managing social and related issues.

Looking longer term, the bank formalized a social response system around the organization. Instructions such as never discussing profits, costs, or revenues to outsiders began to emerge. Clarification developed concerning job responsibilities, interrelationships among the advertising, public relations, and other parts of the newly constituted public affairs department, and other initially uncertain aspects of the departmental interrelationships. Similarly, personnel as a whole became more sensitive to where social issues might arise, consulting the specialists accordingly. Overall, the bank became increasingly confident that its reorganization and associated steps prepared it well for the future social and regulatory atmosphere. If emergencies continued to occur, the organization was in place to deal with them.

DeVito Power

DeVito Power is an Italian company that lost virtually all its market due to the steep rise in crude oil prices around 1973 and 1974. Almost their sole business was the supply of a large proportion of the equipment necessary for construction of fossil and nuclear power generation stations in Italy. Although the severity of the situation was tempered by an eight- to ten-year lead time from order to completion, it was clear at the end of 1973 that almost no new business from its only market (the Italian power generation industry) could be expected for many years.

Vulnerability was even further aggravated by the structure of the Italian domestic power generation station industry. The highly centralized electricity supply organization (government owned) was dominant, holding within its ranks a large amount of the expertise necessary to the construction of a whole station. Manufacturers of the installed equipment, like DeVito, only dealt with their isolated parts of the whole. Their in-house expertise was rather like a mirror of the customer requests that the electricity supply organization made and no more. This structure had been in place since just after the Second World War, so it was well established.

The extremity of the situation was almost as profound to DeVito as was its most obvious solution—to enter world markets in power generation stations. In the near future it was also evident that the specific markets would have to be those of the Middle East and oil-producing nations in general. For all that the answer was apparent, how to set about it was much less clear and proved to be an even greater challenge than almost any one expected. Before the end of this complicated administrative response, DeVito Power was a changed company.

New Customer Requests

Contrary to the domestic customer relationships, Middle Eastern consumers demanded that one contract exist between the purchasing government and the leading contractor. Risk was therefore entirely shifted from buyer to seller, and the integration between the varied aspects of power station construction had to be completely managed within a consortium or sole contractor. DeVito entered the highly competitive market with bids on likely contracts and the company was successful in winning three contracts.

All of them were for small installations—typical, in size and technology of power stations built by DeVito in Italy around the 1950s. This was part deliberate and part serendipity (the emerging countries mainly have small concentrations of population and industry). Certainly the outcome was favorable, because it limited risk but still provided sufficiently valuable learning experiences. Losses were considerable on all the first bid contracts because of unforeseen but expensive difficulties.

Examples of problems that had to be overcome in the early days of the export marketing strategy included the provision of transportation and differences in customer/company attitudes toward cost overruns. Infrastructure had to be built in many cases, including streets, railways, harbors, and boats. Although partly foreseen, the inadequacy of existing facilities in the countries was not apparent until existing facilities were tested. As a result, project budgets were greatly exceeded but customer governments were uncooperative on the matter of compensating for these errors of costing and judgment by the company.

It was a contrasting attitude to that of the power industry in Italy, where cost overruns had always been seen as part of natural risks of business to be discussed and shared with customers according to circumstances. In fact, one purchasing government could not meet final payments. Although the problem was discussed at the level of the Italian government initially, as other problems had also been, DeVito ultimately found themselves in the position of raising money from the international private banking community for their customer. This and other problems were unprecedented in the company's previous domestic experience and were additional to the predictable but continuing challenge of managing consortia and whole projects. It was these more persistent aspects of their new business that had the greatest impact on DeVito Power.

Organization

It was perhaps natural that a matrix organization should be adopted to manage the new challenges. Grouping engineering specialists into teams beneath a project manager with profit responsibility was a logical way of building the gaps in their technology yet imposing financial and commercial discipline. For DeVito, the method did not work well. The frequent traits of the system—full responsibility but limited authority in the hands of the project manager, and the tendency for team members to play off their positions against two bosses—more than offset the benefits of the organizational system.

Instead, experience with early work and early use of matrix organization suggested a different approach. It was found that each project logically split into several phases, as follows:

proposal and negotiation

order initiation (subcontractor quotes confirmed or modified)

final definition and optimization of project details

realization of requirements and final purchasing

on-site erection and commissioning

running and service

Each phase was found to benefit from quite different types of expertise and management personality, and so it was logical to organize around them. For example, more sale-oriented personnel were necessary for the first phase. For definition and optimization, deep engineering skills were necessary, and for on-site work a practical, almost bivouac, attitude was beneficial as well as knowledge of the construction industry.

A structure arose where each phase contained within it people of appropriate character and technical background. Specialized groupings then began to materialize within each function. Thus on-site work split into the functions of planning, erection, commissioning, and start-up, and the engineering area began to separate out into the definition and optimization functions. The structure that emerged can be described as phase-functional.

However, the organization question is rather like the tip of an iceberg—it is merely suggestive of a much deeper set of changes that entry into the new market brought about for the company. Some of the other changes that entry into Middle Eastern markets brought about are briefly discussed below.

Other Changes

Language usage was one of the more apparent changes in the company. In the late 1960s it was an unwritten rule that Italian should be spoken at all times. With most engineers partly trained in the English language it would otherwise have been quite natural to occasionally lapse into English—especially for the many technical words. Young engineers found it necessary to invent translations for *hardware*, *software*, and other words to keep beyond senior management criticism. With the drive into Middle Eastern export markets, use of the English language became at least a necessary evil. As the lingua franca of many of their new customers, it was essential to develop it within the company. The position swung so far that the company provided internal training courses in English, and it became common to hear the language used in meetings and in corridors.

An even more profound illustration of the cultural change that had come about in the company is provided by the breakdown of organizational hierarchies demanded in the matrix structure and the phase-functional form that finally materialized. Previously the company had a highly formalized set of personal relationships bounded by rigid superior subordinate relationships. Such a mechanistic organization would be a reasonable assumption for the company in its original circumstance of a slowly changing and low-risk environment. Now the habits and attitudes that went along with the more comfortable past were put aside in favor of the uncertainty of roles and relationships associated with faster changing environments.

On a more practical level, DeVito Power was now mainly selling smaller, lower technology equipment. Research and development had to be redefined in line with the new needs. Some budgets were trimmed and others enhanced as necessary to the new focus in the business. Similarly the type of engineer and the type of satisfactions that he could obtain from employment in the company changed. At the risk of oversimplification, new personnel tended to be more entrepreneurial, action-oriented engineers. A heavier research emphasis in personnel was more fitting before entry to Middle Eastern Markets, but emphasis on quick, practical solutions to more immediate problems was more appropriate after the entry.

A rather different kind of company came about in a little over five years. At the end of the 1970s the company was beginning to work smoothly again. Lessons were learned from the small, early projects to the extent that some phases, for example, the generation of a proposal, could be completed to a higher quality in one third of the original time. Mistakes were much less frequent and organizational tensions were now at an acceptable level. Reasonable profits were now being made on the export projects to counterbalance termination of cash flows from domestic work.

The account of the response of DeVito Power to loss of its sole market completes the presentation of data collected for response in complex settings. Complex settings were proposed in chapter 3 as organizationally diverse, technically complicated, and culturally rigid, and the details of the five investigated companies seem consistent with these expectations.

It was also proposed in chapter 3 that these characteristics of complex organizational settings would result in relatively complicated response situations. Broadly, this expectation has been met for all the ten responses investigated in complex settings. The implications of a discontinuity were frequently misconceived or, at least, improperly understood, and the technical and organizational aspects were often found to be comprehended only slowly and with difficulty by the managers within the organizations. Decisions were certainly taken in an incremental and testing fashion and usually involved complicated patterns of adoption and dissemination as the various and diverse departments, subsidiaries, and managerial levels interacted in the development of a given response.

With these provisional conclusions relating to response in complex organizational settings, the next chapter continues to explore decision processes but in the context of a divisional organizational setting.

12
Generaltex's Industrial Products Division

T he Industrial Products Division of Generaltex provides the first opportunity in this study to observe responses within a divisional setting. Expectations of organizationally focused, technically controlled, and culturally professional features of a divisional structure presented in chapter 3 can begin to be appraised with this case. Despite this organizational distinction, study of the division's responses to a demand surge, cost inflation, recession, and cash shortage should, according to propositions 6 to 9 of chapter 3, show the same fundamental decision processes as those observed in Prosper and Atlas and the three other researched complex settings. Each response is described in turn in the following pages after a description of the division itself.

The Industrial Products Division

The Industrial Products Division (IPD) generated around $350 million in annual sales in the early 1970s, which supported a net income of about $25 million and accounted for less than 5 percent of Generaltex's total business. There were twenty-five operating units in Generaltex, and they were organized as divisions. IPD was one of the few interests of the company which was not wholly related to the textile industry, although a small part of its business was in the supply of industrial substances for some specialized applications in textile manufacture. IPD was quite distinctive within Generaltex in selling to diverse industrial customers rather than to wholesale, retail, and consumer customers associated with textiles.

The prevailing management philosophy in Generaltex placed heavy emphasis on planning. The planning cycle was annual, both within the operating units and for the company as a whole. Each year, plans were presented to Generaltex's centralized planning group for debate and authorization. When approval had been obtained, the operation of the various divisions was supervised predominantly by means of variances in key variables such as cost and manpower. Although planning was a centralized activity and one that was dominant in the company, practically all other management issues were devolved to divisions.

It is reasonable to describe Generaltex as a highly decentralized company and one that allowed its divisions a large degree of autonomy once charter was defined and planning requirements and procedures were satisfied. The group's commitment to planning had given Generaltex a distinct orientation towards systematic management. Such matters as objectives, resource allocations, portfolios, incentive schemes, manning, financial matters, and other aspects of management had been carefully analyzed and developed into orderly and explicit formulas which applied across the whole company.

The acrophylic substances which IPD manufactured and sold are renowned for their lubrication properties, fire and general thermal resistance, water repellence, and also a molding capability which produces a similar appearance to rubber but has far higher thermal, electrical, and weathering resistance. Among the fields in which acrophylics find application are as engine oil additives, defoaming agents, rust preventatives, hydraulic oils, fire resistant moldings, sealants, and gaskets. These ubiquitous substances find application in almost every industry, but their high cost lends them only to specialized uses. Consequently IPD had a very large number of industrial customers, none of which represented more than 2 or 3 percent of total revenue.

The many properties of acrophylics allowed IPD and its competitors to sustain growth at around 10 percent per annum from the 1950s. New product development had been the primary force behind this growth and had been successful in generating many new applications and in opening up many new markets. In this exercise, the physical properties of acrophylics were important. These substances played an invaluable role in satisfying increasingly more stringent legal and performance requirements in products. The fire resistance and efficient sealing capability of the acrophylics substance led to its use in many consumer and industrial products where fire hazards existed. Increasingly more complex machinery design encouraged the use of acrophylics for their superior lubricating properties and excellent thermal and abrasion resistance in high-speed and temperature situations in manufacturing.

The United States manufacturing and office operations of IPD were all located on one site. IPD's managers described its organizational structure as quasi-matrix. One side of the matrix consisted of three product departments and one international department, and the other side of several functional areas. The full organizational structure is diagrammatically represented in figure 12–1.

Product departments reflected a logical categorization of the acrophylic products in terms of their properties, applications, and customers. The classification of products into departments was: lubricants; moldings; specialized products; there was also an international department. The other side of the matrix constituted the functional areas of sales, finance, research and development, and manufacturing. There was also a set of staff functions designated as personnel,

Figure 12-1. IPD's Organization

planning, and legal advisers. Each of the heads of these eleven parts of IPD reported directly to a general manager who, in turn, reported directly to corporate headquarters. The size of the management team and the nature of its responsibilities enabled its members to work in close proximity. Informal day-to-day communication supported by infrequent meetings was generally adequate to meet integrative needs.

The acrophylic industry was concentrated into a few large suppliers both within the United States and worldwide. IPD held nearly 40 percent of the United States market, and Fisher Corporation, the other large competitor, held just over 40 percent. The two other dominant competitors, General Products and Utility Chemicals, held approximately 10 percent and 5 percent market shares respectively. Worldwide market shares were small. European and Japanese competitors were not as established in their domestic markets as the United States companies were in their home market.

Demand Surge

During the surge in demand in late 1973 and early 1974, the plant operated at peak capacity. At times it was necessary for production managers to improvise equipment or contract out work just to keep pace. Raw material inventories were allowed to expand to insure against material shortages and the possibility of work stoppages. IPD's response to the demand surge is an example of an operating response. Managers reported organizational processes—meetings, corridor communications, and the like continued according to usual formats. Leadership patterns were reported to be as usual. In all the above respects and the basic nature of the discontinuity, this demand surge represents an operating response during which the various elements of the division's operations were realigned to match the revised supply and demand levels. Interesting, however, was an important administrative subresponse that attempted to support the unprecedented but also somewhat contrary position of demand far exceeding the usual manufacturing levels.

Excess demand provided, for the first time, the opportunity to be selective on the seeking and acceptance of orders. It allowed management to attempt to optimize its product mix, but this required a change of thinking within the company. Under investment policies established over more than a decade, IPD had operated with excess capacity. Sales orders were evaluated on an incremental cost basis, and virtually any order which returned a positive contribution was accepted. However, as plant volume increased in the early 1970s and capacity became constrained, orders had to be evaluated not only in terms of the difference between variable cost and price but also in terms of the amount of plant time, labor, and materials required. Consequently, sales efforts became selective for the first time.

Salesmen were briefed to seek and accept orders which met profitability criteria and also those that would more effectively coordinate sales activities with manufacturing capabilities and financial objectives. Sales management began development of a sales incentive program which was later named the profit factor program. The value of the sales per product was to be multiplied by a coefficient which would reflect the margin and other priorities (such as changes in plant volume, raw material costs, and market building) for that particular product for the month in question. The adjusted total sales value would then be the basis for evaluating and rewarding each salesman's performance. As it happened, the profit factor program was not completely in place by the end of the third quarter of 1974 and, because demand had fallen, it was not used for the purpose for which it was devised. It was, however, pressed into service, after some modification, to meet the need to attract orders for which immediate or early payment would be received when this became a priority in the 1975 recession.

This example suggests the possibility of subresponses of a different type being present within a response of a given type. The reason for the development of the profit factor program is simple to find—while the demand surge was an operating response according to all the criteria suggested before, it combined the additional need for a small proportion of nonmanagerial personnel to approach their job from a somewhat contrary perspective. Salesmen had now to think selectively in circumstances of excess demand, where previously their job had been one of aggressively promoting demand unselectively. A reorientation in the thinking and behavior of personnel was shown in earlier case reports to be characteristic of administrative response. It was natural, therefore, that this predominantly operating response be usefully accompanied by a component administrative subresponse to meet the special need for vital reorientation of a small number of nonmanagerial but somewhat autonomous personnel to a very different perspective concerning their jobs.

Cost Inflation

Cost inflation happened simultaneously with the demand surge. Several management actions combined to achieve the substantial price increases necessary to counter the rapid increase in costs. Foremost, however, was a control system implemented by the general manager, designed to bring about a thorough review of prices. This response is, therefore, primarily administrative in permanently amending operations to cope with inflation. It represented a considerable challenge for the division because of unknown demand elasticities and general uncertainty.

From late 1973 and through 1974, total costs increased by about 70 percent. More rises in costs were expected, and it was judged likely that cost inflation would become a permanent feature of the industry. In late 1973, when the surge in demand was experienced, it was also an important objective to raise prices to cover these costs as well as to maximize production and optimize product mix.

Given that the last rise in the average selling price had occurred in 1958, the increasing of prices was a challenge to management. A variety of questions were encountered, many for the first time. Which company would have to be the first in the industry to raise prices? Which items should be marked up and by how much? Which markets were most price sensitive? Should gross margin percentage or total contribution dollars be the main criterion? The first price increase was 2 percent. Although small, it represented a dramatic change in policy. In order to avoid an avalanche of negative reaction, management advised all customers, explaining how the rising cost of materials had necessitated the price adjustment. Two months after this first difficult step, prices were being raised 10 to 20 percent without exceptional caution.

The origin of the need for price increases can be traced back to generalized concern by Generaltex corporate headquarters. Company planners had reasoned that the rate of inflation was soon to become of such an order that productivity improvements without price increases would no longer be adequate to maintain acceptable levels of profitability into the future. As a result, in the early 1970s pricing emerged as an important issue within the group. The significance of this is that it was expected that the problem would be addressed in the plans of each of the divisions and the respective management directed to determine a policy on the issue. Pricing was highlighted at the annual presentation of corporate plans, and the procedure forced general managers to be assessed against their achievement on pricing. The way in which the matter was dealt with by each planning unit in Generaltex varied according to the nature of the cost increases and pricing difficulties which applied in each case.

For IPD the issue was of great importance because of their consumption of oil and energy as principal feedstocks. The full impact of cost increases in early 1974 coincided with the arrival of a new general manager to the division. He recognized that a system had to be developed which would force managers to review their prices. A price change form was devised which was sanctioned by the company lawyer, and antitrust legislation was evoked to reinforce its importance. On the form it was necessary that a price recommendation be made on every product, even if it was to hold prices at current levels. The forms were reviewed by the general manager's office and were personally signed by him if approved.

To smooth market acceptance of the price rises, the general manager made several presentations to meetings of major end-user industries. In Chicago he addressed the "white goods" industry, announcing recently devised new applications for industrials. He also used the occasion to announce that domestic appliance manufacturers should expect a 60 to 70 percent price increase on most products and to explain the reasons for the increase. Such speeches were widely reported in the media, which helped in dissemination. For example, the Chicago speech was reported in Britain in the *Synthetic Rubbers Journal.*

Individual pricing decisions were difficult, particularly in the specialized products segment. For most products the management of IPD was forced to increase their prices before their competitors. It would have been simple enough to raise prices 20 percent across the board. However, markets and products differed in price sensitivity, and not all products had the same profit margins. Prices were raised by different amounts according to these considerations, but in this way many decisions were made hastily on each department's hundreds of products. Some decisions turned out not to be optimal, and some introduced unforeseen complications in competitive reactions.

Some mistakes were inevitable, and foam molding materials for the furniture industry are a prime example. Foam acrophyle is molded to cast woodlike plastic parts for furniture. These products were among IPD's highest margin items and represented a $12 million market in 1973. The furniture industry, however, was hit hard by the recession and could ill afford additional costs. In 1974 IPD raised prices on foam molding products by about one third. Fisher Corporation did not do so, and IPD suffered. In the space of six months, their market share dropped from 75 percent to 50 percent, and they lost over $1 million of business. In October of 1974, when the furniture market collapsed, prices were reduced to meet competition. IPD market share returned to 75 percent in one year, but volume was down about a third. The company later felt that they should have priced for contribution dollars rather than for profit margin, but their emphasis on gross margins affected judgment at the time.

As a result of price increases by all three product departments, the average selling price per pound of finished material rose from $2.70 in 1973 to $3.20 in 1974. These increases reduced the profit squeeze but did not eliminate it entirely, as gross margins dropped 6 percent. As a result of budget pruning, however, net income as percentage of sales was increased slightly.

Margins were also enhanced by process improvements. The 300 and 400 percent increase in raw material costs brought about a reexamination of the efficiency of production methods. Before 1974, around 2 percent waste was created. Engineering modifications later reduced raw material wastage to negligible amounts. The higher cost of raw materials forced the company's engineers to think and design in an entirely different manner. The financial benefit of the investment of $12 million on the revised plant was considerable, showing only a fifteen-month payback.

While the pricing initiatives arose from some definite management decisions, occasional mistakes and false starts were made in accomplishing the full range of price increases. One common feature of the IPD responses presented so far with those of the oil companies' responses is that they contained sub-responses which were, in some senses, trials. Although the IPD's organization and environment were simpler than those of Atlas and Prosper, an equivalently evolutionary route to response formulation and implementation was found in all of the IPD responses.

Recession

Over 1974 and 1975, the dramatic and sudden recession in demand for acrophylic products precipitated a number of rapid actions by IPD management. Decisions were executed by respective functional areas. Integration across the individual parts of the company was accomplished as customarily by informal communications, augmented by some meetings. This account describes an operating response in seeking to maintain operations in the face of a major fall in demand.

Actions tended to fall into two groups: those relating to the need to obtain sales, and those relating to the cost cutting associated with the demand downturn. Their instigation was a mixture of the clarity of the need for certain actions at the level of the IPD functional management, together with the leadership of the general manager and his immediate subordinates. The most important of these actions are listed and briefly described below:

Sales efforts were reinforced and the dire need for sales was stressed throughout the company. Managers of the product departments allocated some of their time to selling. Research and development and other nonselling parts of the divisions were alerted to identify business wherever it might exist. The sales force was temporarily restructured to transfer effort from long-term sales prospects to immediate possibilities. Bargain sales were held at which slow-moving inventory was offered for cash.

Inventories were reduced to free working capital, although this had the potential of adversely affecting sales in removing immediate availability of some items.

Manpower reductions were achieved, mainly by the dismissal of nearly two hundred hourly employees and the resignation without replacement of a proportion of sales force personnel.

Advertising and promotion budgets were drastically lowered to 1 percent of sales from the 3 percent which had been the norm before 1974.

Short term cuts in research and development expenses were put into effect, and work was concentrated on projects with a near-term payoff.

General expenses were heavily restrained. First-class air transport was stopped, and at the height of the recession it was literally impossible to buy a pencil without written approval.

Many customers stopped paying at the same time that they stopped ordering. The recession made many customers illiquid, and there were many bankruptcies. Credit policy was toughened and efforts were strengthened in collecting doubtful receivables. Supply was withheld from bad payers for the first time in the history of the company, although sales revenues were also vital to IPD. The profit factor program was used for the first time with a weighting applied in favor of salesmen securing orders for prompt payment.

Cost-cutting actions described above and others were consolidated in the financial plan for 1975. Original estimates were made in June of 1974, and

Table 12–1
Comparative Income Statements

	1974 Actual	1975 Original Plan	1975 Revised Plan
Sales	380.5	451.0	328.0
Lubricants domestic	126.3	159.9	126.3
Lubricants international	24.6	35.3	26.2
Moldings domestic	75.4	90.2	68.9
Moldings international	18.9	24.6	16.4
Specialized products domestic	90.2	102.5	67.2
Specialized products international	45.1	38.5	23.0
Cost of goods sold	167.3	211.6	154.2
Gross margin	213.2	239.4	173.8
Total divisional expenses	77.1	87.7	56.6
Lubricants	33.6	41.8	23.8
Moldings	16.4	17.2	12.3
Specialized products	15.6	14.8	11.5
Sales Department	11.5	13.9	9.0
Other overhead expenses	75.4	86.1	68.0
Central R&D	.8	.8	.8
Advertising	2.5	4.9	1.6
Other G&A expenses	72.1	80.4	65.6
Income from sales	60.7	65.6	49.2
Other income	3.3	3.3	3.4
Total income	64.0	68.9	52.6
Taxes	31.2	32.8	24.6
Net income after taxes	32.8	36.1	28.0
Depreciation	18.9	22.1	18.0
Dividends	16.4	19.7	14.8

these included sales of $500 million. Sales at that level were expected to require plant and equipment additions of approximately $50 million and significant increases in working capital. By the end of 1974, it was realized that these original sales estimates would have to be sharply reduced and plant and equipment expenditures scaled down. Based on revised sales forecasts received from each product department, a completely revised budget was formulated in late 1974 for 1975. In spite of recent developments, the net income goal for the year was set at $28 million. It was also agreed that fixed plant and equipment investment should be limited to the $12.5 million required for replacement and safety improvements. Tentative plans called for a reduction of working capital investment of approximately $5 million compared to 1974 levels. The actual figures for 1974 and the original and revised plans for 1975 are reproduced in table 12–1.

This operating response bears the same kind of relationship to the company's organization and systems as the two responses to the oil embargo did to the organization and systems of the oil companies. In all three cases, the managers understood their circumstances and proceeded to make subresponses reasonably confidently. For IDP, almost textbook solutions were possible for some problems. Even the upward and downward shifts of authority and responsibility, the revision of priorities, and the faster pace of communications among management occurred at IPD during the recession as at Prosper and Atlas during the embargo. The division had the systems, structure, skills, and orientation needed to execute fully this operating response.

Cash Shortage

Management of IPD during the recession was, for all practical purposes, accomplished without formal interaction with corporate headquarters. This next response, however, employed a fuller interface between the division and the headquarters. The shift from the company's role as a cash recipient to that of the tighter, less growth-oriented role of a cash donor was described by one of the managers as philosophical, in that it changed the way in which managers looked at their jobs. In amending operations, the cash shortage is therefore an administrative response.

A priority was to make the whole company's personnel conscious of the concept of cash flow as quickly as possible. A sensitivity was developed so that within about two years managers were originating and making decisions as necessary to a well-managed cash flow. Other employees also modified the way they performed their jobs so that cash flow would be maximized as a result of the actions of management. This revised mentality towards business was common throughout Generaltex divisions. To help business adjust, Generaltex introduced some corporate-wide management courses on cash flow management.

The newly appointed general manager of IPD quickly established the fresh viewpoint necessary to achieve cash generation in the organization by accordingly modifying the company's goals. He announced that the primary mission for IPD was now to be a strong number two in the industry and not to strive for market leadership, which had been the goal. Financial goals were also modified from an emphasis on maximizing earnings to one of optimizing net income, liquidity, and return on investment through the management of working capital and capacity investment.

The new awareness of cash flow came about in IPD in this and other ways but mainly by the adoption of new or revised administrative procedures and approaches. Recommendations for methods of increasing cash flow were prepared by IPD's corporate planner and reviewed by the general manager. Implementation mainly fell to the financial manager, whose responsibility it became to supervise the design and adoption of revised systems as well as the management of their parameters as the company's environment changed. Recommendations focused on three areas of IPD's operations: (1) working capital conservation, (2) capacity investment strategy, and (3) funds allocation procedure.

Working Capital Conservation

IPD monitored its levels of inventories and receivables in relation to sales volume. Historically the division incorporated a margin of comfort into these levels to insure that no sales were lost due to overly strict credit terms or inventory shortages. With the business downturn, inventories and receivables had climbed sharply and needed to be brought back to below historical norms in order to meet goals of working capital reduction.

In preparing the five-year plan, it was estimated that by instituting tighter inventory controls and utilizing computer programs it would be possible to operate with significantly lower ratios of inventories and receivables. It was calculated that by switching to a lean policy, working capital investment by 1980 would be $17 million less than it would be under the traditional "margin of comfort" policy.

A credit control system was introduced so that shipments could not be released without a customer's credit rating. When the system was installed it became possible to manipulate the selectivity of the credit policy by differently interpreting the allocated ratings according to IPD's working capital position. Equivalent tighter controls were also put into effect on inventories. The lower reordering level and smaller order quantities increased the risk of stock depletion but more accurately reflected the more stringent working capital goals.

Capacity Investment Strategy

Before 1974 capacity investment had always been managed on the basis of building for optimistic assessments of market demand. This had allowed the company to capitalize on sudden spurts of demand, but had produced excess capacity for short periods of time. Lead times for investment varied considerably, from twelve–eighteen months for equipment at the finishing end of the manufacturing process to three years for new reactors and distillation columns.

After consideration, management decided on a level of investment which would link with forecasts of future demand termed the most likely as opposed to the optimistic. It was further decided to opt for a phased program which would be accelerated or decelerated in the face of spurts or downturns in future sales and cash flow. Building in such flexibility would help to compensate for the risk of loss of sales, which was the major disadvantage of adopting a more conservative investment strategy.

Funds Allocation Procedure

Of particular concern in the allocation of funds were those termed creative. These were essentially funds diverted from net income for investment in future earnings through research and development and related activities. In a stringent cash environment the allocation of such funds became all the more critical, and a system had to be developed that would reflect revised priorities.

The company's clusters of products were classified into three groups according to their position on the product life cycle. Lower parts of the cycle were designated as build–push and allocations were to be generous for good prospects. Products deemed to be around the top of the cycle would primarily be judged as sources of current or near-term earnings, and consequently investments would only be made on a selective basis. Products in the decline stage would be systematically managed so that funds were harvested from them for investment in newer products. This method of management of creative funds is considered to have brought about a considerable improvement in margins.

Postscript

From 1975 and onwards IPD experienced new and higher levels of profitability. The return on sales ratio was improved by 25–30 percent over the period 1975–77, and the return on investment ratio by 40–50 percent. IPD management also sought to manage the business through cycles and achieved only a 1 percent swing on return on sales as opposed to the 4 percent swing common before 1975. Management also noted that the old relationship between environmental demands requiring the substitution of acrophylics for materials with lesser properties assisted in this financial improvement. Many new products were developed, of which those employed to meet legislative developments in safety and reduction in weight of automobiles greatly assisted the achievement of these results. Despite these favorable trends, the major reason for the company's success was thought to be the improved attention to margins, price, process efficiency, working capital conservation, and improved funds allocation.

The organizational setting of IPD seems well described as organizationally focused, technically controlled, and culturally professional. The observations made for this case strongly suggest that response in divisional settings is rather different from that experienced in the complex settings along the lines indicated in chapter 3 (table 3–2). The underlying basis of decision processes seems, however, to be largely equivalent to that experienced in the complex organizational settings of chapters 5 to 11. For example, responses involved small steps (relative to uncertainty) from the original conditions (the initial 2 percent price increase before more substantial price increases were implemented), the use of devices already held close by (the techniques used for cash management were already present in Generaltex), the presence of satisficing decisions (many prices were set nonoptimally because of ignorance of demand elasticities) within planning frameworks and analysis, and the presence of a general structure to decisions (typically (1) a warm-up period, such as the corporate discussion on the need to raise prices, followed by (2) the development of a decision or decisions such as the design of the price-change form and the addressing of pricing on all products, followed by (3) the implementation and adjustment of a decision such as price corrections in the face of competitor reactions).

A total of fourteen responses in six companies have now been described—ten responses in five complex organizational settings, and four in one divisional setting (IPD). Three more are now to be described that took place in the National Lighting Division, a divisional setting also.

13
TCA's National Lighting Division

The following three responses in the National Lighting Division of TCA provide further insight into response in divisional settings. "Inflation Beaters" describes how the company revised its marketing approach after energy price increases threatened their market for bulbs. "Far Eastern Vehicle Bulbs" describes how the company reorganized to counter inexpensive imports that risked taking its market. "Safety Legislation" describes how the company responded to challenging safety standards imposed by the United Kingdom government. First, some background to the division itself is to be presented before each of these administrative responses is addressed in turn.

These responses are, however, distinctive to many of the other responses presented in this study. Inflation Beaters and Safety Legislation are largely confined to the respective functions within the division, as were the supply function responses to the oil embargo in Prosper and Atlas reported in chapter 10. This possibility was identified in chapter 3, where it was indicated that such a functional response, although not embodying a usual proportion of cross-organizational interaction, would largely reflect the overall features of the setting as a whole—complex, divisional, or simple. In agreement with these expectations, Inflation Beaters and Safety Legislation display relatively more focused and more orderly responses than would be expected for responses embracing a division as a whole, because of their relative divorce from overall divisional interactions.

Far Eastern Vehicle Bulbs is also somewhat anomalous. Although an organizationwide response, it is exceptional among the other responses investigated in divisional settings in affecting only a highly specialized proportion of the business of National Lighting. Vehicle bulbs constituted less than 5 percent of revenue and a smaller percentage of net income. As a result, relatively greater complexity was found in the response, due partly to the need for cross-functional integration for which there were no formal mechanisms and for which there was relatively little motivation within each of the functions.

The National Lighting Division

The National Lighting Division of TCA Corporation manufactures bulbs, light fittings, and related items. Bulbs predominate, and accounted for almost 80 percent of revenue. The overall market extended to a number of technically different products, end use applications, and customer segments; National Lighting was active in almost all areas. It is estimated that there were nearly five thousand different items offered by National Lighting. The business was characterized by the relatively inexpensive nature of its products, large production quantities (several million per annum), and high mechanization in production.

TCA had widely diversified from its original textile base to include both heavy and light engineering, of which the National Lighting Division was one part. TCA had adopted a strategy of almost complete decentralization. There were very few groupwide formal instructions or directives or centrally organized administrative procedures, and all the fifty or so companies that made up the group had substantial autonomy. The high degree of decentralization, however, was complemented by strong financial discipline. Divisions of TCA were controlled through the frequent reporting and analysis of financial statements at corporate headquarters.

National Lighting was organized along conventional functional lines, as diagrammatically represented in figure 13–1. Excepting the managing director, there were two levels of senior management. Four directors headed up functional areas of managing, marketing, finance, and research and development. At the next level, but still reporting directly to the managing director, were a company lawyer and three managers responsible for distribution, purchasing, and personnel.

Although this organizational hierarchy existed, it tends to misrepresent the reality of the management situation in National Lighting. A philosophy of informal working relationships was promoted by TCA which had been adopted by National Lighting. Distinctions between directors and managers had little meaning in relation to the way the company worked. The management of National Lighting worked as one tightly knit group; managers in one functional area spoke directly and frequently to those reporting within another.

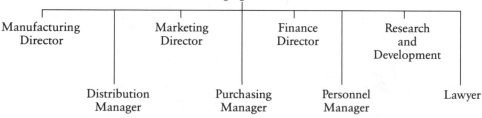

Figure 13–1. National Lighting Division's Organization

Inflation Beaters

The oil price increases of late 1973 and the associated supply difficulties placed the United Kingdom government in the position of having to promote energy saving. Their "Switch Off" campaign on television, through public broadcasts, and other media created an atmosphere of energy consciousness. The great likelihood that customers would use fewer lights and use the remainder for shorter periods of time introduced a serious and unprecedented threat to National Lighting's business. They found that industrial consumers were resorting to measures such as the removal of one bulb in three-bulb units and the removal of entire light fittings that were not absolutely essential. There was every sign that the replacement bulb business was about to experience a serious fall in demand.

Seminars

The energy crisis had built up in terms of its effect on industrial users through November and December 1973. The dark days of January and some scattered industrial action by electric power unions brought the situation to its most extreme point at that time. It was then that a member of the government, driven by concern for energy conservation, suggested that men should shave without artificial light. Members of the marketing department in National Lighting began to realize that if they were not careful they could be without a profitable business in the near future.

No one can be quite certain when or where the original realization arose that a retaliatory effort should be mounted to counteract a reduction in demand. It was over a Friday evening drink that the marketing manager first aired the need to respond to the threat. From this point it emerged that the company had an important story to tell in the use of their products in energy conservation. The basic notion was to begin to persuade customers to replace existing bulbs with those requiring less power. For example, 75-watt bulbs would be used in place of 100-watt bulbs at a 25 percent energy saving. There was also the possibility for encouraging customers to change from relatively inefficient tungsten bulbs to fluorescent tubes in offices, to mercury or high-pressure sodium lamps in factories, and to low-pressure sodium lamps in street lighting.

Savings could be considerable by adopting these replacements. A factory illuminated by tungsten bulbs gets 12 lumens per watt. Replacement with high-pressure sodium lamps gives a rating of 100 lumens per watt at the same energy consumption. That is more than eight times the efficiency. Users could then have the advantage of saving on energy, using fewer lamps, and obtaining more illumination as well. These steps could fulfill the customers' needs for energy conservation in the most functional way, and at the same time stimulate business for National Lighting.

In the winter of 1974, political and general talk was of energy conservation. With public opinion so charged on the subject it seemed natural that National Lighting should promote their views on lighting. The idea of a series of seminars arose within the marketing group. This would be an economical way of disseminating the company viewpoint directly to the leaders of opinion and to sales prospects. One advantage was the speed with which a seminar could be mounted. The development of an advertising campaign or a promotional mail shot would probably have taken a few months. A seminar could be staged in a matter of weeks.

It was recognized in National Lighting that their sales efforts were best directed to the senior management in companies, specifically the managing director, treasurer, and engineering or production managers. The prevailing interest in the topic presented a rare opportunity to carry an effective sales message to such high-level people. Proceedings materialized at a rapid pace, and before the end of January 1974 the first National Lighting seminar on energy conservation had taken place. The company had been fortunate in securing a senior politician with a portfolio for energy to chair this first seminar.

The day's success was readily acknowledged by the participants and showed promise of resulting in a series of sales for National Lighting. The encouraging results endorsed National Lighting's intention of arranging a series of seminars throughout the country, and the operation went into full gear. Invitations went to several thousand "target participants" in a series of letters from the managing director of National Lighting.

The success of the seminars soon made them a regular promotional activity. They were typically run by regional sales managers, with more than a dozen held in most weeks. In this connection the company developed and maintained a large stock of standard up-to-date presentation material. It was estimated in early 1979 that several hundred such seminars had been conducted and that they were still considered a valuable promotional method.

Inflation Beaters Campaign

The soundness of the marketing concept of linking sales with moves to increasing energy conservation was demonstrated by the early seminars. With the confidence engendered by these successes, the decision was made in February 1974 to mount an advertising campaign based on the same concept. In particular, a pull-out pamphlet was designed for inclusion in the general supplements in the national Sunday newspapers. The campaign was found to be very successful, with high response rates and a high conversion to sales. The promotional vehicle was very much one of presentation of case studies of customers who had generated large energy savings using the services of National Lighting.

It is interesting to note that the company had used exactly the same general approach before the sudden increase in energy costs. Their selling message had been one of stimulating sales by encouraging the replacement of obsolete lighting equipment. Although competitors did not exclude this approach to achieving sales, National Lighting had become somewhat distinguished in the industry in adopting this emphasis in their sales pitch. It was perhaps natural that this same approach should be adopted so forcibly and successfully now that the increase in energy costs had, indeed, rendered so many customers' lighting systems redundant. The case-study approach, implying a third-party endorsement of the promotional message, had been used in the past, but now the case studies became even more persuasive. They showed increased savings and were used more often and to greater effect.

As 1974 progressed, the company's situation became clearer. Higher energy costs were very likely to damage the light-bulb market permanently if efforts to counteract that possibility were not sustained by National Lighting or other parties vested with the same interests. On the other hand, the success of the energy conservation marketing initiative had been encouraging, and it had demonstrated a substantial potential. In December 1974, almost twelve months after the idea to accentuate the energy conservation marketing approach, interested members of the marketing team participated in an informal meeting to generate further ways by which the link with energy conservation could be made even more effective. Several ideas emerged from this meeting and from general "corridor conferences" that are a regular feature of the National Lighting management style. The most significant outcome from these debates was the origination of the term Inflation Beaters and the build-up around this expression of a full-fledged marketing campaign. The approach represented an even heavier emphasis on the same concept of achieving sales by promoting more efficient lighting which used less costly energy.

After four or five months of development work, the Inflation Beaters campaign was introduced in May 1975. Its main thrust was the use of multicolored inserts in the Sunday newspaper supplements which had proven so successful with the campaign's predecessor, the energy conservation promotion. Other successful aspects of this earlier campaign were also retained, some in modified form. One example was the *Lighting Review Report* which was supplied to salesmen to itemize proposed improvements and expected cost savings and to distribute to production managers or other personnel at the prospect site. The report was often used by the prospect for presentation to his or her board to gain acceptance for the lighting recommendation.

Evolution

The Inflation Beaters campaign was still in progress at the end of the 1970s. The principle of the retention of the good and rejection of the unsuccessful had been maintained. The evolution had been along three major axes. Probably the most important one was a gradual expansion of the concept of the replacement of existing facilities. The second was the development of even more creative promotions within the overall Inflation Beaters campaign. The third was a gradual differentiation to include subcampaigns targeted at distinct subsegments of the market; the brewing industry is one example.

To expand on the first, the concept of replacement of existing lighting facilities gradually broadened. The original energy conservation campaign had been most seriously concerned with the replacement of existing bulbs with those using less power. The concept then quickly came to embrace replacement of existing bulbs with those of greater efficiency. As time progressed and the company gained confidence in its approach and learned the strength of the message which they were promoting, the concept broadened to include lighting systems for entire plants, sometimes starting from first principles in determining needs. Replacement of entire lighting installations had been undertaken before autumn 1973, but these occasions were rare and more usually coincided with revisions in the operations of the plant or other facility. As energy costs rose substantially and continually, customers and potential customers began to appreciate the importance and benefits of redesigning whole lighting systems, and they welcomed this broad concept.

For the second direction of evolution, that of increasingly more creative promotions within the general Inflation Beaters campaign, a chronological discussion of examples proves instructive. One of the earliest promotional concepts was a paper jigsaw puzzle with pieces from which the recipient could select key matters appropriate to their existing lighting installation. When assembled and carefully turned over, it spelled out the savings that the potential client could realize by substituting more efficient lamps. Another promotional effort was a direct mail-out of a brochure called *Do-it-Yourself Guide to Lighting Economy*. Simple step-by-step procedures were detailed for the replacement of less efficient fixtures with more efficient, modern industrial light fixtures.

"Motto matching" came next, where different executives (those thought to make up the decision-making unit for lighting equipment) in a target firm were each sent slogans through the mail. If recipients matched them up with each other, in order, the first letters spelled the work *money*. This promotion also invited the company executives to send for details regarding how they might save a good deal of money by contacting National Lighting, promising them a small gift for doing so. In short, Inflation Beaters utilized various promotional techniques, and the general idea seemed to have yet more scope in the future.

The National Lighting approach to stimulating demand for bulbs and fittings was not followed by the other three main competitors in the industry for some eighteen months. Four years later, in 1979, the approach was established across the industry, with the trade association mounting a competition among its members for the best lighting system for energy efficiency. From the start of 1974, National Lighting had increased its share of the industrial market from 30 percent to 35 percent in five years, an exceptional achievement in this highly mature industry. The management has no doubt that the basic concept behind the Inflation Beaters campaign made a major contribution to this success.

Far Eastern Vehicle Bulbs

Successes in sales of industrial light fittings described above contrasts with the mass of problems with which National Lighting had to deal in its vehicle light bulb business. The automobile bulb market had traditionally been a low-priority product area for the firm. It only constituted some 5 percent of revenue and, as a below-average margin product area, it constituted less than the same percentage of profit. National Lighting had held 25 to 30 percent market share since the early days of popular motoring. It was number two in the product area among three significant industry participants. Stability in the marketplace became disturbed in the late 1960s and early 1970s as bulbs entered from Eastern (communist) European countries and then from the low-cost economies of the Far East.

The imports from East Europe were priced lower than the domestic product, but their lower quality helped to retain a normal competitive atmosphere. Market share of the Eastern European product found a nonthreatening level at around 5 percent. Market stability really began to be challenged, however, when Far Eastern countries started manufacturing and exporting automobile bulbs around 1972. These inexpensive imports, although of low quality, met with considerable success, until they held a volume share of 40 to 50 percent of the market for replacement bulbs in 1978. The substantial price advantage of the Far Eastern product was a key factor in their rapid market acceptance. Retail buying price was less then the National Lighting factory standard cost of the equivalent bulb.

Marketing and Loopholes

The marketing approach taken by the Far Eastern vehicle bulb importers was particularly damaging to National Lighting. It was strongest and most effective in its early stages at the retail replacement bulb market where National Lighting had a traditional strength. The small size and low weight of vehicle bulbs contributed to the development of the "Automobile Trunk Brigade." One-man operators visited garages and other retail outlets and dealt directly for cash with immediate supply from their automobile trunk. Retail outlets were happy to risk an unknown brand, since most consumers were uninterested in the origin of a low-value, seemingly homogeneous product. Service garages had a double incentive in that any possible consumer resistance was effectively dispelled at the source when the product would typically be fitted without the purchaser even seeing the item.

Legislative loopholes on labeling also assisted the entry of the Far Eastern product. It was allowable in the United Kingdom for a made-up lighting assembly to bear the identification of the country where it was assembled, although all the components may have been imported. It was also legal for imported bulbs sold in the replacement market to be packed in the United Kingdom and sold in cartons bearing the trademark of a domestic company without stating the country of origin of the contents. These laws had contributed to the development of an independent lighting assembly industry which supplied the completely fitted unit to automobile manufacturers or the complete cartons to retailers.

National Lighting Company's response to these developments evolved as the extent of the Far Eastern import operation materialized through the mid–1970s. Initially, from early 1975, efforts were focused on lobbying the government to protect domestic industry from Far Eastern imports. Later, other steps were taken, including cost reduction and management reorganization to implement several related decisions.

Lobbies

The Lighting Trade Association performed several functions to represent the industry's affairs. Probably of grestest importance was its role in the management of industry affairs with government, often taking the form of lobbying for legislative change. Also prominent among its functions was its statistical information service. The association's members furnished details of their business, which were aggregated and circulated to members in a monthly bulletin. The monthly statistical service also collected import data, so there was an awareness of the extent of foreign imports in the marketplace. It was quite natural, therefore, that the Lighting Trade Association should assume the role of government negotiation as imports of vehicle bulbs (and other types of bulbs to a lesser extent) began to take a significant share of its members' business.

Lobbying initiatives by the association proceeded from about the summer of 1975. Antidumping legislation was invoked to persuade the government to impose import controls and defend the home manufacturer from what was perceived as unfair competition. The possibilities of success were difficult to assess, and the slow pace of the government machine on such matters is, of course, legendary. Through 1976 the industry's initial high hopes of some protection from imports began to fade.

Difficulties in Lowering Unit Costs

In order to become cost competitive with the imports, National Lighting put an investment program into effect. The program was aimed at reducing unit costs by decreasing the proportion of labor costs through higher mechanization. Its intention was to reduce operator levels from the seven or eight persons required for present machinery to three or four. This ambitious plan required the mechanization of operations that had only been done manually in the past. The company set about the purchase, design, and manufacture of machines in their customary way. Except in rare cases the engineering group, who held a high reputation for their abilities, designed, built, installed, and maintained machinery in all the company's factories.

The engineers encountered a few difficulties in meeting the challenge of mechanization required to fulfill these new objectives. As a result, the completion date slipped back from the intended installation during the two-week summer factory closing of 1976. Some six months later, at the end of 1976, with the machinery ready to be installed, the removal of the old plant necessitated a temporary stop in production. Options were either to replace each of the four machines in service one at a time, thus minimizing production disruption, or to shut down and reopen with all-new plant and equipment. The decision was made to lose some production and replace all four machines in one operation. This allowed a concurrent remodeling of floor layout. It was thought that the loss of production could be more or less offset from stock.

Unfortunately, the installation and running-in period did not proceed according to plan. These machines were found to be particularly troublesome, and minor breakdowns were frequent, especially when high speeds were approached. Quality was inconsistent and reject levels were above normal.

Production problems accumulated until supply could not be satisfied. Important customers experienced shortages, and retail and marketing channel intermediaries were without adequate stocks. These supply difficulties intensified through most of 1977 while production improvements had still not reached a level where current demand could be satisfied, least of all where accumulated order backlogs could be tackled. An atmosphere of confusion was developing. Localized difficulties in terms of specific order expedients were clashing with production programs required to regularize the difficulties of the machinery.

Extending order backlogs made priorities progressively more difficult to determine in a production environment which was unaccustomed to irregularities of this order. Traditionally, market stability and several stocking points had made the production task a simple scheduling and programming exercise. The increasing gravity of the situation led to a special meeting convened by the managing director of National Lighting. All the factory and production management were present, as were the product manager and development engineers. The disarray in vehicle bulb operations became highly evident in this more concentrated and formal atmosphere.

Coordinator

After this meeting, the managing director finally became convinced, in searching for a solution to the apparent chaos, that a coordinative manager was required. In his mind as a suitable appointee was one of the more promising young development scientists in the laboratory who had been involved in vehicle bulbs research for some years. In that capacity he had worked closely with the automobile manufacturers and had acquired considerable knowledge that would be useful in the proposed coordinative role. He had also worked as a supervisor and foreman in the factory and had an instinct for that side of the business. The position would serve a second purpose of providing a vehicle for his personal growth towards further management responsibilities.

The appointment was to be temporary. There had been only one other appointment as a coordinator in the history of the company, and there was a feeling that such an appointment should be unnecessary in the normal operation of the business. It did represent, after all, an additional overhead charge in a cost-sensitive company. It would, nevertheless, present an opportunity to test a revised management structure for the company. The managing director decided that the new coordinator should report to him directly. The coordinator's salary and related costs were to remain allocated to his old department's budget, that is, to the laboratory.

The job title was to be simply Coordinator—Vehicle Bulbs; he was to have no staff and no formal authority over the managers in the functional areas of the company on whose services he was going to have to depend. He was to act as a liaison with marketing, production, engineering, and other departments. The performance standards for the appointment were to resolve current production difficulties, reestablish the moter vehicles bulb business as a profitable operation, and regain the market standing of National Lighting vehicle bulbs. Unit production costs had to be reduced to profitable levels, and some marketing initiatives were seen to be necessary to achieve the long-term viability of this sector of National Lighting's business.

Manufacturing Teams

The coordinator identified an immediate priority to be the satisfaction of outstanding orders. A related, but less immediate, need was to manufacture the bulbs more efficiently, so that the best return was obtained from the recent investment in the machinery. To achieve these two goals, he set about developing special project teams. Two teams were formed (one for each of the two factories that made vehicle bulbs), comprising representatives from the engineering development departments, production superintendents, work study experts, fitters, and similar people responsible for technical factory floor operations. In a sense these teams had existed before the coordinator's initiative, in that their various efforts were dependent upon each other. The coordinator's efforts gave new momentum to their teamwork and focused efforts on the problems of vehicle bulbs that were usually of low priority to these personnel.

The gravity of the supply situation at the end of 1977 is illustrated by a telegram received by the managing director from National Lighting's major customer: "You are 500,000 bulbs in arrears. Some orders have been outstanding for more than six months. Inform us how you propose to rectify this situation." With hindsight, it is possible to reflect that the receipt of this telegram was probably the turning point for the recovery of the company's production. It supplied a sense of urgency and reinforced the need for determined effort by the relevant staff. A program was developed by the coordinator with the teams that succeeded in clearing the outstanding situation in seven weeks. From this point through 1978, production speeds and quality were progressively improved. At the autumn of that year, the new plant was thought to be working almost to its full potential.

Marketing Initiation

As production problems were gradually resolved, the coordinator's attentions turned to marketing activities. To deal with marketing problems, the coordinator worked in tandem with the product manager for vehicle bulbs who had full financial responsibility for the marketing performance of the brands. A review was carried out by the two managers on the economics of selling direct in an equivalent manner to the competitor's automobile trunk brigade.

It was decided to give the selling method a trial. For this purpose, a group of twelve salesmen were seconded from the regular sales force on an experimental basis. This initiative was not successful. The company discovered that the costs of running company automobiles and the apparently lower productivity of a regularly employed sales force rendered the operation inviable. It is probable that the vastly lower overheads and the possibility of tax avoidance by independent trunk brigade salesmen provided a comfortable profit, but that the method of operation could not be commercially sound for a full-fledged company such as National Lighting. Another method had to be found.

A decision was made next to give the ordinary sales force some freedom in negotiations. Previously the automotive sector of the business had sold on the basis of a fixed price. It was expected that increased negotiating discretion for salesmen would lead to reduced margins but to increased volume. Apart from the direct incentive to purchasers, the move was also designed to increase the attention and motivation of the sales force. Independent wholesalers were targeted as the priority sector. These institutions supplied the smaller retailing outlet where imports had been most successful in displacing National Lighting.

Sales aids were constructed to act as talking points for the salesmen. The most aggressive one consisted of a small display of Far Eastern Imports which had been purchased at retail and were blatantly defective in their manufacture. A small brochure was also produced which outlined the dangers of this cheaper Far Eastern product.

At the end of 1978, the coordinator was beginning to focus on irregularities in the order-processing system. An order that could not be met by a depot had always been referred to central stores. If they were unable to supply it, a form was dispatched to the plant requesting production. This method had proved to be unresponsive to the pattern of trends in the marketplace. Uneconomic order quantities were often produced; conversely, quantities were sometimes produced that were too large in relation to average demand. Some orders were occasionally withheld before a convenient production run could be programmed, but at the loss of important customer goodwill. The product range was rationalized somewhat, and information flow was improved so that demand planning could be accomplished more satisfactorily.

The other area of special attention in the early part of 1979 was renewed government lobbying to bring in some control over Far Eastern imports. Partly under the coordinator's instigation, the research laboratories undertook some testing of the quality of foreign imports. They were surprised by the findings themselves. It was found that, of the imports tested, one-third yielded less than 75 percent of the rated light output. Even where the light output reached the rated level, the life of the bulbs was significantly shorter than that of the domestic product. It was also becoming clear that the imports did not meet safety standards. These findings renewed hopes that the government might still be persuaded to take action on controlling low-cost imports, but opinions on the prospects of success were divided.

Safety Legislation

While government agencies appeared to be slow in reacting to market threats, implementation of safety legislation was affecting both production systems and costs. Study of National Lighting's response to the introduction of stringent safety legislation provides the first researched example of a social change in a divisional setting. The response process is found to be comparable in many important respects to the others that have been examined.

After several years of debate and satisfaction of certain formalities, the Industrial Safety Legislation of 1976 finally came into effect on December 1st of that year. It had three main aims. The first was concerned with improving safety in the workplace, including manufacturing machinery and other matters such as the safety of gases. The second was concerned with establishing effective systems of safety control within manufacturing plants and a generally increased awareness of safety. The third concern was to achieve an adequate level of training in safety procedures and standards among the work force.

Requirements

Safety legislation had, of course, already been in existence for many years, but this new legislation represented a major tightening of standards and of safety control systems, and it promised to hold serious consequences for most manufacturing operations. A factory inspectorate already existed for the purpose of enforcing the requirements of earlier laws, but that group was inadequately staffed to take on the task of implementing the new legislation. As a result, the factory safety inspectorate was strengthened through increased manpower and training, and it was vested with greater powers to enforce compliance with the new legislation.

The key part of the new legislation was concerned with establishing safety committees and responsive systems of accident and hazard reporting. The demands were exacting in terms of the constitution of the committees and the form of the reporting system. National Lighting had operated a safety committee with periodic meetings and inspections since the 1930s. Systems were established already in the plants for reporting and investigating safety problems and accidents. The company's existing arrangements came close to meeting the requirements of the new legislation, and only small revisions were necessary, such as revised membership of some safety committees and details of accident and hazard reporting systems. Other changes at National Lighting were chiefly directed at giving the existing arrangements more force to meet the full intent of the legislators. More responsibility was devolved to the safety representatives, and efforts were made to disseminate word of their supplemented authority around the factory. For example, color pictures of the safety representatives were posted at appropriate points so that all operators knew, by sight, the person to whom they should report safety matters.

The training requirements of the legislation were also simple for National Lighting to satisfy. The company had a strong local reputation for its training activities from apprentice and operator level up to foreman and fitter level. Safety had always been a matter of importance in National Lighting training. A satisfactory safety record was essential to securing and maintaining the workforce, apart from the pressing humanitarian concerns. Again, the introduction of safety training required only minor variations in content and approach to satisfy the needs of the new legislation.

It was on the issue of machinery safety that the new legislation had the greatest effect on National Lighting. The government's safety inspectorate visited the company in late 1976. As is required by the law, they arrived unannounced and proceeded to inspect the entire factory for nearly a week. The report consisted of comments on the safety weaknesses of machinery, and it was couched in the language of suggestions and comments rather than imperatives. Emphasis was on what are termed pinchings, that is, areas where moving parts mesh and where a hand or other object could be carried into the machinery. Although the addition of guards was a reasonable and simple request, the engineering difficulties in providing many guards were, in fact, considerable. This could be expected to be the case, since the safety consciousness of the company in the past had avoided as many pinchings, and installed as many guards, as technically and economically possible.

Not only did much of National Lighting's machinery work at high speeds, but often there were high localized temperatures designed to weld hard metals (tungsten and platinum, for example). Hard glasses used in bulb manufacture are delicate, and complex mechanical operations have to be performed with thin sections of the material at high speeds. Guards placed around such operations often hampered the operating speeds and dependability because of heat build-ups and other factors. Most important were the problems of adjustment that were introduced by the fitting of guards. In many cases, the machines had been adjusted while in operation. Now the same adjustment necessitated stopping the machine, removing the guards, and then adjusting at a standstill. Not only was this procedure costly and time-consuming, it was often not possible to adjust the machinery as finely as before, reducing manufacturing efficiency still further. It is ironic to note that the provision of guards on some machines actually decreased their safety. Less exact adjustment and absence of continuous observation rendered these machines more likely to break down, thereby increasing the risk of flying glass.

Engineering

The engineering task for existing machinery was a question of making do as well as possible within the technical constraints and the regulations imposed by the factory safety inspectors. Ingenuity was occasionally necessitated, but in the main, the engineering task was to come up with a set of straightforward modifications. The government had produced a copious volume entitled *Codes of Practice* to give clear instructions in the ways specific and commonly occurring safety problems could be dealt with.

Engineering for the design of new machinery was more demanding. Full implications of the newly legislated safety requirements were an overlay to the usual design parameters. Before the new legislation, the engineering designers typically would have confined attention to the technical machine concept and, when it had been constructed, a method would be devised to guard it. This approach was no longer acceptable, since there might not be a satisfactory means to guard the machine. Also, the newly mandated guard standards could easily alter the economic and technical assumptions underpinning machine design. The optimally efficient machine became one where adjustment and maintenance were required less often; that is, greater reliability had to be engineered into design. Guarding also had implications for machine layout in order to avoid heat build-up and other problems. In the future, machines were to be designed with safety legislation implications determining parameters from the ground up.

Engineers had to be trained in the legislative requirements and their translation into machine design. A number of methods were used to alter the orientation of the design engineers and to bring about an efficient adoption of safety factors into machine design. Normal persuasion and feedback managerial methods were, of course, utilized as an everyday process. In addition, engineers were sent to seminars on the technical problems associated with meeting the demands of the safety legislation. Other sources were available and were used, including institute publications, visits to exhibits of operating machines embodying certain principles, and so forth.

Efforts at developing an inching facility on machines is representative of a small number of machine attributes which were improved for the purpose of meeting the design challenges of the new legislation. Inching is a method by which the fitter can switch on a machine for a very short period of time and make adjustments on the basis of his observation. Before the legislation a similar feature had often been available on machines, but the actual sweep of the movement was not precisely controlled. The new safety legislation demanded that an inch had to conform exactly to a predetermined part of an operation. The company was therefore involved in some extra conceptual development work to improve on the accuracy of the device.

Consultants on safety-related technical problems were also brought in to offer novel solutions to problems. A case in point was a series of packaging machines which were guarded by the use of photoelectric cells. Breaking of the narrow beam of light caused the machinery in question to stop immediately. Photoelectric cell technology had not previously been employed by National Lighting. The traditional National Lighting solution of using guards would have been impractical and expensive. The photoelectric cell could have been fitted independently by National Lighting, but on balance, the use of consultants was less expensive and more efficient.

Meeting the safety legislation, as articulated through the safety inspectorate, took National Lighting about two years. By the middle of 1978 all requirements had found technical solutions, and National Lighting was well ahead in implementing all the requirements within the imposed time limits. As well as the nuisance aspect of dealing with what was, effectively, an additional set of management concerns, the exercise had cost the company some improvements in productivity. The routine 3 or 4 percent increase in productivity per annum for the two years since the operation started had not been sustained. It was expected that the old annual increase in productivity would again be attainable once the safety requirements were fully implemented.

Although embracing very different types of situations, there are commonalities among the three responses in National Lighting, as well as between them and those responses recounted in earlier chapters. In all the cases, an evolutionary route to response completion, and the crucial role of specific situational factors to how responses took shape, was observed. As in other cases, trial and error and learning by doing often preponderated over planning or prior analysis.

The three cases presented from National Lighting also illustrate that responses tend to be formed from reemphasizing or bringing into the limelight skills or attributes already held in the corporation before the need for response. Nothing in National Lighting or in the previous cases was invented from scratch for the purpose of response. All of the responses in this corporation grew from some starting point that already existed by accentuating certain products (energy-saving bulbs) or skills (safety engineering), focusing dispersed skills (vehicle bulb manufacture and marketing), or adopting ideas held elsewhere (use of the photoelectric cell).

While the responses in National Lighting were recognized to be somewhat anomalous with regard to others investigated in this study, findings were consistent with those of other responses—given some additional "simplicity" for the functional responses that took place only within the marketing and engineering departments and some additional "complexity" for the response where relevant activities were diffused and initially lacked organizationwide resolve.

The next chapter details five more responses of various types within another four divisional structures.

14
Further Responses in Divisional Settings

Each of the following examples illustrates a response in divisional settings resembling those of the Industrial Products Division and the National Lighting Division. The response of two broadly comparable divisions in the package holiday industry in the United Kingdom, the Carolvale and Ronson Divisions, to a severe fall in demand that occurred in their 1977 summer season are to be recounted first. The response of a division in the welding industry, Weld Division, to a demand fall is to be recounted second. The response of a division in the cardboard container manufacturing industry, Container Division, to (1) a demand surge and (2) the imposition of a three-day work week by order of the United Kingdom government are to be recounted last. These five responses presented here, when added to the seven responses researched in Industrial Products and National Lighting, make a total of twelve responses in six divisional settings.

Carolvale Division and Ronson Division

Carolvale Division and Ronson Division are two of the leading European companies in the package tour business. In this industry, air transport, accommodation, meals, and other vacation items are packaged at one inclusive cost for customers. The accounts describe how the two companies executed operating responses to meet a major fall in demand.

In 1975 to 1976 the pound sterling devalued in relation to most European currencies by about 30 percent. For an industry purchasing several months ahead in stronger currencies and receiving payment in a generally declining currency, difficulties were considerable over that period. Other more detailed matters, however, further increased the challenges to financial prosperity for the researched companies in 1977. The following descriptions relate how Carolvale Division and Ronson Division responded to a major anticipated downturn in demand.

The Package Tour Industry

Business peaks over the summer months for the package tour companies, but most sales are contracted some months earlier, after Christmas and during January. The winter is therefore one of considerable activity as companies strive to attain a high share of the market over the major contract period. As the different companies release their plans for the season, competitive behavior often becomes intense as each company tests the effectiveness of its programs and amends, counters, or repositions its programs according to the results in the marketplace.

Almost all the companies in the industry in Britain produce lavish catalogues of their inclusive offerings which must be available at the end of December of the previous year. Allowing for production and printing, programs specifying flight arrangements, hotels, and all prices must be concluded some months before December. Consequently, at least outline commitment has to be made for aircraft seats and hotel space some eleven or twelve months before the customer actually takes his or her holiday. Several participants in the industry have realized advantages of vertical integration and have acquired their own fleets of aircraft as well as hotels. With these substantial fixed capital investments (around 80 or 85 percent of costs are fixed for some high-volume packages), the operating leverage of package tour companies is high.

A more volatile element in the business arises from the fact that over half the costs are incurred overseas and usually contracted with hotels and airlines in local currency. With many commitments to suppliers made up to a year before payment, and with many customer purchases made six months or more before the vacation takes place, the package tour companies are vulnerable to currency fluctuations at both ends of their business. The impact of costs increases (through foreign currency appreciation or otherwise) on demand can be considerable for this price-elastic luxury purchase. Unfortunately, currency devaluation is often coincident with economic recession, and the combination of both puts double pressure on demand. It was under such circumstances that the package tour companies looked to the industry's summer 1977 prospects in the period before and during Christmas 1976.

Potential problems were further aggravated around 1976 and 1977 by the recent history of the industry. The quadrupling of the oil price in the last months of 1973 dramatically increased industry costs while at the same time reducing aggregate disposable income and, therefore, lowering demand—2.2 million packages were sold in 1973 but only 1.25 million in 1974. The industry leader was forced into liquidation, with many of its customers losing substantial prepayments for their vacations. As a result, consumer confidence was at a low ebb as the industry moved towards its 1977 season.

Nineteen Seventy-Seven

From the day after Christmas to about the 5th of January is the critical time in the package tour industry. Early reservations are taken as an indicator of the quality of the season as a whole and as a testing of competitive strategies. For Carolvale, the ten-day test was alarming, with a 65 percent shortfall in demand over the same period a year before. The corresponding shortfall for Ronson was 35 percent.

It was reported that some package holiday companies were experiencing a 40 percent drop in the number of reservations, but the average drop was thought to be around 20 to 25 percent. The low level of demand reflected the weakness of the national economy, lack of consumer confidence in the industry, resistance to ever-increasing price levels, and fear of price increases between contract and departure (some costs increases were often passed on to the customer as supplemental charges).

An innovation had, however, been introduced to the industry in the summer of 1976. Cosmos, one of the leading package tour operations, had stimulated strong demand by overcoming much of the consumer resistance by guaranteeing prices. As the British arm of a Luxembourg-based, Swiss-owned company, it was perhaps natural that Cosmos should apply its international perspective to foreign currency matters. Using strong Swiss currency to pay suppliers (and presumably hedging in the future currency markets), it was able to insulate itself from the pound sterling devaluation to which its competitors were more vulnerable. It was natural that Cosmos should promote guaranteed pricing in 1977 after its success in gaining market share in the summer of the preceding year. Cosmos's price guarantee strategy therefore exacerbated the more general demand and cost challenges facing Carolvale and Ronson for 1977. Carolvale's response to its early reservations downturn will be described, and then Ronson's will be compared to it.

Carolvale

As might be expected for such a fast-changing market, Carolvale makes extensive use of market information systems (including a real time computer reservation system whose output is analyzed daily), market research, and market analysis. These devices were designed to track early signals of market changes. The possible downturn in the summer 1977 market was detected by Carolvale in November 1976 from assessments of the general economic situation and consumer research.

A premium was placed on rapid communication within the Carolvale organization. An open door policy was maintained by managers, telephone lines were kept busy as personnel and external contacts exchange information, and newspaper cuttings were constantly circulated on their day of publication by managers. More systematic communications were also well established. There was an informal (although regular) meeting of the senior management each week (after the previous week's reservations had been compiled) and a formal meeting in the third or fourth week of the month (after the previous month's accounting figures for operations have been determined).

At the series of weekly meetings through November 1976, the expected downturn in the market for the 1977 summer season was the main topic of discussion. There were two possible decisions in the face of the market downturn:

1. to promote and therefore maximize sales
2. to cut back by returning airline space and hotel space to suppliers and by finding an alternative use of company-owned aircraft space and hotel space

The promotion route would necessitate that the company move early, so that any new packages could be designed, any revised arrangements could be made with airlines and hotels, and promotional literature could be printed and distributed. Cutting back could be done much later, say one or two months before delivery, without serious financial loss except for contracted options with airlines and hotels. Loss of goodwill could, however, be considerable for this latter course of action.

The promotion option was decided upon. Balancing of risks and potentials together with the relationship of marginal cost to marginal revenue clearly suggested that it would prove to be the correct decision. It was decided, in particular, to put together a number of special programs that would be likely to suit better the character of the forthcoming summer season. An example of the type of special package was one offered at a lower price to the consumer but not allowing him or her to select the actual hotel. Carolvale would allocate vacationers to available accommodation upon their arrival at the resort. In this way Carolvale created additional flexibility, allowing the company to optimize hotel capacity according to local and short-term conditions while selling a cut-price product to a consumer who might not otherwise be enticed to purchase in 1977. Another special promotion was a group of packages termed the Fair Deals, where inexpensive transport and accommodation of less than hotel standard were offered at very low prices to a segment of the market that otherwise could not have afforded a foreign holiday in 1977.

Investigation into the possibility of introducing price guarantees was also proposed at the November meeting of the board members. Giving price guarantees to consumers promised a way to counteract low levels of consumer confidence and a way to maintain market share. Carolvale could not proceed, however, to direct implementation of price guarantees. Uncertainties existed about their legality under Bank of England regulations as they applied to the Carolvale Package Tour Division and to the Carolvale Corporation as a whole. There was also a need to assess the likely future parity of the pound sterling with other currencies important in the Carolvale operations. Both the legality issue and the foreign exchange forecasting were made the responsibility of the financial director and later became routine work for his department. Following the finance department's investigations, the board members agreed in the second week of December to give consumer price guarantees for the 1977 summer season.

At the end of February 1977 the response was beginning to produce optimistic returns from the market. At the end of the 1977 season Carolvale had sold 3 percent more packages than in 1976, despite a 7 percent decline in the market as a whole. The price guarantees did, however, affect margins, reducing trading profit as a percentage of turnover from 6 percent for the 1976 season to less than 3 percent in 1977. Carolvale's market position, however, strengthened.

Ronson

Many of the differences between the response of Carolvale Package Tours and Ronson Package Tours can be traced to differing relationships between each division and its holding corporation. Carolvale Package Tours is one of several unrelated, diversified, and completely autonomous businesses in the Carolvale Corporation. By contrast, Ronson Package Tours constitutes part of a vertical integration strategy by Ronson Airlines. Although administered as a division, its interdependence with the other (mostly larger) divisions of Ronson, together with its divisional role as, among other things, a means of obtaining marginal revenues, imparts a less aggressive character to the company.

The airline culture imbues Ronson Packaging Tours with a gentler management character than that of Carolvale through more systematic career progression, greater employment security, less stringent attitudes to overhead costs, more formal internal communications, and other characteristics. The link between Ronson Package Tours and Ronson Airlines is, however, the major explanation for how the response to the 1977 summer season shortfall over the early reservation period materialized.

As with Carolvale, Ronson Tours used extensive market research. Consequently Ronson also suspected weak demand in the early reservation season (from Christmas through January) during the preceding November and December. Response to the demand fall became a specific topic addressed by the December 1976 management meetings. The management committee was the key plenary and integrative device in the division and met weekly. The committee consisted of the divisional managing director, the sales development manager, the advertising and promotions manager, a representative of Ronson airline's hotel reservation department, and a representative of the airline payload department (which managed aircraft seating capacity). The committee came to several conclusions in these meetings as follows:

1977 would be a "late booking year." It was expected that consumers would be unwilling to commit themselves to summer package tours until they were more confident that they would have the necessary money, but that regular consumers would eventually decide to purchase a package.

The company would continue to offer only better than lowest price and lowest quality packages. In particular, a policy statement was reiterated that they would continue not to make substitutions. It was common among many package tour operators under financial stress to alter hotel arrangements or other details at the last minute. Although the savings could be considerable for the operators, Ronson had always resisted the practices. In part, emphasis on maintaining quality reflected the links with Ronson Airlines, which promoted service rather than price.

Price guarantees would be introduced if competitors introduced them. With Cosmos and Carolvale entering with price guarantees on December 26, Ronson announced its equivalent scheme in early January. As an international airline familiar with foreign exchange management, and with a substantial proportion of revenues already denominated in strong currencies, the issue did not require any significant legal investigations or research.

Despite the assessment that the 1977 market would show only a modest fall on 1976 in overall terms, Ronson felt the need to stimulate demand. Their efforts had two related intentions:

1. to create some excitement in their market and thereby increase consumer awareness;

2. to offer some extra values to court marginal consumers who would not otherwise purchase.

It was decided to offer 10 to 15 percent price cuts on a few of the lower price and more popular packages. It would be the first time that price cuts had been publicized by Ronson or by other companies at this level in the market. It would be newsworthy, therefore, and would contribute to effective advertising and public relations campaigns that would help to stimulate demand.

At the end of the 1977 season the Ronson Division had sold a few less packages than in the previous year, but management reported that promotional arrangements had reduced margins by about 10 percent. Their performance was better than the industry average, and managers were well satisfied with the actions they had taken. The managers' key conclusion that 1977 would be a late booking year, rather than one with an aggregate lower demand, was largely fulfilled, particularly for their segment of the market.

Contrasts between the decisions of Carolvale and Ronson can be traced to the relationships of each division to its particular corporation. Differences also applied to the manner in which the response was formed in each company. Ronson was more relaxed and timely in its actions, reflecting its links with an international airline but also reflecting the less elastic demand in its segment and the less crucial relationship of financial results in Ronson's Package Tours to the well-being of its managers and the corporation as a whole. The atmosphere in Carolvale was controlled but was also more urgent and faster moving than that of Ronson, reflecting the division's greater financial independence and the closer link between the well-being of the managers and the success of their decisions.

Weld Division

Weld Division is an autonomously managed subsidiary of an engineering company based in Britain. The division's principal product is a range of welding sets that are used on-site for heavy steel engineering work associated with oil field development, bridge building, shipbuilding, and other types of construction. There are many suppliers of heavy welding sets, because the technology is simple: the manufacture of electrical parts and assembly with a heavy diesel engine supplied by engine manufacturers. Providing only limited opportunity for product differentiation and almost no scope for proprietary technology, the market for welding sets behaves rather like that for a commodity. Competition is based mainly on price.

Following the oil price increases of 1973 and 1974, the world market for welding sets experienced a surge in growth as numerous heavy engineering projects began to take off in the Middle East, especially projects associated with oil field development. Times were particularly auspicious for Weld Division because the changes in oil price had led (indirectly) to devaluation of the pound sterling. As a result, the company could offer lower prices on world market than competitors and proceeded to enjoy considerable prosperity for some three years. But then fortunes changed.

In the middle of 1977, surpluses of oil on world markets brought about a reappraisal of exploration, oil field development, and pipeline construction by the oil producer governments and the eventual cancellation of much activity. Although Weld Division actually sold to British construction and engineering companies, their major ultimate customers were the governments of the Middle Eastern oil producers that control oil field construction. This account describes Weld's response to a sudden demand fall of 30 percent in sales volume and 50 percent in sales value arising from the above causes. It is an operating response.

Weakening Demand

The general manager of Weld Division set aside one day each month for a series of meetings. In the morning he met with the senior managers, including those responsible for marketing, production, purchasing, and accounting. In the afternoon he met with the shop stewards and charge hands. In the evening he met with the workers' council, which is a formal body involving elected and appointed officials from all levels of the company. The state of the business was reviewed in these monthly meetings, and future decisions were discussed. This pattern of regular meetings kept an open exchange of information around the company which proved valuable for the circumstances of the response which are about to be described.

The marketing director, who was routinely responsible for monitoring order intake, first identified the possibility of a drop in demand. The first indication was a drop in forward orders and an associated fall in inquiries. Generally there is a two- or three-month period from forward orders to order confirmation.

This weakening order position was reported to the regular monthly meeting of the senior management. This omen, however, was difficult to interpret and act upon in the early stages of the fall in demand. Weld Division was one step removed from the final user, either because their major contact was with chief contractors or consulting engineers for home sales or because they used agents for export sales, obviating direct contact with the users. It was difficult to sense whether "hard luck stories" were genuine reactions to a fall in demand or part of a normal process where agents attempted to reduce the prices they were charged by Weld Division.

The decision was made at the March 1977 senior management meeting to scout the world market to determine the extent of the easing in demand. This involved scanning reports from company salesmen currently overseas, independent overseas agents, and company-operated overseas agencies (for example, in Singapore). They found that the activity level had "fallen through the floor." At about this time, Saudi Arabia actually stopped the whole development of some oil fields until an extensive examination of the world oil market had been completed by officials in that country.

An emergency meeting of the senior management was held in the middle of March 1977 when the potential gravity of the situation became known. As always in uncertain circumstances, a balanced reaction had to be found. An overreaction might do more damage than the fall in demand itself. Two emergency decisions were taken:

1. to stop all production overtime
2. to stop all possible orders and deliveries of components

Crisis

A month later it became evident that demand was to be weaker than expected at the emergency meeting. The position prompted several additional actions:

1. to attempt renegotiations or temporary amendment of long-term supply contracts
2. to encourage departure of workers
3. to permit a dramatic drop in prices to about 60 percent of the levels holding before the fall in demand
4. to seek out additional orders at any "sensible" price
5. to introduce a new product which had been in a state of readiness for market for some months but had been held up by worker and management objections

While the first three of these actions represented rather simple steps in terms of implementation, the last two presented more taxing challenges.

While export orders (which excluded orders from British companies that were used abroad) had often averaged about 10 percent of sales over several years, they rose to 90 percent in some months during the crisis. One order, in particular, averted very serious financial consequences for Weld Division. The company's few export salesmen felt they were on a wild-goose chase trying to find markets with which they had only limited dealings previously. Venezuela turned out to be a savior where a large order (equivalent to one month's usual production) was available but would require complete manufacture in less than two weeks. Emergency meetings were held within the company where the message was clearly spelled out to all levels of employees that securing and completing this order was vital to the survival of the company.

Agreement was given by all levels of the company that this order should be taken and that they should seek to manufacture the products in two weeks rather than the month that would usually be required. The work force took on the task and completed it in eleven days. While the manufacturing was helped by the backlog of stocks of many components arising from the slowdown, in some ways it was made more difficult by the absence of stock buffers at intermediary stages of the production process. Downtime was actually higher than usual, but people worked through the night, including those among the work force who had declined even modest amounts of overtime on previous occasions. The cooperative atmosphere fostered by management in the workplace and their long-term policy of open communication and consultation through all levels of the company paid off in achieving the accomplishment of this special order.

New Product

Introduction of a new product during the crisis was also something of an accomplishment, although it is ironic that the adversity actually helped to move along its development. The new product was a relatively inexpensive, portable welding machine that incorporated a number of features not formerly available on smaller machines. It had been in a state of readiness for some months but held up in its development by trade union negotiation and by certain practical details that many managers felt could be resolved quickly if there was cooperation among the work force. Faced with the reality that getting the new product into the manufacturing process was vital to continued employment, many of the most substantial obstacles of a year before began to disappear.

Time showed, however, that the fall in demand reflected a longer term situation than had been thought formerly. The market never recovered to 1976 levels through 1977, 1978, and 1979. Oil field development (the principal ultimate market for Weld Division in 1976) did not return to comparable levels in the Middle East, and North Sea development slackened. The industry became active in Mexico and the United States, but Weld Division was not in a good position to service these markets because of stiff domestic competition in the United States and limited European or pound sterling credit lines to Mexico. Another reason, however, exacerbated problems for Weld Division with the rapid appreciation of the pound sterling. It floated to levels in 1980 which positioned it at 1968 parities with the United States dollar and in similarly strong positions against other currencies. Without the defense of product differentiation or proprietary technology, Weld Division was at a substantial disadvantage compared to companies operating from other manufacturing nations or other divisions of the same parent company which operated in more differentiable markets.

Container Division

Container Division is one of several subsidiary companies organized and managed as divisions within an international paper-manufacturing company. The autonomously managed division is situated in Great Britain and mainly manufactures cardboard containers supplied to the food industry. The company made two substantial responses around the time of the OPEC oil price increases of 1973 and 1974. The first was a response to a demand surge when orders in hand went from an industry norm of about five days' production to between six months' to a year's work. The second response occurred in the next year and centered around a three-day working week legislated by the government in order to save energy during a coal-miners' strike. These are both examples of operating responses.

Demand Surge

The demand surge ran counter to all previous experiences over recent decades. Historically, in an industry selling to a buyers' market and buying from a buyers' market, Container Division found itself in much of 1973 selling to a sellers' market and buying from a sellers' market. Accustomed relationships in the business therefore inverted, with consequences for top management, salesmen, and production hands alike. This unprecedented situation arose largely from panic buying issuing from a widespread concern for the supply of raw materials in the wake of oil supply uncertainties.

Container Division was one of four divisions in the total company that each used paper as raw material (mainly supplied from the parent company) and converted it to finished products available to end users. While each of the companies was managed independently, it was natural that consultation among the divisions was frequent. In particular, there was a routine two-day meeting every month. The challenge of the demand surge was recognized first in these meetings and found to be threefold:

1. how to cope with lack of raw materials
2. how to turn business away
3. how to minimize unprofitable orders

Most actions were independent, but there was one major collaboration initiated by headquarters management. At one point over the period of exceptional demand, Container Division had a stock of papers that would supply production operation for less than five days. Stock levels usually approximated nine weeks. The parent company agreed, therefore, to jointly purchase a quantity of special (low) quality paper from Japan on special terms. The headquarters company also arranged a scouting of Scandinavian mills for any paper that might be available outside of usual channels (the parent company supplied most of the paper to its divisions).

A private airplane was leased by the company for this survey of Scandinavia. A system of swaps between the divisions also was organized by and through headquarters. Most of Container Division's competitors ran out of stock over the period, but all the parent company-owned paper conversion divisions were able to produce without interruption.

Turning away business, however, was found to be more difficult than would be imagined ordinarily. It was soon clear that it would probably hold long-term implications for the business if management refused customers and therefore forced them to go elsewhere for their requirements. As well as the risk of losing business, there was the opportunity to gain business as hard-pressed buyers of cardboard containers reached throughout the entire industry for supplies. To establish priorities among these competing claims, it was decided to refer to short-term and long-term goals.

A simple allocation procedure was adopted for each long-standing buyer as a proportion of the prior year's purchases that reflected paper availability to Container Division. New business was accepted only if it fitted into the division's long-term goal. Any remaining supplies were then allocated competitively.

There were, however, other devices available to management to improve service to their customers during the demand surge. Management described the process as one of escalation. As the situation became more intense, decisions became more stringent and more widely based. A series of decisions was made that culminated as follows:

> About thirty different grades of paper board were customarily available to customers. The selection was reduced to about half that number, but customer choice also was limited in another way. Ordinarily, if a reel of one grade of board was not fully used for an order, the remainder would be stored until another order was received for which it could be used. To avoid downtime, the decision was made to use all the contents of a reel whether it exactly matched an order or not. The customer was asked to pay the extra cost for a higher quality board if that was all that was available.
>
> Similarly, the number of inks available to customers was reduced from nearly eighty to just eleven standard inks. This decision partly reflected the lack of availability of dyes that the demand surge had also created.
>
> Traditionally, Container Division (as well as its competitors) had stocked finished products for their customers. This practice was eliminated completely.

All the decisions were made as a result of emergencies brought about by the demand surge that was recognized as an inevitably temporary phenomenon. The set of circumstances enabled Container Division to rid itself of almost all unprofitable business over the period. Benefits of the temporary reversal of power between buyer and seller persisted beyond the response itself. The number of grades of boards and number of inks did not return to levels pertaining before the demand surge for some years. The previously routine practice of holding stock for customers did not return at all. In addition, senior management took a permanent step to safeguard Container Division and its sister companies from another shortage of raw material. A 15 percent ownership stake was secured in a company that processed waste paper back to board usable by Container Division. Together with the waste that the parent company supplied to the waste conversion company, this stake was believed to be adequate to ensure a sizable supply of raw material to the parent company in the event of a future demand surge.

The Three-Day Week

In January 1974 the United Kingdom demanded that industry work a three-day week so that the use of energy would be minimized. For Container Division, as all production companies in the country, the aim was to achieve five days' output in three. The challenge for the general manager at Container Division was more formidable, perhaps because its fully unionized closed-shop work force was known for its truculence.

Here was a problem that was perceived by headquarters management and by divisional management as one benefiting from consultation. A special meeting was held at headquarters (following the same kind of format as the regular monthly meetings) to discuss the issues. It was evident that two courses of action should be followed immediately:

1. An application should be made to the appropriate government agency for a special disposition to permit a five-day week.
2. Arrangements should be made for each plant to work three days of twelve-hour shifts per week in lieu of the normal five days of eight-hour shifts per week until permission for a five-day week was obtained or until the crisis diminished.

The director for personnel (headquarters) assumed responsibility for preparing the application to the government, and the director of marketing (headquarters) assumed responsibility for assisting him with the task. With administrative arrangements in place for the government application at headquarters level, the divisional general management returned to their respective plants to implement the three-day week.

After a few hours' thought, the general manager of the Container Division called a meeting of his four functional managers together with their immediate subordinates—a total of about twenty people. At the meeting he presented his recommendations. Under the circumstances only minor matters seemed unclear, because the three-day, twelve-hour shift was the only configuration that could result in as near to the normal forty hours as possible. Effectively the decision was "top down," with the general manager delegating subdivisions of the task according to the respective normal responsibilities of his managers and their subordinates.

The next step was to call a meeting of the joint union management committee, which always met weekly and included all the shop stewards and their deputies together with all the top operations managers at Container Division. A crisis meeting was called at a special time, which served to emphasize the need for special actions. Ideas were debated and agreed upon.

The results of this meeting were then disseminated throughout the organization. The shop stewards met individually with their memberships and worked out how to organize the details—exactly who should work on what shift, and so forth. The operations management met with their foremen and supervisors and discussed exactly what actions were being taken and why.

After three weeks, the government approved Container Division as one of the companies that could operate on the normal five-day week schedule. (The basis of approval was that the company mainly supplied food manufacturers—the food industry was demarcated as a priority industry that could continue to work a normal routine). There was, however, a sequel in that the work force had found the emergency work program so convenient in personal terms that they refused to return to the five-day week. The regional representation for the largest trade unions was called in by management to persuade the workers to return to the usual hours, and the impasse was thereby resolved.

In some senses, many of the management also were sorry to see the end of the three-day week. Both productivity and morale had increased over the period. It had to be remembered, though, that all machines were operated continuously, which would not be possible over a long period of time, and many expedient steps had been taken that would not have allowed the high pace of work over a sustained period.

This chapter has provided a further five examples of operating responses. Results are similar to those of the operating responses in Generaltex's IPD and also to those of Prosper and Atlas's responses to the oil embargo. In all cases the response involved the realignment of operations to different levels. Also characteristic for these operating responses as well as for administrative and corporate response was a combination of direct action and prior planning. Planning and analysis were present when uncertainties and data were such that quite reliable predictions were possible (Ronson and Carolvale demand estimates) and when financial conditions could be or were mandated to be defined and budgeted ahead of action (IPD's reponse to the recession). Action taking place somewhat ahead of fully articulated plans was also present, such as when circumstances were so exceptional that models were not available (Container Division's air tour of Swedish pulp mills), and where operating uncertainties were so extreme that it made more sense to press ahead than try to consider detailed implications (Container Division's manufacturing for the demand surge). Thus, planning and analysis and trial-and-error approaches were used in combination, depending upon the respective opportunities provided for the use of each and the particular attributes that each could bring to a situation.

This chapter also concludes presentation of the total of twelve responses in divisional settings. In chapter 3 (table 3–2) it was stated as expected that divisional settings would be organizationally focused, technically controlled, and culturally professional. In absolute terms as well as in terms relative to the complex settings described in chapter 5 to 11, these expections were broadly substantiated by the accounts of chapters 12 to 14. These characteristics of divisional organizational settings were suggested in chapter 3 to affect the nature of response in ways that were termed overall as systematic. With the possible exception of the response of National Lighting to the loss of market share in vehicle bulbs through low-price imports (discussed at the end of chapter 13), expected features of response in divisional settings noted in table 3–2 were found to be characteristic in the field. Impacts of discontinuity on the divisions was generally immediate, involved the whole division, and was sufficiently unambiguous in its meaning to require little of the extensive interpretative debate on the nature of the environmental change found in the responses in complex organizational settings. Problems were usually sufficiently well defined for investigations to be singular and reasonably conclusive and for relatively comprehensive solutions to be devised and implemented. In the next chapter, attention is turned to response in simple organizational settings.

15
Responses in Simple Settings

S imple settings were described in chapter 4 (table 4–3) as organizationally simple or incomplete, technically confined, and culturally personal.
The fieldwork reports which follow give more meaning to these terms
and their associated descriptions. The reports also afford the opportunity to
draw some conclusion on the special impacts of simple settings on response
to be compared with conclusions drawn from the preceding reports on responses
in complex settings and divisional settings.

Each of the following examples presents results of fieldwork conducted
in relatively lesser depth. The responses of an iron ore mining company, Jackson
Mines, to (1) a major strike and labor relations problem, and (2) a demand
fall are recounted first. The second response is that of a pet-food manufacturer, Schumacker, to a salmonella outbreak. The response of a specialist
automobile manufacturer, Suza Cars, to a marked shift in market demand and
component supply is the third case reported in this chapter and also concludes
all the data collected for this study of managing response.

Jackson Mines

Jackson Mines is a North American iron ore mining company. It mainly supplies Japanese and United States steel mills and is partly owned by the companies that buy its production. The capacity of the mining facilities was
increased from twenty million tons per year to just over twenty-five million tons
per year in 1976. As suppliers to the burgeoning Japanese steel industry, the
company's growth prospects looked good when investments in extra capacity
were made. In the later part of 1977 and the early part of 1978, the company
was faced, however, with a 30 percent decline in customer orders compared
to outline agreements arrived at only a few months before.

Another major challenge faced by the management a little before this
demand fall was a period of highly adverse labor relations. The experiences
of the management and employees during the protracted angry strikes and the

bold initiatives taken by both sides in the disputes constitutes a response in its own right, and also provides essential background for an understanding of the demand fall. Management of the labor relations problems before the demand fall reoriented thought and action in the company and constituted an administrative response. After the demand fall, operations and behaviors essentially returned to those prevailing prior to the response—the demand fall is an operating response.

Labor Relations

Trade unions are powerful in the part of North America in which Jackson Mines operates. In fact, unions had been unduly uncooperative, in the assessment of many managers in that region, and labor relations were particularly acrimonious at Jackson Mines. As an isolated mining community of just five thousand people, most of the labor force were single males determined to bargain for high pay. Circumstances came to a head in the summer of 1976 with two exceptionally bitter six-week strikes within a little more than three months. The owners' losses totalled more than twenty million dollars in lost production. Problems for Mr. Jackson, the company's general manager and descendant of the discoverer of the iron ore deposits, were aggravated by the fact that much of the equity was owned by the customer steel mills. Losses to the steel companies included the trouble and expense of buying ore on the near-term market. More important was that the disruption in supply threatened their rationale for investment in Jackson Mines. Jackson had been a dependable and constant supply of ore for a steel-making process which necessitates even production flow.

With the experience of these protracted strikes, pressures became urgent for Mr. Jackson to find a solution to the poor standard of labor relations at Jackson Mines. To rectify the problem, he spoke to colleagues and read through business periodicals for some technique that would alter management/worker relations. Management by Objectives[1] surfaced as a possibility, but when it was tried on a limited basis it was a disaster. The exercise of establishing objectives did, however, illustrate the massive gap in attitudes that had developed within the organization. It showed that a more far-reaching solution was necessary.

Just as Mr. Jackson was beginning to suspect that a technique-oriented solution would not be up to the task, a long-time friend in another company suggested the Robert R. Blake and Jane S. Mouton Grid (Blake's Grid).[2] Nominating his financial manager (Mr. Jackson's right-hand man) to accompany him, the general manager attended a two-day introductory course on that management technique. Provisionally convinced that this might be the answer, Mr. Jackson checked out the lecturer's credentials and his record in employing Blake's Grid. Reassured of the worth of the technique and the lecturer's skills,

Mr. Jackson decided to try out the method, and appointed the lecturer as organization development consultant with the brief of creating more constructive working relationships at Jackson Mines.

The timing proved critical. Naturally the strike had resulted in a large backlog of orders, and this afforded the opportunity to improve worker attitudes. After the summer strikes, the company worked through September and October at breakneck speed, succeeding in topping all previous company mining records. Such effective teamwork improved morale from the trough in August to the highest level that had been experienced in the company by October. In the meantime, 280 of the company's 800 employees had graduated from the Blake's Grid courses. As a result, a different culture had arisen in Jackson Mines that was recognizable to everyone. These two months of high spirits and improvement of working relationships were crucial to the way the company met the impending decline in demand.

Demand Fall

Recognizing the likelihood of a future drop in the size of contract orders from January 1978, the general manager's first step was to obtain revised purchasing commitments from customers for the next three months. It became clear that the commitments would show about a 30 percent decline from previous commitments that were close to average levels. Costs would have to be reduced by at least 25 percent to achieve an acceptable financial performance.

Variable costs such as energy, transportation, and so on could be brought down to the level required by the demand downfall by simply holding off orders and not using equipment. The challenge to the company came from labor costs, where a 35 percent reduction was necessary. Part of this requirement could be met through natural wastage—labor turnover had run at nearly 30 percent per annum over recent years. Nonunion workers could be dismissed without fear of reprisals, but it was only necessary for the general manager to dismiss two people, as the action motivated others to leave in line with requirements. The critical managerial challenge rested with the once-truculent union work force, who would have to accept a 25 percent reduction in take-home pay to meet company goals. Never in the company's history had any change of this size been accomplished without massive strikes and disruption, but in 1978 Mr. Jackson achieved the required reduction in take-home pay without obstruction. The new culture introduced by use of Blake's Grid was felt to have played its part in the satisfactory outcome.

Openness with the trade unions was the hallmark of the approach. The stand was one of stating the inevitability of the situation, and trade union officials and workers were involved in the decisions that had to be made. Awareness of the impending demand fall and cutback was high in the work force. From August 1977 there had been substantial preconditioning, not only within the company but also outside the company. Local press comment on the situation had been thorough, and several statements issued by local and regional politicians had received considerable publicity. The widespread realization and acceptance of the worldwide slump in steel making made for a more cooperative atmosphere.

Mr. Jackson practiced a technique that had been made known to him by the organizational development consultant. After thorough consideration of the problem from every point of view, he constructed a single, one-page written statement of the demand situation and the policy he was going to take to manage it. This statement was then used as the basis for all written and verbal communication to all involved parties, including staff, trade union officials, workers, wives, managers, journalists, and others.

It was clear that a 25 percent reduction in labor costs would require that no overtime be worked and that a shorter working week be introduced with all pay at standard rates. Mr. Jackson also considered exactly how he was to manage communication of these policies to the work force. In the end he used just two meetings to accomplish worker acceptance of cancellation of all overtime and acceptance of the shorter working week at standard rates. First, the leaders of the trade union were informed in a consultative way in personal conversation with Mr. Jackson. Second, one week later, the trade union secretaries were informed directly by Mr. Jackson at a lunchtime meeting where alcoholic beverages flowed freely. The trade union leaders and secretaries then promulgated the arrangements to the work force without any disruption arising.

Mr. Jackson considers that a large part of the success of the moves was his direct contact, as general manager, with the trade union officials. Such action was without precedent in the mining industry in that part of the world. The trade union officials and the industrial relations specialists in Jackson Mines were all unhappy about this approach, but no major problems ensued as a result. The reason for its acceptance is thought to be attributable to the new culture that had developed in the company in the preceding months.

It is Mr. Jackson's view that if it had not been for the Grid, implementation of the production cutback would have been a shambles and eventually would have necessitated a heavy-handed redoing of the organization. The Grid also showed the necessity for some long-range planning, particularly social planning, to obtain more stability in the company. One intention, for example, was to attract more women into the company. Mr. Jackson looked forward from 1978 to a period of high prosperity and increasing stability.

Schumacker

All food-product manufacturers fear a salmonella outbreak, but small family businesses such as Schumacker face the gravest consequences from such an outbreak. In June 1972, survival of the Schumacker company was in balance after a baby had died of salmonella. The death had been attributed to the baby having eaten dog food supplied by Schumacker, although there was no direct evidence that this was the cause. With just one product and one factory, the company was facing risk of bankruptcy. Without the skillful management of Mr. Schumacker (owner and general manager), his fifty employees would have had to have been terminated despite his deep sense of responsibility to them. The company was started by his father, so at least two generations in the small Northern German town in which the company was situated had been dependent on the Schumackers for their livelihood. As a sudden dislocation in understood circumstances, this is an operating response.

Crisis

On the 8th of June, the high-circulation evening newspaper in Northern Germany carried the story of the baby's death from salmonella and attributed it to Doggy, Schumacker's only product. Evening radio and television took the story, and it was headlined in national newspapers the next morning. Doctors could not be certain that the salmonella had come from the dog food, although the baby's father was insistent that this was how the fatal illness had come about. Salmonella is not harmful to dogs.

The next day Schumacker was deluged by telephone inquiries from the public, the media, and their retailers and distributors. It is federal law in Germany that all products suspected of salmonella poisoning must be removed immediately from the market at all levels of trade—manufacturer, distributors, and retailers. It would take at least four weeks for the alleged contamination to be investigated by the respective government agency. Cessation of revenues put Schumacker under risk of bankruptcy, but the threat of distributors and retailers returning their product for refund would have ensured collapse of the company.

Response

A project team was formed, including Mr. Schumacker, an advertising consultant, the company's main food broker (an intermediary who takes title to the goods and distributes them to wholesalers and retailers), and a legal adviser. Priorities were soon established. The most important initial consideration was the members of the distribution channels. To avoid return of the product, a message was sent by telephone and telegram, and later by letter, to retailers and distributors. The message advised them that Schumacker Dog Food may contain salmonella but that it was not yet certain. They were advised further that if any dog food was contaminated, it was suspected that only a very local part of Northern Germany would have received the consignment. Although no one could be certain of the latter point, it allayed distributors' fears and helped avoid returns, despite the legal necessity for retailers to remove the product from the shelves in their stores.

The next priority was to determine the source of salmonella, or prove that there was no contamination. Although the problem was complicated by the absence of Schumacker's technical director, who was in the United States, the deduction was made that it would be most likely to arise from the bone-meal constituent in the dog food. The company immediately set about a different formulation for the product that avoided use of the bone meal. Government approval of the new product would be required before it could be sold, and this would take time. The hope was to have a new product ready to sell before government findings on possible salmonella contamination were released. It would be a way of deflecting attention from the considerable harm that confirmed salmonella contamination would inflict on Schumacker's reputation.

With priorities established and put into action, attention of the project team turned to less immediate but equally crucial matters. Most critical was that the distributors and retailers not lose patience and begin to return their stocks during the four weeks necessary to resolve the problems confronting the company. Patience was proving difficult to maintain, because the media had persisted with an aggressive campaign against the company. Problems were aggravated further by reported illnesses in several babies across Germany that parents and the media readily attributed to consumption of Schumacker's dog food.

With tensions running high, several steps were taken to prevent the retail trade from panicking:

It was decided that it might be helpful to present Mr. Schumacker to the public through the media. He is a man of obvious sincerity, and his television interview succeeded in drawing sympathy from the public. The media became aware of the vulnerability of this single-product family business and began to run a series of moderate articles on the firm and its predicament reflecting this change in viewer sentiment.

A small advertising campaign was placed in the national newspapers. The advertisements were directed at consumers, but were also designed to reach the store owners and strengthen their loyalty to Schumacker.

The food broker on the project team systematically maintained personal contact with all the large multiple chains.

The company's personnel were carefully briefed with a specific reply to give to the public, the media, and the trade at all times. Several employees were assigned to telephone duty to answer the large number of calls made to the company during the period of salmonella suspicion.

One unsuspected factor was working in Mr. Schumacker's favor. Dog owners were becoming progressively more restless with the nonavailability of the product because their dogs were reluctant to accept substitute products. An exceptional case of consumer loyalty!

Conclusion

A major concern was that the government report on salmonella contamination might be adverse and might precede government approval of the newly formulated product. As events turned out, the former was published first, one day before the expected government approval of the new Doggy product. The report confirmed the existence of salmonella, and that it arose from the bone meal constituent that had been excluded from the new product's formulation. This ingredient originated from a large manufacturer who also supplied the company's competitors, so that if Doggy was affected it was quite likely that competitors were at risk as well.

The company took a calculated risk. They had a copy of the government report condemning the bone meal, but they believed it had not yet been received by the media. They did nothing and hoped that the press would not contact the government. The next day, Schumacker was granted approval for its new product, and by that evening television news programs carried the launch of New Doggy with the general manager introducing the new product against a background of dogs consuming it voraciously. After six months, Doggy had almost regained its original market share. Today the company is much larger and sells a wider range of both dog foods and cat foods.

Suza Cars

At the time of this account, Suza Cars was still one of the few independent, specialist automobile manufacturers in Europe. In the middle 1970s the company put a range of quality sports cars on the market that replaced an older product line which had become, through the years, more difficult to produce and less profitable to sell. Suza Cars had only one small product line manufactured on the same line and using many common components. These three products also were sold through the same channel to essentially the same market segment. The original founder still exerted an almost singular force on the development of the company, as he had done for thirty years previously. The response described in the following pages is administrative in nature.

The Setting

Suza's reputation was well established at the beginning of the 1970s, having been won with a range of sports cars offering exceptional performance and glamour for their owners at an attractive price. At this time, however, their appeal was waning—not so much for the consumer but for the Suza company itself. Several trends had reduced the rationale for the range of cars over the 1960s:

> As a small manufacturer, Suza purchased many of its conponents from large automobile manufacturers and associated tire and glass suppliers. Many of these parts were becoming difficult to acquire because they were no longer produced in large volumes by the manufacturers. Supply of many parts was becoming less dependable as well because of repeated strikes at the manufacturers.

> The original Suza aluminum-bodied cars were made obsolete largely by safety legislation in the United States. The United States was a key market for the company.

> Cost inflation had become a major force and had resulted in an erosion of margins for Suza's product range.

The decision was made in 1970 by top management (formulized through a board commitment to the necessary investment) to design a new range of cars that would solve the above problems.

The challenge was ominous, because it usually takes five years for a company like Suza to build a production car from ground up. The greatest challenge, however, was to find a light body that would withstand the United States safety collision tests. A traditional steel body would not be feasible for Suza's small manufacturing volumes and would compromise at the high performance characteristics for which Suza was famous. The cars' reputation almost wholly arose from a high-power, lower body weight design concept achieved by use of an aluminum body. Although the way in which an aluminum body could be designed to meet the safety regulations was not apparent to top management, the decision was made to incorporate it into the design and to find a solution to the problem later.

Dubbing the new car Felicity, management defined two major parameters for the new range to guide its development. These may be summarized as:

1. to minimize bought-in components by designing and manufacturing in-house all possible elements of the car (including air conditioning and upholstery)
2. to develop a high-quality, dependable, luxurious, and prestigious high-performance automobile

In this setting, the project moved into development.

Development

Mr. Suza, the founder and majority owner of the company, played the dominant role in the development met of the new product range. As an automobile engineer par excellence, he was the most qualified to mastermind the project. The first step was Mr. Suza's briefing of a stylist (an outside consultant), and within two weeks sketches were available for consideration.

The research and development group at Suza Cars then took over and designed the layout and configurations of the engine, transmission, and other mechanical elements into the shape described by the sketches. The outcome was then revised until a design emerged that satisfied the requirements of styling and engineering. After the car reached the prototype stage, it was shown to the press and dealers for comment. The reception was mainly favorable, which encouraged Suza to continue development along the same lines.

Detailed design work then became the order of the day. Intensive consultation was necessary between team members because of the high interdependence of parts in a high-performance car and because of the especially stringent design problems arising from limited space and low tolerances for a sports car. Such problems were particularly challenging because of the discipline to design to an efficient manufacturing cost, which involved extensive debate with production engineers. Project work of this type has a natural tendency to exceed time scales and exceed budget. Alert to the problems from previous, although smaller, design projects, top management exerted tight control over time and money. Most designers and draftsmen frequently worked seven-day weeks to meet the need to bring the range to market as soon as possible.

The most critical challenge in the development of the new range of cars was, however, the need for an innovative solution to the technical problem of building stresses into the aluminum body in order that the car could withstand the collision and rollover tests demanded by the United States safety legislation. Conventional extrusion technology was not feasible on cost and other grounds for pieces of metal the size of car body panels (especially when rigorous aerodynamic considerations had to be satisfied). Eventually Mr. Suza's creative genius solved the problem. After a restless night he determined to go to the factory and conduct some experiments. By dawn, a solution had been tried on a small scale and was successful. In about two more weeks, the solution had been proven at production scale and production speeds.

Launch

The new Suza car met with an enthusiastic reception when it was launched, but problems for the product were not yet over. Offered at a price almost double that of its forerunners, introduction of the new Suza carried many additional challenges. The car would, after all, have to be sold to a different type of customer—an affluent senior executive rather than a young motoring enthusiast. Better quality and better service were necessary. This upmarket move affected almost all areas of the company. Some examples of implications for the company and its distributors are noted below:

> Public relations and advertising materials had to be upgraded. In the general field of public relations, telephonists had to be trained to present a higher quality image and better service.

> Quality control and production supervision had to be strengthened in manufacturing.

> Prior to the new models, the dealers were mainly small, privately run firms. The new range dictated the choice of larger companies and motor groups who would provide adequate finance for the stock of cars and spares as well as suitable premises and locations. This reduced the number of dealers by half.

Events in the world at large seemingly added to the appeal of the new Suza. As a lightweight, high-performance car of dependable quality, it was ideally suited to the new era of high energy costs. The oil price increases of 1973 and 1974 were, however, disadvantageous to Suza. Demand for luxury, high-price automobiles declined about 50 percent in the mid–1970s compared to 1970. While the Suza's high energy efficiency helped the company to withstand the situation, sales fell below anticipations. Coupled with the high costs of developing the new range and a series of unprofitable years, Suza Cars continued to be proudly independent but remained only marginally profitable.

Suza Cars is the twenty-sixth and last example of response presented in this study. The three simple organizational settings of Jackson Mines, Schumacker, and Suza Cars seemed to corroborate expectations of a small, single, functionally structural independent operational unit with strong leadership, relatively unformalized systems, and medium to low operating complexity as discussed in chapter 3 and summarized in table 3–2. Expected implications of these characteristics on the decision processes in response seemed also to be largely substantiated by the evidence of the four responses investigated in these three cases. The discontinuties were readily interpretable for their significance. Although needed outcomes were relatively simple to identify, in all three cases the situations were more directly threatening to the survival of the organization than those in complex and divisional settings, and how the challenge could or should be met was generally less evident for the simple settings. These conclusions can be compared with those drawn for response in complex settings at the end of chapter 11, and with those drawn for response in divisional settings at the end of chapter 14.

This chapter completes the presentation of data collected for this study of managing response. The next task is to pull together and analyze what has been observed, and to draw implications. Part III of this book follows, where five chapters outline the findings of this study and the final chapter discusses the practical implications for managers and reserachers.

Notes

1. John W. Humble, *Management by Objectives* (London: Industrial Education and Research Foundation, 1967).

2. Robert R. Blake and Jane S. Mouton, *The Management Grid* (Houston: Gulf Publishing, 1964).

Part III
Analysis and Implications

Can the Ethiopian change his skin, or the leopard his spots?
—Jeremiah 13:23

Let the great world spin for ever down the ringing grooves of change.
—Alfred, Lord Tennyson,
Locksley Hall

Part III of this book presents an analysis of the field observations summarized in the foregoing textual accounts of part II and draws implications for management, the organization, strategy, and research. Initially, this third part follows the same structure as the propositions developed and stated in chapter 3. First, the preliminary propositions 1 to 5 are to be addressed in chapter 16. These include the basic model and characteristics of response, the three distinct types of response (corporate, administrative, and operating) and the three possible organizational settings (complex, divisional, and simple).

Chapters 17 to 20 constitute the core of the decision processes aspect of the study, dealing, in turn, with each of the four decision process propositions 6 to 9 of chapter 3. To be suggestive of the actions found to be taken in response, and to be somewhat descriptive of the four most evident sets of processes occurring in response, these four chapters are titled, respectively, finding solutions, solving problems, developing initiatives, and using situational factors. While some logic is intended in the sequencing of the chapters, in practice all four sets of processes occurred concurrently and continuously throughout the duration of all responses, although certain aspects were often more conspicuous or formative at particular times. Direct managerial implications are briefly noted at suitable junctures through each of the chapters.

Rather than a simple refutation or acceptance of the propositions, the analyses of chapters 17 to 20 go deeper to generate findings of practicable resolution for management practice and of sufficient definition for the development of testable hypotheses for subsequent research. This is achieved by the addressing of more specific research questions posed by finer-grain examinations of relevant literature and more detailed logical development of the general propositions in directions indicated to be important through the field research experience.

Chapter 21 presents the implications of this study for managers, the organization, strategy, and research by extending the analysis and specialized implications of chapters 16 to 20 into overall implications for managerial action and by suggesting directions for future research. Response is shown in this study to be intrinsically a whole situation, impossible to render as checklists, linear sequences, or in other relatively mechanical formats. A more general approach is required in terms of an overall managerial style that releases the decision processes found to be successful in response. *Responsive management* is the term used to describe this approach.

It is argued in chapter 21 that managers dealing with response should adopt a style that is practical, active, flexible, and sensitive (inducted from the findings of chapters 17, 18, 19, and 20, respectively). Equivalently, the implications for the organization are that a response process should be engendered that seeks to stimulate initiatives and selectively adopt those initiatives considered the most promising (inducted from the findings for response in complex, divisional, and simple organizational settings [chapter 16], those relating to the overall structure and development of response [chapter 19], and elsewhere). Implications for strategy are also drawn and address inculcating responsive management within an organization in overall terms. Implications for research to further test, deepen, extend, and apply the findings of this work are discussed in the final section of chapter 21.

16
Reviewing Response

T his chapter reviews the three sets of background propositions before subsequent chapters address the four aspects of decision processes under discontinuity selected for study. In chapter 3, four sets of propositions were stated, the first related to identifiable steps common to responses, the pattern of responses within a corporation, and the main characteristics of discontinuity and associated response. The second set was concerned with identifying three distinct types of response, and the third set with addressing expected organizational contingencies for response. These three sets were regarded as essential background to consider properly the fourth and core set related to decision processes under discontinuity. It is the purpose of this chapter, the first in the analysis section of this book, to address each of these three sets of background propositions in turn, and state the main managerial implications that seem to follow from the findings.

Response and Discontinuity

The Response Model

In chapter 3, a model of response was logically deduced from base literature mainly concerning the behavior and conditions of the environments of organizations (briefly addressed in chapter 1) and embracing also some understandings of general systems theory as well as input from elsewhere. A proposition concluded the development:

> *Proposition 1.* The process of discontinuity and response can be represented as a model of (1) an environment of an organization possessing an incipient capacity for discontinuity, this capacity potentially resulting in (2) a discontinuity that (3) exceeds the flexibility or adaptation of the organization so that its members' goals can no longer be satisfied adequately, making (4) a response necessary that

(5) involves a collection of subresponses to (6) realize a viable organization whose members' goals are, once again, satisfactorily met.

Can this proposition be refuted or is evidence from this study sufficient to support the provisional acceptance of this model? Data presented in chapters 5 to 15 were examined to pinpoint each of these phenomena and conclude whether each was observable in the order specified and that the various elements neither overspecified nor underspecified the basic model of response to discontinuity.

Table 16–1 offers descriptive terms for each investigated situation for the environmental capacity, the resulting discontinuity, whether the discontinuity exceeds flexibility or adaptability, and some of the main subresponses involved. Inspection of table 16–1 in conjunction with the data of chapters 5 to 15 demonstrates that in all cases it was straightforward to identify unambiguously all the elements of the proposed model. The model seemed to provide a full specification of the various entities of which discontinuity and response were composed, and the implied sequencing of the elements was found in the data also.

Response countered the new environmental capacity and the associated discontinuity with a new organizational capability. This permitted the organization members' goals to be satisfactorily attainable once again. Thus, the Industrial Products Division countered severe cost inflation with a new sensitivity to pricing. Similarly, when the Industrial Products Division faced the cash squeeze, it developed a new efficiency in cash-flow management. Weakening demand at National Lighting was met by imaginative marketing in the Inflation Beaters campaign. When National Lighting experienced low-priced foreign competition in vehicle bulbs, it countered by installing newly cost-effective machinery together with newly aggressive marketing.

Managerial implications suggested by the above model may be summarized as:

> The presence of incipient capacity as a necessary precondition for discontinuity to arise means that predictability and preparedness for discontinuity may both be possible in general terms but not in particular details. Ability to reason the range of future discontinuities was admirably illustrated by the scenarios developed at Atlas nearly a year before the oil price increase and embargo occurred. The taking of actions ahead of a discontinuity would, however, seem ill-advised, because generally the costs and associated risks of taking definitive actions ahead of an event would exceed those of waiting until the nature of the "new environment" is both confirmed and more exactly shown. Action in the sense of preparedness for a range of outcomes suggested by the possibility of an imminent discontinuity may, however, be more feasible. Atlas, as a result of incorporating scenarios as part of the capital investment appraisal process, often embodied greater flexibility into projects and chose them or designed them to be more adaptable to possible changes in the general character of the environment of the business.

Recognition and initial calibration of discontinuities and the associated need for response were a function of the aggregate goals of the management group. Higher goals and situations, where projected performances against goals were more stringently monitored, seemed to show the need for response and what was required for response more clearly, and possibly sooner—the corporate context of the Industrial Products Division was demanding on both these counts, and response occurred promptly and with more refined conceptual development than for many other situations investigated in this study.

Multiple subresponses were typically required to achieve a response—both several subresponses at a point in time and later subresponses building from earlier subresponses.

Relation of Response to Discontinuity

In chapter 3 it was reasoned that when a complex organization is affected by a discontinuity it affects the organization unevenly. It was argued further that situational specifics at each point in time and space originate highly individual responses or subresponses asymmetrically across the organization. Consequently, a discrete response to a discontinuity is likely to be fragmented into specialized parts and, when viewed as a whole, the response is likely to embrace, therefore, some compensating synthetic or dissemination processes. To restate the relevant proposition 2:

> *Proposition 2.* The pattern of overall response, particularly for more complex cases, is likely to display some fragmentation into asymmetric and situationally specific parts (subresponses) and embody correspondingly some syntheses of these respective parts or dissemination of subresponses to one or several parts of the organization.

For corporate and administrative responses in the more complex organizations, the proposition was irrefutable; in fact, no contrary cases were found. As responses leaned toward simpler situations, either simpler organizational settings or simpler operating responses, the expected attributes were displayed less conspicuously.

At the most aggregate level in the data collected for this study, it was shown in both Prosper and Atlas that a mix of responses across the total organization was necessary to deal with a suddenly differently functioning environment. Atlas's and Prosper's entries to the coal industry, construction of refinery projects, introduction of management systems, and rescheduling of supply activities formed parts of a whole mix of responses. Several reorganizations also were occurring in both Prosper and Atlas in the early 1970s, several other entries to new businesses were being pursued, and several other operating responses

Table 16–1
Researched Responses

Corporation/Response	Capacity/Discontinuity	Discontinuity Exceeds	Some Major Subresponses
Prosper Oil			
Coal diversification	Diminished crude availability/ Anticipated need for coal liquidation	Adaptability (corporate)	Search for acquisitions and other coal business liaisons
Catalytic cracker investment	Substitution of coal for fuel oil/Price differential between light and heavy products	Adaptability	The catalytic cracker proposal
Rotterdam pricing system	Excess capacity/Need to add value	Adaptability	Internal control system in the Netherlands
Supply crisis	Embargo/Dislocation of supply	Flexibility	Revised supply schedules
Atlas Oil			
Coal diversification	Diminished crude availability/ Anticipated need for power over energy supplies	Adaptability (corporate)	Coal exploration efforts
Scenario planning system	Constrained demand and uncertain supply/Lack of investment confidence	Adaptability	Original scenarios in the futures study
Supply crisis	Embargo/Dislocation of supply	Flexibility	Revised supply schedules
Interoil			
Foreign exchange system	Movement to floating exchange rates/Devaluation of the United States dollar	Adaptability	Foreign exchange control system/Approval of top management
Columbus Bank			
Reorganization	Trends in the environment/ Social action	Adaptability	Reorganization/Handover of branch to black banking business

DeVito Power Entry to Middle East markets	Oil price increase/Fall in domestic power generation needs	Adaptability	Export sales efforts
Industrial Products Division			
Demand surge	Economic boom/Supply shortages	Flexibility	Raw material inventories expanded
Pricing initiative	Raw material cost increases/Margins threatened	Adaptability	The price change form
Demand stimulation	Economic recession/Withdrawal of demand	Flexibility	Senior management sales program
Cash systems	Cash shortages at corporate level from economic circumstances/Cash recipient to donor	Adaptability	Management training courses
National Lighting Division			
Inflation Beaters campaign	Energy price increases/Suppression of customer demand	Adaptability	Marketing programs/Educational seminars
Vehicle bulbs initiatives	World industry competition/Loss of domestic market	Adaptability	Experimental sales force/New machinery/reorganization
Safety improvements	New safety legislation/Arrival of government inspectors	Adaptability	Machinery modification/Safety committee reorganization
Carolvale Division Demand fall (operating crisis)	Consumer confidence lags and price increases/Demand falls	Flexibility	Research of exchange control legislation
Ronson Division Demand fall (operating crisis)	Consumer confidence lags and price increases/Demand falls	Flexibility	Marketing programs
Weld Division Demand fall (operating crisis)	World economic slump in oil production equipment/Demand falls	Flexibility	New prices/Lower production levels/Export order

Table 16–1 continued

Corporation/Response	Capacity/Discontinuity	Discontinuity Exceeds	Some Major Subresponses
Container Division			
Three-day week	Energy shortages/Government legislated three-day week	Flexibility	Average bonus paid despite low production level
Demand surge (operating crisis)	Anticipated shortages/Panic buying	Flexibility	Reduced ink and paper variants
Jackson Mines			
Demand fall (operating crisis)	World economic recession/Demand falls	Flexibility	Reduced take-home pay
Blake's Grid	Attitudes of work force/Repeated strikes	Adaptability	Application of Blake's Grid
Schumacker			
Demand cutoff	Suspected salmonella content/Halting of customer demand	Flexibility	Public relations campaign
Suza Cars			
Product range	Safety legislation and supply problems/Market and product availability threatened	Adaptability	New car layouts/"Discovery" of new process

took place, particularly to withstand working capital shortages as the price increases of suppliers needed to be met before accounts had been received from customers. A total situation was, therefore, asymmetrically distributed across the organizations depending upon specifics in time and place.

The formative role of situational specifics on decisions was significant in many ways, as indicated in the proposition. (This matter is to be treated further in chapter 20.) The general manager of Jackson Mines, because of his training, perceived labor relations problems in broad, cultural terms rather than in repeated operating responses that would have dealt individually with symptoms rather than with root causes. But situational specifics were observed in some cases to influence not only how problems were perceived but also where, in the more complex organizations, they were first addressed and with most effectiveness. It was no accident that the problems of competition from inexpensive retail oil products should reach significance in the Netherlands before other national markets because of the presence of the oil refining complex and spot markets of Rotterdam. Other things being equal, it was natural also that the first solution to this problem general to Prosper throughout Europe should arise in that market where the harshness of the situation and the capacity for solutions were both most strongly present. Further, the use of Rotterdam prices for internal control and motivation was a natural outgrowth of the predisposition and particular experience of the manager following his extensive experience as a trader at the Chicago Board of Trade. It would have been very unlikely that a specialist in organizational motivation would have recommended this free market solution that worked so well and became a model for the other Prosper subsidiaries in Europe.

Thus, parts of responses sometimes took place unevenly in various suborganizations within a company, according to which parts of the total organization were most affected or best able to respond. A response, when viewed as a whole and especially in the more complex cases, can be seen as a synthesis of these quasi-independent activities that took place around the organization. For most cases, and particularly for operating responses, this synthesis often fitted the classical model of coordination of the respective functional areas of the business—marketing, manufacturing, and so on. Sometimes this activity was more subtle, such as the careful incorporation of skills and resources held through the oil businesses of Prosper and Atlas into the fledgling coal business. Another process concerned with dissemination was observed where subresponses proven at one point in the organization spread around the organization at large. For example, the techniques of scenario planning gradually spread around the whole of Atlas from very local and specialized beginnings.

Managerial implications of the asymmetric response of organizations according to the pattern of local conditions in the company, and the synthetic or dissemination processes that accompany them, are various:

In more difficult situations it is probably more effective to facilitate apparently useful initiatives from suborganizations particularly affected or particularly motivated to make suitable changes, rather than attempt a centralized analysis of the overall environment and seek to implement universally the recommendations of that analysis. Better information is probably available at selected parts of the institution, together with local environments especially rich in the phenomena of concern and providing, therefore, particularly fertile grounds for the formulations of relevant solutions.

It may be dysfunctional to limit idiosyncratic initiatives, because possibly the intense situational and distinctive character of those initiatives may be of particular value to the wider organization where unprecedented flexibility or adaptability is required.

It may be beneficial to manage consciously the relatively late phase of response that is largely overlooked in present literature that uses synthetic processes to (1) coordinate subresponses within a suborganization, (2) integrate subresponses across a wider organization, or (3) disseminate subresponses from one suborganization to another.

To conclude, the asymmetric and fragmented nature of response across a whole organization generally implied a less deterministic and more facilitative approach to management.

Character of Response and Discontinuity

The third proposition was stated in chapter 3 as:

> *Proposition 3.* Discontinuity and the associated response are characterized by novelty, instability, and compression.

All three characteristics were present in all the researched cases and seemed adequately to describe the circumstances of response. Inspection of the data showed that for every response there was the presence of (1) phenomena issuing from the environment of the respective organization that were of a magnitude or character previously not experienced (an expectation governing selection of the sample), (2) a succession of recurring disruptions around and after the discontinuity, and (3) a need for actions to be taken against the possibility of significant financial loss—the threat of loss being immediate and generally severe in operating responses and one of an opportunity cost for other responses because of the need to grasp opportunities or adapt to change promptly in competitive environments.

Novelty in the sense of the unprecedented obviously applied to all cases (a criterion for acceptance in the sample). Novelty in the sense of a different nature applied to all but the more linear operating responses (typically those dealing with demand falls) where managers perceived situations largely as major extensions of established activities or more extreme examples of past occurrences.

Instability, or the capacity for the situation to provide a series of unpredictable variations subsequent to the discontinuity, was common throughout. Again, however, this tendency was least for operating responses concerned with sudden falls in demand. In more taxing operating responses and in administrative responses, instability impacted decision-making considerably, as the difficulties of analyzing environmental developments and of interpreting the results of preceding actions were compounded by instability.

Compression was found characteristic of response also. Urgency applied with most force to operating responses, but for administrative and corporate responses the importance of the situations pressured organization members for timely results.

Only some very general managerial implications concerning novelty, instability, and compression are to be drawn here, because these characteristics, intrinsic to response, color many of the findings of subsequent chapters relating to decision processes themselves. These characteristics, for example, mean that initial subresponses or collections of subresponses formulated to reconcile some aspect of a discontinuity are likely to require subsequent adjustment or additional subresponses because of recurring instabilities. Where novelty is highest, provisional or exploratory initial efforts may be especially appropriate. Skillful leadership creating well-directed energy in the organization when and where required seemed a particular benefit under time pressure. The managers' abilities at the Weld and Container Division and also at Jackson Mines to exceed production records when external conditions required it present three examples of apparently effective action under compression.

Corporate, Administrative, and Operating Responses

The preceding data enabled evaluation and deepening of the observations made on the three distinct types of response when they were introduced in chapter 3. For convenience, proposition 4 is repeated here:

Proposition 4. Three distinct types of response exist (corporate, administrative, and operating) and the details and circumstances of the response situations differ according to each type. In particular:

Proposition 4.1. Corporate response involves an added structure, clear overall goals, and loosely defined subresponses. Special arrangements are necessary to obtain needed expertise, and the overall atmosphere is one of learning and experiment.

Proposition 4.2. Administrative response involves revisions to structure, unclear goals, and emergent, uncertain subresponses. Needed expertise requires revised thinking from present organization members; introspection and reeducation characterize the general atmosphere.

Proposition 4.3. Operating response involves expedience around an existing structure, apparent goals, and sometimes obvious but generally extreme subresponses. Response is managed by prior organization members and, while tasks may be clear, ingenious solutions employed under high pressure are often characteristic.

Table 3–1 and the accompanying text explain the meaning of these general terms. The above propositions could not be rejected.

Corporate Response

The corporate responses involved addition of distinctly new operations and a separate organizational structure. A clear ultimate goal was expressed, for example, "entering the coal industry and achieving net sales of at least 5 percent of total corporate net sales within five years" (stated by both Prosper and Atlas managements), but detailed intentions were not specified. The level of ignorance concerning the coal industry was high, and something of an opportunistic attitude prevailed in the early years. Both Prosper and Atlas grasped opportunities as they emerged, without adhering to a detailed set of prior formulated programs. Problems of limited expertise were solved by assembling a team in each case that comprised technical knowledge and managerial skills thought necessary for the coal diversifications. Special and sometimes outside consultants and other personnel were required to compensate for the missing expertise in these teams, but both Prosper and Atlas managed their responses with a minimum of outsiders, and consultants were only secured in highly technical areas. Overall, the corporate responses were characterized by a clear mission (to enter the coal industry) with learning and experiment to cope with ignorance and uncertainty. For example, it was reported in chapters 5 and 6 that the company's managers were learning about the coal industry as they went along, and trying ideas out on a small scale before adopting them fully.

Corporate response required a balancing of the competing needs for sheltering and supporting the infant organization while, at the same time, allowing the infant organization to achieve its own distinct character as necessary to succeed in the new venture. Success seemed significantly determined by:

1. an independent and strongly supported management
2. a symbolically managed separateness (even though the diversifications were fully dependent on their parents for resources)

3. an organizational freedom only constructively bounded as necessary by the parent company

The selection of personnel for each stage of growth of the diversification appeared critical, with entrepreneurs preceding professional managers. When the diversification became professionally managed, it was possible to establish a structure and group of executives that appeared, at least, to reflect more nearly the overall values of the parent companies. Development of professional management put the businesses on a firm footing but did increase the possibility of transferring unsuitable ways of operating from the corporations' main businesses, and of encouraging or allocating excessive overheads.

Administrative Response

Structure, in the sense of patterns of authority and communication and the information and data that flow around the organization, was amended in all the administrative responses. This was achieved in one or more of three different ways:

1. introduction of a new management system, such as that devised at Interoil to minimize foreign currency exchange losses, or new guidelines, such as the new safety engineering specifications at National Lighting
2. reorganization, such as the formation of the new large and powerful public relations department at Columbus Bank
3. the implementation of new marketing campaigns (such as the Inflation Beaters campaign at National Lighting), or the construction of new manufacturing facilities (such as the catalytic cracker at Prosper) that amended relationships of members of the total system of organization and environment

The administrative responses tended to take place within unclear goals. This was because it took time and effort for all the managers essential to the implementation of a given administrative response to accept and understand the ambiguities that the often perplexing challenges presented. It was usual, therefore, for intentions to materialize in only an uncertain and evolving fashion as different aspects of the situation gradually became clarified among local groups of managers. The adoption of Rotterdam prices by Prosper and the adoption of scenario planning by Atlas management probably most fully illustrates this uncertain, evolving process, but it was also evident at the Industrial Products Division (which probably faced the clearest set of challenges) in their management of cash flow and in their management of the recession.

Expertise necessary to administrative responses was generally held within the company or division. The key question was one of the managers' recognizing and understanding their circumstances. The same managers were involved (although there is evidence that outsiders helped in the process of recognition and understanding in some cases) in administrative responses; there were seldom special project teams, as occurred in the two corporate responses. Overall, administrative responses were characterized by introspection as managers groped to understand the challenges, and by reeducation as managers adjusted to new ways of working. Prosper's catalytic cracker and Rotterdam pricing, and Atlas's scenario planning probably represent this introspection and reeducation most fully among the responses researched in this study, but the general observation holds true for all the other administrative responses.

Managing administrative responses well seemed, on the basis of the data collected here, to be primarily a matter of:

1. encouraging early recognition of the need for response
2. assisting managers to educate themselves on the implications presented by the need for response
3. achieving consensus at a critical level for discrete subresponses that can lead the organization to the needed development

Early recognition can be assisted by insisting upon the provisional interpretation of difficulties as symptoms of a root cause rather than isolated incidents. Managers can be assisted in educating themselves on the implications of a given challenge by a host of means, such as the circulation of critical documents written by experts and attendance at management meetings and seminars. Achieving consensus to execute needed behavioral and physical changes can be assisted by careful manipulation of power within an organization, the shifting of personnel, and the holding of personal and group meetings engineered to create dialogue and eventual action. Examples existed in the data of all these various devices, and all seemed constructively to influence events.

Operating Response

In operating responses the structure remained the same but expedience prevailed around it. The Prosper and Atlas patterns of authority and communication altered for response, as operators and lower managers temporarily held more authority and sometimes communicated directly to top management. Patterns of information and data flow altered also, as special information was provided and different data went to different locations in the organization. The goal, often just to keep operations going, was clear during operating responses, but how to accomplish that goal was usually not so clear. Thus, while the Carolvale Division and Ronson Division managements were both clear about their goal (essentially to minimize losses), both deliberated anxiously on the different impacts of general or selective price cuts, on foreign currency guarantees, on when to act on promotional offerings, and on when to hold back and reserve their position.

While operating responses were a novel experience for many of the corporations researched in this study, suitable management expertise was available. Decisions related to operations that were typically well understood, and trained managers were instinctively aware of the need to cut costs in the face of poor demand, to stimulate sales where additional revenue exceeded additional costs, and to keep operations running as smoothly as possible at the highest economic level. Thus expertise already held in the organization was usually adequate for operating response unless the structure was somewhat incomplete, such as at Schumacker where experts were brought in from outside. Overall, the atmosphere in operating responses was one of clear tasks (although ones that were often extremely challenging), a search for ingenious solutions among everyday resources and managers, and expedient, high-pressure working conditions as tight deadlines were met and opportunities were maximized as nearly as possible. This general atmosphere was observed in all the researched examples of operating responses.

Managing operating responses apparently benefited from recognition of businesses as being a coalition of workers, customers, suppliers, and perhaps others such as government bodies. An operating response was required when the smooth working of this coalition broke down, and successful management of an operating response revolved around maintaining the coalition so that it could operate at the highest possible level in the circumstances. In the better managed operating responses, management focused its efforts on the members of the coalition whose cooperation was most critical to maintaining operations as near as possible to the required level. Thus, encouraging customers to purchase was critical in the Carolvale Division and Ronson Division demand falls, and finding additional supplies was critical in the Container Division demand surge. To maximize financial results, an important skill was one of soliciting the required additional support from the critical members at the lowest cost. For example, the Carolvale Division and Ronson Division promotions were carefully targeted to specific groups of consumers so that needed sales could be won at the lowest cost. Careful management against a time scale was also important in maximizing financial results. For example, Weld Division offered progressively greater price discounts and progressively deeper cuts in production rates as their demand fall worsened. Weld Division strived to balance the competing risks of over- or under-production against an uncertain future.

Complex, Divisional, and Simple Settings

In chapter 3 it was reasoned that three distinct types of organizational settings could be distinguished within which response could take place. The relevant proposition read as follows:

Proposition 5. The form and nature of response is contingent upon the type of organization setting within which it takes place, of which three types can be differentiated: complex, divisional, and simple (excluding the multinational and infantile cases).

Proposition 5.1. In complex settings, the response can be termed loosely as *complicated.*

Proposition 5.2. In divisional settings, the response can be termed loosely as *relatively systematic.*

Proposition 5.3. In simple settings, the response can be termed loosely as *improvised.*

Table 3–2 and the accompanying text explain the meaning of these general terms.

Experience indicated that the classification of organization settings was found to be reasonably sound, but five of the twenty-six responses, in particular, seemed somewhat anomalous. The responses of Prosper and Atlas to the oil embargo (chapter 10) were noted to be more centrally coordinated and led more directly than the other responses in those companies. Those responses were recognized to be examples of what were termed functional responses, expected in chapter 3 to follow the characteristics typical of the overall corporate settings without the need for cross-organizational interaction. Inflation Beaters and safety legislation responses at National Lighting also were recognized as functional responses, but were identified in chapter 13 as being somewhat simpler than the other divisional responses which pervaded the whole organization. Also, the response at National Lighting to the major loss of market share in their vehicle bulbs business was recognized as unrepresentatively complex for a divisional setting, as well as inconsistent with expectations for response in divisional settings proposed in chapter 3.

A further weakness in the general notion of a site of a given type resulting in responses of the equivalent type was also demonstrated in the collected data. Many responses in Prosper and Atlas arose from and through subresponses arising individually in suborganizations that were akin to simple or divisional settings, and through processes expected to be more characteristic of simple and divisional settings. Notable, for example, is the first use of Rotterdam prices for an internal control system in the essentially divisional Netherlands subsidiary of Prosper. Also, note the first development of the scenario methodology at Atlas in the corporate planning department—more nearly a functional (sub)response. These weaknesses of the simple contingency model according to the three organizational types (complex, divisional, and simple) stimulated a deeper analysis of the possible organizational contingency determining response.

An Amended Conceptualization

The above cases demonstrated that, in the last resort, it was the nature of the relation of the response to the involved aspects of the host organization that determined the real setting within which the response took place. In the overwhelming majority of cases, the general classification of the organizational setting yielded a response correspondingly. Thus a complex setting yielded a "complex response" and a divisional setting a "divisional response." But these anomalous cases showed that a more precise definitional statement would be one that necessarily embraced as one whole or ensemble the needs of response and the exact details of the organization relative to those needs. Thus, for example, one characteristically complex response occurred in a division when the conditions generated by the relationship of the response to the organization satisfied broadly those of a complex organizational setting (the vehicle bulbs response of the National Lighting Division).

The expectations of chapter 3 for an organizational contingency for response were amended, therefore, to describe more precisely the three patterns of organizational circumstances that apparently governed the progress of a response, rather than the three general types of organization in which responses arose. Table 16–2 presents the features of complex, divisional, and simple settings as amended in the light of the above findings. The term *complex setting,* for example, is now reserved for conditions where the determining organizational features exist, even if the surrounding organization is of divisional or simple form. A complex setting is now said to exist where several quasi-independent operational units are involved, where there are probably many levels of management and some staff functions involved, where rewards are diffuse and gently enforced, and where actual leadership is probably dispersed and somewhat amorphous. Such conditions existed at National Lighting in the case of the response to the surge of imported vehicle bulbs, although the site itself was definitively a division in every way, even by name.

Divisional settings are now recognized from table 16–2 as those, independent of the overall host organization, that are generally centrally coordinated and responsible within a medium scope of activities, involve a medium number of levels of management in medium relative complexity, experience a focus and commitment of managerial efforts and professional leadership, and where performance measurements are reasonably tightly defined and strictly enforced. *Simple settings* are now recognized as those within which a response takes place that meets the conditions of a single operational unit of simple or inexplicit organizational form, a small number of managers, medium or low technical complexity, that revolves around leading personalities, and possibly includes strong personal leadership administered on informal and personal grounds. If the above conditions apply, it is to be recognized as a simple organizational setting, irrespective of whether the overall organization can or cannot be described in those terms.

This amendment of the meaning of complex, divisional, and simple organizational settings removes the anomalies to the model presented in chapter 3 for the five responses where the prior model was found insufficient. Also, the

Table 16–2
Features of Complex, Divisional, and Simple Settings, as Amended

	Complex Setting	*Divisional Setting*	*Simple Setting*
Organization	*Diverse*	*Focused*	*Simple or incomplete*
Involved organizational units	Several organizational units involved of broad scope, acting relatively independently	Centrally coordinated and responsible organizational field of medium scope	A single, small operational unit of simple or explicit organizational form
Involved hierarchy	Probably many levels of management and many staff functions involved	A medium number of levels of management	A small number of levels of management
Technicality	*Complicated*	*Controlled*	*Confined*
Operations	High relative complexity	Medium relative complexity	Medium or low relative complexity
Culture	*Rigid*	*Professional*	*Personal*
Leadership	Distributed leadership exerting only contextual influence	Focused commitment with few sacred cows and a professional leadership	Revolves around leading personalities with possibly strong personal leadership
Rewards and performance measurements	Diffuse and relatively gently enforced	Tightly defined and strictly enforced	Largely unformalized or administered on personal grounds
Discontinuity/ Response	*Complicated*	*Systematic*	*Improvised*
Discontinuity	For corporate and administrative responses the significance may be misconceived	Usually immediate, with alternative managerial views on the nature of the problem relatively rare	Extreme, immediate, and readily interpreted for its significance
Comprehension	Difficult to comprehend because of diverse organization and complicated technical circumstances (external and internal)	Relatively straightforward to comprehend because of focused organization and controlled technical circumstances	Simple to identify but perhaps difficult to understand because of limited expertise and resources
Response	Substantial and wide-ranging in the organization. Decisions taken in an incremental, testing fashion in high complexity and high uncertainty	Problems investigated and relatively comprehensive decisions put into effect, with difficulties that arise dealt with as necessary within moderate uncertainty	Large investment of time and other resources (relative to organization), tightly managed under high risk because of vulnerability and limited expertise
Programs	Difficult to implement within a complicated structure of many levels and many departments, subsidiaries, etc. and operations of high complexity	Relatively straightforward to implement within a complete, well-regulated structure and operations of medium complexity	Implementation tests ingenuity because of organizational limitations, although operations are of medium or low complexity

amendments remove the need to separately identify functional responses. Under this new schema, the supply department responses to the oil embargo occur within what can be recognized straightforwardly as a divisional setting. The Inflation Beaters and safety legislation responses in National Lighting more nearly fit the divisional setting as described in the amended model than the prior model. Further, the vehicle bulbs response in National Lighting can now be admitted within the new schema as occurring within a complex organizational setting. Other responses and subresponses recounted in the data also more consistently meet the requirements of their respective classification according to this slightly amended view of organizational setting.

Responses in Complex Settings

Complex settings were described in chapter 3 and table 16–2 as organizationally diverse, technically complicated and culturally rigid. Chapters 5 to 11 reported responses in complex settings. Prosper, Atlas, (except the supply function responses to the oil embargo), Interoil, Columbus Bank, DeVito Power, and the vehicle bulbs response at National Lighting represented examples of this classification of organizational setting (as amended). Consistent with expectations, the response process within complex settings tended to be relatively cumbersome and the management challenge somewhat unwieldy.

For example, the corporate responses investigated in Prosper and Atlas showed a process that was slow, iterative, and opportunistic. The administrative response through all complex settings showed a natural, evolving kind of process where later actions reflected the results of earlier, more circumscribed actions.

It seemed from the responses studied here that the managerial differences between the three organizational settings were most conveniently illustrated by the relatively distinctive roles of senior management and of lower management for each setting. In the investigated complex settings, senior management problems were observed to be relatively unwieldy. Senior management, because of the wide distribution of power in complex settings, tended to manage response by conceptualizing and communicating issues and inviting initiatives to take hold from lower levels. Thus, the role of lower management was to recommend actions within the general terms of reference laid down by more senior management. In some complex settings there were many corporate specialists, so that the expertise necessary for responses tended to exist in-house.

Response in Divisional Settings

Divisional settings were described in chapter 3 as organizationally focused, technically controlled, and culturally professional. Industrial Products Division, National Lighting Division (except the vehicle bulbs response), Carolvale

Division, Ronson Division, Weld Division, and Container Division were reported in chapters 12 to 14 and represented examples of discontinuity and response in divisional settings. Under the amended conceptualization, the supply function responses at Prosper and Atlas to the oil embargo may be recognized as examples of divisional responses also. The response process tended to be orchestrated, and the management problems tended to be capable of instrumental resolution rather than the rather less interventionist approach apparently usual in complex settings.

As a result of the focused organization and narrowly defined business of divisional settings, the impact of discontinuities tended to be direct. Vulnerability to discontinuity for a particular division may be high, but the fortunes of the corporation as a whole may continue to be secure because the corporation would probably include several divisions that might not be affected.

Because of the focused organization and controlled technical circumstances, as well as the often complete, well-regulated management organization, management action generally proceeded according to some centralized logic. Senior management was able to identify and delegate tasks to progress responses, and the role of lower management was, therefore, to follow such delegated tasks. Operating responses were, for example, often achieved by coordinated actions that were well controlled by the senior and professional management. Administrative responses were the subject of more iterations and complications, but also generally proceeded with the benefit of relatively comprehensive decision making.

Response in Simple Settings

Simple settings were described in chapter 3 as organizationally simple or incomplete, technically confined, and culturally personal. Jackson Mines, Schumacker, and Suza Cars were presented in chapter 15 as examples of this type of organizational setting. In chapter 3 it was reasoned that response in a simple setting would tend to be rather improvised, and the field experience demonstrated that this was generally true.

The two administrative responses investigated in simple settings showed considerable determination and ingenuity as small management teams put themselves on the line against tight and compelling deadlines with rather limited understandings of what form the final response would take. Operating responses tended to be highly coordinated because of the few people involved, but nevertheless often involved a large number of irregular steps rather than linearly smooth action because of (1) limited expertise, and (2) the risk of corporate failure. Senior managers just got on with the tasks at hand, and less senior managers tended to be in an assistant capacity to the strong, personal, perhaps owning senior manager. Specialists were used to compensate for organizational inadequacies.

This chapter examined several features of response. A model of response, and a pattern of overall response, was found characteristic of the data collected for this study concerning discontinuity and associated response. Three types of response and three organizational settings also were reviewed in this chapter for their influence on managing response. With this background it is now possible to look in depth in subsequent chapters at how decision processes were managed in discontinuities.

17
Finding Solutions

I n chapter 3 proposition 6 stated "decision processes find solutions close to the experience of the decision maker(s) and represent small steps from the status quo." This proposition was developed from prior research findings and from well-accepted theoretical foundations. Is it possible, with the evidence of the field experience and with the recorded data in part II of this book, to refute this proposition?

Accepting the propositon would be consistent not only with the varied sources used to develop the proposition but also with other bodies of literature. For example, Richard M. Cyert and James G. March (1963) describe search as problemistic, problem-motivated, simple-minded, and biased.[1] Similarly, Henry Mintzberg, Duru Raisinghani, and André Théorêt[2] found a general tendency for search to occur initially with familiar sources in local or immediately accessible areas. Only if memory or passive search fails, Mintzberg et al hypothesize, do decision makers search in more remote and less familiar areas and consider custom-made solutions rather than ready-made solutions.[3] The proposition also generally endorses relevant aspects of the incrementalist view on decision processes as small, partial, and somewhat gradual steps from the status quo[4] and is consistent with much that is known of individual decision-making as well.[5]

To examine the validity of the proposition, all the subresponses identifiable in the recorded data were examined for the solution that was employed and for the source of that solution. Without exception, the solution employed in every subresponse was found to exist previously in some form, somewhere. All solutions came from an existing organization, from suborganizations with which there were close or parallel working relationships, or externally from organizations of which one or more of the involved decision makers had direct experience.[6] There is no evidence whatsoever in the data collected for this study that would provide any basis for refutation of the proposition. Instead, data suggest overwhelmingly that the proposition be accepted "that solutions employed were close to the experience of the decision maker(s) and represent small steps from the status quo."

This general proposition needs, however, to be deepened and refined to be of practical consequence for managers. Reasoning from first principles, there can be only three general ways by which elements of an organizational system can be moderated within this accepted proposition:

1. by *realigning* existing elements into a different but still common pattern
2. by *reemphasizing* the relative importance of the existing elements with respect to each other
3. by introducing new elements into the system, *replicating* them from elsewhere

A pattern of sources and uses of solutions can be postulated. In an operating response, it may be assumed that the pressures for close-by and familiar solutions is greatest. Operationally, the need is to realign the factors of production and sales to the most favorable alternative balance. Within the available time period the factors can be:

1. *rebalanced* by boosting, cutting, hastening, or slowing
2. *intensified* by selective attention to new and temporary interdependencies in operations

It was shown in the data collected for this study that operating responses were concerned with meeting the organizational need for flexibility in the face of discontinuity.

The longer run adaptation of the organization to its environment was the domain of administrative responses. There were three ways by which this adaptation can be achieved through reemphasis:

1. by *accelerating* selected development projects and allowing others to lapse
2. by *accentuating* the relative importance of newly preferred resources or skills over others
3. by *focusing* certain sets of desired resources or skills formerly dispersed or overlooked

Two ways were also provided for achieving adaptation from existing resources and skills by replicating those held elsewhere:

1. by *transferring* them from within the same corporation
2. by *adopting* them from outside the corporation

Each of the subresponses identified in the field data collected for this study were evaluated against the three general cases (realignment, reemphasis, and replication) and their seven subcases (rebalancing, intensifying, accelerating, accentuating, focusing, transferring, and adopting). Examples of all the postulated cases were found in the data, and every subresponse could be assigned to one of the eight categories without ambiguity.

To summarize, the researched reports showed that although novelty was a characteristic of all discontinuities, the solutions found for responses already existed in some form, somewhere. In fact, solutions were found by (1) realigning what already existed, or (2) reemphasizing what already existed, or (3) replicating what already existed. Taken together, these were dubbed the Three Rs.

A company that was healthy before a discontinuity had developed skills or resources useful even after a discontinuity disturbed the prevailing equilibrium. Cash-flow management had been a consideration in other Generaltex companies before it became of importance to Industrial Products Division. Energy efficiency in lighting units had been a concern before it achieved its importance at National Lighting Division after 1973, as had safety issues before the new legislation of 1976. Weld Division had been selling in export markets for many years, but the 1976 demand pattern amplified the importance of export sales. Similar examples of some relevant prior experience occurred for most responses. In those cases where no prior experience could be called on internally, consultants could offer the necessary skills, as at Schumacker, Jackson Mines, and elsewhere. Although the needed capability did not exist in-house, other companies had previously experienced comparable changes, and suitable expertise was therefore available externally.

The Three Rs

A comparison of the three Rs—realignment, reemphasis, and replication—is presented in table 17–1. The table summarizes for each of the three general ways of finding solutions (1) the basic mechanism involved, (2) the alternative or complementary constituent methods employed, (3) the overall outcome achieved in terms of the strategic change to the organization, and (4) the respone situations in which the method of finding solutions was usually dominant. Basic distinctions between the Three Rs are explained below.

Realignment was concerned with adjusting the present operations of a business so that they could become viable at a new level. Faced with a suddenly lower level of demand, for example, managements had no alternative but to realign operations by cutting costs and, if possible, by boosting sales so that activities could subsequently proceed viably at this lower level. Thus, realignment was essentially concerned with operating response and was often the first line of attack for a company confronted by a discontinuity. When the major international oil companies were faced with substantial oil price increases in 1973 and 1978, the most urgent need was to realign distribution so that

Table 17–1
Finding Solutions: The Three Rs

	Realignment	*Reemphasis*	*Replication*
Basic mechanism	Realignment of existing resources	Reemphasis of skills and resources already held by the company	Replication of skills or resources already existing elsewhere in the company or externally
Constituent methods	Rebalancing Intensifying	Accelerating Accentuating Focusing	Transferring Adopting
Overall outcome	Brings about a higher or lower level of viable operations	Change of fit of organization and environment	Introduces new skills
Situations where usually dominant	Operating response	Administrative and corporate response	Administrative and corporate response

operations would proceed as smoothly as possible and meet the excess of demand over supply as optimally as possible. The deeper, longer run implications of an industry working under a different pattern of supply and demand was a matter for more reflective consideration, and for which reemphasis and replication provided the most suitable means of finding solutions.

Reemphasis found solutions for response by (1) relatively varying the rate at which different projects were developed; (2) increasing or decreasing the importance of certain products, departments, individual managers, or other resources or skills; or (3) consolidating formerly dispersed skills or resources. By adjusting the emphasis of the various attributes already under development or in existence in the business, an improved longer run fit between the business and its environment was accomplished.

Replication was concerned with the introduction into an organization of products, systems, or skills in existence elsewhere but previously absent in that organization. Sometimes this involved the transfer of certain ideas, systems, products, or other items held in one part of a company to another part of that company, and sometimes the adoption of such items from outside of the company.

Each of these three distinct methods of finding solutions was selectively employed, singly or in combination, according to the needs of the situations. For example, the demand surges researched in this study tended to use realignment to maintain operations as viably as possible, and to use reemphasis to satisfy the different mix of products and the different mix of salesmanship, purchasing, and other managerial skills demanded by the situation. The diversification reported in this study involved variously, for example, reemphasis in consolidating the previously dispersed coal interests within the companies, replication in introducing several work operations of other companies and in modeling structure and systems on those present in the oil companies, and realignment, after the coal businesses were established, to meet the problems of strikes and other disruptions. Reemphasis and replication tended to represent long-run changes because (1) they were more complex and needed more time to implement and (2) they were relatively more expensive in real terms and in opportunity terms.

The dominant way of finding solutions for each of the strategic responses investigated in this study are recorded in table 17–2 as a brief statement of the source of the solution that was employed in each case. While much variation existed in the data, it was possible to distinguish typical management considerations that applied for realignment, reemphasis, and replication. Further, it was often possible to draw some conclusions on what actions seemed relevant to managing the situations well by comparing responses and by logically evaluating the facts of the researched situations.

Realignment

Realignment usually jointly required the following two activities:

1. rebalancing of operations
2. intensifying of selected operations

Rebalancing involved the cutting of costs and the stimulation of sales (in the case of a demand surge, the inverse held), and intensifying involved the extra efforts that such rebalancing demanded at specific parts of the company. Essentially, these efforts represented more hard work rather than a revised way of working.

Rebalancing

A rebalancing of existing operations played a major role in many responses. The commonest examples among the responses collected for this research were falls in demand. Response typically involved a realignment aiming to increase sales and reduce costs until a new balance was achieved at the lower level of activity. Carolvale Division and Ronson Division provide examples where marketing programs were introduced to attract customers and costs were cut in line with revised demand forecasts. Similarly, Weld Division manipulated prices to stimulate sales for its products while also cutting costs where it was feasible. Jackson Mines had limited marketing freedom but attempted to

Table 17–2
Use of the Three Rs in the Researched Responses

Company/Response	Realignment	Reemphasis	Replication
Prosper Oil			
Coal		Consolidation of existing minor interest in coal such as geologist and goodwill in Africa	Enthusiastic adoption by various foreign subsidiaries (South Africa and Australia)
Cracker			Use of design engineers and manufacturers familiar with these crackers
Rotterdam pricing			Equivalent market prices adopted for control and motivation by most European subsidiaries in lieu of transfer prices
Embargo	Existing operations intensified and rescheduled	Older operators led in need for manual as opposed to computer systems	
Atlas Oil			
Coal		Consolidation of existing minor interests in coal as a) hydro-carbon research and b) mineral exploration	Proposal "propelled" through adoption by overseas subsidiary companies
Scenario			Adopted for capital investment appraisal by management from academic usage
Embargo	Existing operations intensified and rescheduled		
Interoil			
Foreign currency system		Development of expertise on floating exchange rates	
Columbus Bank			
Social outcry		Reorganization focused skills regarding public relations	
DeVito Power			
Exploit Middle East markets		Existing plans for small power stations reworked	

Industrial Products Division		
Demand surge		Sales incentive program
Pricing initiative	Existing skills and resources applied to new circumstances / Use of legal counsel invoking antitrust laws	
Recession	Realigning of operations	
Cash squeeze		Systems of cash control known in Generaltex
National Lighting Division		
Inflation Beaters	Existing products and marketing elements refocused to energy efficiency	
Vehicle bulbs	Temporary reorganization focused efforts	
Safety legislation	Existing skills enhanced on machine design and safety	Photoelectric cells introduced by consultants
Carolvale Division		
Demand fall	Adjustments to marketing programs	
Ronson Division		
Demand fall	Adjustments to marketing programs	
Weld Division		
Demand fall	Strenuous use of resources and skills	
Container Division		
Three-day work week	Strenuous use of resources and skills	
Meeting demand surge	Revised emphasis on marketing, purchasing, and other areas	
Schumacker		
Salmonella outbreak	Marshalling of existing skills and public relations (consultant)	
Jackson Mines		
Demand fall	Adjustments to operations	
Poor labor relations		Other users of the managerial grid
Suza Cars		
New range	Technology and skills in engineering	

maximize demand while reducing the work force and cutting costs. Thus, the joint steps of stimulating sales and cutting costs characterized rebalancing.

When stimulating sales, companies included in this research expended their efforts on attracting the "next possible sale." They worked at the margin, that is, using advertising, salesmanship, or a combination of both to attract the nearest target. For example, Weld Division pursued export markets where they had been formerly only weakly represented. Carolvale Division sought customers who had probably been purchasers of their vacation packages in earlier years but who did not have the resources to purchase a full-price vacation in that lean year of 1977. Thus, the careful and systematic identification of the nearest potential sales was characteristic.

Cutting costs also proceeded at the margin, that is, the most expendable items were cut first. But how the cost cutting was achieved was more interesting than what items were cut. Most critical was accommodation of the unpleasant realities of reducing take-home pay or of removing people from the organization. Two measures seemed useful to accomplish tasks successfully which affected people adversely:

1. wide publicity of impending problems
2. wide consultation with those affected

The impending slump in the world steel industry was well known and understood at Jackson Mines as a result of wide publicity, and the work force was therefore more willing to accept the need for reduced pay or dismissal. The work force at the Weld Division was widely consulted before the export order with the close deadline was accepted by the company, and this achieved commitment that had the order leaving the factory in record time.

Intensifying

Several responses used some intensifying or lessening of resources, personnel, managers, and information. For example, the responses of Prosper and Atlas to the 1973 OAPEC embargo of crude oil to certain nations were achieved through an intensifying of operations in some regards but a lessening of operations in other regards. Certain shipping routes such as Venezuela to the United States, certain storage facilities such as those in Northern Europe outside of the Netherlands, certain oil fields such as those of Iran and Venezuela, and certain ships were used intensively, while others were used less than normally or not at all. Certain personnel, such as those skilled in manual scheduling in Prosper, and certain managers, such as those most able to deal with extreme situations, played a major role, while others with less useful abilities for response receded in their importance over the period of the supply disruption. The same observation can be made of information channels, where some were "running hot" while others were suspended temporarily. Board involvement in operations was intensified to one of crucial importance in the embargo, while contact between the board and operations is very limited in normal times. A similar but less pronounced pattern of intensified and lessened use of resources, personnel, managers, and information also was observed in the other operating responses.

Response required, therefore, the intensive efforts of some personnel. How did management secure these efforts? The experience embraced in this research suggests that organizational loyalties and pride in the job may be sufficient to accomplish response. In most cases, no extraordinary incentives were provided—the spirit was very much one of expecting that employees and managers would do their duty in the hour of need. To assist commitment, managers often consciously engendered an esprit de corps. After the event, some reward was often made. For example, a bonus payment was made to a group of workers for their special efforts, although it was not solicited by the workers nor promised beforehand. In another case, the department that was used intensively in a response and stretched to the full received the approbation of a two-page feature in the company's annual report. The feature showed that special service was recognized, and set an example for other departments to follow in the future if that should be required of them.

One reason for the usual absence of any special payment for exceptional service rendered in response was the fact that those exceptional services were often perceived by the employees as necessary to keep their jobs. Perception of job insecurity coupled with a spirit of uniting against adversity were often factors in successful response, and managers usually lost no time in creating and exploiting such perceptions to engender a constructive atmosphere.

Reemphasis

In reemphasis, new ways of relating within the company or with its environment were brought about. This was achieved by emphasizing some part or parts of the corporation over others. As briefly noted above, the research showed that reemphasis could be achieved in a number of ways:

1. varying the rate of development of existing projects, termed *accelerating* or *decelerating*

2. increasing or decreasing the importance of some of the company's more suitable products or skills, termed *accentuating*

3. consolidating formerly dispersed skills or resources, termed *focusing*

Accelerating

In several situations the challenges presented by the discontinuity were partly countered by a simple acceleration or deceleration of activities that were already proceeding in the companies. Acceleration meant an added effort committed to the development so that it could come to fruition sooner than otherwise. Deceleration was a subtracted effort from ongoing developments so that they either came to fruition later or possibly not at all.

For example, Prosper's total response to the 1973/74 oil price increase involved the following accelerations in development:

> The planning and organization review committee published its report on the move to autonomous marketing subsidiaries sooner than would otherwise have been the case.

> Increased investments were made in the development and search for non–OPEC oil.

> Moves to diversify were hastened, such as entering the coal industry.

Several decelerations also took place in Prosper at around the same time. Some examples include:

> Capital investment was minimized in crude carriers and traditional refineries. Investments in these facilities that were already contracted were slowed to the maximum possible extent, and all optional related expenditures were curtailed.

> Manufacture of less profitable products was less strongly pursued, as allowed by the company's total supply, demand, and capital equipment position.

To achieve response, therefore, managers should review their situation for developments that are underway that should be accelerated or decelerated—organizational development, planning, research and development, and so on. Those deemed relevant to the company's new circumstances should be accelerated, and those deemed less relevant should be decelerated. Although the exact outcome of this exercise may not be discernible beforehand, it can pitch the company in constructive directions that can help to show ultimately the detailed steps that need to be taken.

Acceleration and deceleration were brought about in a number of ways, including (for acceleration):

> senior management intervention to bring about more strenuous pursuit of a particular development

> the establishment of tighter deadlines, the calling of more meetings, the more timely reporting of minutes or position papers, the use of larger time slots for meetings, and the use of more prestigious venues

closer supervision of the leader of the respective development

enhancement of the power or status of the leader of a development group or of the group as a whole

freer control of expenditures

Accentuating

Responses were sometimes achieved by accentuating some of the company's resources. For example, some discontinuities gave some products more potential in the marketplace than formerly—accentuating those products therefore helped in response. Similarly, some managerial skills (or other skills) became more relevant in the new circumstances—accentuating those managerial skills therefore helped in response.

In the Inflation Beaters response of the National Lighting Division, some products were accentuated to resurrect depressed demand in the face of higher energy costs. The most energy-efficient lamps in the company's product range were gradually emphasized over others. As a result, customers revised their buying behavior and actually began to replace existing lighting installations as an investment option. DeVito Power provided another example where small power stations (long obsolete in the domestic market) were brought to the fore as the main sales item in the new Middle Eastern Markets. Old drawings were literally taken out of archives and adapted for use in these new export markets.

An accentuation of skills occurred at the National Lighting Division also. To meet the new safety legislation requirements, existing safety engineering abilities at the National Lighting Company were expanded and applied more forcefully in machine design and rebuilding. Pressure to implement the new specification was the main managerial action to bring about a reemphasis of the skills, but it was supported by sending engineers to specialized courses and by other means.

Accentuation often was achieved at managerial levels by the making of management appointments that were deliberately designed to accentuate some skills in the organization that were required for response, but which were formerly only poorly represented. In the Atlas entry to the coal industry, the head of the operation was selected according to the needs of the fledgling company. The manager who was first appointed to head up the coal venture was politely referred to as an iconoclast and seemed encouraged to be defiant in fighting for the individual needs of the new business within a dominating corporation. His successor was a professional manager selected for his ability and interest in integrating the diverse operations as a unified, accountable, smoothly functioning business. The next appointment as head of the Atlas coal venture had a background in oil trading. The reason for the appointment was to bolster and improve the coal-trading side of the business, which was an appropriate bias to bring to the present stage of the infant international coal industry.

Where accentuation was used to achieve strategic change, progress was usually pursued on several fronts simultaneously, with each front supporting or extending other fronts. Specific techniques varied according to whether accentuation of products or other physical items was sought or a more general accentuation of particular managerial skills or perspectives. To accentuate products within a given product range, the process seemed to be one of a combined set of steps that gradually revised the importance of desired products: selective advertising, targeted salesmanship, increased production capacity, and so on. To accentuate skills within an organization, the researched examples suggested that managers should set goals on which the work force could concentrate their efforts, insist on reasonable progress toward target standards, make examples of successes, reward originators of successes, and reinforce required skills by job swapping, course attendance, and so on.

Focusing

In many responses, managers found solutions by taking what already existed in the organization but focusing it through reorganization as necessary to the new circumstances. Elements of a coal business existed in both Prosper and Atlas before steps to diversify into the coal industry were formalized. Prosper had coal activities in a small joint mining venture in which its South African subsidiary was a partner, and they had an influential coal geologist on the payroll. In Atlas, the research and development laboratories had been experimenting with some technical opportunities, such as coal slurry conversion, for many years, and geologists had been involved in contract coal exploration for client companies. In both Prosper and Atlas, occasional discussions on the possible move had spanned more than a decade among corporate planners, board members, and senior management, generally. The decision to enter the coal business partly represented a focusing or consolidation of activities and skills that were already present in the companies but scattered and unrelated.

At National Lighting, the appointment of the coordinator and the associated bringing together of the company's various interests in vehicle bulbs served several purposes in the company's response to the risk of losing the vehicle bulb market to foreign imports. Previously, vehicle bulbs had various and minor places as a small part of a total company marketing effort and a few manufacturing lines in a large, multiproduct factory. The reorganization concentrated attention on the vehicle bulb problem, increased commitment to resolution of the difficulties (particularly with the president's mandate behind the appointment), brought together efforts that would otherwise have taken much longer to coordinate effectively, and devoted more management time to a problem which would otherwise probably have remained organizationally marginal (vehicle bulbs represented less than 5 percent of the performance targets of each manager in the previous structure). Without this focusing of efforts on the problem by the general manager through a minor and temporary organization change, the response would have proceeded with less effectiveness and efficiency.

Another example was provided by Columbus Bank. Focusing through reorganization was crucial to the bank's response to the various and seemingly irrational social challenges that the bank was facing from time to time. Appointment of the senior executive as head of all the bank's customer contact departments (including marketing and public relations), with the chairman's conspicuous support, created a coordinated center of expertise more capable of managing social and related challenges.

These findings suggest, therefore, that if the new capability demanded by response was dispersed through the organization, managers should seek to find solutions by bringing about a focusing of these separate efforts through reorganization. In each of the three examples cited above, a task group or a person was appointed with senior management support for the purpose of carrying out the change. That person or group was given full responsibility to solve the problem at hand, and given at least some access to the respective parts of the organization which needed to be embraced to accomplish the response. The group or person was given considerable authority, either by direction of the most senior management or by virtue of the standing of the person or persons involved. It was necessary for the integrator to assume power within the organization in order to achieve essential cooperation from personnel in separate parts of the company who did not report directly to the integrator.

The group or person assigned for the task needed a grasp of the range of expertise necessary to completion of the task for which the focus in reorganization had been devised. For example, the coordinator at National Lighting had experience in most of the areas of the company critical to the success of their attempts to combat the foreign imports of vehicle bulbs (the exception was marketing, and efforts seem to have been less successful in that area). A similar breadth of experience was present also in the groups put together for both of the coal diversifications and also in the appointment of the senior manager at Columbus Bank to coordinate the response to social issues.

Replication

In replication, solutions were found for response by replicating or copying devices already used elsewhere. Sometimes the model existed in the same company and sometimes outside of it. In the former case, replication involved the transfer of already quite well understood models, and the problems were largely those of easing the adoption into a similar organization and making the detailed modifications to the general system that were necessary. In the latter case, rather less well understood models were introduced to an organization within the company for the first time with the increased likelihood of more major organizational disruption, unexpected consequences, and the need for more major adaptation of the model. Replication of models already held within the corporation was termed *transferring* and replication of models from outside the corporation was termed *adopting*. Examples of responses from this research that most conspicuously displayed replication were those concerned with the design and incorporation of management systems to motivate revised managerial behavior, although it is believed that the general concept applies also to products, machines, and other skills and resources.

Transferring

Prosper provided an example of transfer of solutions within the same company. Use of free-market prices for internal control and motivation first happened in the Dutch subsidiary. The idea and its implementation was a response to the specialized supply and competitive position that existed in the Netherlands, but global trends were following broadly the same lines of development. As the needs of the whole company shifted in sympathy with those previously experienced in the Netherlands, so one European subsidiary after another replicated what Prosper Netherlands already had in place, and thus achieved more independent marketing operations.

Another example was provided by Atlas. In the middle 1970s one subsidiary after another introduced scenario planning, and later its use spread to routine evaluation of capital investment projects. In these cases, the users had only to copy the model first introduced by the corporate planners in 1968 with its later refinements. This important scenario planning response to uncertainties in the oil industry came about after its initial adoption by the corporate planners by simply replicating the system as it then existed within the company.

The management challenge in the transfer of models held within the same company appeared in the evidence of this research to be smoother generally than the adoption of models from outside. Otherwise, problems and management considerations of replicating by transfer and by adoption were observed to be equivalent and will be discussed in the next section.

Adopting

How did the original free-market price system come about at Prosper Netherlands, and how did the first use of scenario planning come into being in Atlas? In fact, these original models were also developed by replication from models available outside of each company. The Chicago Board of Trade provided the prototype for the use of free-market prices in Prosper Netherlands, and widely published futures studies of the late 1960s provided the prototypes for scenario planning in Atlas.

The copying of established models from outside the companies was present in many of the researched responses. Although a challenge to Prosper, construction of the large catalytic cracker was a replication of similar capital projects already completed by other oil companies with a more substantial refining emphasis. Skills of consulting engineers, plant suppliers, building companies, and other essentials to the project were available to Prosper. Adaptation of earlier works and existing products that had been commissioned by others was largely all that was required of their various suppliers. Another example was the adoption of the Blake and Mouton Grid at Jackson Mines which was modeled on its successful implementation in other, sometimes quite similar companies.

Apart from the obvious question of a judgment on the suitability of a particular model considered for adoption, the fieldwork showed that two joint processes were also important:

1. modification of the model so that it suited the organization and the exact purpose for which it was intended
2. preparation of the organization for the model to be applied

It was necessary, therefore, to establish:

1. a clear understanding of the conceptual meaning of the system to be adopted
2. a sensitive and detailed understanding of the specific circumstances in the organization (or suborganization) within which the model was to be implemented
3. a process of education to accompany implementation of the replicated systems

A few examples will be used to explain the importance of understanding the conceptual meaning of the system. It was not until the Rotterdam pricing system, introduced in the Netherlands, was fully understood as representing opportunity costs that it was possible to appropriately modify the general concept to other European subsidiaries of Prosper. Similarly, adoption of the scenario planning system in Atlas proceeded apace only when the conceptual problems were smoothed out, such as the need for scenarios to be conceived by management as a range of possible outcomes. Also, the foreign exchange control system at Interoil was readily adopted only when the conceptual facts were established that foreign exchange problems should be dealt with by line management and that the treasury department should take only an advisory role.

The importance of a sensitive and detailed understanding of the specific circumstances in the organization (or suborganization) is indicated also. Use of opportunity costs for motivation and control purposes in Prosper's European subsidiaries was heavily dependent on the modification of the system exactly to the local conditions—to the Swiss company's option of purchasing from Italy, to the Scandinavian companies' alternative supply from markets other than Rotterdam, and to the realities of a refinery in the German company's financial statements. Similarly, the successful adoption of the Blake and Mouton Grid at Jackson Mines was partly testimony to the consultant's careful introduction of the system in a way that respected, and was sensitive to, power structures and past incidents that had colored perceptions of the workers and junior management.

It was noted also that an extensive educational process accompanied the introduction of the management systems observed in this research. The concepts and problems behind Rotterdam pricing gradually became better understood through experience with it and through observation of situations where it was already in operation, and study of these situations helped prepare its introduction to other parts of the Prosper company. The practical matters associated with using scenario planning in Atlas for individual business plans and capital investment proposals were monitored and evaluated, and the corporate planners found themselves frequently acting in a tutorial capacity with line managers. In other cases, the educational process was managed systematically by providing courses. Thus Generaltex provided several courses on cash management for various levels of management and staff to which the managers of the Industrial Products Division sent many of their employees, as did the managers of other divisions of the parent company.

Thus, solutions were found in response in practical ways, by taking what already existed somewhere and realigning, reemphasizing, or replicating it. There were good reasons for using what was already available and close-to-hand. Usually those solutions were tested and understood, and the risks of applying them were therefore less. It was often good judgment for managers to accept solutions that were known to be partial, inelegant, apparent, imperfect, and nonoptimal, because they could be relied upon to work. Managing their known or more limited deficiencies was a small price to pay for solid management that probably allowed a response to proceed more efficiently to a more effective result.

Although it was important to understand where solutions were found for responses, it was also important to understand how problems were solved in response. While some situations could be managed in deliberate terms, other seemed more temperamental. Why did Atlas make one or two false starts in its coal venture? Why did DeVito Power pursue its goal without a detailed sense of what was necessary to its achievement? Analysis of the responses showed two distinct means of problem solving. Much of the heterogeneity in how the researched responses were managed was explained by recognizing the complex coupling of two complementary but contrasting approaches. The following chapter elaborates.

Notes

1. Richard M. Cyert and James G. March, *A Behavioral Theory of the Firm* (Englewood Cliffs, N.J.: Prentice–Hall, 1963), pp. 120–122.

2. Henry Mintzberg, Duru Raisinghani, and André Théorêt, "The Structure of 'Unstructured' Decision Processes," *Administrative Science Quarterly*, June 1976, p. 255.

3. Ibid.

4. Charles E. Summer, *Strategic Behavior in Business and Government* (Boston: Little, Brown, 1980), p. 123.

5. See, for example, Hillel J. Einhorn and Robin M. Hogarth, "Behavioral Decision Theory: Processes of Judgment and Choice," *Annual Review of Psychology*, No. 32 (1981), pp. 53–88.

6. Michael D. Cohen, James G. March, and Johan P. Olsen, "A Garbage Can Model of Organizational Choice," *Administrative Science Quarterly*, Vol. 17, No. 1 (1972), pp. 1–25, suggest, for example, that some activities within some organizations can be viewed for some purposes as "solutions looking for issues to which they might be an answer," among other things.

18
Solving Problems

A s the research data was investigated for how each response was managed, two contrasting approaches to solving problems surfaced. On the one hand there was a systematic route that employed prediction, recognition of goals, planning, control, and other known steps to problem solution. On the other hand there was a more experimental route that stressed activity over detailed thinking and preferred less structured solution of problems. It was found that both modes always existed in combination in each response, and that each provided mutually supportive uses in response.

In chapter 3 it was noted that the normative, planned, synoptic approaches to decision making that dominate the literature of management would be of limited value in managing response. As a result, it was proposed:

> *Proposition 7.* Satisficing and other nonoptimal approaches to decision processes better describe solving problems in response, but depend upon some analysis and also upon rational frameworks for coherence.

This chapter logically develops characteristics of solving problems in decision making appropriate to managing response by conceptualizing the *analytic mode* and the contrasting *derived mode.* The features of these two hypothetical modes are to be conceptualized from prior studies in the light of the proposed characteristics of response presented in chapter 3. The expected general roles to be played by each of these modes in response are to be hypothesized also. Occurrences of the two modes were determined for each of the responses, and the uses that each provided characteristically across the data were determined. Overall, this two-mode formulation was found to be a useful explanatory view of what actually transpired in the researched cases.

It has long been known that decision makers do not optimize but rather satisfice, that is, find good enough solutions rather than any one best solution.[1] The reasons cited for this behavior are numerous, including the cognitive limits of decision makers,[2] the coalition character of many organizations, requiring trade-offs,[3] the presence of several conflicting goals,[4] the conscious and unconscious bias in expectations,[5] and the impact of multiple organizational levels,[6] among others. Pursuit of a fully analyzed solution to a problem would involve, at the extreme, a usually fruitless search for a consensus on goals or values, the collection of masses of data of great complexity and probably continued insufficiency, and a potentially unlimited expenditure on data analysis.[7] Clearly, there are limits concerning the rationality of attempting to analyze a business situation fully, and it might be presumed that this limit reflects the circumstances of the organization involved, the researchability of the situation, the importance of the decision, and also the level of uncertainty present.

While many works have offered alternative models of decision and organizational action as being more realistic descriptors of actual processes,[8] others have shown the presence of two or more distinct and coherent alternative theoretical conceptions. As already noted in chapter 3, several writers have accepted the existence of different modes of decision making or policy or strategy making, and suggested generally that strategy and planning approaches are suited to circumstances of lower uncertainty and that the more incremental approaches to policy decisions are suited to situations of greater uncertainty.[9] For example, Michael B. McCaskey, in 1974, distinguished between "planning with goals" and "planning without goals."[10] In the latter case, the planner identifies a general direction or domain within which the organization works and where the specific direction emerges from the actor's favored styles of perceiving and doing. This "directional planning" was claimed to be appropriate in unstable environments and in more organic (as opposed to mechanistic) structures because it possessed greater flexibility and the ability to make the best of unexpected opportunities.

Two other writers are prominent, however, for showing the existence of separate and distinct modes but arguing that the modes should be considered jointly to achieve an improved explanation of decision making. Thus, Graham T. Allison explains the Cuban missile crisis by means of three models, (1) the rational actor, (2) organizational processes, and (3) governmental politics, and John D. Steinbruner explains the rise and fall of the multilateral nuclear force (1956–1964) with (1) the analytic paradigm and (2) the cognitive paradigm (cybernetics as amended by cognitive theory).[11] The governmental dimensions of Allison and Steinbruner are clearly of indirect relevance to this study within business organizations. Harold A. Linstone claimed, however, that the conceptualizing of distinct perspectives and the use of these multiple perspectives for analysis is a general tool, suitably adaptable to particular needs.[12] The general approach of conceptualizing one or more modes to explain jointly the decision processes in response was used, therefore, to address proposition 7 concerning the nature of decision making in managing response.

The Analytic and Derived Modes

A two-mode model was formulated—one embracing the analytic mode and the other a derived mode. Allison's organizational processes model, Steinbruner's cognitive paradigm, and similar conceptions from elsewhere were inspected to conceptualize the features of the derived mode, addressing directly the relevant characteristics of response to discontinuity noted in chapter 3. The analytic and derived approaches to response so developed are summarized in table 18–1 and commented upon in the following paragraphs.

The analytic mode as described in the literature assumes rational decision making with the elegance of systematic thought but without organizational action being confounded by uncertainty or the characteristics of novelty, compression, and so forth. Planned, systematic approaches to solving problems, therefore, characterize the analytic mode. Abstract or modeled reasoning makes possible detailed preparation and planning. Intellectual processes allow generation of alternatives, which can then be subjected to evaluation and comparison to arrive at a choice of the most suitable course of action. Programs can be constructed for detailed implementation of the chosen decisions, and management action can proceed accordingly.

Use of the analytic mode requires satisfaction of at least two conditions. First, it requires knowledge of variables, their future behavior and their interrelationships in the face of change. Second, it requires a capacity for the consistent calculation of outcomes.

The novelty characteristic of discontinuity was reasoned to impose the need for an experimental and reactive approach to meet expediences or irregularities, to confine the risks of possible excessive action, and to test unknown and puzzling conditions. Further, it was considered that compression limits the possibilities for thorough documentation before action, and novelty tends to make such documentation impractical.

Table 18–1
A Comparison of the Analytic and Derived Modes

Analytic	Derived
Reasoned, planned	Experimental, reacting to events
Formalized as precise proposals, settled before embarking on the task	Instrumental resolution of problem—attacked without being fully planned
Intellectually modeled with plans often committed to paper	Trial and error within broad purpose without commitment to detail
Relevant aspects well understood	High uncertainty with many unknowns
Fits within existing structure and observes established formalities	Irregular fit with existing structure and established procedures

The character of decision for the derived mode was surmised, therefore, to be one of trial and error, small steps taken critically as instabilities cause erratic movements in the environment and novelty engenders circumspection concerning the validity of many actions. Also, it was judged that while the pre-existing structure must condition how problems are recognized and solved by the organization, the novelty, asymmetry, and other tendencies in response result in an irregular fit between needed actions and the host organization structure and its established procedures.

It was hypothesized, therefore, that both the analytic and derived modes would be present in all the researched responses. It was hypothesized also that the analytic mode would be observed particularly at junctures within a response where situations:

1. were foreseeable with sufficient certainty to enable detailed specification before action

2. needed to be defined directionally and in overall terms as a framework within which the derived mode could then take place

3. mandated established procedures laid down within the sites

4. mandated presentation of financial budgets or controls prior to embarking on a course of action

Further, the derived mode was hypothesized to be present whenever conditions demanded action but where uncertainty could be further reduced economically or feasibly by further application of the analytic mode.

The data collected in this study and presented in chapters 5 to 15 were analyzed for incidence of the analytic and the derived modes. Examples of the presence and uses of the two modes are presented in table 18–2. These and other examples are to be used to illustrate the findings given later in this chapter. The features of the analytic and derived modes as they were found from the data are to be examined first. Later the uses of the analytic mode and the derived mode are to be reviewed in the light of the above hypotheses.

General Results

Instances of the analytic and derived modes were clearly identifiable in the data collected for this study. Their respective nature was found to be in accord with the expectations noted above. The following sections elaborate.

The Analytic Mode

Analysis, as an activity, occurred frequently and intensively in several responses and was perhaps more characteristic than the derived mode in those responses that were less complex, situationally, conceptually, or organizationally. In analysis, intellectual modeling of variables and their interrelationships took place as a precursor to action. Conditions where this activity was most pronounced were those where knowledge of the variables relevant to a situation was greatest, and where the interactions of those variables was understood most confidently.

Examples included the relatively simple responses of the Ronson and Carolvale Divisions to their demand falls, the internal analysis of the well-understood and even computer-modeled refinery options at Prosper in connection with the catalytic cracker investments, and the development and implementation of the various cash flow management techniques at Industrial Products for which similar systems had been designed and implemented previously within other divisions of Generaltex. This method revolved around the generation, evaluation, and selection of alternative courses of action, although only in the catalytic cracker case were alternatives explicitly stated and exhaustively evaluated. Generally, only one alternative was worked through to completion, but this did not necessarily mean that the earlier rejection of other alternatives before this full development led to a nonoptimal result (particularly in the minds of the decision makers).

Many advantages of the approach existed beyond those of simple rationality and measurability. First, analyses could be committed to hard form— both as computer models and as paper proposals—permitting iteration, updating, and fine-tuning. Second, analyses could be made within established organizational structures and procedural frameworks, permitting formal approvals and progress by understood patterns of managerial authority, delegation, and specialized skills.

The Derived Mode

Instead of relying on modeled reasoning, measured methods, and established procedures, the derived mode substituted what may be loosely described as trial and error. Facing uncertainty, this approach tried possible solutions and observed whether or not they worked. Consideration of outcomes led to the successful parts of an initiative being retained and improved, and the less successful being abandoned. Information on the problem was gathered by experiment. A problem was solved step-by-step through apparently irregular modes.

Learning by doing and *trial and error* are useful descriptive terms for the derived mode. Prior reasoning did not generate precise plans for action but rather a broad understanding that a problem existed or that a goal had to be achieved. How the needs of the situation were to be met was less clear and, because of uncertainties, could not be specified beforehand. Instead of procrastinating in the analytic mode, executives boldly attempted the unknown with what seemed logical steps toward the goal but carried risks because their

Table 18–2
Some Instances of the Modes in Each Response

Company/Response	Analytic	Derived
Prosper Oil		
Coal		
Cracker	Formal proposals	Details of the coal business
	Identification of need	
	Development of capital investment proposal	
Rotterdam pricing	Analysis as an opportunity cost system	Implementation of Rotterdam market prices in the Netherlands subsidiary for control and motivation
Embargo	Scheduling	Hour-by-hour revisions
Atlas Oil		
Coal	Original proposals and subsequent approvals	Details of the coal business
Scenario	Development of corporate scenarios	Incorporation of the scenario perspective in investments
Embargo	Scheduling	Hour-by-hour revisions
Industrial Products Division		
Demand surge		Attempt at sales factor system
		Other assorted activities such as inventory expansion and improvising production
Pricing initiative	Corporate level identified need	Some reversals, for example the furniture foam molding materials
	Approach to implementation planned and executed at Industrial Products	
Recession	Prediction and revision of finances	
Cash squeeze	Required actions reasoned at Industrial Products and corporate levels	
National Lighting Division		
Inflation Beaters		Evolution of the marketing campaign
Vehicle bulb imports		Most of the tasks of the coordinator
Safety legislation	Proposal and implementation of machinery for lower unit cost production	
	A planning exercise by machinery engineers	

Interoil Foreign currency systems		Recognition that treasury department should not be responsible for foreign exchange transactions
Columbus Bank Social outcry	Reasoning for new organization	Management of the social demonstrations
DeVito Power Exploit Middle East markets		Most activities associated with Middle East business
Carolvale Division Demand fall	Economic prediction and adjustment of resources	Assembling cut-price packages
Ronson Division Demand fall	Economic prediction and adjustment of resources	
Weld Division Demand fall	Economic prediction and adjustment of resources	Seeking of new export sales
Container Division Three-day work week	Situational assessment and adjustment of resources	
Meeting demand surge		Miscellaneous novel activities associated with excess demand, purchasing from Japanese and Swedish mills, etc.
Jackson Mines Retrenchment	Economic prediction and adjustment or resources and labor expectations	
Poor labor relations		Labor relations skills and modification of corporate culture
Schumacker Salmonella outbreak	Advertising and public relations campaign	
Suza Cars New range		New aluminum car body concept

consequences could not be fully predicted. Commitment to solving immediate problems was the primary motivation, and the derived mode was practical and instrumental to that end without details being worked out to completion before action was taken.

As was not the case for the analytic mode, knowledge of variables, their future behavior and interrelationships in the face of change were recognized to be less than properly understood. Practitioners admitted to an inability to assess circumstances in a measured way. Consequently it was also accepted that decisions could not be committed to hard form—at least in more than general or tentative terms. Thus, simulated testing of possibilities was impossible. Only the alternative of experimenting and evaluating in practice was possible. The open-ended and uncertain character of the problems and the derived route to solution tended not to fit easily within formal organizational structures.

Combining the Analytic and Derived Modes

Reasons why the analytic and derived modes cannot occur independently may be found readily. Any situation that can be fully satisfied by prediction, planning, and control would be one so free of risk as to be unworthy of the response mode. Similarly it would be inconceivable for any manager to embark on a course of action purely through the derived mode. Some preliminary assessment, together with sufficient confidence in the value or success of intended moves, would be mandatory for good practice.

In some cases it was found that the analytic mode was little more than a shell or framework within which the response materialized by the derived mode. In others, more extensive analysis was possible, and the uncertainty and risk surrounding the needed action was limited. For them, the role of the derived mode was less because most actions could be substantially planned in advance, with only minor irregularities incurred in their implementation.

Uses of the Analytic Mode

Inspection of the data showed four senses in which the analytic mode was used:

1. where the situation was plannable—that is, where uncertainty was limited or, at least, constrained within manageable bounds

2. where there was conscious and explicit attention given to the overall goal and the general approach to be used to pursue that goal

3. where considerable sums of money were involved, and a capital investment proposal procedure was both advisable and probably mandated by corporate constitution

4. where financial budgeting and planning was employed to control and measure the impact of changes on income statements and balance sheets

An example of plannable situations was provided by the response of the two package tour companies to their demand falls. Although predictions were impossible in accurate terms, the situation was mainly understood at Carolvale and Ronson. Stability in assumptions as well as in the interrelationships of environment and corporation made the analytic mode dominant in these responses. Controlled steps were possible because outcomes could be quite reliably predicted. These conditions also made existing organizational and decision-making structures adequate to the task.

Where detailed planning was not possible, there was usually evidence of some skeletal or directional planning. Goals or objectives, in the sense of the general direction desired, and a general idea of how they were to be attained existed or were formulated for each of the responses. Thus, while the entries to the coal industry reported in chapters 5 and 6 showed no detailed planning in the early stages of the new ventures, there was careful deliberation in both cases concerning the precise goal that was appropriate, and intense debate as to how, in general terms, the challenge was to be approached—joint operating ventures, owned land and exploration, trading or mining, steam coal or metallurgical coal, and so forth.

Prosper's catalytic cracker and coal entry responses provided examples of the third use of the analytic mode. Those responses were required to follow set procedures for capital investment appraisal, as were all other large commitments of corporate funds. For the cracker it was possible and necessary to form a definitive capital investment proposal despite the high uncertainty that the company perceived. For the coal entry the formal arrangements were satisfied, although the proposal sensibly reflected uncertainties by presenting a general statement of what was intended with bounds that were not to be exceeded.

The fourth use of the analytic mode was where financial consequences were appraised as revisions to internal control statements. This step was present in most responses but was most evident in those where computer simulations were used. Prosper's planning models were rerun after the 1973 oil price changes to assess consequences of the changing situation. Prosper's linear programming models of supply (and related models) were used liberally in developing the catalytic cracker proposal. The detailed revisions to forecasts and budgets at Industrial Products in the face of the recession provides another good example.

Uses of the Derived Mode

Five rationales for substantial use of the derived mode were found in the researched responses:

1. where circumstances were acute
2. where there was operating uncertainty

3. where predicaments were unclear
4. where solutions were unclear
5. where solutions were clear but the route to them was unclear

Each of these rationales seemed to correspond to situations where uncertainty was generally unremovable economically by more extensive analysis. The above conditions are discussed below with the aid of examples from the responses.

Acute Circumstances

In many cases, exceptional circumstances triggered a derived route to problem solution. The more exceptional the need, the greater the motivation to push for imaginative solutions by any mode that became apparent. The general manager of Jackson Mines would probably not have sought so strenuously and resourcefully for a solution to the industrial relations problems without the acuteness of the situation. The company achieved a different culture through modes that the general manager could not have envisaged at the start of his zigzag path to solving the problem.

Other companies enacted measures that would not otherwise have occurred to management without acute circumstances. Unprecedented demand levels and difficulties in obtaining paper raw material prompted the management of Container Division to derive answers that had never been tried before in the industry. Airplanes had not previously been commissioned to tour Swedish paper mills, and Japanese supplies had not previously been sought. Similarly, the short-term inversion of usual channel power relationships afforded the opportunity to rationalize the offered number of inks and grades of paper. Restricting customer choice would have been unimaginable without the extremity of the situation.

Operating Uncertainty

Several responses took place in such dynamic circumstances that even the near-term operating problems could not be anticipated in advance of action. It was clear from discussion with the executives involved that often decisions were taken that were thought likely to bring about further operating uncertainties, but managers persisted actively with the decisions and chose to react to ensuing matters as they arose.

In the demand surges experienced by the Industrial Products Division and Container Division, strain on the production facilities created the need for imaginative solutions to maintain machinery at full spate. The problems of overloading could not have been understood in detailed terms and, in any case, many unnecessary precautions might have been taken if full anticipation of problems had been attempted. Rather than detailed analysis, it seemed better to embark on the courses of action and deal with irregularities as they arose.

Parallel observations may also be made concerning Atlas's and Prosper's management of the supply embargo. Although considerable planning was possible, the dynamic nature of the situation necessitated that the seemingly most sensible decision be made at a point in time with the expectation that erratic consequences would occur and be dealt with later. As particular ships became available to unload, and as particular refineries became threatened with uncontrolled closure, so improvisations had to be constantly made. Neither the problems nor the possible solutions could have been anticipated in plannable terms before the events.

Unclear Predicament

The predicament in which managers found themselves because of discontinuities were often unclear and perplexing to the point where opposing opinions were sometimes held within the same organization on the likely nature of the future. For example, some managers in Prosper and Atlas even questioned whether a new era of high-price oil had, in fact, come about. Some top managers (and some lower managers) whose judgment was respected and had been correct in the past held the conviction that the OPEC cartel would collapse, and that prices would quickly return to former low levels. This conviction accounted for much of the resistance, diffidence, and risk of about-turns which punctuated many of the responses in Prosper and Atlas. Such differences of opinion also influenced other responses researched in this study. For example, managers in Carolvale Division and Ronson Division had widely differing opinions on the likely shape of the 1977 season for vacation packages. Some thought the low early sales probably suggested only a late purchasing season which did not merit decisive action, and others thought that the season would be poor and merit some major adjustments.

The way managers in the oil companies dealt with this inability to even define the predicament confidently in terms that were widely accepted was to allow some progress in several different directions. By giving some opportunity to several schools of thought, risks were hedged against any reasonably foreseeable outcome. Once solutions were taking form in this largely derived way, the managers were better able to see what the true predicament was, and in the meantime some feedback had been obtained on the quality of the initiatives that had been taken. In other responses (such as those in the Carolvale Division and Ronson Division), one set of decisions was agreed upon which reflected a compromise between opposing opinions and achieved, in practice, an objective of hedging bets against the risk of either outcome.

Unclear Solution

In some cases the problem was clear and a need for action was apparent, but exactly what actions were necessary was unclear. The way such situations were managed was to start and allow steadily increasing familiarity with the problem to suggest solutions. In Interoil, for example, the need for more efficient management of foreign exchange transactions was clear, but how it should be accomplished was unclear. The treasury department committee was set up without a sense of the kind of recommendations that would emerge and, in fact, worked for several months before it was even recognized that a solution would need implementation above and beyond the jurisdiction of the department. Comprehension of the consequences of floating exchange rates, evaluation of their detailed impacts on the company, and analysis and documentation of the decision process for international transfers were all preliminaries to recognition that the solution to the problem had to be beyond their domain.

Unclear Route to Solution

In other cases the solution was known but the route to its solution was unclear. In situations of this type, the answer was to get on with the job and allow experience to betray the route to solution as well as to expose the problems which that route created. For DeVito Power, it was clear that they needed to enter the Middle Eastern market for power-station machinery in order to survive. Implementing the decision brought about a series of complex problems, many of which were not foreseen, and for which a large number had no plannable solution. Getting on with the job was the only way to expose the difficulties and to solve them. When the company had experienced completion of a few such contracts, it became apparent that construction of infrastructure was a necessary part of such work, as well as planning contingencies against a customer's possible inability to pay and other matters. Eventually, organizational structure and ways of working in the company became modified in line with the nature of the new market.

Both Prosper's and Atlas's entries to the coal industry were accomplished with a clear goal but without any established sense of how the goal was to be accomplished. Many initiatives were commenced with an uncertain idea of what problems they would present and how they would be solved. Atlas's early attempts to enter coal trading provided an example where problems of securing sources of supply, chartering shipping, and so on met with several false starts and ultimately could not come to fruition when the 1973 oil price increase removed all uncommitted tonnages from the market. Similarly, Prosper embarked on coal ventures without management's previously acquiring relevant knowledge. Prosper's managers were conscientiously learning the definition of terms for coal deposits and coal qualities while negotiating joint ventures and acquisitions. Atlas appointed a junior executive with a hydrocarbon research and development background to compile a manual on the coal industry for involved personnel, but before this task was in hand the company was already exploring for coal and had made several capital investments.

Balancing the Modes

This research showed, therefore, that formal analysis had only a balanced role in managing response. To place too much emphasis on analysis would have impeded solution of problems in urgent and complex situations. To insist upon detailed analysis or planning would have proved wasteful and ill-fitting to the uncertainties and unfamiliarity surrounding responses. Too much specification would have inhibited managers from pursuing opportunities that could not have been identified through desk work, and too much specification could have risked overcommitting managers to certain directions when unforeseeable events might have shown them to be of lessening appeal.

The findings of this chapter suggest some direct implications for managers. In circumstances of response, extensive analysis and an appropriate following of formal organizational processes and systematic problem solving needs generally to be accompanied also by the taking of selected actions ahead of what would ordinarily be considered completed analysis, and possibly the use of compromised and exceptional organizational arrangements.[13] The data suggest that it may be possible to determine at critical junctures, when proceeding according to the analytic mode is constructive. Generally the analytic mode applies when situations are sufficiently knowable, when overall goals or parameters need to be established, and when bureaucratic or control issues demand it. Similarly, it may be possible to determine when use of the derived mode is necessary or desirable to the progress of a response—generally when uncertainty was best removed by action rather than continued analysis which arose when a whole complex of operations were incomprehensibly disturbed, when near-term operating situations could not be predicted, when contrary opinions seemed almost equally plausible to remedy a situation, when solutions were unclear (despite analytic efforts) but goals were clear, and when needed solutions were apparent but how to achieve them could not be unambiguously resolved by further analysis. Many responses seemed to require the simultaneous application of both the analytic and the derived mode, and the relative combination of both differed according to the stage of development of the responses and the different roles that each was able to play in the response.

In the responses investigated in this research, it was much more helpful to use an active management style, allowing the derived mode to rise to its proper importance and not allowing the derived mode to be unnecessarily restricted by an overcommitment to the analytic mode. This predominantly learning-by-doing and trial-and-error approach to problem solving respected the uncertainty and complexity characteristic of response. Thus, solving problems often demanded that the derived mode be dominant, and this amounted to willing ness of managers to take risks where analysis could not provide answers, a willingness to boldly attempt the unknown because analysis could not predict outcomes, and a willingness to readily experiment to find out things that could not be analyzed in detailed terms.

Notes

1. Herbert A. Simon, *Administrative Behavior: A Study of Decision-Making Processes in Administrative Organizations* (New York: Free Press, 1976, first published 1945).

2. James G. March and Herbert A. Simon, *Organizations* (New York: John Wiley and Sons, 1967).

3. Richard M. Cyert and James G. March, *A Behavioral Theory of the Firm* (Englewood Cliffs, N.J.: Prentice–Hall, 1968); Edward R. Freeman, *Strategic Management: A Stakeholder Approach* (Marshfield, Mass.: Pitman, 1984).

4. Richard M. Cyert and James G. March, op. cit., pp. 115–118.

5. Richard M. Cyert, William R. Dill, and James G. March, "The Role of Expectations in Business Decision Making," *Administrative Science Quarterly*, December 1958.

6. Eugene Carter, "The Behavioral Theory of the Firm and Top-Level Corporate Decision," *Administrative Science Quarterly*, December 1971, pp. 413–428.

7. D.E. Regan, "Rationality in Policy Making: Two Concepts, Not One," *Long Range Planning*, October 1978, pp. 83–88.

8. Examples of works offering models of decision making as more realistic descriptors than the rational, analytic model include David Braybrooke and Charles E. Lindblom, *A Strategy of Decision* (New York: Free Press, 1963); Amitai Etzioni, *The Active Society: A Theory of Societal and Political Processes* (New York: Free Press, 1968); and H. Edward Wrapp, "Good Managers Don't Make Policy Decisions," *Harvard Business Review*, September/October 1967, pp. 91–99.

9. See note 14 in chapter 3 for some writers who have argued that incremental processes are more appropriate for unstable environments and that formal synoptic processes are more suitable for stable environments.

10. Michael B. McCaskey, "A Contingency Approach to Planning: Planning With Goals and Planning Without Goals," *Academy of Management Journal*, Vol. 17 (1974), pp. 281–291.

11. Graham T. Allison, *Essence of Decision: Explaining the Cuban Missile Crisis* (Boston: Little, Brown, 1971); John D. Steinbruner, *The Cybernetic Theory of Decision* (Princeton: Princeton University Press, 1974). Two other important models employing the technique of isolating distinguishable modes are those of Henry Mintzberg, "Strategy-Making in Three Modes," *California Management Review*, Winter 1973, pp. 44–53, and J. Arthur Kuhn, "Organization Design and General Motors versus Ford Motor, 1918–1937," a paper presented at the joint TIMS/ORSA Conference, 1976, and reported in Roger L. Hall, "The Natural Logic of Management Policy Making, Its Implications for the Survival of an Organization," *Management Science*, August 1984.

12. Harold A. Linstone, *Multiple Perspectives for Decision Making, Bridging the Gap between Analysis and Action* (New York: North Holland, 1984), pp. 25–37, provides a review of various identifications of the multiple perspectives approach to analysis.

13. Henry Mintzberg ("Patterns in Strategy Formation," *Management Science*, May 1978, p. 944) notes: "We hypothesize then that the planning mode will normally lead to what can be called 'main-line strategies,' typical and obvious ones for the organization to adopt."

19
Developing Initiatives

T he nature and general structure of decision processes was proposed, in chapter 3, to be complex and irregular, and describable only as general conceptual patterns (Proposition 8). Literature concerning the structure of decisions is abundant and catholic, but dominant among both normative and descriptive works is the assumption of some sequence of phases around which decisions take place. Typical is the three-phase model of Herbert A. Simon: (1) intelligence, the searching of the environment; (2) design or inventing, developing and analyzing possible courses of action; and (3) choice, the selecting of a course of action.[1] These are stated to be "closely related to the stages in problem-solving first described by John Dewey: What is the problem? What are the alternatives? Which alternative is best?"[2,3]

Simon, however, recognized that the relationship between intelligence, design, and choice was not simple, and described the three phases in a given decision as "wheels within wheels within wheels."[4] In a major study of 233 decision processes, Eberhard Witte tested for the presence of five distinct phases in decision making he identified in the literature.[5] After exhaustive testing on data gathered from written documents held within companies, Witte comments: "We have reason to start from the opposite hypothesis: Complex and innovative decision-making processes have a constant relationship between the activities of information gathering, development of alternatives and choices over the total time period."[6]

Witte's data and analysis did, however, show some tendency for an overall pattern. For example, he found a greater incidence of choice in the latter stages of a decision and a more frequent display of all the five phases per relative unit time period both at the beginning of a decision and towards the end.

Henry Mintzberg, Duru Raisinghani, and André Théorêt[7] studied twenty-five "important decisions" and showed clearly, however, that the Simon trichotomy of intelligence, design, and choice did usefully describe the overall structure of their data, but with a qualification: "We find logic in delineating distinct phases of the strategic decision process, but not in postulating a simple, sequential relationship between them."[8] They describe decisions as being arrived at "only by groping through a recursive, discontinuous process involving many difficult steps and a host of dynamic factors over a considerable period of time."[9] Any possible simple sequence was moderated by a collection of complicated forces to include control of the decision process itself, various communication routines that provide input and output information necessary to maintain the decision making, and political considerations that enable a decision maker to work his or her way to a solution in an environment of influencing and sometimes hostile forces. The dynamics of the decision process investigated by Mintzberg and his coworkers were also subjected to interrupts, scheduling delays, timing delays, speed-ups, feedback delays, comprehension cycles, and failure cycles.[10]

This empirically based literature and other works reviewed in chapter 2 concerning complex decision processes suggest, therefore, three general conclusions of apparent importance to this study of managing response:

1. Activities of intelligence, design, and choice may be expected to function continuously throughout formation of a response, consistent with the principal conclusion of Witte[11] and sympathetic to Simon's expectations as to their functioning in decision.[12]

2. An overall phase structure can be expected that resembles the original trichotomy of Simon[13] that was "corroborated" by Mintzberg et al.[14]

3. The relatively simple structure proposed above is significantly complicated in the field by the changing pace and intensity of forces and events (environmental and organizational) that cause repeated modifications to the progress of the response.

To examine these expectations, the data of chapters 5 to 15 were analyzed accordingly. Constant activities equivalent to intelligence, design, and choice were found at all junctures of all decisions, but observations suggested that the terms *evolution, contribution,* and *choice* better describe the nature of these constant decision processes in response. The influences of environmental and organizational forces and events on these processes was found to be considerable. The presence of an overall structure common to all the responses was then investigated. Breaking the responses into smaller elements, and inspecting these elements for their nature and how and when one set of apparently related elements proceeded to a set of elements of slightly different nature, suggested a three-phase model that showed an overall structure consistent with the Simon trichotomy,[15] but suggested also a different articulation to best describe observations in this study. The three phases identified in this study are termed *antecedent, development,* and *maturation.* This chapter elaborates on these findings.

A Constant Process

Responses developed by evolution from smallest origins through to a final, fully adopted form over a stretch of time. This is a trivial statement in itself,[16] but this evolution was at the heart of how decisions came about, because the intelligence gained at each increment of evolution provided the basis for further increments. Evolution represented, in the cases researched in this study, an intelligence-providing and an intelligence-driving activity. Contribution of management effort to particular initiatives drove the development of responses to their conclusion. It was only through the conscious allocation of time, resources, and sometimes exceptional commitment that the essential inventing, developing, and analyzing came about. Choice as to what initiatives managers would pursue led to the success of some initiatives over others. Beyond routine administrative duties, most managers had considerable freedom as to the development of projects.[17] It was this "voting with the feet" for one course of action over others at a particular time that caused contributions to the design of certain initiatives to take place and the design of others to be overlooked or pursued with less effort.

These three related activities of evolution, contribution, and choice were judged equivalent to the well-grounded intelligence, design, and choice trichotomy of Simon.[18] Use of the Simon trichotomy to describe this constant interaction throughout a decision is much less usual than its use to describe the overall structure of a whole decision process. This conclusion does, however, reflect Witte's belief that "human beings cannot gather information without in some way simultaneously developing alternatives. They cannot avoid evaluating these alternatives immediately, and in doing this they are forced to a decision."[19]

Evolution

The elapsed time that responses took from conception to full form spanned several years for most cases that were not operating situations. If reactions to E. Ralph Biggadike's study of new ventures is typical, it may come as a surprise that a span of seven to ten years for a response was common.[20] The following examples from Prosper and Atlas serve to illustrate both the scale of elapsed time and the modest beginnings from which most responses began to gain form.

> The idea for Prosper's entry into the coal industry can be traced back to the middle 1960s as one of several items ventured in a corporate planning review. It was not until the middle to late 1970s that Prosper's coal business was a formalized operating company.

Atlas's coal business (now among the largest in the world) evolved gradually through two committees, beginning with indefinite terms of reference. Again, it took seven years from the initial exploration efforts to the formation of an organizationally stable company.

The catalytic cracker investment first "took off" as a muted suggestion at a Prosper executive committee review meeting early in 1974. Despite top priority attached to the project by many senior managers, formal approval (itself contentious) came three years later and the plant came on stream only some four years after that.

Introduction of Rotterdam pricing for motivational purposes started as only a threat by the president of Prosper Netherlands to his marketing managers. It took five years from then for the use of Rotterdam pricing to become widespread throughout Prosper.

Scenario planning originated innocently as a convenient method of reasoning and exposition in the *Look Ahead Committee Report*. It took a decade of gradual but uninterrupted adoption before the approach was almost universally used throughout Atlas for planning and capital project appraisal purposes.

The evolutionary sense of a minor beginning progressively escalating to a full development is discernible even in the operating responses, despite their relatively collapsed time scales. For example, localized oil shortages occurred some five or six months before OPEC's unilateral October 1973 pricing decision. Prior to that October, there were many indicators that gradually firmed through the preceding summer and into the early autumn—tanker availabilities, shipping rate increases, and so on. With hindsight, the oil price increase of 1973 can be seen as a natural outgrowth of the already near doubling of the price of crude oil in 1971. Even after the moment of the embargo, the impact on the operations of the oil majors was somewhat graduated, as existing inventories and supply operations already in force provided some buffering or slack. The several demand falls and the two demand surges embraced in the data showed also a warming-up period before obtaining their full form.

Central to this evolutionary process was a series of discrete initiatives that represented areas of attention on which management focused effort—taking initial ideas to some tangible end point. Implementing these initiatives or merely discussing them with colleagues provided feedback concerning what aspects of the initiative were helpful and which were less helpful. With this improved knowledge, managers could then set about the design and implementation of additional initiatives, with these in turn displaying the effective and ineffective. In this way, response materialized step by step through a series of partial solutions.

Thus, evolution of the responses may be seen as the sum of a number of initiatives from the first idea that is proposed through the numerous other initiatives that take responses from a general sense of need to a final form. The pricing initiative of the Industrial Products Division is an example of this phenomenon as one of the less complicated responses researched in this study but also one where the discrete initiatives were simple and conspicuous. A sense of the need for a reaction to cost inflation initially emerged at Generaltex, the corporate parent. The goal transpired in the initiative to make management of prices a performance criterion for the general manager at Industrial Products. The idea of the initiative of the price change form materialized and encouraged each subordinate manager to take certain pricing initiatives. Subsequent pricing initiatives were then necessary in some cases in the face of competitive reactions.

The evolutionary process was further explained by the sequence of events that occurred in parallel in the environment and the organizational processes that those events engendered within the corporation. Managers constantly sought to (1) interpret these uncertain and confusing events for their significance, (2) progress or impede initiatives as appropriate to the perceived significance of the events, and (3) adjust details of a response to the vested interests of a particular manager or group of managers. Discussions, debates, negotiations, and learning proceeded to read meaning into the complex pattern of events that surrounded and drove the formation of response:

Discussion often took place to hasten understanding of confusing events in the environment. Internal contradictions were often apparent to involved managers, such as the need for a high price for fuel oil to justify Prosper's coal diversification but the need for a low price for fuel oil to justify the proposed catalytic cracker. Flexible discussions among managers helped to resolve these issues.

Debate often occurred on the relative merits of alternative courses of action, such as the extensive debate on whether Atlas should enter the coal business through exploring of undelineated coal reserves, through establishing coal-trading operations, or through acquiring existing coal businesses.

Negotiations often took place between the competing interests of different parts of an organization, such as the conflicts between the national marketing subsidiaries and the refining and shipping companies at Prosper on the impact of the use of Rotterdam prices on capacity utilization.

Learning took place as the environmental issues became better understood. Learning often slowed adoption of initiatives, such as the delay in using the scenario planning technique in Atlas by various subsidiaries whose managers did not recognize its value or properly comprehend its conceptual basis at the start.

As time went by, the circumstances governing response became better understood by the managers in the organizations. First, trends in the environment became revealed, thereby resolving many contentious issues. Second, debates among managers also gradually improved understanding and prepared the basis for action. In at least one case, an event gave a final stimulus to the way of thinking of a company by pointing the way to the future. The pronounced increase in the price differential between low and high distillates that occurred in 1975 was judged by many members of the management to be a key factor in the board's final approval of Prosper's catalytic cracker project. The event provided a clear illustration of the supply trends and economic impacts that would probably apply in the future and that were detailed in the capital investment proposal.

In the large organizations, alliances of managers formed around different initiatives, but as the uncertainties gradually became resolved or better understood, some initiatives were gradually found inappropriate while the vision of others increased in value and the respective alliances of managers around initiatives correspondingly expanded or reduced. Events in the environment together with internal debate promoted this evolutionary process. The stronger, more suitable initiatives survived and were strengthened, while the weaker, less suitable initiatives receded or were eliminated. Thus, those initiatives found to be appropriate as uncertainties were resolved gained ground, while those initiatives found to be inappropriate as uncertainties were resolved lost ground. This evolutionary process ran throughout the data collected for this study, as a few examples demonstrate:

> In Atlas's entry to the coal industry, environmental trends and internal debate confirmed the wisdom of some approaches over others. The ownership and exploration initiative and its associated alliance fell from the limelight, the trading initiative and its associated alliance was temporarily halted and put into abeyance, but the initiative and associated alliance for buying into existing coal businesses gained ground and became dominant.

> National Lighting's moves to counter the penetration by Far Eastern importers into the division's vehicle bulb business took several directions, including lobbying the government and a " trunk brigade sales force," before the right combination of organizational, manufacturing, and marketing initiatives emerged as the appropriate answer.

> Blake's Managerial Grid was only adopted by Jackson Mines after numerous other techniques had been rejected at an early stage and after "Management by Objectives" had been tried and found to be inappropriate.

> Many variations of layout and configuration were contemplated and tested before the final decisions were made for Suza Car's new product range.

Ambitious managers recognized this process and therefore strived to succeed within it by allocating their time in the most effective way. Executives sought, therefore, to invest their time in the development of those initiatives that they perceived would benefit them most. A typical manager who wished to prosper in an organization was particularly aware of concentrating on those initiatives favored by superiors. The various manager's elected contributions and choices helped them accomplish their goals, and at the same time brought about the evolutionary process within response.

Contribution

Responses may be distinguished from the general run of activities of management. As the data of chapters 5 to 15 demonstrated, the development of responses may be seen as an additional set of actions by management extra to day-to-day affairs (although the operating responses were integral to usual operations, they may be described as a differentiable burden). While day-to-day managerial issues were being dealt with regularly, responses were being developed contemporaneously in many parts of the organizations.

Two general observations can be made:

1. Development required some contribution of effort from a number of executives in various segments of the companies and, for many responses, at several junctures.
2. To do so required many executives to elect to use time in the development of a possible response.

Without such a commitment by management, generation of ideas, consideration of proposals, intellectual development, trials, and the host of other activities necessary to a response development would not have come about.

As development work was invested, so a response became established. Two aspects were strengthened: first, details of the response allowed it to become more effective and efficient in its application; and second, broader understanding permitted wider adoption by the organization. From tentative or primitive beginnings, responses were gradually transformed to definite and reliable form and more general use. The willing commitment of time and effort by managers was indispensable to the selection and development of initiatives and therefore to the needed development of the response to its final form.

Choice

With the exception of obvious, formal approvals of capital projects (the coal entries of Atlas and Prosper, the catalytic cracker at Prosper, and the acceptance of the Suza Car's prototype are some examples in the data), selection from formally enumerated alternative courses of action were quite rare in the data collected for this study. More substantive in the evolution of responses was a gradually increasing support generated by executives choosing between alternatives in the allocation of their scarce disposable time. The final form a response took, therefore, tended to be the result not of a single major choice based on the best available information but rather a de facto result of a large number of individually small but collectively decisive choices made by single managers as to where, when, and how they chose to invest their time and effort.

Managers, for good reasons and often through subtle means, chose to instigate, filter, or veto possible intiatives. Probably of greatest importance was the fact that managers at lower levels often saw the need for particular initiatives and chose to instigate them themselves. For initiatives coming from other sources in the organization, and perhaps strongly supported by more senior management, some were adopted with alacrity while others were moderated. Initiatives also were frustrated by managers choosing to slow the pace at which they were embodied, or initiatives were, at the extreme, politely rejected by managers. Some of these choices were exercised without any ostensible resistance to top-management initiatives. It appeared, for example, that the coal group at Atlas, perhaps unwittingly, chose to frustrate development of the coal business in terms of purchasing and developing undelineated reserves while they chose to pursue the coal-trading option with enthusiasm.

The constant process of choice by managers was, therefore, often subtle and diffuse but imparted distinct form on the development of a response. Choice in managerial work, as observed in this study, was not so much that of selection of a course of action from a range of independently enumerable options, but a case of whether an executive chose to constructively participate in or approve development of a response. A process that may be loosely termed voting with the feet brought about those responses that materialized. Conversely, an unwillingness to commit effort to a problem or an idea led to the frustration of the development of a response. The role of choice was, therefore, reduced to a series of individually minor but collectively decisive elections by managers as to how their scarce time was most usefully deployed among competing claims.

The Phases of Response

In common with most other research and writing concerning decision structure, several phases of response are suggested by the data collected for this study. Selection of three phases seemed to best group the variation within the data into homogeneous units. While bearing some relationship to the phases identified by others, the model proposed here offers some subtle but important distinctions. The first phase suggested by the data for this study resembles those of Mintzberg et al.'s recognition routine,[21] William F. Pounds's problem finding,[22] and Marjorie A. Lyles's formulating of strategic problems.[23] The evidence of this study is that it is useful to distinguish separately *antecedent* behavior prior to the development of conscious efforts in some general direction. This first phase of response involved an unsystematic perusal and consideration of unordered stimuli received by organization members. When these stimuli were interpreted in some way that implied the need for action, an organization process was begun that moved the development of the response into a different and more definitive phase, but not one that necessarily followed from completion of a diagnosis or formulation of what the problem actually was. It is known that unstructured decision situations frequently recycle through a problem identification stage several times.[24,25]

The second phase identified by this research is termed *development* and was conceptualized to include the relatively homogeneous decisional activity that proceeded from the moment a definite commitment was made to formulating a response, to the point where a prototype was tangibly defined and accepted in a workable form. This phase therefore embraces both design and choice. The reasons for this are twofold. First, choice was a continuous activity integral with the step-by-step design of responses as described earlier. Second, formal choice among well-defined and evaluated alternatives was a special and untypical case. Even where formal authorization was necessary, this tended to be a formality. While the existence of an authorization hurdle might well have influenced details of what was presented for authorization, no fully designed recommendation was made to a higher authority in this research without extensive discussion and informal acceptance prior to the formal authorization.

A third phase shown by the data of this study was termed *maturation*. Once a tangible entity had been developed and accepted, this third phase worked on this prototype and incorporated it within the organization. This phase was strongly displayed and was important to an understanding of response in organizations because many key aspects were not resolved until this point. Despite the importance of this phase and its distinctiveness compared to the earlier phases, it has received scant or negligible attention in prior investigations. For example, Peer O. Soelberg identified "implementation and feedback and control" for his theoretical model, but did not take field work beyond the choice phase.[26] An organizational process characterized this phase where revision and modification were the order of the day.

Table 19–1 compares each of these three phases of response along selected criteria. Table 19–2 distinguishes each of the different phases for all the responses investigated in this study. The next three sections further explain each of the phases.

Antecedent

The antecedent was the pattern of conditions that created problems requiring response at a particular time and place within an organization, that motivated

Table 19–1
The Three Phases Compared

	Antecedent	Development	Maturation
Description	Conditions prior to development of the response essential to its origination	A definite management commitment was made to response and a tangible entity was created	Responses moved to full adoption and to full technical refinement
Mechanisms	Problems became conscious, and the need for solutions began to be considered	Solution to need was developed satisfactory to the involved managers	Demonstrated benefits and known practical difficulties carried response into its fullest form
Character	Anticipation, confusion	Initially problematical, uncertain	Deliberate with trials

a search to identify the problem, and that suggested a step that could be taken to begin to more systematically examine the situation. The antecedent was a period where storm clouds were gathering, where management consciousness was being raised, and where the need for decisive action was being evaluated. The character of the antecedent phase was often one of anticipation as weak indicators of inclemence were inspected for their significance.

The nature of the antecedent phase differed somewhat depending on the type of response. For corporate responses, the antecedents were long-term and distant in nature, for administrative responses the antecedents were medium-term and threatened the current business, for operating responses the antecedents were near-term, and often precursors to the discontinuity were directly experienced through the operations of the organizational unit.

The oil company responses illustrate these distinctions according to corporate, administrative, and operating responses and how they influenced the antecedent:

> For the coal diversifications, the antecedent was the long-term sense of the finite supply of crude oil in the coming decades, as well as the consciousness of the success of the coal route followed by other international oil companies.

> For Prosper's catalytic cracker response, expected supply shortages of light distillates and the possible associated profit opportunity prompted the antecedent.

> For Atlas's scenario planning response, uncertainties in the oil industry created the look-ahead study which ultimately led to the full adoption of the scenario technique because uncertainties were inhibiting confidence in capital investments and demanded consideration of multiple futures.

For Prosper's Rotterdam pricing response, the antecedent was the threat to management performance issuing from the inability to show profits on the internal accounting statements of the Prosper Netherlands subsidiary. Its spread within Prosper reflected these same conditions in other subsidiaries and senior management's wish for improved measures of performance.

For the embargo, at both Prosper and Atlas the vulnerability to supply disruption had been demonstrated several times before and the spring and summer of 1973 had been replete with warnings of the possibility of an impending disruption. The combination of circumstances formed an antecedent showing possible imminent disruption but where a decision to act was inappropriate until an emergency arose.

Equivalent observations concerning antecedents may be made for all the researched responses, as indicated in table 19–2.

Development

The development phase applied from when a definite management commitment crystallized from the antecedent in favor of formulating a response to the point where a tangible entity was created which could act as the pattern or prototype for the subsequent full definition of the response. A definite commitment was recognized as a significant decision or action that arose when managers determined that a real problem existed for which a response needed to be sought. A tangible entity existed when managers had found a pattern or formula that was agreed upon (formally or informally) by the involved management as satisfactory for the purposes of the response—examples included a proposal detailing the form of response, a working control system (perhaps an acceptable pilot system), or a definite product (perhaps an acceptable prototype product). The development phase embraced the period of response from the decision to act until a general method had been agreed upon from which the finer details could be settled and from which full incorporation across the affected parts of the organization could proceed.

Definite Commitment. Sometimes a definite commitment came about informally without written or voted consents. When responses were urgent and self-evident, such as in operating responses, it was unnecessary to make any formal commitment to obvious exigencies. In less urgent circumstances, a range of steps consolidated commitment according to corporate custom and needs. This critical step, taking response from a general assessment of a possible problem to a specific act that committed resources in a definite way, took several forms in the researched responses, for example:

Table 19–2
The Commencement of Each Phase in Each Response

Company/Response	Antecedent	Development	Maturation
Prosper Oil			
Coal	Perceptions of finite crude supplies	Appointment of the coal group and approval of financial backing	Acquisition of coal mining companies
Cracker	Consciousness of price differential between heavy and light distillates, together with company (and wider) supply constraints on the more valuable light outputs	Approval for examination of the project in the corporate planning function to approval of initial proposal	Widening support or compliance with the proposal as it moved toward funding
Rotterdam pricing	Netherlands dilemma of "statement losses" on marketing activities	Introduction of the system in the Netherlands	Adoption of the system by other subsidiaries with technical refinements
Embargo	Vulnerabilities to supply difficulties in the spring and summer of 1973	Supply disruption triggered inception through to an understanding of the implications for the organization	Revised roles, systems, and parameters of supply disruptions become known and the response managed more confidently
Atlas Oil			
Coal	Perceptions of finite crude supplies	Appointment of the six-member coal committee to where the pattern of entry was agreed	Acquisitions made of various coal mining and trading companies
Scenario	Success of existing scenario plans in 1973 and need for a systematic approach to future uncertainty	Commitment to wider and fuller use in managing the company after October 1973	Assumption of the method in subsidiary plans and capital investment appraisals
Embargo	Vulnerabilities to supply difficulties in the spring and summer of 1973	Supply disruption triggered inception through to an understanding of the implications for the organization	Revised management hierarchies and communication became better understood, as well as details of supply circumstances
Interoil			
Foreign currency system	Shift to floating exchange rates	Foreign exchange losses by the company to development of a proposal	Dissemination of recommendations contained in the proposal

Columbus Bank Social outcry	Closure of competitors' branches	Negotiation with state regulation bodies and local action groups	Reorganization for social responsiveness
DeVito Power Exploit Middle East markets	Imminent collapse of home market	Decisions to enter Middle East markets to successful sale of early contracts	Execution of early contracts to ultimate reorganization and sale of new contracts
Industrial Products Division Demand surge	Purchasers' panic actions	Realization of extent of demand surge and management resolve to take extreme actions to determination of response parameters	Profit factor program, etc.
Pricing initiative	Cost inflation and lack of uniform policy	Appointment of general manager with mandate to resolve pricing problems; Instigation of the price change form	Implementation of price increases and later fine-tuning
Recession	Previous demand surge	Realization of extent of recession and management's resolve to take extrme actions	Implementation of cost-cutting and sales stimulating measures
Cash squeeze	Reduced profitability of Generaltex corporation	Corporate instruction to become a cash donor; Promulation of revised goal to be number two in the industry	Implementation of the three new cash conservation systems
National Lighting Division Inflation Beaters	Energy cost increases	Government recommendations on energy conservation; First seminar and advertising campaign; Telegram received from main customer; Appointment of the coordinator	Subsequent advertising campaigns and their refinement
Vehicle bulbs	Commercial success of Far Eastern manufacturers; Attempts at lower cost manufacture		Manufacturing and marketing changes
Safety legislation	Passing of Safety at Work Act	Visit of factory inspectorate; National Lighting recommendations for additional safety requirements	Machinery design modifications and so on

Table 19–2 continued

Company/Response	Antecedent	Development	Maturation
Carolvale Division			
Demand fall	Trends in cost inflation and consumer disposable income	Decision to research sterling guarantees and special packages and their planning	Putting into effect the sterling guarantees and the special packages
Ronson Division			
Demand fall	Trends in cost inflation and consumer disposable income	Decision to promote some packages and to instigate sterling guarantees depending upon competitors' actions together with their planning	Weakly displayed, implementing public relations and advertising campaigns
Weld Division			
Demand fall	Level of activity in oil field construction and similar engineering projects	Decision to research world position and formulation of cost cutting and sales stimulation actions	Securing and execution of foreign order
Container Division			
Three-day work week	Government imposition of three-day week	Meeting of division managers	Actions necessary to make arrangements with factory personnel
Demand surge	Panic buying by customers	Realization of extent and intensity of demand surge to determination of parameters for response	Management actions through the demand surge
Jackson Mines			
Demand fall	World trends in steel manufacture	Receipt of revised demand estimates from customers	Meetings and agreements
Labor relations	Two bitter strikes	Attendance at the presentation on Blake's Grid	Inculcation of a revised culture through the organization
Schumacker			
Salmonella outbreak	Vulnerability to salmonella	Assembly of a response team	Public relations and advertising campaigns and new product formulation
Suza Cars			
New range	United States safety legislation and increasing component supply difficulties	Decision to design and build a new range, formalizing of organizational arrangements to construction of prototype	Completion of production model and establishing of new distribution and other details

Task groups were formed in the moves into the coal industry by Prosper and Atlas.

Formal arrangements were made for the corporate planning function at Prosper to investigate the need for cracking capacity in the company.

Formal goals were given to and accepted by the general manager for resolving the pricing problems in Industrial Products.

The appointment of a coordinator was made by the managing director of National Lighting to bring about a response to the division's receding fortunes in the vehicle bulb market.

Specific decisions were made to take action such as to research the question of sterling guarantees and special holiday packages by Carolvale Division.

In many corporate and administrative responses, events triggered action in management that had been considered for some time. For example, the declaration of unilateral pricing by OPEC stimulated a renewed determination to develop coal businesses; the telegram received by National Lighting from its major customer concerning arrears on vehicle bulb deliveries precipitated concentrated action by the managing director; and receipt of the sharply reduced forecast of iron ore requirements received by Jackson Mines from the company's customers underscored the need for quick and major action by the president.

In some operating responses, the development phase was started by a sudden incident in the organization's environment. For example:

the declaration of the OAPEC embargo

the baby's death attributed to accidental consumption of Schumacker's dog food

In other operating responses, commitment followed a period of build-up until previously hypothetical fears were confirmed as meriting action, as in the demand falls experienced by the Carolvale Division and Ronson Division and as in the demand surges experienced by the Industrial Products Division and the National Lighting Division.

To bring a response into development necessitated a critical mass of support or consensus within the management group. For simple organizational settings it was sufficient for one person to hold the opinion that launched development. For complex settings and most divisional settings, a number of people nearly always was required. Thus a mandating vote was needed to form the coal groups in Prosper and Atlas as well as to recommend the development of a proposal for cracking facilities in Prosper. In other responses the commitment was often less formal, but a sufficient consensus to move the company into the development phase was essential in all cases.

Tangible Entity. Following a definite commitment by management, the development phase took development to the point where a tangible entity—a pattern or formula for response, such as a proposal, modus operandi, pilot working system, or prototype product—was formed. Initiatives were being generated and tested in this time, and management commitment was growing from the critical mass required to start development to an order of commitment necessary to proceed to the tangible entity (also requiring a critical mass of support). Incomplete understanding of the implications of change made many early initiatives in response exploratory in nature, but as management efforts clarified uncertainties and the nature of the environment gradually unravelled, initiatives became more accurate, more effective, and more closely allied to the real needs of the situation.

In some cases the tangible entity marking the end of the development phase was clear, as the initial proposal for the catalytic cracker investment at Prosper and the prototype automobile for Suza Cars. In other cases the point of demarcation was not marked by a precise event, but more by a sense in the management group that a critical juncture had been reached where the situation was adequately understood and a sufficiently good answer to the situation had been found. Examples of the latter situation were the eventual sanctioning of an acquisition or merger route to enter the coal industry at Atlas, and the decision to repeat the successful design of the Inflation Beaters seminar and the associated promotion campaigns at National Lighting.

Maturation

The maturation phase took the tangible entity to its full adoption and full technical refinement. It was important as the phase when the potential value of the response, as a tangible entity, was maximized across the organization. Maturation confirmed the efficiency and importance of this response over competing alternatives for management attention. This phase was when details and refinements crucial to maximizing the success and value of the response were devised, tested, and incorporated. It was also when variations were introduced so that the response could be applied to all situations where its perceived benefits outweighed its full costs.

While there cannot be a definitive end point to adoption or technical refinement, a time was reached where a sense of completion was attained—when the objective of the response was generally agreed to have been accomplished. Such completion took many forms, depending upon the particular response.

For example, the coal businesses at Prosper and Atlas may be said to have reached that point when those businesses were recognized as fully fledged sub-sidiaries within Prosper and Atlas, the scenario planning response at Atlas was "complete" when the method was used routinely through most of the host com-pany, the demand surge responses at Industrial Products Division and Con-tainer Division accomplished their respective purpose when they had overcome the difficulties of managing the discontinuity, and the demand fall response at Jackson Mines was fully accomplished when the meetings with the unions had taken place and the agreements had been made and executed.

By the time the maturation phase had been entered in the researched com-panies, most of the learning associated with a response had already taken place. At this stage the benefits of the response had been quite clearly demonstrated, and the practical difficulties were known and understood. It was therefore possi-ble for the maturation phase to be pursued deliberately and with some confi-dence. Thus National Lighting's Inflation Beaters campaign proceeded from strength to strength, and the manufacture of Weld Division's challenging export order was executed in record-breaking time. Many were also characterized by trials as well as by deliberation as the solutions completed in the development phase were tested in the field. Thus Industrial Products had to readjust some of its prices after the company's first efforts at price increases, and Suza Cars had to test their new products against the opinions and preferences of distribu-tors and consumers.

A manager involved in response was, therefore, engaged in developing initiatives appropriate to the complex of a changing environment and organization. The three phases of response were the result of an evolutionary, initiative-centered process driven by managers constantly contributing efforts and choosing where, when, and how to invest those efforts. To cope with these surroundings, a flex-ibility was required so that minds could be changed in the light of contrary information, so that mistakes could be recognized, admitted, and learned from, and so that there was a receptivity to unexpected shifts that could take place in the environment or in the organization.

The content of this chapter does, however, also indicate how responses were managed by senior managers who did not have direct involvement in a response but who had ultimate responsibility for the success of the work of others. The need was to engender the practical approach to finding solutions, the active approach to solving problems, and the flexible approach to develop-ing initiatives. How this was done was to deliberately encourage the stimula-tion and selective adoption of initiatives from subordinates and allow the gener-ation and pursuit of many initiatives to show the ultimate way. Key to encouraging that process was the use of situational factors. The next chapter is to show how situational factors affected response.

Notes

1. Herbert A. Simon, *The Shape of Automation* (New York: Harper and Row, 1965), pp. 54–56.

2. Ibid., p. 54

3. John Dewey, *How We Think* (New York: D.C. Heath, 1910).

4. Herbert A. Simon, op. cit., p. 56.

5. Eberhard Witte, "Field Research on Complex Decision-Making Processes—The Phase Theorem," *International Studies of Management and Organization,* Summer 1972, pp. 156–182.

6. Ibid., p. 180.

7. Henry Mintzberg, Duru Raisinghani, and André Théorêt, "The Structure of 'Unstructured' Decision Processes," *Administrative Science Quarterly,* June 1976, pp. 246–275.

8. Ibid., p. 252.

9. Ibid., pp. 250–251.

10. Ibid., pp. 260–266.

11. William R. Dill, "Administrative Decision-Making," in *Concepts and Issues in Administrative Behavior,* ed. Sidney Mailick and E.H. Van Ness (Englewood Cliffs, N.J.: Prentice–Hall, 1962), pp. 29–48; Eberhard Witte, op. cit., p. 180.

12. Herbert A. Simon, op. cit., pp. 54–56.

13. Ibid.

14. Henry Mintzberg et al., op. cit.

15. Herbert A. Simon, op. cit.

16. Eberhard Witte, op. cit., pp. 172–173.

17. Rosemary Stewart, *Choices for the Manager* (Englewood Cliffs, N.J.: Prentice–Hall, 1982).

18. Herbert A. Simon, op. cit.

19. Eberhard Witte, op. cit., p. 180; also quoted in Henry Mintzberg et al., op. cit., p. 252.

20. E. Ralph Biggadike, *Entry, Strategy, and Performance* (Cambridge: Harvard University Press, 1976).

21. Henry Mintzberg et al., op. cit., pp. 253–254.

22. William F. Pounds, "The Process of Problem Finding," *Industrial Management Review,* Fall 1969, pp. 1–19.

23. Marjorie A. Lyles, "Formulating Strategic Problems: Empirical Analysis and Model Development," *Strategic Management Journal,* Vol. 2, No. 1 (1981), pp. 61–75.

24. Henry Mintzberg et al., op. cit.

25. Marjorie A. Lyles, op. cit.

26. Peer O. Soelberg, "Unprogrammed Decision Making," *Industrial Management Review,* Spring 1967, pp. 19–29.

20
Using Situational Factors

S ituational factors explained how responses started, developed, and acquired many specific details. Situational factors imparted essential character to responses. Rather than being negative, details that arose from parochial considerations were important because the response had to fit those particular circumstances closely to be effective. Comparably successful responses would have been less likely to emerge without the influence of situational factors. In fact, managers fitted responses within situational factors, and adjusted or interpreted situational factors to facilitate the development of response. The proposition 9 given in chapter 3—"Situational factors are determinants of decision processes and outcome"—can be accepted.

Alfred D. Chandler was able to report some common situational attributes guiding the development of a divisional structure at DuPont, General Motors, Standard Oil of New Jersey, and Sears Roebuck.[1] He showed that the organizational innovators were those "closest to the problem who were given or took time away from operating duties in order to concentrate on this significant entrepreneurial problem."[2] In particular, the personality and training of the involved executives and the "attitudes existing within the enterprise itself" in favor of a "rational, analytical view of the problems of business and industrial administration"[3] were concluded to be of paramount importance. Alfred P. Sloan, Jr. in his autobiography indirectly corroborates this view by noting that the great strength of General Motors was that the organization did not get "lost in the subjectivity of personalities" but adds that "sometimes it is necessary to build an organization . . . around one or more individuals rather than to fit individuals into the organization."[4]

Joseph L. Bower, in his study of the resource allocation process, spoke of a structural context that "shapes the purposive manager's definition of business problems by directing, delimiting, and coloring his focus and perception"[5] and determines his or her priorities. Structural context embraces "the influence of the organization, the measurement and information systems and the reward and punishment system,"[6] which are all controllable by top management. It was the use of structural context which was shown by Bower to progress the resource allocation process within the divisional corporation which he studied. Bower also recognized a situational context of personal and historical factors of great significance and "critical to the solution of any particular problem because it is in large measure the substance of the problem," but, as Bower states, "The problem with situational context, however, is precisely that it is unique to the situation; one cannot generalize about it."[7]

The analysis of a decision or other organizational process as the result of specific situational forces has been employed rarely. However, it is widely recognized that strong or strengthening organizations are typically those with consistent "bundles" of cultural, organizational, and other features relative to the characteristics of their environments.[8] Since it is known that organization structure links with environmental features, it may be presumed also that organizational processes assume different form depending on the characteristics of a particular organization structure. It follows, therefore, that an organizational output is conditioned by the environment, structure, and culture of the organization from which it issues. It is also widely accepted that decisions are conditioned by personal values and the theoretical notions or "conceptual maps" that decision-makers hold.[9]

The conjunction of these environmental, cultural, organizational, personal, and conceptual forces may, therefore, be provisionally concluded to impart form on a response as a whole. However, the conditioning applied by situational factors during response formation may be concluded to be uneven during the progress of a response. In their study of twenty-five strategic decision processes, Henry Mintzberg, Duru Raisinghani, and André Théorêt drew a fundamental distinction, "the difference between what psychologists call convergent and divergent thinking. It is one thing to find a needle in a haystack, quite another to write a fugue."[10,11] The development phase of response was found by Mintzberg et al. to be characterized by divergent thinking and the later phase by convergent thinking.

Situational factors (environmental, cultural, organizational, conceptual, and personal) are proposed, therefore, to impart form on a response according to three distinct foci. First, a *contextual focus* that applies throughout the response and determines fundamental matters such as which responses occur, their overall character, and how they are managed. Second, a *start-up focus* that applies during the antecedent and especially during the development phases of response and determines initial possibilities resulting from who can inspire certain initiatives where. Third, a *maturation focus* that applies over the later phase of response and convergently determines final details of the response according to the vested interests and motives of the various parties impinging on these last stages.

Contextual Focus

Research has indicated that situational forces encourage certain behavior and exclude other behavior. External, cultural, and theoretical forces dominated in the contextual focus, but organizational and personal forces also played a part. Context was found to shape responses in three particular ways:

1. *Which response, when.* Corporations and their particular circumstances created specific needs at specific points in time, and these were found to determine which response materialized and when.

2. *Character.* The corporation's character prejudged the general character of the responses that materialized.

3. *Management.* The managerial philosophy applying in each corporation influenced how the responses were managed.

Which Response, When

Over recent decades, supplies of crude oil to marketing operations have been abundant for Prosper but relatively scarce for Atlas. The "crude long" position of Prosper (abundant supply) and "crude short" position of Atlas (limited supply) explained a great deal about what responses were enacted by each company, as well as when the particular response was enacted.

A context was created in which Atlas's managers were sensitive to adding value through secondary refining earlier than Prosper's managers. Although details of how a series of hydrocrackers (a more technical plant for increasing the proportion of light products than a catalytic cracker) were installed throughout Europe was not researched in detail, it was evident that external, cultural, and theoretical forces were in step to promote this development five or so years before Prosper. It became urgent for Atlas to add value to its limited crude supply well before the oil crisis, while it was still good sense for Prosper to sell lower value products at high volume.

Having constructed a full complement of cracking facilities, it was natural that Atlas's managers were working under a different set of external and theoretical forces in the middle 1970s. When most executives in Prosper were glad that their large catalytic cracker would soon be on stream, some executives in Atlas were speculating that technical developments would soon diminish the benefits of secondary refining. Potential oversupply of light products from excess secondary refining capacity was not the basis for their major argument.

To Atlas's managers, greater utilization of natural gas liquids and also more efficient blending of oils afforded by introduction of microprocessors presupposed a much less vigorous demand for light distillates. Atlas desisted from investing in crackers or their equivalents through most of the seventies as "almost the only oil company not marching in step." The Prosper planners were also aware of these technical developments that risked long-term attractiveness of secondary refining, but differences of time and the relative state of development of each business explained the different interpretation of significant trends. Thus, Prosper managers attached different and higher importance to constructing secondary refining capacity in the 1970s than did Atlas managers.

Existence of the scenario planning response at Atlas is testimony to the external, cultural, and theoretical circumstances in the company. Consideration of technical, social, and political trends is more strenuous in Atlas than in Prosper. An answer can be found for this difference between the two companies in the relative supply positions also. Atlas was thrust more forcibly into the intricacies of international politics and, because of its tighter supply position, was more vulnerable to outcomes than Prosper. Thus, consideration of the contextual focus helps to explain also the greater development of scenario techniques in Atlas, where greater store was placed on analysis of environmental issues. Nonformation of a scenario response in Prosper partly reflects that the situational forces auspicious to its development in Atlas did not exist in Prosper because of the company's more stable position at that time.

A pattern is shown where, reflecting crude oil supply, Atlas was more conscientious in analyzing its circumstances on longer term matters, but it does not follow that Prosper was trailing in general terms. Prosper, too, experienced high growth and high profitability and counted many major successes. It does, however, help to explain Atlas's earlier initiatives in entering the coal industry, together with an earlier commitment to a series of nonoil diversifications. The coal entries are also interesting because of the part situational factors played in creating their quite different development process.

Character

The character of the coal businesses that Prosper and Atlas formed reflects the nature of the host companies. Rather than establishing a fully integrated coal business, Prosper emphasized acquisition of coal resources and their subsequent production. This emphasis reflected the bias in Prosper's oil business, where distribution and marketing traditionally took a backseat to the acquisition of resources and production. Atlas, on the other hand, is developing a strategy for their coal business, of vertical integration supported by high research and development expenditure at all stages of production, transportation, handling, and distribution, as well as creating added value by manufacturing final consumer products. Atlas's stance in their coal business mirrors the robust and highly successful strategy employed in their oil business.

The contrasting methods by which Prosper and Atlas accomplished the decoupling of the respective parts of their oil business also arose from the general nature of each company. Historically, Prosper's top management had emphasized central control more than the top management of Atlas, who had to contend with a wider, larger, and more disparate organization and operation. To achieve a partial divorce of marketing from the other functions at Prosper required a high level committee (the policy and organizational review committee) and associated stringent measures. Implementation both brought about and required, however, the use of somewhat artificial free-market prices (the

Rotterdam pricing system) for internal control and motivation of the company's marketing subsidiaries.

The "looser federation" of subsidiaries in Atlas, together with the cultural and organizational embodiment of substantial autonomy for the subsidiaries over many years, made disaggregation into separately assessed profit centers a more natural development for the Atlas organization than for the Prosper organization. Independent purchasing of crude oil and products had been widely accepted in Atlas on a selective basis in subsidiaries and in the company's supply function for many years. Appointment of personnel and some minor restructuring was all that was necessary to achieve a decoupling of the formerly integrated oil business. The general nature of the two corporations prejudged the character of the response.

Illustrations of the influence of the general nature of corporations on the character of responses may be surmised from other researched cases. A member of the top management of Suza Cars commented that with the company's proprietary technology in lightweight bodies and high power-to-weight engines, it would have been more rational to design and manufacture a high-volume "commuter car" than a low-volume sports car. The fact was, however, that no one in Suza Cars would want to commit part of their lives to what would have been considered a dull project.

Similarly, it was natural that National Lighting Division should seek to counter the loss of market share to inexpensive foreign imports of vehicle bulbs by investing in their domestic operation rather than overseas. While the division had foreign manufacturing operations, the perspective of the management was firmly oriented to retaining domestic manufacture rather than foreign manufacture. The commitment to the principle was almost ideological and appeared to exclude even the consideration of supply from lesser developed countries, despite the clear cost advantages. It was also natural that the company should lean towards its customary and successful means for the development of its business, namely, the internal design and manufacture of production machinery. It was found that the general nature of the corporations and of their management were a determinant influence on the character of all the responses that were studied.

Management

How responses were managed arose from the dominant managerial philosophy that applied in each company. Prosper is a more aggressive company than Atlas, and its approach to problems is less restrained. It is true to cultural bias that Prosper used acquisition as its method of entry into the coal industry. Atlas, conversely, largely developed its coal business from within. Although several methods were used, internal development was favored by the senior management. When the desire for entry accelerated with the oil supply problems of

1973, exigencies prevailed and coal companies were acquired. The method, however, was gradual. Usually companies cooperated with Atlas as independent partners in the early stages, with equity stakes slowly increasing as links naturally became stronger and as trust developed between the managers of the respective companies.

How the coal responses came about was also conditioned by contrasting theoretical conceptions on coal availabilities. Atlas proceeded on the theoretical assumptions that good-quality coal deposits could be found in nonindustrialized countries and that such an exploration and ownership route would be more desirable than a strategy based on known and understood reserves in industrialized nations. Prosper, and most other companies, did not develop or proceed upon a theoretical set akin to Atlas. Actions were different as a result and revolved around direct acquisition of existing businesses.

The catalytic cracker serves as another example of the influence of the contextual focus on the form that response finally took. The cracker's large size, rather sudden conception, and the boldness with which it was developed and progressed through Prosper's approval systems for capital investments reflected the decisiveness and adventurousness that so commonly issued from Prosper's corridors and executive suites. Discussions with Atlas executives tell of a gentler sequence in that company, with the gradual formation of a group of technologists to implement a high-technology secondary refining capacity.

A notable example of the influence of the contextual focus (as created by environmental, cultural, theoretical, organizational, and other forces) was provided by the response of Carolvale Division and Ronson Division to the demand fall in the package holiday industry. For the Carolvale Division, the more focused attention on profit and performance and more elastic demand led to a more urgent and determined management attitude. For the Ronson Division, the greater financial and personal security provided by the international airline, as well as a break-even point in operations that was both lower than that for Carolvale and shared with other parts of the airline, made the management style more gently paced.

Conclusion on the Contextual Focus

Thus, the contextual focus influences which responses develop and when, the character they take on, and how they are managed. Managers should be aware of three implications that arise from the contextual focus:

1. Responses that are infeasible within a realistic interpretation of the effects of the contextual focus will be unlikely to succeed and will present exceptional troubles if they are attempted.

2. Management should seek opportunities where its contextual focus provides competitive advantage and not handicaps. This statement applies to the development of existing business as well as to the search for new business.

3. Where the contextual focus results in minor problems for a total response which is otherwise sound, management should be sensitive to when and how these minor problems might arise and prepare for them accordingly. Often a convenient interpretation that rationalizes weaknesses into strengths might be useful, but often manipulation of situational factors as they relate to the start-up or maturation focus will be useful.

Start-Up Focus

Responses started at the point in the organization where changes had the first significant impact. Needs were identified there and translated into appropriate solutions. Forces focused to generate the background necessary or were auspicious to generation of individual initiatives. It might be presumed that responses would not have materialized without these sets of local conditions, or, if they had later materialized, might have taken on a slightly different form. These influences on response will be discussed below as the "where?" of response.

Responses took on a general shape that reflected the local conditions at their start-up but particularly reflected the people who were involved at this impressionable time in the creation of responses. Many of the ideas influential in the responses and many of the options that were exercised in the responses flowed from the personal backgrounds of the decision makers. These influences on response will be discussed below as the "who?" of responses.

Where?

Start-up took place where trends were first recognized as possibly affecting corporate well-being, and this often took earliest decisive form at the top levels. The experiences of the oil companies provide several examples:

The Atlas coal diversification grew out of the new enterprise group that the board commissioned.

In Prosper, the decennial plan for 1971–1981 noted that the long-term supply position for petroleum was likely to be constrained, and focused attention on coal as a possible substitute for oil. A board president gained approval from his peers for the establishment of a coal study group in 1974.

The Prosper catalytic cracker investment proposal first gained recognition in discussions on the corporate planners' review published in 1974. The board then sanctioned development of a full proposal, and positioned it in the corporate planning department. Any other organizational arrangement in Prosper would probably not have resulted in the rapid development and completion of the catalytic cracker investment.

Scenario planning grew out of the board-sponsored look-ahead committee, which used scenario planning. Repeated publication of environmental trends as scenarios in the annual review played a part in adoption of the scenario planning method in Atlas.

It was in these localized circumstances of time and place that needs were first understood, thus motivating managers to embark upon the initial phases of response creation.

Some responses started at lower levels. An example is the use of Rotterdam prices in Prosper Netherlands. Specific circumstances applying in the Netherlands most particularly affected Prosper Netherlands' profit potential and performance. The proximity of the lower cost Rotterdam market (only a local telephone call away) worsened inequities in the previous transfer cost method of assessment for the Dutch subsidiary's financial performance more than for any other part of the worldwide Prosper Company. It was natural that irregularities in Prosper's control system should stimulate action first at that relatively junior point in the organization.

Similarly, the responses to the embargoes were enacted primarily at the level of the supply functions. It was there that cut-offs had their first impact, and it was at that point that responsibility lay for acquisition of supplies. The board also participated in the embargoes, however. Top management was instrumental in setting conditions that imparted determinate form at the early stages—such as the allocation procedures and details of relations with oil-producer governments.

The same relationship of response starting at the point in an organization where discomfort was encountered first applied to all the other responses investigated in this study. Thus the Industrial Products Division responded first to the demand surge and the recession but the Generaltex corporate management had some involvement in stimulating the wider issues of the pricing initiative and the cash squeeze. At Interoil the problems of foreign exchange losses were investigated by the treasury department (where the organization structure attributed the losses), although it later became apparent that the solution had to be implemented through general management.

Who?

Personality, background, and training of individual executives played a determining role in many responses—both at start-up and afterwards. Personal orientations and preferences seemed to make a difference to the shape and progress of responses. Presumably because of their unique perspectives, the involved decision makers identified and rationalized circumstances in ways particular to themselves.

The most evident example is that of the President of the Dutch subsidiary of Prosper. His many years dealing in commodity futures at the Chicago Board of

Trade gave him a unique view on oil company operations. His understanding of free markets and his predisposition towards business reflecting such realities, was an essential factor in his adoption of Rotterdam prices. Without the presence of this particular executive with his particular viewpoint, it is possible that the way Prosper dealt with the related issues of transfer prices and the motivation of subsidiary management would have been quite different and perhaps less timely and less effective.

Another example is provided by Atlas in its scenario planning response. The strong intellectual bias in the corporate planning function, and the members' frequent reference point in the world's finest universities, were important to the response's identification and its later development and success. One person, in particular, earned the respect of his colleagues for an individual contribution to the conceptual refinement of scenario planning as it is now applied throughout Atlas. The details that made the technique such a useful and respected tool within Atlas issued from a unique brand of intellect and personal commitment of one person.

Conclusion on the Start-Up Focus

Thus, the start-up focus shows that responses usually start where the sudden change has its first major impact, and that the personal backgrounds of those who actually start the response may be both influential in starting the response in the first place and in giving the response a good deal of its character.

Managers involved in developing a response should be aware of two implications that arise from the start-up focus:

1. The organizational forces within which they work and their personal backgrounds may (a) hold back recognition of the need for a response, and (b) lead them to overreact or to distort ambiguous situations relating to sudden change.

2. The organizational forces within which they work and their personal background may sway details of the response. There are times when this personal bias should be allowed and other times when it should be restrained. Third parties, such as respected colleagues or good consultants, can offer more objective opinions when such matters are in question.

Managers responsible for a response but who wish to achieve the response through others in the organization should be aware of two implications that arise from the start-up focus:

1. Responses are likely to originate when and where impacts of the sudden change are first felt in a significant way. As a result , organizational forces can be adjusted to facilitate early detection and commitment to response. For example, sensitive measures of adverse conditions in the environment,

reinforced by penalty systems linked to their consequences, will assist in early detection and early action. At the extreme, these arrangements may also result in overreaction, but that might be the healthier bias because the sunk costs of a response that was started and then terminated in start-up are likely to be small.

2. Careful positioning of a particular executive within the organizational structure can accomplish earlier detection of the need for response and help to give the response some helpful bias.

But once the response has attained tangible form and enters the maturation phase, situational factors come to bear in slightly different ways. This is discussed in the next section.

Maturation Focus

A mix of people and groups slowing, impeding, encouraging, and altering response development was common to all the more complex responses that were researched. Situational forces created needs and suggested solutions according to the diverse vested interests of those people involved in development of, or of those people affected by, a response. These vested interests often competed, resulting in certain choices being made over other choices. It was in the maturation phase that these competing forces had the greatest impact on the form that the responses finally developed. In the earlier phases the political ramifications were either not evident or were insufficiently pressing to cause people and individuals in the wider parts of the organization to influence initiatives decisively.

Parties

Figure 20–1 shows a simplified "map" of people and groups prominent in Atlas's coal venture. As the figure illustrates, influence from vested parties played a number of roles. Some groups encouraged development, such as the subsidiaries in countries B, C, and D where their local governments had a policy of development of their coal industry. Wider parts of the Atlas corporation such as the geologists, research and development department, the government of country A, and other national governments all moved the response in certain directions and all influenced how the response developed.

Figure 20–2 shows a simplified "map" of people and groups prominent in Prosper's Rotterdam pricing response. Development of the response took place despite the resistance of the shipping and refining departments concerning the idea of using Rotterdam prices for internal control and motivation. Continued influence from the Netherlands subsidiary and personal relations between

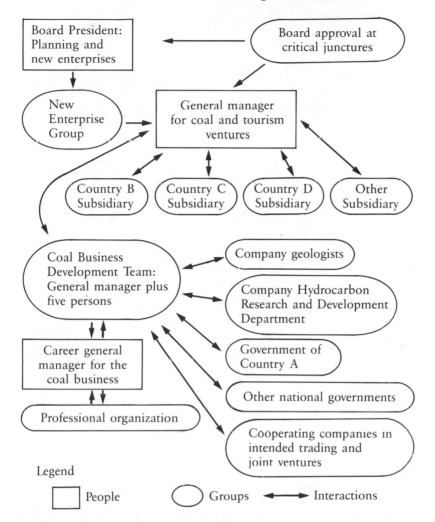

Figure 20–1. A Map of People and Groups in Atlas's Coal Venture

its management and headquarters management were central to response impetus. Finer points of the response, which were essential to its wider adoption, took place as the Swiss subsidiary and others made their contributions to development of the response and, thereby, played their part in finalizing the response's ultimate form as an opportunity cost system.

Similar maps of vested parties acting as sources of influence in development of responses may be constructed for all the researched responses, especially those in complex structures. In the Prosper coal diversification, the sponsoring board president, task force, cooperative governments, and other

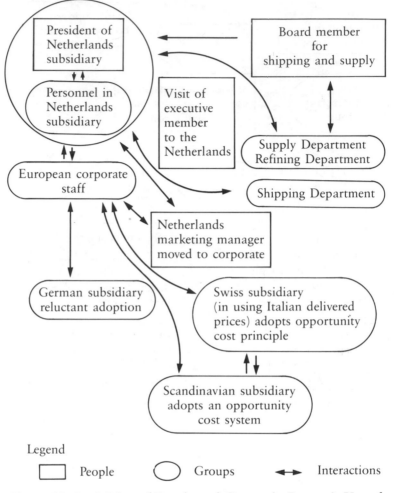

Figure 20–2. A Map of People and Groups in Prosper's Use of Rotterdam Prices

influential vested parties played important roles. Adoption of scenario planning at Atlas required involvement of the corporate planners, subsidiaries, headquarters management, and the board, among others.

Motives and Interests

The parties in each response sought to influence the outcome of the response to satisfy their motives or, at a minimum, to defend their interests. Table 20–1 details the parties that were involved in Prosper's Rotterdam pricing response, together with the various motives and interests that each person or group of people had in the response. Each party exerted its influences to meet its own motives and consequently affected the responses in a number of ways. The effects of these patterns of situational forces on the final form of the response are also given in table 20–1, and extensive further comment will not be made in this text. Just as the form of the Rotterdam pricing response was influenced by the patterns of situational forces on parties and their subsequent need to satisfy their respective motives and interests, so the forms of other responses were influenced also.

The Atlas coal diversification was heavily influenced in its early stages by competing claims on its direction of development. Situational factors induced commitment to a slow ownership route among senior management who wanted an ultimately strong and secure coal business, and commitment to a fast entry into the trading area of the coal industry among the coal team who wanted some action and some early results. The final outcome carries some respect for both of the schools of thought and also for the alacrity with which some foreign subsidiaries supported the development of a coal business in Atlas. Vertical integration and acquisition of many ancillary functions, such as coal-handling equipment, reflect the interests of the research and development department and other technical functions of the company.

Technical details, size, and other aspects of Prosper's catalytic cracker investment betray many trade-offs between competing interests. Following the recommendations of the planning and organization review committee, the supply function would take full profit-and-loss responsibility for the large proposed additional secondary refining investment. With existing capacity utilization at around 60 percent at the time of the decision, there was reluctance to accept the corporate planners' recommendations. Resolve was further intensified by the intention to build a facility that would be larger than anticipated needs for some years. Structure, especially in terms of the conditioned viewpoint of the supply department, heavily influenced the decision process. Without the existence and forceful enthusiasm of the corporate planning function, the recommendations probably would not have materialized for many more years.

Conclusions on the Maturation Focus

Thus, the maturation focus shows that responses are influenced by the parties and their vested interests on whom its successful development to full adoption depends. Two implications of the maturation focus are significant:

1. Skillful implementation of a response requires that the response be steered through the vested interests of the affected parties. A tailoring of the perceptions of resistant parties where possible, a negotiation of vested interests

Table 20–1
Parties, Vested Interests, and Effects on Prosper's Rotterdam Pricing

Parties	Vested Interests	Effects on Response
President, Netherlands subsidiary	To progress within Prosper and therefore to generate noticeable accomplishments and build a successful company.	The original challenge that his marketing executives should make a real profit above actual oil prices or risk dismissal.
Personnel in Netherlands subsidiary	To progress as individuals and as a group through a viable company and with good relationships, especially with the president.	Support for idea and cooperation in implementation.
Board member for shipping and supply	To maintain high capacity utilization of extensive fixed assets in shipping and refining. Position reinforced by recently implemented financial accountability for operations.	Restraining adoption of Rotterdam prices, specifically in terms of mandating 70 percent internal purchasing by subsidiaries from the supply function.
Supply department, shipping department	A broader representation of the interests of the board member above.	Broader support of the above position and company policy.
European corporate staff	Need for comparative data on the performance of the numerous subsidiaries. Concern for the possible demotivational consequences of the transfer price system on marketing companies "obligated" to show losses in the mid–1970/72 environment.	Support gradually given but after evaluation of the Netherlands experience.
Executive committee member	Success of foreign marketing subsidiaries. Impressed by the interpretation of the Netherlands company results expressed in free-market prices.	Encouragement for adoption beyond the sole example of the Netherlands.
Manager in Netherlands moved to corporate	Self-progress helped by support and promulgation of successful developments.	Encouragement for adoption of Rotterdam prices by other European national subsidiaries.

Swiss marketing subsidiary	Need for evaluation of performance on grounds other than transfer price so as not to be at a relative disadvantage to other subsidiaries. Italian supplies are usually less expensive than those from Rotterdam and favor the Swiss company profit performance.	Conception of internal motivational and control system as one of "opportunity cost" therefore permitting employment of the more beneficial Italian refined prices.
Scandinavian and some other subsidiaries	Equivalent motivation to the Swiss subsidiary (above).	After reluctance to adopt Rotterdam price, ready acceptance of the principle of opportunity cost.
German subsidiary	Inclusion of under-capacity refinery in financial statement made use of any free-market price unattractive.	Modifies system (internal to German company) to reflect full use of self-refined product.
French subsidiary	French government regulations necessitate a margin above costs.	Unnecessary for French company to adopt the system because "profitable" activities are mandated by government. Consequently, subsidiary autonomy maintained on Rotterdam pricing as on other issues.

(perhaps including some wider issues), and an adjustment of details to meet reservations might be necessary. A clear sense of the conceptual meaning of the response, of the impact it will have on the affected parties, and of the aspects of the response which are essential to its success will assist in steering or negotiating the response to full adoption.

2. The situational factors determining the vested interests of the respective parties sometimes can be adjusted to facilitate adoption of a response. Introduction of different criteria for the assessment and reward of managerial performance more in line with the changes that the response will bring about may, for example, achieve compliance where it was not previously forthcoming.

Subject to a feasible and advantageous fit of a response with the contextual focus, this chapter indicates two conclusions:

1. that situational factors influence start-up of a response, and that these can usually be adjusted to improve the effectiveness of a response

2. that situational factors influence the maturation of a response, which requires that vested interests be sidestepped or negotiated, or that situational forces themselves be adjusted so that vested interests can be aligned to the needs of responses

To accomplish response in and through the influences of situational factors requires, therefore, a sensitive awareness of the interests of others, and an alertness to how responses can affect people on whose cooperation the success of the response depends.

Notes

1. Alfred D. Chandler, *Strategy and Structure: Chapters in the History of the American Industrial Enterprise* (Cambridge: MIT Press, 1962), pp. 369–400.

2. Ibid., p. 375.

3. Ibid., p. 394.

4. Alfred P. Sloan, Jr., *My Years with General Motors* (Garden City, N.Y.: Doubleday, 1963), p. xvi.

5. Joseph L. Bower, *Managing the Resource Allocation Process* (Homewood, Ill.: Irwin, 1972), p. 73.

6. Ibid., p. 261.

7. Ibid., p. 71.

8. For a demonstration of the influence of environment on management, see William R. Dill, "Environment as an Influence on Managerial Autonomy," *Administration Science Quarterly*, Vol. 2, No. 4 (1958), pp. 409–443. See note 68 of chapter 2 for a summary of works linking organization structure with environment and variously showing the consistent bundling of organizational and environmental characteristics.

For discussions of the possible conditioning of cultural features on organizational outcomes, see Terence E. Deal and Allan A. Kennedy, *Corporate Cultures: The Rites and Rituals of Corporate Life* (Reading, Mass.: Addison–Wesley, 1982), and Charles E. Summer, *Strategic Behavior in Business and Government* (Boston: Little, Brown, 1980).

9. The central position of personal values has long been recognized in the formulation of strategy. See for example Kenneth R. Andrews, *The Concept of Corporate Strategy* (Homewood, Ill.: Irwin, 1980), pp. 79–85, and William D. Guth and Renato Tagiuri, "Personal Values and Corporate Strategy," *Harvard Business Review*, Vol. 43, No. 5 (1965). The idea of conceptual maps is presented by Michael B. McCaskey *The Executive Challenge: Managing Change and Ambiguity* (Boston: Pitman, 1982), who notes: "Our conceptualizations, or representations, of the parts of reality we have learned to see as meaningful, interesting, and important guide our actions and our work with others."

10. Henry Mintzberg, Duru Raisinghani, and André Théorêt, "The Structure of 'Unstructured' Decision Processes," *Administrative Science Quarterly*, June 1976, p. 255.

11. William R. Reitman, "Heuristic Decision Procedures, Open Constraints, and the Structure of Ill-Defined Problems," in *Human Judgments and Optimality*, ed. W.W. Shelley and C.L. Bryan (New York: John Wiley and Sons, 1964), pp. 282–315. Also cited by Henry Mintzberg et al., ibid.

21
Implications

This chapter presents the implications of this study for managers by extending the findings of earlier chapters into the style and character of processes that managers should employ in response. Collectively the observations are to be termed *responsive management*. Implications for research are to be presented after those for managers and stress a number of different types of studies that would further test, deepen, and apply the findings that were presented in the preceding chapters.

The decision to express the managerial implications of this study in terms of general approaches for managers to adopt follows from the nature of the research topic and from the nature of the findings. A set of step-by-step procedures would be unlikely to fit the unique features upon which successful management of a specific response depends. A set of planning forms, or other ready-to-hand instruments, also would not embrace the particular complexities and dynamics of a specific response. Since this study focuses upon the most challenging circumstances that managers are likely to face, and upon the decision processes that accompany those challenges, it was perhaps inevitable that the implications should take the form of prescriptions relating to managerial processes which then can be interpreted as appropriate to particular circumstances.

What should managers and researchers do in the light of these findings? Chapters 17 through 20 (in particular) showed responses to be (1) *practical* in that they used what was close-to-hand and already existent through realignment, reemphasis, or replication (chapter 17); (2) *active* in that responses predominantly used a derived, iterative, or experimental approach rather than detailed analysis for solving problems (chapter 18); (3) *flexible* in that responses employed constantly three simple processes according to three distinct phases within a dynamic organization and environment (chapter 19); and (4) *sensitive* in that responses arose from and were steered through a complex of situational factors (chapter 20).

For managers, three perspectives are to be examined in turn in discussing the implications of these findings:

1. Implications for management takes the perspective of an involved manager who is "managing a response" and examines each of the four characteristics of responsive management indicated above (practicality, activity, flexibility, and sensitivity).

2. Implications for the organization takes the perspective of a more senior manager who is "managing a response process," and describes how responsive management can be managed in subordinates by the stimulation and selective adoption of initiatives (the process that was mentioned briefly at the end of chapter 19). The four characteristics of responsive management (the practical pursuit of realignment, reemphasis, and replication, the active use of the derived mode, the flexible developing of initiatives, and the sensitive steering within or manipulation of situational factors) are the instruments with which senior managers stimulated initiatives and selectively adopted preferred initiatives.

3. Implications for strategy takes the perspective of a senior manager who is concerned with "managing a corporation through environmental change," and wishes to institute responsive management and understand its relationship to strategy, planning, and other commonly used methods for the management of corporations.

The next three sections correspond to each of the above three perspectives. Subsections are to be introduced by a series of quotations made by respondents in this study.

Implications for Management

The research findings may be summarized as showing that when managers were faced with the need for response, they should get on with the job at hand and not procrastinate unduly in a search for the ideal. Managers were found to use practically what was close-to-hand and either realign, reemphasize, or replicate accordingly; to derive actively the answers to many problems by testing and experimenting; to move initiatives flexibly through a continually shifting organization and environment; and to mold sensitively the shape and form of initiatives to the personal, organizational, and other forces bearing on the initiative.

All the above processes were accomplished in an "on-line" manner, because the uncertainties that surrounded the affected managers were difficult for them to interpret. Interacting with the problems was found to be the most efficient route to solution, because it led to an increased understanding of the situation—often a superior understanding to that which could have been achieved with desk work alone. Circumstances in response dictated, therefore, that usually managers should manage practically, actively, flexibly, and sensitively. These terms are to be explained and expanded upon in the next four sections.

Managing Practically

> In the crisis, we just dealt with each of the issues as they came up. It was the only way we could do it.
>
> —*A Container Division executive concerning its demand surge*

> It would be easy to write an account of our diversification that would appear thoroughly planned and precisely executed. In fact the outcomes were more a matter of propinquity and accident.
>
> —*A Prosper executive on its coal diversification*

The way solutions were found in response, that is, by realigning, reemphasizing, or replicating what already existed, as described in chapter 17, usually implied practical actions or decisions that were often uncertain. Data collected for this study and presented in chapters 5 to 15 showed that circumstances of response were customarily complex. Often they embraced a great many variables which could adopt a wide range of values, and usually these had interactions that were unwieldy and improperly understood. Rather than searching for single, encompassing answers, research has shown that managers sometimes should be satisfied with practical and perhaps incomplete solutions. "Will it work?" rather than "Is it the panacea?" was the healthier of the two extreme possibilities. Evaluation of the data indicated that five properties of decisions or actions reflected this practical need to use what already existed and what was close-to-hand. These five properties were termed partial, inelegant, apparent, imperfect, and nonoptimal, and together characterize the practical ways by which responses were managed.

Partial solutions were appropriate when more comprehensive solutions were impossible to visualize or execute. By solving parts, some imponderables were removed or factored out of the complexity. Outstanding issues could then be identified more readily and similarly rectified in practical terms. Whole solutions materialized step-by-step and often in a zigzag or circuitous fashion. The Container Division managed its demand surge by a series of steadily escalating actions from reallocations of paper raw material between divisions, through special, low-quality purchases from Japan, to hastily arranged private tours of Swedish paper mills. The revised relationships with its customers eventually reduced the service demands on Container Division with respect to stocks, inks, lengths of runs, and so on.

Responses often inclined to the inelegant rather than the refined. There was not usually a premium for the use of modern or fashionable management techniques or for the application of technical or rigorous problem solution procedures. What mattered was a good answer; correlation between quality and the method used did not necessarily exist. Circumstances often demanded and benefited from inelegant solutions, perhaps more quickly formulated but reinstating the company's balance with its environment sooner. Thus, Prosper's management of the embargo found elegant linear programming solutions to the company's supply situation abandoned in favor of the old-fashioned manual methods. The older personnel who had the skill to manage the problems without computer solutions enjoyed renewed status for skills that had become redundant formerly.

Clever solutions were often not the most appropriate. The apparent or close-to-hand deserved to be preferred when they were feasible. They had the advantage of being better understood, which meant that risk was more limited and that management skill in applying them was likely to be higher. Managers were frequently better off settling for an obvious solution and making it work, rather than searching for one that might have been more intellectually satisfying but which may have carried greater risk, may have encountered greater resistance in use, and may have proven less effective in aggregate terms. It was probable, for example, that National Lighting might have been better off, even in the long run, with less ambitious automation plans for the manufacture of miniature automobile bulbs. Market share and quality-related goodwill might well have been better served with a less ambitious solution implemented faster and with fewer problems associated with it.

An imperfect solution (with known deficiencies) or a nonoptimal solution were accepted for response where practical circumstances dictated. Although many inefficiencies and shortcomings were expected, benefits often sufficiently outweighed undesirable side effects. Practical considerations suggested that solutions that would normally be judged as unsatisfactory were considered when a more attractive option was not available.

Accepting the imperfect or nonoptimal had other rationales besides pros cancelling cons. Taking such actions led to a wider or fuller understanding of the problem by displaying more symptoms of underlying causes and permitting a more thorough diagnosis. With increased experience, a more viable path was generally revealed.

Probably everyone involved with the introduction of the Rotterdam pricing system for the purposes of internal control and motivation was aware of the many imperfections and the nonoptimality of the concept. The weight of opinion, however, was firmly in favor of its introduction (with modifications) for most European subsidiaries. Such commitment reflected a view that the use of Rotterdam prices would probably do quite well and was probably the best implementable option available, although judged far from perfect. The first introduction of the system did greatly improve many senior managers' understanding of the need to make national marketing subsidiaries more responsive to their markets rather than to the output of products supplied to them from the refineries.

Managing Actively

> We have been long on analysis but too short on action in that business.
> —*An observation on National Lighting's vehicle bulb business*

How I learned to measure the hardness of steel was accidental. During my experiments the hammer missed the punch on one occasion. The hammer blow made a perfectly smooth impression in the ingot. It was then that I realized that the impression would permit the use of ultrasonics for measurement. The answer emerged from just getting on with the job in hand!

—*A Weld Division manager*

We had to go to the Middle East to find out the problems—we could not have imagined all the difficulties before we got started.

—*A DeVito executive on its entry to Middle East markets*

Chapter 18 showed that responses were accomplished through two approaches, which included a derived mode employing experiment, iterations, and other more intuitive aspects of management, as well as the more commonly reported analytic approach. This derived mode was generally more important and was largely accomplished by managers just getting on with the job at hand. Activity, or a commitment to getting things done, rather than an inclination to thoroughly consider things abstractly, resolved most issues. Although careful reasoning was always observed, the research data in chapters 5 to 15 showed that there was a need to act in circumstances that were only partially understood and that an appropriate managerial style was therefore one that incorporated:

1. a willingness to take limited risks
2. a boldness in attempting the unknown
3. a readiness to experiment

Risk was inevitable in response, and a willingness to meet it was essential. Circumstances were often so unpredictable that it was necessary to act rapidly rather than to allow uncertainties to be fully removed by the passage of time. Managers often, therefore, were not afraid of making decisions where there was some risk of their going awry. Taking a balanced and necessary risk was often unavoidable. The pricing issue at the Industrial Products Division was a case in point. It was clear that prices had to be increased substantially, but by how much for each product line and for each end use represented a set of many decisions which were impossible to make without accepting the risk that mistakes were to be made. Competitor reactions could, in theory, have caused the loss of major market shares, as happened in the area of foam molding materials for furniture, where the company's market share dropped from 75 percent to 50 percent in six months.

Similarly, a boldness was required to gain success attempting the unknown. Responses often took place in situations that were only fragmentarily understood. Sometimes decisions were made that carried the company into the future with blind spots still present. The option to wait until the future revealed itself was often less rational than to move preemptively. An example was provided by DeVito Power, where the company entered the Middle East markets largely by just getting on with it. Their bold contracts contained plenty of blind spots of which the company's managers were aware in general terms but of which they could not be aware in specific terms. DeVito's management was unable, therefore, to predict exactly what the blind spots were or what impact they would have. Ultimately, the company found itself constructing whole docks, negotiating with large communist nations for special permissions to use transport routes, and arranging loans for its customers in the international money markets so that DeVito's fees could be payed by their client state-owned corporations.

In many responses, uncertainties and unknowns were most usefully countered by a readiness to experiment with a response or part of one. Tentative or restrained commitments confined some risks and maintained the balance of unknown quantities, but served also to spur understanding and avoid waiting. Doing nothing until a situation became more clearly understood was sometimes infeasible, because competitors or others could steal initiatives in the meantime. Prosper's and Atlas's entries to the coal industry contained the above features. In both diversifications the management tested out the ideas on their foreign subsidiaries, some of which took up the invitation to enter the coal industry. Small investments were approved by both Prosper and Atlas whose outcomes were very uncertain. This testing of the water gave Prosper its first direct experience in coal mining after a fruitless joint venture in exploration. For Atlas, its first initiatives in the coal industry clearly displayed the problems of entry through the acquisition of undelineated reserves and also the problems of entry into coal trading. The company's readiness to keep trying, despite the early setbacks, eventually provided a formula for buying into newly constructed coal mines by prepaying for later supplies. This formula, once proven by experience, formed the basis for further, substantial participation in the coal industry.

Managing Flexibly

There was a reluctance to admit the facts of the radical change in demand patterns in the company—estimates were maintained until patently they applied no longer.
> —*An Atlas executive on the supply and demand position in 1974 and 1975*

Although our market share was sliding down on that product, we felt we had to make a stand and therefore waited a quarter before putting our prices back to where they were before. Once we got our prices back to where our competitors had kept theirs, our market share position improved but has never returned to where it stood.
> —*An Industrial Products Division executive concerning its response to cost inflation*

Chapter 19 showed that the development of response was a simple process of gradually increasing support for particular initiatives. The progress of an initiative was susceptible, however, to the dynamics of organization and environment such that the initiatives may be accelerated, amended, truncated, or delayed depending on how events proceeded. As environment and organization evolved in complexity, so the unexpected sometimes occurred, or the expected occurred with unpredicted intensity. As chapter 19 described, in such circumstances decisions could be quickly outmoded or their inefficiencies quickly exposed. Conversely, previously infeasible or unimagined initiatives could become attractive. Thus, under such circumstances, as illustrated by Prosper's and Atlas's coal diversifications, for example, it was useful for managerial style to incorporate flexibility as:

1. preparedness to change one's mind
2. willingness to learn from mistakes
3. receptivity to shifts in the organization and environment

Changing one's mind is often perceived as a weakness. The presumption is that matters should have been thoroughly investigated beforehand and a decision made without later vacillation. Responses typically involved such intense dynamics that arriving at the optimal decision before it had been tested was as likely to be due to serendipity as to good judgment. A preparedness to change one's mind in the light of experience and wider developments seemed a prerequisite to effective management of response.

As well as changing one's mind when expectations did not materialize, there was also a need to learn from mistakes. It was necessary to analyze past beliefs objectively and to relate their meaning to the future. An appropriate management style incorporated a willingness to recognize mistakes, interpret them, and apply lessons learned from them.

In many cases the prevailing situation was not a dire need to change one's mind or a sudden need to remedy conspicuous mistakes, but a gradually emerging revision of expectations. As events shifted, so it was necessary for managers to move accordingly. An important part of response was management's receptivity to making appropriate modifications to decisions or to their own general outlook as events marched on.

It is reasonable to speculate that Atlas's entry to the coal industry could have proceeded more smoothly, more quickly, and less expensively if there had been a greater willingness of management to alter opinions in the face of experiences, to learn from their mistakes, and to be more receptive to shifts in the organization and environment. Some respondents, for example, reported that the original exploration route (especially as exemplified by the company's first experiences in exploration) was firmly held onto by management well beyond the time when it was understood that a policy of acquisition of undelineated reserves was not likely to be successful for coal. However, mistakes were learned from and eventually a strong coal business was developed at reasonable cost. As the coal surplus dried up in 1973, and as the financial attraction of investment in the international coal industry increased, so decision makers shifted their positions in appropriate directions.

Managing Sensitively

His opposition to the new management system became so vehement that he made statements that I considered illogical time and time again. After some "careful handling" the new system became accepted eventually despite his opposition.

—*An Atlas executive*

We consider it more important that we have the ability to respond to change than that we expend a great deal of effort in predicting what might or might not happen.

—*An Industrial Products Division executive*

Chapter 20 described how situational factors were critical to response: exactly who was involved, the time and place of the response, and how it was managed could all have a crucial bearing on the shape and form of the response and its effectiveness. Careful management of these situational factors was necessary, and accomplishing it demanded a sensitivity to surrounding circumstances and to how they were changing. The experiences of managers recounted in the field work showed that the successful molding of a response depended upon a style of management that was:

1. aware of the interests of others
2. alert to shifts in organization and environment as they affected persons

Responses depended on the cooperation of people. Managers needed to enlist and not to unwittingly affront the persons and the organizations essential to successful execution of response. Incorporation and satisfaction of the interests of others involved in response was necessary to smooth and efficient development. Awareness and sensitivity of these interests was a crucial attribute of response management.

In changing circumstances, the impact of decisions on people in an organization altered through time as responses matured. Perceptions of impacts by affected persons was a major influence on behavior, and often impacts were perceived as increasingly threatening as the consequences of change were gradually comprehended and became more immediate. Efficient management of response was as alert to the shifts in organization and environment as these affected persons, so that timely and sensitive accommodations could be made.

Prosper's catalytic cracker investment provided a notable example of managing sensitively. Despite major dissent from the supply function and by those responsible for refinery operations, the capital investment was gradually steered through the "minefield." When the time came for taking the proposal to the board (usually a routine matter at that stage), a willing proposer did not exist. Skillful maneuvering was necessary to find two co-proposers who would share the risks. Similarly, it was apparent that opportunities for progress of the proposal provided by shifts in the organization and the environment were not missed. The 1975 approval by Prosper's executive committee that a catalytic cracker proposal be developed was apparently strongly influenced by the demand and price pattern of oil products that emerged in that period which was highly favorable to the lighter products refined by crackers—a point that was heavily stressed by the project's proponents around that time.

Implications for the Organization

The foregoing discussion took the perspective of managers involved in the response. What were the ramifications for more senior managers who wish to solicit and guide a response? The need was to bring about required behavior in lower levels, perhaps without direct involvement in the work. In principle, the task was to encourage the involved managers to responsibly adopt the responsive management described in the preceding pages of this chapter. How that should be done may be less obvious but, again, it was found to be generally a matter of style and not reducible to checklists or linear models.

The key process in developing a response was mentioned in chapter 19 to be one of first stimulating a series of suitable initiatives from the organizations and, second, supporting and adopting the most constructive initiatives. The former brought about a pool of ideas and initiatives that were tried and which could lead to further and better initiatives. The latter achieved a selection from these numbers so that the best could be incorporated.

The overwhelming majority of ideas and initiatives went unrecorded and unremembered, but their role in response seemed, nevertheless, to be potentially crucial. Although many initiatives were not used directly, without the generation of the ideas and their testing, other solutions would not have become apparent. Rather than addressing the waste behind unused initiatives, the need seemed in the uncertain circumstances of response to be one of stimulating many initiatives so that an evolution of thought could be achieved and so that a final selection could be made from a large collection of experiences or from wide-ranging discussions.

Stimulating Initiatives

Get adrenalin in the organization by generating a crisis atmosphere.
—*A Container Division executive on the demand surge*

The idea of using Rotterdam prices as an internal system of control and motivation emerged after long discussions. Anything new was a long process going through various levels.

—*A Prosper executive*

From the data collected for this study, three organizational attributes seemed to assist in stimulating initiatives and generating the kind of management action that has been termed above as practical, active, flexible, and sensitive, and which reflects response as described in previous chapters. These organizational attributes are to be termed a *free atmosphere,* a *supportive climate,* and a *loose structure,* and are explained below. Liberal use or evidence of these three organizational attributes seemed particularly important in the earlier antecedent and development phases of response.

An open-minded, permissive, uncensorious set of attitudes among the group of people involved in a response characterized a free atmosphere. Only in such circumstances was it reasonable to expect the kind of wide-ranging, creative, and, at times, iconoclastic communications necessary to achieve an understanding of the unprecedented. There was often a need to generate a solution that went beyond previous experience and ways of thinking. An organizational atmosphere sufficiently free to condone the exceptional seemed generally to be more successful in stimulating initiatives of useful number and variety.

The generalized and unspecific recommendations of the planning and organization review committee at Prosper provides an example. The general recommendations left the way open for any number of initiatives, proposals, or solutions to the general need for more decentralization. The use of Rotterdam prices which had become so important to the achievement of the goals of the planning and organization review committee's recommendations could not have been foretold by them, but the committee deliberately kept an open mind to allow such devices to surface for the purpose.

Similarly, a supportive climate in the organization—one where justifiable mistakes were tolerated—seemed helpful to response. The need was to create a milieu where initiatives were encouraged within reasonable bounds even if they were partial, inelegant, imperfect, or if they held risks, seemed bold, or appeared experimental. Prosper's coal venture was characterized by this kind of climate where a great many initiatives—from the purchasing of coal from East Europe to the proportion of steam or coking coal that could be secured—were stimulated and considered respectfully. Only by discussion and testing of inconclusive initiatives, often containing a sensible proportion of the above characteristics, was it likely that the most useful one would be found. Cultures that were tolerant of warranted changes of mind and of civil differences of opinion also seemed particularly relevant to the more complex response situations. Flexibility and sensitive accommodation of vested interests was thereby provided, which was shown in chapters 19 and 20 to be important in response.

A loose organization seemed relevant to response in that those conditions could foster initiatives more readily. The best ideas were as likely to arise from the bottom levels as from the top, and from outside of the group as from within it, as was shown repeatedly in the case data. Prosper's response using Rotterman prices, represented diagrammatically in figure 20-2, is particularly memorable in this regard. Different jobs, different interests, and different experiences created contrasting perspectives that led to a unique capacity to launch a good idea. Further, the successful response relied for its efficiency on the support and accommodation of others. If all levels were embraced in creating and developing initiatives, then an alliance was forged concomitantly and was well prepared for any subsequent implementation. For the purpose of response, formal authority patterns were often best subdued, and departments encouraged to cooperate. A combination of perspectives and viewpoints through a loose structure for response was likely to trigger the imagination of all sides as well as to engender a necessary understanding of the implications of decisions beyond a particular manager's organizational level and specialized responsibilities.

Adopting Initiatives

Do you know the concept of osmosis? Well, that's exactly how decisions were made in companies.
        —*A Prosper executive on the catalytic cracker investment*

Manager: What happened to the ideas your department had for synthetics?
Subordinate: Well you nipped them right in the bud at the presentation—we could tell you didn't like the ideas from your intonation.
        —*Another Prosper executive*

The situational forces identified in chapter 20—environmental, cultural, organizational, conceptual, and personal—inevitably constrained and guided both stimulation and adoption of initiatives. For managers responsible for the development of response through others, the need was to adjust or present those forces so that they operated as constructively as possible. Two particular ways were available to accomplish adoption of desirable initiatives: (1) manipulation of organizational and personal forces, and (2) persistent, day-to-day use of personal forces (and possibly others) for the encouragement of the constructive and discouragement of the unhelpful and the destructive.

Manipulating organizational (structural and informational) and personal forces could motivate required behavior in response management as implied in chapter 20. They could be used to stress one part of a company (a skill, an individual, a product group, or whatever) over others. Adoption of appropriate initiatives was hastened or made more likely by, for example, introducing or stressing new measures for evaluation of management performance that biased those involved in favor of the initiative. Adoption of appropriate initiatives was also hastened or made more likely by personnel changes, such as new or strengthened appointments which reinforced selected abilities and perspectives as necessary to adoption.

Another powerful tool for guiding the adoption of initiatives arose from simple day-to-day management of personal forces. Rewarding subordinates for success and penalizing (or just not rewarding) them for failure is an age-old formula to bring about required behavior. Adjustment of monetary and status rewards occurred in the researched responses, but uncertainty in the situations often made early use of such instruments impossible or ill advised. It was often impossible to reliably understand exactly what specific type of behavior was relevant to solving problems, and thus more subtle or ambiguous means were more relevant. The operators at both Prosper and Atlas who managed oil supply during the chaos of the 1973 embargo received special recognition by both companies. One gave a monetary bonus, and the other gave the supply function an extensive mention in the company's annual report. The reward was retrospective in both cases, however.

In practice, a gentle process was observed to be dominant in the data presented in part II and as described by the managers in the field work, where superior managers constantly reacted to initiatives and persons. Subordinates often strove to court favor within the system. It was by a casual remark, by a critical question displaying previously unapparent weaknesses, by a corridor smile, by the inclusion of a name on a meeting agenda, and by similar subtle means that senior managers nipped some ideas in the bud or allowed others to blossom. It was through such subtle means (that were often necessarily ambiguous or inconsistent because needs were uncertain) that some initiatives had their paths cleared of obstacles and were permitted to proceed smoothly, while others encountered a quiet resistance. The process was gentle in that it seldom required definitive action of senior management. Some responses could form and others decline without serious conflict in most instances.

Implications for Strategy

The purpose of this section is to take the perspective of a senior manager who wishes to institute responsive management in a corporation and who wishes to understand the relationship between responsive management, strategy, planning, and other commonly used methods for the management of corporations through environmental change.

Instituting Responsive Management

At the start I suppose we were just a group of guys, but our people were our only asset.

—*Atlas executive on entry to the coal industry*

Corporate made the divisional president of Industrial Products responsible for sorting out the pricing problems. That was his job, he accepted it, and he was measured and rewarded according to his performance.

—An Industrial Products executive

It was a long time before we realized that the foreign exchange losses could not be averted by our actions in the treasury department, although senior management held us accountable for them.

—An Interoil executive

Instituting responsive management on an instinctive, continuing basis seemed largely a matter of establishing an appropriate culture within the organization. Research experince showed three factors to be important, but they are offered tentatively as somewhat beyond the controlled evidence of this study. They may be summarized as:

1. freedom for constructive management action
2. unobscured exposure to problems
3. motivation systems that encouraged managers to confront problems and that were sympathetic to justifiable failure

For response, management should be free to act as necessary rather than be hidebound through overly restrictive corporate regulations or previous commitments. Such freedom for constructive management action seemed necessary because the problems often were beyond normal experience in terms of severity or nature. Existing systems, methods, attitudes, and even organizational hierarchies could therefore impede response because they were designed or they evolved for a different kind of problem solving to the novel needs that may be necessary to achieve response. A suitable hands-off approach permitted managers the freedom of action they needed to make changes outside of the usual as they became necessary and not to be hesitant or stalled in their actions. Only when such freedom existed was it likely that early warning signals of imminent change could meet with the managerial response that they merited, and only when such freedom existed was it likely that risks appropriate to the challenges could be taken.

A structure and its associated information flows apparently become tailored precisely to the usual run of business, but blind spots can exist when a new problem arises which can obscure the proper recognition and understanding of such problems. In other cases, aspects of a situation have actually sheltered and cushioned managers and their employees from outside adversities—employment tenure, import restrictions, union closed shops, suppressed energy costs, and guaranteed pay increments or bonuses provide some examples that exist in the data collected for this study. To incorporate responsive management, organizational arrangements should ensure that management is given unobscured exposure to the problems of discontinuities in the world at large as they relate to the organization.

This work has shown that boldness, risk taking, and experimentation are necessary, among other things, to the successful management of response. An organization seeking to incorporate responsive management needs to ensure that motivation systems of reward and penalty are proportional to the task at hand, to encourage managers to confront problems. Without incentives that match the size of the challenge and the associated personal risk, it is unrealistic to expect bold initiatives that may be essential to the achievement of response. The appropriate motivation must be sympathetic to the nature of the challenge. While success deserves reward, so does appropriate management action that may have turned out to be unsuccessful. While it is difficult to differentiate skillful management in the face of failure, it is likely to be a necessary responsibility of senior management if it wishes managers with proven abilities who no longer need to take risks to improve their careers, to take responsibility for high-risk situations such as those of response.

Strategic Planning

> This company has gone for strategic planning hook, line and sinker. It's like working for the government now.
>
> —*A Generaltex executive*

> In general, people who do well in this company wait until they hear their superiors express their view, and then contribute something in support of that view.
>
> —*Attributed to W. Niskanen, former executive at Ford*[1]

What has been described as the responsive management style is seemingly at odds with the measured approach to management that has predominated in management thinking and writing. One might be tempted to consider that what has been observed in responses constitutes no more than sets of circumstances patently needing the application of strategic planning or similar systematic methods to order them. Is the experimental, interactive character of decision processes observed in this study no more than a relapse to the less systematic management of corporations that preceded the adoption of strategy and planning?

Managing environmental change may be understood as a number of responses at a point in time as well as a series of responses through time. The concept of strategy and others advocates statement of objectives, which in turn provides the framework for a sequence of formulated decisions implemented according to a schedule. A scattered and less systematic approach, centered around individual responses, has been observed in the organizations investigated in this study. The less rigid, response-centered approach to managing environmental change worked well because this approach fitted the intrinsic nature of the situations that were managed and for which previously defined positions could not have been determined.

It is improbable that even the most prescient of top managers or corporate planners could anticipate all possible events and developments in the environment that surrounds an institution. Ideal solutions might well be those not apparent to the mainstream decision makers if their perspective is embedded in the past, routine development of the institution and not inclined to the novelty characteristic of response. An overly censorious attitude toward the fit of initiatives within existing strategy brings the risk of filtering out a variety of initiatives that might otherwise provide the unexpected solution to an environmental challenge. What then should an executive charged with custody of an institution (or part of an institution) do in these situations?

The problems which strategy addresses are shown to involve constantly many different parts and combinations of parts of institutions and embody widely differing time frames. Strategy formation is shown in this study to be an organizationally diffused process rich in synthesis and dissemination and inevitably incremental, uncertain, evolutionary, and situational. This enormously complex process has to be the result of both the quality of the conception of a particular direction and character held within an institution and the quality of the decisional and managerial processes that realize that direction and character.

The evidence of this study suggests that the rational, analytic, and procedurally systematic approaches to strategy formation are necessary and desirable but are also insufficient and, indeed, perhaps dysfunctional when pursued without a balanced appreciation of managerial and decisional processes. It should not be a surprise that the application of strategic planning rubrics at the expense of the decisional and managerial processes found in this study fosters the frequently reported unimplementable plans, rigidity, blind spots, and frustrating rituals. Disenchantment should not, however, be directed at the concept of strategy or the philosophy that underpins it, but rather at the primitiveness of the model of strategy formation as it has largely been represented. It is an unrealistic and intellectually arrogant assumption that any abstractly analyzed strategic conception can supplant organizationwide variety and ingenuity.

Adverse environmental change constitutes, inevitably, disintegrative forces on an institution's ingrained strategy, but long-run prosperity requires that these forces be suitably countered, harnessed, or sidestepped. The concept of strategy provides a whole view that allows an institution to identify and discriminate among its options so that efforts cumulate and integrity is maintained. Contemporary and likely future challenges mean that managers need to achieve progressively more sensitive and timely responses to meet increasingly novel disintegrative environmental pressures. Approaches to these issues that exclude decisional and managerial processes can be expected to prove increasingly insufficient and dysfunctional, because it was through these processes that such challenges were first recognized, understood, and effectively met. Realization of the decisional and managerial processes described here is necessary to overcome ingrained conceptions reinforced by custom and habit, and to generate the anomalies, idiosyncracies, and inconsistencies appropriate to novelty. Response recognizes enduring dimensions of institutional identity and strategy, but also allows diversity of actions to institutionalize gradually a variety of initiatives and their synthesis and dissemination across the organization.

Response and responsive management deals with challenges to an institution's established strategy and planning framework. Discussion of the sources of discontinuities argues that such challenges will become increasingly common, indicating that adopting responsive management incorporating the incremental, uncertain, evolutionary, and situational decision processes described here will become increasingly necessary. Responsive management introduces many decisional and managerial phenomena unincorporated in present treatments of strategy, but does benefit from the strategist's concepts of goal formation and methods for analyzing the corporation and its environment. Responsive management supplements the concept of strategy to provide a fuller and more operational theoretical conception of particular importance as assumptions underlying strategy ingrained in an institution are broken or weakened by environmental change. Responsive management running hand-in-hand with strategy is necessary to the prosperity of institutions in the future. The issue is not one of building systems where disorder once prevailed, but one of adopting a model sufficiently accurate and comprehensive to accomplish flexibility and adaptability concomitant with the developing instability of the environment.

Implications for Research

The more valuable theory will be that which accepts assumptions on organizations, people, and so on as they exist in reality. Such a philosophy has guided this research, and the implication for other research is conceived in similar terms. Heeding the above provisos, the findings of this research imply several different types of studies that would further test, deepen, or apply the concepts identified in the preceding chapters.

Testing Studies. This work presents an elaborate set of potential hypotheses ripe for further testing in other sites. While some may be expressible in unambiguous deductive statements and tested statistically, it is envisaged that most will benefit from a *broader gauge* methodology, reflecting the need to examine complex wholes in order to read meaning of value to managers.

Follow-up Studies. Without the advantages of large numbers, it is impossible to assess with statistical confidence whether this research experience is representative of general phenomena. While the work's findings are faithful to a range of data and intuitively legitimate, there is a need to look at many other cases. As such work accumulates, it should be possible to understand further relationships concerning response to environmental change and to identify variations according to more types of organizations, of environmental change, and of response.

Detailed Studies. Some of the topics separately distinguished in this study may be capable of detailed, independent study. The danger in such an approach is that the whole is lost, but a careful delimitation and careful method should be able to avoid that risk. Topics that would most likely be amenable to such treatment could include finding solutions (chapter 17), solving problems (chapter 18), developing initiatives (chapter 19), and using situational factors (chapter 20).

Effectiveness Studies. Implications for managers presented earlier in this chapter were deduced from the findings for response described in the study. Research is desirable to examine whether these deductions correlate with instances of efficient or successful response behavior. Determining a suitable dependent variable or variables to use as a measure of effectiveness will present difficulties but, with the insights provided in this study, it should be possible in practical terms if not in conceptually fully satisfying terms.

Corporate Growth Studies. A distinguishing characteristic of this research has been a focus on responses. It is tempting to view the growth of corporations in such terms where operating responses provide challenges and betray problems, where administrative responses add systems, capital investments, new products, and so on, and where corporate responses add new operations. A fit with three stages of corporate growth is suggested where small businesses are more vulnerable to operating situations but where administrative responses gradually take the company to a larger size and full structure. Further administrative responses may then successively answer the challenges presented by growth, while corporate responses take the company from a single business to a fully fledged diversified company. Detailed study along the lines of the method used in this work as to how important general aspects of this growth process are achieved might show interesting returns.

Portfolio Response Studies. It has become common practice to manage the constituent businesses of a corporation as a portfolio. In the various conceptions that characterize the viewpoint,[2] identifiably different strategies are suggested for each respective business in terms of improving, maintaining, or dropping the relative competitive position of the business or acquisition or divestment of a business. Careful, descriptive studies of several comparable situations employing a methodology such as that for this study could throw useful extra light on how these critical and commonplace strategic actions are executed by management.

Separate Studies. The research questions guiding this study were concerned with developing corporate skills as necessary to an increasingly turbulent environment. Work with several companies and with several variations of the challenges confronting managers in this era has allowed some general observations to be made. The broadbrush stroke has suggested a bedrock of basic concepts and some ways in which they may be more specifically focused. Separate studies of more corporate, administrative, and operating responses could use these concepts in deriving a deeper understanding specific to each type of response. Categories of response situations could also be investigated, such as administrative responses that incorporate systems, administrative responses that incorporate organizational change, and administrative responses that incorporate capital investments.

Another study could be that of the development work associated with incorporating the management of response as illustrated in this work into corporate systems so that responsive management is continuous and routine. Responses would then become as continuous and systematically managed as necessary to counter threats or exploit opportunities. Exactly the most efficient way to accomplish this goal would need careful thought and inquiry (the derived mode would be important because of the uncertainties).

It may be tentatively supposed that an inventory of probable environmental changes could be compiled. These could then be monitored for their evolution in the environment on a periodic or continuous basis. An inventory of complete or ongoing responses across the corporation could show where needed skills might be available. Checklists could be used to enhance appropriate progress through the early stages of the response. Gradually the skills of manipulating situational forces, stimulating initiatives, and so forth could be carefully developed through the logging and evaluation of experience.

Systematizing the response process may be useful but it would also risk a major flaw of putting the cart before the horse. This work has strongly implied that the diversity in corporations, the wide range of environmental challenges, and the idiosyncrasies of many effective solutions mean that responses should embrace more than the top level of management or a group of strategic planners. Rather than a central brain regulating the management of environmental change, the challenge is to maintain a form of management that stimulates individual initiatives. A loose rein is crucial for the management of strategy and response. It is better that some horses falter en route to a changing but increasingly appealing destination than that a few prime drays plod nervously through an environment that is moving too fast to comprehend toward a destination of receding appeal. Let the racehorses pull the cart this time!

Notes

1. Steve Lohr, *The New York Times Sunday Magazine,* January 4, 1981, p. 45.
2. Arnoldo C. Hax and Nicolas S. Majluf, "The Use of the Growth–Share Matrix in Strategic Planning," *Interfaces,* February 1983, pp. 46–60, and "The Use of the Industry Attractiveness—Business Strength Matrix in Strategic Planning," *Interfaces,* April 1983, pp. 54–71; Charles W. Hofer and Dan Schendel, *Strategy Formulation: Analytical Concepts* (St. Paul: West, 1978), pp. 182–184.

Author Index

Ackerman, Robert W., 14
Ackoff, Russell L., 11, 12
Adelman, Morris A., 113
Aldrich, Howard E., 19, 26, 27
Allison, Graham T., 262
Anderson, Carl R., 36
Andrews, Kenneth R., 12, 25, 296
Andriole, Stephen J., 20
Ansoff, H. Igor, 5, 6, 12, 26, 36
Ashby, W. Ross, 19, 26, 27, 36
Athos, Anthony G., 13

Barber, Noel, 113
Barnard, Chester I., 19, 25, 46
Basil, Douglas C., 19
Bauer, Raymond A., 43
Beer, Stafford, 27
Bell, Daniel, 5
Bertalanffy, Ludwig von, 44
Biggadike, E. Ralph, 279
Bonge, John W., 31
Bower, Joseph L., 14, 18, 295, 296
Braunstein, Daniel N., 27
Braybrooke, David, 14, 26, 262
Bryan, C.L., 296
Burns, Tom, 19, 36

Carr, Donald E., 66
Carter, Eugene, 262
Caves, Richard E., 19
Chandler, Alfred D., Jr., 14, 15, 17,
    18, 28, 31, 295
Channon, Derek F., 31
Churchill, Sir Winston, 113
Cohen, Michael D., 243
Coleman, Bruce P., 31

Cook, Curtis W., 19
Cyert, Richard M., 14, 26, 44, 243,
    262

Dauman, Jan, 11
Davis, Stanley M., 19
Deal, Terence E., 296
Declerck, Roger P., 12
Dewey, John, 277
Dill, William R., 262, 278, 296
Donavan, Neil B., 12
Dyer, Davis, 19

Einhorn, Hillel J., 243
Emery, F.E., 4, 11, 25, 44
Etzioni, Amitai, 262
Evan, William, 25

Faulkner, John C., 12
Foote Whyte, William, 47
Ford, Jeffrey D., 19
Forreser, Jay W., 11, 27
Fouraker, Lawrence E., 31
Frederickson, James W., 36
Freeman, Edward R., 262

Galbraith, Jay R., 19, 26, 31, 36
Gore, William J., 15, 17, 18
Grant, John H., 25
Guth, William D., 296

Hall, Richard H., 31
Hall, Roger L., 262
Hamilton, Adrian, 141
Hargraves, Basil John Alexander, 11
Harrison, Frank E., 28

Hatten, Kenneth J., 36
Hax, Arnoldo C., 13
Hayes, Robert L., 12
Higgens, G.W., 19
Hill, Peter, 141, 144, 146
Hofer, Charles W., 13
Hogarth, Robin M., 243
Horwitch, Mel, 66
Hunger, J. David, 25

Johnson, Michael L., 12

Kahn, Herman, 5, 109
Kennedy, Allan A., 296
King, William R., 25
Kotler, Philip, 25
Kotter, John P., 20, 25
Kuhn, J. Arthur, 262

Lawrence, Paul R., 19, 26
Lenczowski, G., 143
Lindblom, Charles E., 13, 14, 26, 262
Linstone, Harold A., 262
Lohr, Steve, 326
Lorsch, Jay W., 19, 26
Lyles, Marjorie A., 284, 285

McCaskey, Michael B., 13, 262, 296
Mailick, Sidney, 278
Majluf, Nicolas S., 13, 329
March, James G., 14, 15, 17, 18, 26, 44, 46, 243, 261, 262
Miles, Raymond, 19, 20
Mintzberg, Henry, 13, 14, 26, 31, 36, 46, 243, 262, 273, 277, 278, 284, 285, 296
Mitchell, Terence R., 36
Morse, John, 19
Murray, H., 19

Nathanson, Daniel A., 31
Normann, Richard, 14, 15, 17, 18
Nutt, Paul C., 36

Olsen, Johan P., 243

Paine, Frank T., 36
Pascale, Richard Tanner, 13
Paul, Ronald L., 12
Penrose, Edith, 142
Perrow, Charles 19

Pfeffer, Jeffrey, 4, 5, 19
Pollock, A.B., 19
Pounds, William F., 284

Quinn, James Brian, 13

Raisinghani, Duru, 14, 26, 46, 243, 277, 278, 284, 285, 296
Regan, D.E., 262
Reitman, William R., 296
Rhenman, Eric, 15

Salancik, Gerald R., 4, 5, 19
Sampson, Anthony, 141
Schendel, Dan E., 13, 36
Schon, Donald A., 11
Schumpeter, Joseph A., 15
Scott, Bruce R., 31
Selznick, Philip, 15
Shelley, W.W., 296
Simon, Herbert A., 13, 14, 15, 17, 18, 19, 26, 46, 261, 277, 278, 279
Sloan, Alfred P., Jr., 295
Slocum, John W., Jr., 19
Smart, Carolyn, 20, 26
Smith, Richard Austin, 20
Snow, Charles, 19, 20
Soelberg, Peer O., 285
Sommerhoff, G., 25
Sparkes, John R., 13
Stalker, G.M., 19, 36
Steinbruner, John D., 14, 26, 262
Stewart, Rosemary, 279
Stopford, John M., 31
Summer, Charles E., 243, 296

Tagiuri, Renato, 296
Taylor, Bernard, 13
Taylor, James W., 12
Terryberry, Shirley, 4, 36
Thain, Donald H., 31
Théorêt, André, 14, 26, 46, 243, 277, 278, 284, 285, 296
Thompson, James D., 19, 25, 28
Toffler, Alvin, 26
Trist, E.L., 4, 11, 19, 44
Tugendhat, Christopher, 141

Ungson, Gerardo R., 27

Van Ness, E.H., 278
Vernon, Raymond, 141, 144
Vertinsky, Ian, 26
Vielvoye, Roger, 141, 144, 146

Weiner, Anthony J., 5, 109
Wheelen, Thomas, 25
Witte, Eberhard, 26, 277, 279
Woodward, Joan, 19
Wrapp, E. Edward, 13, 262

Content Index

Accelerating, 244–245, 251–253

Accentuating, 192, 244–245, 251, 253–254

Active, 9, 222, 273, 293, 313, 314, 326–318

Adaptation, 4, 93, 107, 121; discussion, 25, 26; evaluation, 224, 244; examples, 226–228; implications, 224, 230; introduction, 4; propositions, 27, 223

Administrative response, 52, 56, 62, 104, 135, 148, 168, 177, 206; definition, 28; discussion, 29–30; evaluation and implications, 233–234, 244; examples, 93–104, 109–115, 122–129, 151–155, 156–159, 159–162, 167–168, 168–171, 173–175, 179–183, 183–188, 188–191, 210–211, 215–218; introduction, 8; propositions, 30, 231–232

Adopting, 192, 244–245, 257–258

Analytic mode: combining/balancing with derived mode, 268, 273; definition, 263–264; development, 261–262; evidence, 264–265; introduction, 8; managerial implications, 273; tabulated examples, 266–267; uses, 268–269, 317

Antecedent phase, 8, 176, 278, 285–287, 322; tabulated examples, 288–290

Asymmetry, 26; discussion, 37, 264; evaluation, 225, 229; implications, 229–230; propositions, 27, 225

Atlas, 50–53, 80–82; cracking capability, 105–106; entry to coal industry, 52, 79–92; response to embargo, 53, 135–149; scenario planning, 52–53, 107–119

Autonomy: in corporate response, 65, 75–76, 80, 232; in divisional settings, 166, 197, 199, 202

Capacity, incipient, 25; evaluation, 224; implications, 224; propositions, 27, 223

Career risk, 84, 89, 326

Carolvale Division, 55–56, 193–197

Choice, 9, 118, 278, 279, 283–284

Coal, 65–67; reserves, 72–73, 83, 85

Columbus Bank, 50–51, 53, 155–159

Complex setting, 50–53, 62, 67–68, 80–82, 136–140, 162; amended conceptualization, 235–239; definition, 31; discussion, 31–34, 238; evaluation, 239; introduction, 8, 27; propositions, 35, 235–236; revised definition, 237

Compression, 27, 37; discussion, 36–37, 263; evaluation, 230–231; implications, 231; propositions, 27, 230

Container Division, 55–56, 202–206

Contextual focus, 296–301; managerial implications, 300–301

Contribution, 9, 118, 278, 279, 282–283

Corporate response, 52, 62, 104–105, 135, 148, 206; definition, 28; discussion, 28–29; evaluation and implications, 232–233; examples, 69–76, 83–90; introduction, 8; propositions, 30, 231

Decision making: novelty in, 26, 36–37; rational, 3, 13, 14, 36, 263; real, 14, 16–17; school, 7, 13–18

Decision phases, 8, 278, 284–293; tabulated examples, 288–290

Decision processes, 3, 14–18, 36–37, 46, 62, 93, 114–115, 118, 218, 277–284, 296; choice, 278, 279, 283–284; in complex settings, 163; contribution, 278, 279, 282–283; in discontinuity, 14; in divisional settings, 176; evolution, 278, 279–283; proposition, 37

Delphi analysis, 113

Derived mode: combining/balancing with analytic mode, 268, 273; definition, 263–264; development, 261–262; evidence, 265, 268; examples, 77, 79, 92, 176, 192, 206; introduction, 8; managerial implications, 273; tabulated examples, 266–267; uses, 269–272, 317

Development phase, 8, 176, 278, 285, 286, 287, 291–292, 322; tabulated examples, 288–290

DeVito Power, 50–51, 53, 159–162

Discontinuity, 6, 14, 25–27, 62, 113–114, 162, 206, 218, 225, 229–231, 263, 271; definition, 26; discussion, 36–37, 223–231; evaluation, 224; propositions, 27, 223; tabulated examples, 226–228

Dissemination: evaluation, 225, 229; examples, 163; implications, 229–230; propositions, 27, 225

Divisional setting, 53–56, 62, 165, 176, 177, 193, 206; amended configuration, 235–240, definition, 31: revised, 237; discussion, 31–34, 238; evaluation, 239–240; examples, 165–167, 178; introduction, 8, 27; propositions, 35, 235–236

Environment, 4–6, 19, 25; environmental change, 26, 207, 264, 326–328; organizations within, 19, 25–26, 36, 44; propositions, 27, 223

Evolutionary: discussion, 239, 278, 279–283; examples, 118, 168–171, 192; introduction, 3, 9

Flexibility, 313, 314, 318–320, 322; discussion, 25, 26, 222, 293; evaluation, 224, 244; implications, 224, 230; introduction, 3, 9; propositions, 27, 233; tabulated examples, 226–228

Focussing, 192, 244–245, 254–255

Foundation, conceptual and propositional, 7

Fragmentation, 26; discussion, 26, 36; evaluation, 225, 229; implications, 230; propositions, 27, 225

General systems theory, 19

Generaltex's Industrial Products Division, 53–56, 165–176

Goals, organization member's, 25–26; discussion, 262; evaluation, 224; implications, 225; propositions, 27, 224

Incrementalism, 36, 37, 118, 132, 163, 176, 192; discussion, 13, 36, 243, 262; introduction, 3

Initiatives, 279–284, 292, 293; adoption, 4, 9, 222, 314, 321, 323–324; examples, 74, 84–89, 318; facilitation, 230; stimulation, 3–4, 9, 222, 314, 321–323; support, 4, 319

Instability, 27; discussion, 37, 264; evaluation, 230–231, implications, 231; propositions, 27, 230

Intensify, 244–245, 247, 250–251

Interoil, 50–51, 53, 151–155

Jackson Mines, 58, 209–212

Managerial implications, 258, 273, 293, 300–301, 303–304, 307, 310, 313–324

Maturation focus, 296, 304–309; managerial implications, 307, 310

Maturation phase, 8–9, 176, 278, 285, 286, 292–293; tabulated examples, 288–290

National Lighting Division, 53–56, 177–192

Normative theory, 4, 6

Novelty, 26; discussion, 36–37, 263–264; evaluation, 230–231; implications, 231; propositions, 27, 230

OAPEC, 52–53, 114, 135, 291
Observations, field, 6, 7
OECD, 65, 96
OPEC, 52, 86, 96, 98, 114, 116, 141–142, 271, 291
Operating response, 52, 56, 62, 135, 148, 206; definition, 28; discussion, 29–30; evaluation and implications, 234–235, 244; examples, 142–148, 167–168, 171–173, 196–197, 197–199, 200–202, 202–204, 204–206, 211–212, 213–215; introduction, 8; propositions, 30, 231–232
Organization, 19–20, 25; Atlas's, 80–82, 90–91, 139; classification, 31–35; DeVito Power's, 160–161; Generaltex's IPD, 165–167, 176; implications for, 314, 321–324; National Lighting's, 178; organizational studies school, 7, 18–20; organizational theory, 19; Prosper Nederand's, 123; Prosper's, 67–69, 74–75, 138; responding to discontinuity, 26–27, 36, 44

Planning, lack of detailed, 77. *See also* Derived mode
Post industrial society, 5
Practical, 9, 222, 258, 293, 313, 314–316
Preparedness, 224
Propositions: discussion, 61–62, 223, introduction, 7; proposition 1, 27, 223–225; proposition, 2, 27, 225–230; proposition 3, 27, 230–231; proposition 4, 30, 231–235; proposition 5, 35, 235–240; proposition 6, 37, 118, 243–245; proposition 7, 37, 118, 261–264; proposition 8, 37, 118, 227–278; proposition 9, 37, 118, 295–296
Prosper, 50–53; catalytic cracker, 52, 93–106; entry to coal industry, 52, 65–77; response to embargo, 53, 135–149; scenario planning, 117–118; use of Rotterdam prices, 52, 121–133

Realigning, 146–147, 206, 244–247, 258, 314, 315; tabulated

classification, 246; tabulated examples, 248–249
Rebalancing, 244–245, 247, 248
Reductionist approach, 11
Reemphasizing, 192, 244–247, 251–255, 258, 314, 315; tabulated classification, 246; tabulated examples, 248–249
Replicating, 244–247, 255–258, 314, 315; tabulated classification, 246; tabulated examples, 248–249
Research: approach, 7, 43–50; concept, 44–45; data base, 46–58; data collection, 46–48; design, 43–50 implications for, 328–330; interviews, 46–47; method, 7; middle time period, 45; phases, 45; sites, 50–60
Response, 6–9, 26–27, 36–38; decision processes in, 278–284; definition, 26; in different settings, 31–35, 239–240; evaluation of model, 223–225, 229–231; examples in complex settings, 50–53, 62, 67–76, 80–90, 93–104, 108–117, 122–132, 151–155, 155–159, 159–162; examples in divisional settings, 53–56, 62, 167–176, 196–197, 197–199, 200–202, 202–204, 204–206; examples in simple settings, 56–58, 62, 209–212, 212–215, 215–218; managing, 315–321, 321–328; nature of, 77, 118, 191–192, 206–207, 273, 295–296, 300–301, 303–304, 307, 310; phases, 284–293; propositions, 27, 223; relation to discontinuity, 225, 229–231; tabulated examples, 226–228; types, 27–30, 231–235; as unit of analysis, 44; *See also* Corporate response; Administrative response; Operating response
Responsive management, 4, 222, 313–328
Ronson Division, 55–56, 193–195, 197–199

Sample design, 48–50
Satisficing, 3, 14, 118; discussion, 36–37; proposition, 37, 261
Schumacker, 58, 212–215

Sensitive, 9, 222, 301, 310, 313, 314, 320–321, 322
Settings, 31–35, 235–240. *See also* Complex setting; Divisional setting; Simple setting
Simple setting, 56–58, 62, 209, 218; amended configuration, 235–240; definition, 31; discussion, 31–35, 238: revised, 237; evaluation, 240; examples, 209, 212–213, 215–216; introduction, 8, 27; proposition, 35, 235–236
Situational, 37, 122–123, 132, 192, 320, 323; discussion, 26, 36–37; evaluation, 225–226, 229, 295–296; examples, 118, 226; implications, 230, 310; introduction, 3, 9; propositions, 27, 37, 225, 295
Solution finding, 36, 243–247
Startup focus, 296, 301–304; managerial implications, 303–304
Strategy, 3, 11, 26; definition, 25; in discontinuity, 12–13, 77; implications for, 314, 324–328; Prosper's coal venture, 74, 77; strategic planning, 3, 326–328; strategic management, 12; strategy and planning school, 7, 11–13
Subresponse, 26; discussion, 36; evaluation, 224; examples, 167–168, 168–171; implications, 225, 230–231; proposition, 27, 224; tabulated examples, 226–228
Suza Cars, 58, 215–218
Synthesis, 26; evaluation, 225, 229; implications, 229–230, proposition, 27, 225

Teams, 65, 70–72, 83–84, 105
Time pressures, 27, 37
Transferring, 244–245, 256

Uncertainty: discussion, 37, 65, 262–265, 273, 282, 314, 315; examples, 168–171, 270–271; introduction, 3, 6
Unit of analysis, 44

Weld Division, 55–56, 199–202

About the Author

R. Jeffery Ellis is an associate professor at Babson College, Wellesley, Massachusetts, specializing in corporate and business strategy formulation and implementation. In addition to academic appointments, Dr. Ellis has worked in strategy consulting, marketing, and selling. His degrees were earned in England: a Ph.D. in management policy from the Cranfield Institute of Technology; an M.Sc. in management from Salford University; and a B.Sc. in chemistry from the University of Nottingham. He came to the United States as a visiting scholar at the Harvard Business School, and his major commitment to synthesizing research method, pedagogy, and consulting with management practice has taken him to diverse programs in France, Britain, Sweden, and Germany. Several of his papers and case studies have been published and are used widely.